Customized Version of

Spreadsheet Modeling *for* BUSINESS DECISIONS

Third Edition

JOHN F. KROS

Designed Specifically for the University of San Diego

Kendall Hunt
publishing company

Kendall Hunt
publishing company

www.kendallhunt.com
Send all inquiries to:
4050 Westmark Drive
Dubuque, IA 52004-1840

ISBN 978-1-4652-6887-7

Printed in the United States of America

CONTENTS

CHAPTER

1 The Art and Science of Becoming a More Effective and Efficient Problem Solver

LEARNING *Objectives*

- Describe the process of quantitative problem solving
- Describe the use of business decision modeling in quantitative problem solving
- Understand the application of business decision modeling in a real situation
- Discuss problems using quantitative problem solving techniques
- Be cognizant of computer and spreadsheet use in business decision modeling

CHAPTER *Outline*

Business Decision Modeling in Action

Algorithm? What the Heck Is an Algorithm?

Business Decision Modeling throughout the Ages

A Brief History

Business Decision Modeling Behind the Scenes

The RAND Corporation

Business Decision Modeling in Action

Algorithm? What the Heck Is an Algorithm?

Introduction

Algorithms, algorithms, algorithms everywhere! What is an algorithm? Where does this stuff come from? This question probably takes you back to those nasty word problems in math class, remember, "If a train leaves Chicago at 6 A.M. traveling at 60 mph and a train leaves Omaha at 7 A.M. traveling at 80 mph. . . ."

Algorithms = step-by-step solution process

Even though some of us may not have very fond memories of these sorts of problems, we use algorithms on a daily basis. Algorithms are really step-by-step methods for solving a problem. Algorithms are set in motion when you order a hamburger at a fast food restaurant or when you book your airline reservation.

Algorithms, Computers, and Problem Solutions

How does this apply to us today as future managers, supervisors, and entrepreneurs? Well, with the advent of the computer in the 1940s and the further proliferation of that concept onto our desktops, the way we use mathematics to solve problems is getting a huge boost. The power of today's computers has added a new dimension to using algorithms to solve problems and to solve problems more effectively and efficiently.

Faster, Cheaper, and Better

Algorithms have allowed businesses to solve problems faster and to provide goods and services cheaper and better.* The study of these algorithms for problem solving is called quantitative methods (business decision modeling), management science (MS), or operations research (OR). This text will provide a solid foundation in what business decision modeling is and give numerous examples of how it is used to solve problems. This text will give you the ability to solve complex problems effectively and efficiently out in the real world.

* Kevin Maney, "Higher Math Delivers Formula for Success," *USA Today*, December 31, 1997.

The Art and Science of Using Business Decision Modeling to Become a More Effective and Efficient Problem Solver

The art and science of becoming a more effective and efficient problem solver is what this book is all about. Readers are invited to develop skills and judgment in becoming more effective and efficient problem solvers. Sections on the communication of results are introduced to aid in the decision and writing process. Real-life problems are addressed throughout the text to integrate the theory with practical applications.

Techniques as well as mathematical models are presented for seeking solutions to these problems. The ability to produce professional-quality reports is a major goal of the text. The text strives to educate managers in the science of problem solving using critical thought and judgment. This process will aid in the management of real life, unstructured, messy situations.

Definition of Quantitative Business Decision Making

What is business decision modeling? There are actually a number of different words used to describe the business decision modeling discipline and a number of different definitions used to characterize it. A few are listed below:

> "[Business decision modeling] is the application of a scientific approach to solving management problems in order to help managers make better decisions."

Business decision modeling is the application of a scientific approach to solving management problems.

> ". . . is the application of quantitative analysis to managerial decision making."

> ". . . may be described as a scientific approach to decision making."

> ". . . is the study of decision making in the operations function."

So which do we follow? Which is correct? Before we try to decide this, let's take a quick look back at those definitions and scan them for any similarities. There are many similarities that exist.

- All definitions mention the idea of decision making.
- Those in charge of the decision making are managers.
- The managers are making decisions on the basis of a scientific approach or set of rules.

These definitions are not the only definitions. When looked at as a whole, however, the different definitions do have a common theme. What about the different names being used? In actuality, business decision modeling tends to be referred to by numerous monikers. In fact, we see the following names used in just the four definitions used above:

- Management science
- Quantitative analysis
- Operations research
- Operations management

The terms management science, quantitative analysis, operations research, and operations management are at times used interchangeably to describe the discipline.

At times, business decision modeling and the aforementioned names are used interchangeably. Just take a look at the name of the course, what department and what school the course is taught in, and the terminal degree of the professor teaching the course. You can start to get a feel for how closely all these names are interchangeable. It should be noted that even though each of these monikers has similar elements, there are subtle differences between the definitions and names.

Overall, as we travel through the text, challenge yourself to begin to make your own definition of what business decision modeling is with respect to your own background, field of study, industry, etc.

Areas of Business Decision Modeling Application

Armed with these definitions, a student of business decision modeling needs to think next about areas where business decision modeling concepts and techniques are used.

Table 1.1 provides a description of the types of industries that use business decision modeling and its uses. The areas listed below are just a sampling of the places business decision modeling concepts are employed. In the process of studying business decision modeling, one should begin to see the numerous applications that affect our everyday lives. Each day as you drive to school, go shopping, access the Internet, or go on vacation, stop and take a look around and ask yourself is business decision modeling at work here?

TABLE 1.1 *Areas of Business Decision Modeling Application*

INDUSTRY	INDUSTRY
Banking	Airline and travel
—Banking and credit card management	—Reservation ticketing
—Loan portfolio management	—Flight and crew scheduling
Manufacturing	Marketing
—Inventory and capacity planning	—Consumer preferences
—Quality control	—Market research
Entertainment	Information technology
—Queuing/crowd control	—Computer programming
—Demand forecasting	—Networking efficiency

TABLE 1.2 *Companies Using Business Decision Modeling*

COMPANY NAME	OPERATIONAL ACTIVITY
SABRE Decision Technologies	Airline reservation systems
Capital One, GE Capital, Providian	Banking and credit card management
CSX and Union Pacific Railroads	Rail shipping
Matson Ocean Liners	Over-the-water freight shipping
McKinsey, Accenture, Ernst & Young, AMS, Boston Consulting Group	Management consulting

Companies Using Business Decision Modeling Concepts

Business decision modeling techniques and models are used in many areas that affect our everyday lives.

As we look around to recognize areas where business decision modeling concepts are applied, we also need to be aware of companies involved in these applications. Many companies directly associated with the areas listed in Table 1.1 use business decision modeling. Table 1.2 contains a brief list of companies using business decision modeling in their daily operations.

This list is by no means exhaustive. There are many more companies that use business decision modeling concepts in their everyday operations and that affect us in our everyday lives. The challenge for the student of business decision modeling is to keep your eyes open and continually observe if the companies that provide you with goods and services use business decision modeling.

The Business Decision Modeling Process

The previous sections included a definition of management science as a rational systematic approach to problem solving. In addition, areas of business decision modeling use were detailed and companies that use business decision modeling in their operational activities were listed. Overall, as students begin to become acquainted with the discipline, it should become clear that business decision modeling is actually a process for solving problems. This process resembles what is called the scientific method for solving problems.

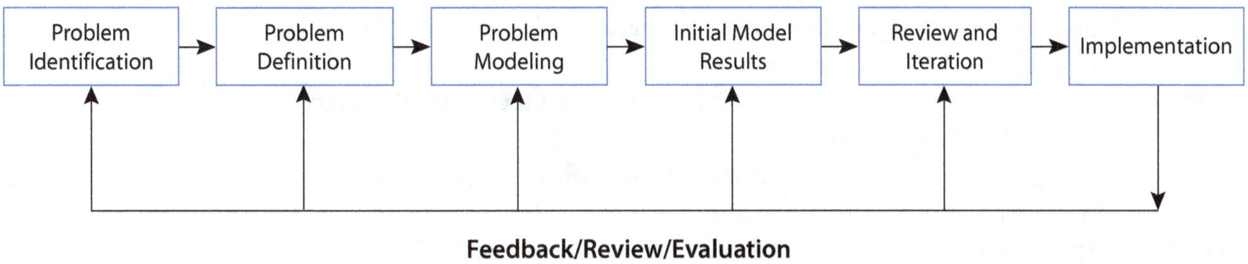

FIGURE 1.1
Business Decision Modeling Process

The business decision modeling process, depicted in Figure 1.1, follows these general steps (1) identification of the problem, (2) definition of the problem, (3) modeling of the problem, (4) initial model solutions and feedback, (5) review and iteration, and (6) implementation. Each of the six steps will be analyzed individually after a brief history of business decision modeling.

The Business Decision Modeling Process

Quantitative Methods/Management Science Time Line

Time	Major Milestones or Accomplishments
1890s	▪ Frederick Taylor develops the field of "scientific management."
1900s	▪ Henry Gantt develops a charting process widely used today. The Gantt charting process is the precursor to packages such as MS Project.
1910s	▪ A. K. Erlang investigates waiting time for telephone callers and formulates the first measure of average waiting time in queuing theory.
1920s	▪ Walter Stewart introduces the concept of quality control charts, the precursor to employee empowerment through total quality management.
1930s	▪ John von Neumann and Oskar Morgenstern develop the fundamental concepts for decision theory and analysis.
1940s	▪ The field of operations research comes to the forefront with the advent of World War II.
	▪ The first electronic computer is developed.
1950s	▪ The Operations Research Society of America (ORSA) and The Institute of the Management Sciences (TIMS) are founded to foster further study of operations research and management science.
	▪ Scheduling and project management techniques, PERT and CPM, are developed by DuPont, Sperry-Rand, U.S. Navy, and Lockheed.
1960s	▪ Large corporations begin to use operations research techniques to solve problems more efficiently and effectively as computers become common tools in industry.
	▪ The Decision Sciences Institute is formed to further the study of teaching and research in the field of decision science.
1970s	▪ The Apple microcomputer and VisiCalc, the precursor to the common spreadsheet, are developed.
1980s	▪ The personal desktop computer is widely marketed and specialized business decision modeling software packages begin to proliferate (e.g., Lotus123, Quattro Pro, and Excel).
1990s	▪ TIMS and ORSA merge to form the Institute for Operations Research and Management Science.
	▪ Laptop computers now run complex software and tackle problems larger than the best computers from the past.
2000s	▪ Students of business decision modeling can gather data, perform complex analysis using their home computers, and communicate the results via the World Wide Web at speeds unseen in the past.

Business Decision Modeling throughout the Ages

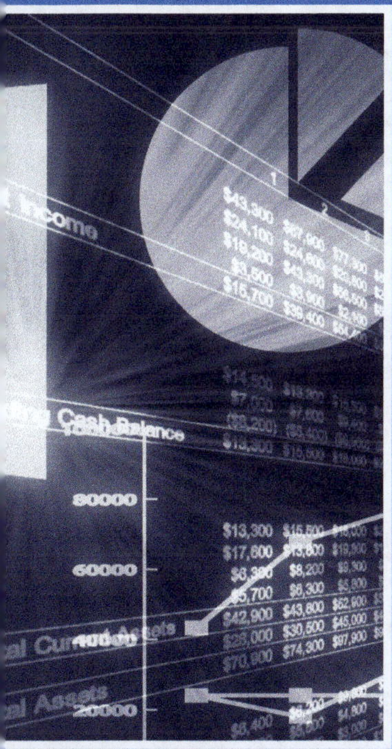

A Brief History

Historical Objective

Until the middle of the last century, most industrial enterprises employed only a few workers. As companies expanded, however, it became less feasible for one person to manage all of the new managerial functions of the business effectively. New scientific methodologies were developed to provide assistance to each new type of managerial function as it appeared.

As more specialized forms of management emerged, so did more specialized subfunctions, such as statistical quality control, equipment maintenance, marketing research, and inventory control. Whenever a managerial function is broken down into a set of different subfunctions, a new task—the executive function of management—is created to integrate the diverse sub-functions so that they serve efficiently the interests of the business as the whole. The executive function evolved gradually, as did organizations themselves. However, increasing demands were made on the manager, who in turn sought aid from outside the organization, which gave rise to management consultants.

Origins of Business Decision Modeling

Business decision modeling can be partially attributed to World War II, since many operations sought to bring mathematical or quantitative approaches to bear on military operations. Business decision modeling has characteristics that include economics (known as econometrics), psychology (psychometrics), sociology (sociometrics), marketing (marketing research), and corporate planning problems. The growing complexity of management has necessitated the development of sophisticated mathematical techniques for planning and decision making.

Some areas of business decision modeling, such as inventory and production control, and scheduling theory, have grown into subdisciplines in their own right and have become largely indispensable in the modern world. The potential of computers and information systems as new tools for management forced the non-technically trained executives to look for help in the utilization of the computer.

Optimal Information Area

Operational Research Society website
http://www.orsoc.org.uk/home.html

OpsResearch.com website
http://www.opsresearch.com/OR-Links/index.html

Professor Hossein Arsham's Applied Management Science
http://ubmail.ubalt.edu/~harsham/opre640/opre640.htm#rintsites

Step 1: Problem Identification

Identifying the problem that exists is the first step in the business decision modeling process. Many experts believe this is the most critical step. If we do not identify the problem correctly all of the subsequent steps are worthless. A statement of purpose, thesis, or set of goals is generated here.

Step 2: Problem Definition

Once we have identified the problem we must clearly define the pertinent variables, those variables' parameters or limits, and any assumptions regarding the real world that apply to the situation at hand. If we do a poor job of defining the problem, our model may be inappropriate. Definitions regarding the problem must be linked to the problem identification and set of goals established therein.

Step 3: Problem Modeling

Problem modeling can take on two common forms: the abstract, or high-level, model and the numeric, or concrete, model.

Models can be of a high-level/abstract nature or a more numeric/concrete nature.

Individuals or groups attacking a problem many times begin with the abstract model and work towards a more specific model.

ABSTRACT, OR HIGH-LEVEL, MODELS

Examples of abstract models are flow diagrams and charts or graphs that physically describe a system or set of components or put structure to the definitions created in the problem definition section. Figure 1.2 is an example of a high level flow diagram used to model the transfer and shipping of goods in a particular region.

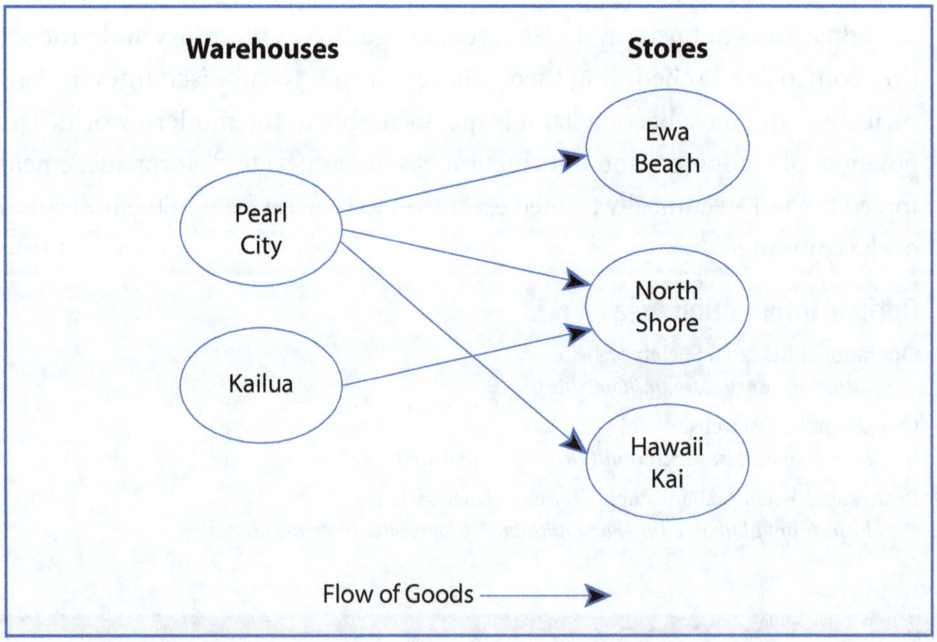

FIGURE 1.2
High-level Flow of Goods Model

NUMERIC, OR CONCRETE, MODELS

High-level models are used primarily in the early stages of the business decision modeling process but many times are carried forward, added to, or modified and also used in the specific modeling stage. Most often the specific models used in business decision modeling are mathematical in nature. These models consist of mathematical relationships that integrate the variables, parameters, and assumptions from the problem definition step into a set of mathematical numbers and symbols. A simple example of a specific model is the relationship of revenues and costs to profit. The numeric model that computes the profit the firm generates is in general,

Financial profit is defined as revenues less costs and is considered a basic financial model.

$$\text{Profit} = \text{revenue} - \text{costs}$$

In fact, businesses use the equation for profit all the time.

Overall, models can become very complex and can include numerous mathematical equations and relationships. The individual topics covered in this textbook will present numerous models for solving many different types of problems. Some of the models we will study tend to be very specific with strict assumptions and definitions, while others are general and can be applied across many situations, scenarios, and disciplines.

Step 4: Initial Model Results

After the problem has been identified, defined, and modeled, business decision modeling techniques are used to generate an initial solution. The word *initial* is used here because the next step in the business decision modeling process is the review and iteration step. Any business decision modeling professional would agree that rarely do we get everything perfect and generate the exact answer the first time around. Moreover, in real life problems are messy and unstructured, and it may take a number of attempts to generate a model that is adequate and/or produces a satisfactory solution. In sum, as students of business decision modeling, we must develop the critical process and not a set of individual stand-alone techniques.

Step 5: Review and Iteration

Managers must review model solutions, or "do a reality check," on the output.

The review and iteration step is a time for what some call a *reality check*. Why should we as managers take a step back?

As you probably noticed in the earlier examples, mathematical formulas and simple algebra were used to create solutions or recommendations. The term *reality check* is used here because of the underlying theoretical nature of mathematics, the mathematical relationships developed in the modeling step, and the earlier definitions and assumptions made in the problem definition step. The review and iteration step encompasses the concept of critical thinking. To be an efficient and effective problem solver, we must develop critical thinking and judgment with regard to the solutions and recommendations that result from the models used.

This critical thinking or judgment is manifested in this step by literally stopping, reviewing the last four steps, and asking yourself a series of questions like the following:

- Does everything look okay? That is, does it all check with reality?
- Did we get an answer that pertains to the problem/goals we identified in step 1?
- Have any of the assumptions or definitions from step 2 changed, or should new assumptions be introduced?
- Is the model we developed functioning properly; i.e., are the answers we obtain feasible and applicable to the real world?

Overall, one of the most compelling reasons for the review and iteration step is to avoid making recommendations or presenting solutions that have no basis in the real world. We must also note that no model is ever perfect, so it is advisable to conduct sensitivity analysis. Good business decision modelers always do a best-, most likely, and worst-case analysis. There will be numerous discussions of sensitivity analysis throughout the upcoming chapters.

Step 6: Implementation

Implementation of the model, solutions, and recommendations is the last step in the business decision modeling process described in Figure 1.1. As future managers, we will be using the models developed and/or the results and recommendations from those models. In the business world, managers must make decisions in order to keep their businesses running, sell products, and service customers. This is in stark contrast to what many academicians or theorists consider the last step of the process.

The implementation step, although the final and possibly the most critical step in the process, is often ignored. At times, necessary changes to a so-called normal way of doing business are revealed and in turn certain individuals may choose not to adopt the results or recommendations of the process due to reluctance for change. This way of thinking needs to be avoided. If the process solution is not implemented; the entire process was a waste of time and money.

Basic Financial Models

Most of the basic business decision modeling models arising in business and economics applications involve the use of the profit equation. The next sections will detail the general profit equation and discuss cost and volume models, revenue and volume models, profit and volume models, and break-even analysis.

Basic financial models such as profit = revenue − cost are used in many places in the real world.

Business Decision Modeling Behind the Scenes

The RAND Corporation

The RAND Corporation was established during World War II to further and promote scientific, educational, and charitable activities for the public welfare and security of the United States. In the early years, RAND's efforts were focused on national security issues, but as time passed, RAND aimed to tackle society's most pressing problems. The unique assembly of researchers, scientists, engineers, humanists, mathematicians, aerodynamicists, physicists, chemists, economists, psychologists, and members of other professions collaborated routinely and effectively to address problems and concerns of people around the world and at home.

The key players in the formation of RAND included General H. H. Arnold; Edward Bowles of MIT, a consultant to the Secretary of War; General Lauris Norstad, then Assistant Chief of Air Staff; Major General Curtis LeMay; Donald Douglas, President of Douglas Aircraft Company; Arthur Raymond, Chief Engineer at Douglas; and Franklin Collbohm, Raymond's assistant. RAND became a nonprofit private organization on May 14, 1948, and was able to obtain loans from Wells Fargo Bank and Union Trust Co. Later, in July 1948, it received further funding on an interest-free loan basis from the Ford Foundation for an amount of $1 million. Four years later, the loan from the Ford Foundation enabled the establishment of the RAND-Sponsored Research Program, which furnished staff with the means to conduct small nonmilitary research projects. This marked the beginning of the diversification of RAND's agenda and was the first of many grants to RAND by the Ford Foundation to support important new initiatives.

Some of RAND's early contributions include providing the foundation for the U.S. space program, digital computing, artificial intelligence, and even laying the building blocks for today's internet technology. Theories and tools for decision making under uncertainty were created, and basic contributions were made to game theory, linear and dynamic programming, mathematical modeling and simulation, network theory, and cost analysis.

RAND Corporation's website is at http://www.rand.org/

Three Parts of the General Profit Equation

The general equation contains three parts: profit, revenues, and costs. The general equation looks like this:

$$\text{Profit} = \text{revenues} - \text{costs}$$

Profit, revenues, and costs are related to the volume of items produced and sold. Algebraically all three parts are functions of the volume of items produced, volume of items sold, and the prices of those items. Each part of the general equation can be broken down into a mathematical equation detailing the specific relationships that profit, revenue, and costs have to volume.

Financial cost is generally made up of fixed and variable components.

Cost and Volume Models

The cost of producing a product comprises two major cost components, fixed and variable. Fixed costs are the portions of the total cost that do not depend on the level of production volume. Fixed costs do not change, hence the name fixed costs. Variable costs are the portions of total cost that are dependent on the level of production volume. Total cost is the sum of fixed cost and variable cost.

Total costs tend to rise as volume of production increases.

Let's take a surfboard manufacturing firm as an example. The firm, Surfboard Inc., knows it takes \$100,000 to set up the shop for the production of the surfboards. This cost doesn't change as the number of surfboards goes up or down. It is considered fixed and is incurred even if no surfboards are made. The firm also knows that it takes \$100 in labor and materials to produce a surfboard. Therefore, \$100 is the variable cost associated with how many surfboards are produced. The resulting cost volume model for producing x surfboards is written as

$$\text{Total cost} = \$100{,}000 + \$100x$$

where x = number of surfboards to be produced
Total cost = fixed + variable costs of producing x surfboards

The total cost for the firm can now be calculated by using the equation presented above. For example, if the firm decides to produce at a volume of 100 surfboards, or $x = 100$, the total cost is calculated as

$$\text{Total cost} = \$100{,}000 + \$100(100) = \$110{,}000$$

Business analysts and economists use this model to describe how the total costs of a firm change as the volume produced changes. This is called marginal analysis. In the case of costs, the marginal cost is defined as the rate of change of the total cost with respect to the volume produced, or x in our equation. From the total cost equation above, we can see that for each extra surfboard produced, the total cost would rise by \$100. The marginal cost is equal to the variable cost in this case.

Revenue and Volume Models

Managers are also concerned with the revenue stream associated with producing products. A model relating revenue and volume produced can be created. Let's use

Surfboard Inc. again as an example. The firm realizes \$300 for each surfboard it sells. Therefore, the total revenue for the firm can be written as

$$\text{Total Revenue} = \$300x$$

where x = number of surfboards to be produced.

In general, revenue is the price of a unit multiplied by the quantity of units sold.

As in the case of costs, business analysts and economists use this model to describe how the total revenues of a firm change as the volume produced changes. Once again, this is called *marginal analysis.* In the case of revenues, the marginal revenue is defined as the rate of change of the total revenue with respect to the volume produced, or x in our equation. From the total revenue equation above, we can see that for each extra surfboard produced, the total revenue would rise by \$300. Obviously, if the firm sells one more surfboard it would receive another \$300 in revenue.

Profit and Volume Models—Putting It All Together

As we have discussed already, profit is made up of revenue minus cost. The last two sections detailed the relationship between revenue, cost, and volume. Since profit is made up of revenues and costs, then profit must also be related to volume. On the assumption that the firm can sell all the surfboards it produces, we can develop an equation for profit based on volume.

As was stated earlier, profit equals revenue minus cost, and if we combine the revenue and cost volume equations, the total profit equation can be written as

$$\begin{aligned}\text{Total profit} &= \text{revenue} - \text{costs}\\ &= \$300x - (\$100{,}000 + \$100x)\\ &= \$200x - \$100{,}000\end{aligned}$$

Therefore, we can see that total profit is related to the volume of surfboards, x, that the firm produces.

Break-Even Analysis

The managers of Surfboard Inc. have been asked to figure out how many surfboards the firm must produce and sell to break even. The term *breakeven* refers to the relationship between revenues and costs. Specifically, breakeven is the level of production and sales at which revenue and cost equal each other. After developing the relationship between profit and volume of surfboards produced, the managers can answer this question, using the profit equation and some simple algebra.

Breakeven refers to the point at which total costs equal total revenues.

Using the profit equation derived above, let's attempt to find, by trial and error, the break-even point. First let's allow volume of surfboards to be produced and sold to equal 400, i.e., $x = 400$, and calculate profits as follows:

At the break-even point, the firm sells enough product to cover total costs, but neither garners a profit nor incurs a loss.

$$\begin{aligned}\text{Total profit} &= \$200(400) - \$100{,}000\\ &= -\$20{,}000\end{aligned}$$

The manager would conclude that at a volume or level of production and sales of 400 surfboards, the firm would incur a loss of \$20,000. However, if the volume of surfboards to be produced and sold is equal to 600, i.e., $x = 600$, profit is calculated as follows:

$$\begin{aligned}\text{Total profit} &= \$200(600) - \$100{,}000 \\ &= \$20{,}000\end{aligned}$$

Break-even analysis can be modeled graphically or numerically.

One can see that at a level of production and sales of 600 surfboards, the firm would realize a profit of \$20,000. Using simple logic, the manager can conclude that the break-even point must lie somewhere between a production and sales level of 400 to 600 surfboards. We can develop a simple equation to help us find the break-even point of any profit equation. The first step is to set revenue equal to cost. This is done by using the profit equation and setting it equal to 0. The resulting equation is

$$\begin{aligned}\text{Total profit} = \$200x - \$100{,}000 &= 0 \\ \$200x &= \$100{,}000 \\ x &= 500\end{aligned}$$

The manager can conclude that the firm must produce and sell at least 500 surfboards to cover all costs and break even.

GRAPHICAL BREAK-EVEN SOLUTION

This relationship between revenue, cost, and profit can be graphed to show all possible combinations of volume and resulting profits. Figure 1.3 displays this graph along with the firm's break-even point, fixed cost, total cost, total revenue, profits, and losses.

In addition, a general relationship for computing the break-even point can be established. If we allow x to equal the number of units produced and sold (i.e., the

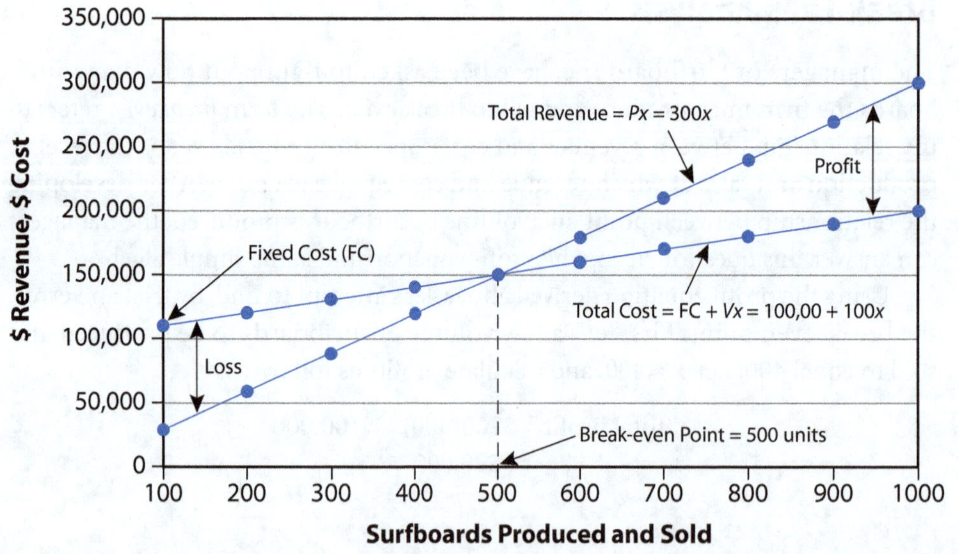

FIGURE 1.3 Graphical Break-even Analysis

volume) and we allow P to equal the selling price per unit, then total revenue can be written as

$$\text{Total revenue} = Px$$

Cost can also be represented in the same manner, where fixed cost is represented by FC and variable cost is represented by two symbols, Vx. The x is the same x as stated above and represents the number of units produced and sold. The V is equal to the variable cost associated with producing an extra unit. Total cost is written as

$$\text{Total cost} = \text{FC} + Vx$$

Combining these relationships, we can write total profit as

$$\text{Total profit} = Px - (\text{FC} + Vx)$$

The break-even point is calculated by setting total profit equal to zero and solving the resulting equation for x, as follows:

The general equation for numerical break-even analysis is

$$x = \frac{\text{FC}}{(P - V)}$$

$$\text{Total profit} = 0 = Px - (\text{FC} + Vx)$$

$$\text{FC} = Px - Vx$$

$$\text{FC} = x(P - V)$$

$$x = \frac{\text{FC}}{(P - V)}$$

Given this relationship, a manager who knows the firm's fixed cost, sales price, and variable cost per unit can easily obtain the firm's break-even point.

Crossover Analysis

The managers at Surfboard Inc. have been approached by two companies selling two different surfboard shaping machines. The first machine would cost Surfboard Inc. \$5,000 up front (i.e., fixed cost machine 1) while the second machine would cost \$2,500 up front (i.e., fixed cost machine 2). Although the first machine costs more up front it does have a lower cost to run. The variable cost to run the first machine is \$5 per surfboard shaped while the variable cost of the second machine is \$12 per board shaped.

For Surfboard Inc. an analysis of where the two machines cross over, or where the unit volume at which the cost of the two machines is equal, needs to be completed. This crossover analysis enables Surfboard Inc. to identify the point (in number of units) where they would be indifferent to the costs generated by the two different machines.

The volume of surfboards shaped dictates the long run cost of each machine. To find the crossover point Surfboard Inc. can use the following formula, where FC = Fixed Cost, VC = Variable Cost, and x = # of Surfboards Shaped:

$$\text{FC Machine 1} + (\text{VC Machine 1})x = \text{FC Machine 2} + (\text{VC Machine 2})x$$

Surfboard Inc. is interested in finding the value of x, which equates these two sides of the formula. Solving for x the formula becomes as follows:

$$x = \frac{\text{FC Machine 2} - \text{FC Machine 1}}{\text{VC Machine 1} - \text{VC Machine 2}}$$

Using the numbers provided by Surfboard Inc. the crossover units in Surfboards is then

$$x = \frac{\$2{,}500 - \$5{,}000}{\$5 - \$12} \approx 357 \text{ surfboards}$$

At approximately 357 surfboards the total cost of each of the two machines is equal. Above and below that volume of surfboards, one machine is preferable to the other. A crossover graph should be developed to assist with this analysis. Plus the graph will better illustrate the risks involved with choosing one machine over the other.

CROSSOVER GRAPH

Figure 1.4 depicts the crossover graph for Surfboard Inc.

It can be seen from the crossover graph that when Surfboard Inc. shapes more than 357 surfboards that the lowest cost machine is machine 1 (e.g., the cost line for machine 1 is lower than machine 2 at volumes greater than 357 units). On the other hand, if Surfboard Inc. shapes less than 357 boards than machine 2 is the best choice (i.e., lowest cost).

When the number of surfboards to be shaped is low (e.g., 50) or when the number of surfboards is high (e.g., 700) the choice of which machine to choose is not a difficult. However, when the number of surfboards to shape lies close to the crossover point, then the decision becomes more difficult. In this case, some trade-off and risk analysis must be done.

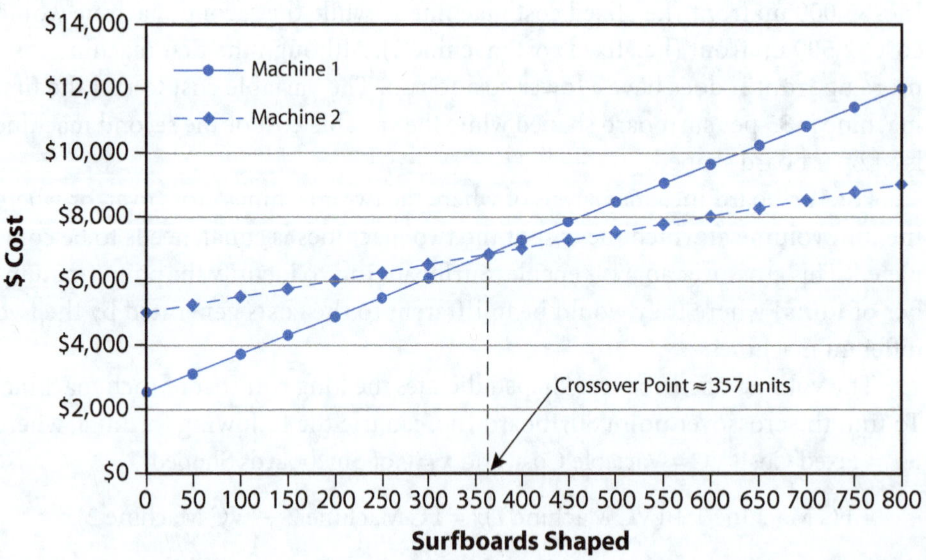

FIGURE 1.4
Graphical Crossover Analysis

One way to analyze the problem when the number of units is close to the crossover point is to ask the question "What happens to the cost of my choice when the opposite of what I thought would happen, happens?" For example, Surfboard Inc. may believe they will shape around 350 boards but then as business is booked they end up shaping more like 450 boards. In this example, Surfboard Inc. was counting on volumes lower than the crossover point and most likely chose machine 2. However, they ended up shaping more boards than the crossover point and would have had lower costs if they had chosen machine 1. Some may chalk this up to chance, shrug it off, and move on, but if Surfboard Inc. estimates incorrectly it could cost them a lot of money in the long run.

So a good question to ask here is what are the risks of underestimating and/or overestimating units shaped. Simply put, if Surfboard Inc. believes that their business will grow in the future they may be willing to take a risk in purchasing machine 1, paying higher costs for volumes lower than the crossover point for a while, but then benefiting from the lower costs of machine 1 when volumes rise above the crossover point. Conversely, if Surfboard Inc. is a custom shop that in the vast majority of times shapes lower levels of boards and stays below or close to the crossover point, they might be better served by machine 2, as it will offer lower costs below the crossover point. Remember that this analysis assumes that Surfboard Inc. can forecast the volume of boards to be shaped with some accuracy. In addition, this basic analysis does not take into account differences in shaping quality, speed, or reliability between the two machines.

Computer-Generated Solutions Using Spreadsheets

Computer spreadsheets have made solving problems such as break-even analysis much easier for managers.

Throughout the text business decision modeling problems will be modeled and solutions proposed by using computer software packages. In some cases, all the student must do is follow the instructions, input a set of data or parameters into a model template, click a solve button, and then interpret the resulting solution output.

In other cases, students will be asked to model problems by using whatever method they believe is adequate. This type of activity develops the critical reasoning and judgment skills needed to effectively and efficiently solve more complex problems.

Solving Complex Problems Using Spreadsheets

With the advent of the personal computer and the basic spreadsheet program, managers now have at their fingertips the tools to analyze a vast range of real-life problems. As we progress through the text, it will become apparent that spreadsheets are a powerful means of formulating, modeling, and solving complex problems. We wish to promote the use of spreadsheets as a logically self-contained and simple method to model problems. By no means, however, are we advocating that spreadsheets are the be-all, end-all solution to business decision modeling and/or real-world problem solving.

Students will find that the text starts out with simple model-building concepts and spreadsheet solutions and builds toward higher-order models with more complex formulations. Some models will be built from the ground up and others will be generated by using spreadsheet add-ins or specialized software. This progression is meant to help students develop modeling, critical thinking, and judgment skills as well as to introduce them to numerous business decision modeling techniques.

The author firmly believes that students must understand the underlying business decision modeling process and not just "point and click" their way to computer-generated solutions. At times the business decision modeling discipline has been accused of supplying students with software or spreadsheet models that spit out problem solutions, while students understand neither how they were generated nor how they should be interpreted. This text provides a foundation in the construction of models, including those developed in conjunction with spreadsheets, the use of specialized software, and the ability to interpret the results that these software packages generate.

Spreadsheet Solution for Break-Even Analysis Problem

The break-even analysis problem given above can also be solved by using a spreadsheet program such as Excel. The following steps illustrate how the surfboard break-even problem can be modeled and solved in an Excel spreadsheet.

1. Open Excel and a new Excel worksheet.
2. In cell A1, type **Break-Even Analysis for Surfboard Inc.**
3. In cell A3, type **Fixed Costs** =. Proceed to cell B3 and type in the value associated with the fixed costs of manufacturing surfboards. For our example, type in **$100,000.**
4. In cell A5, type **Variable Costs** =. Proceed to cell B5 and type in the value associated with the variable costs of manufacturing surfboards. For our example, type in **$100.**
5. In cell A7, type **Price** =. Proceed to cell B7 and type in the value associated with the selling price of a surfboard. For our example, type in **$300.**
6. In cell A9, type **Break-Even Point** =.
7. In cell B9, type in the following formula for the break-even point: **=B3/(B7–B5)**

Cell B9 will then contain the break-even point for our surfboard example. Figure 1.5 displays how this will appear on an Excel spreadsheet.

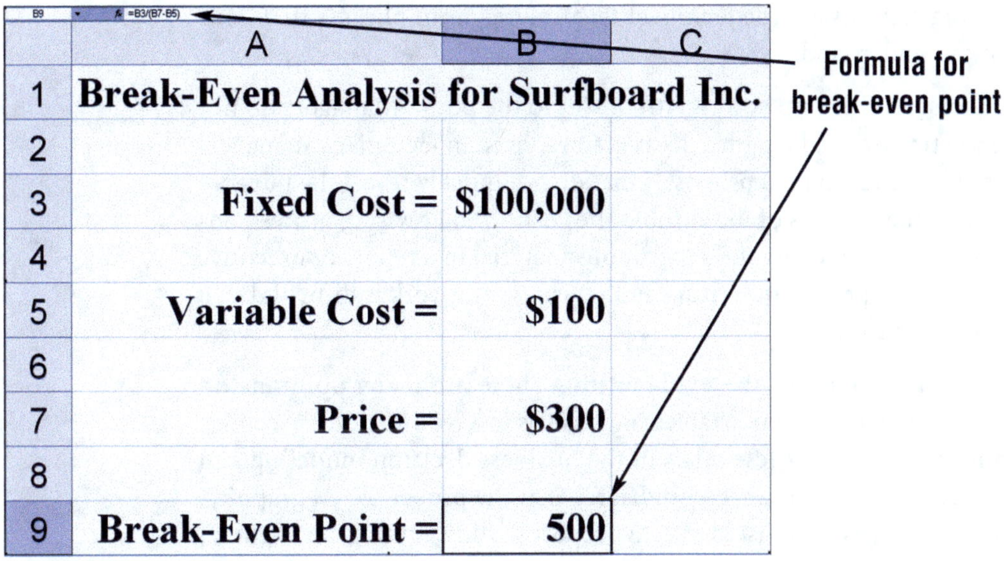

FIGURE 1.5

Excel Spreadsheet for Break-even Analysis

Writing Business Decision Modeling Reports for Business

Reports comprise analysis, conclusions, and recommendations. The quality of the final report is a function of the quality of the content and the quality of the packaging. A beautifully packaged report that has meaningless analysis is as worthless as a powerful analysis that is packaged so poorly that it never gets read. You must have both quality content and packaging to present an effective report.

General Rules of Thumb

It has been said that people tend to be persuaded more easily if a story or anecdote is used to prove a point. In many cases, managers must provide statistics or numbers to convince a client. However, most conclude it is more effective to give a short anecdote before providing the statistics.

There has been much written about business report presentation. There are a few areas that definitely apply to business decision modeling reports. These areas are crucial to helping your client understand your analysis. Areas of utmost importance when writing business decision modeling reports are:

1. **Use common, everyday language.** The terminology and symbols used in business decision modeling at times are very complex. Your client may not be familiar with this terminology or the symbols used. If possible, avoid the use of technical jargon but use your knowledge of business decision

modeling to translate the technical terminology into phrases that your client can understand.

2. **Be concise; tighten up your writing.** Get to the point. Managers do not have the time to read lengthy, ill-written reports. In fact, many managers will not continue to read proposals that do not quickly reveal the purpose and recommendations of the author. The writing and revising process aids dramatically in reducing the superfluous material in a report or executive summary. The process of writing and revising your work is difficult but a very rewarding task.

3. **Use graphics to aid in the explanation.** There are many opinions on whether to include graphics, tables, and visuals in a report and/or executive summary. Overall, professionals in the business decision modeling and technical writing disciplines would agree that the proper use of graphics, tables, and visuals is a must in effective report writing. A few general guidelines do apply:
   - **Labeling.** All charts, graphs, and tables must be labeled.
   - **Size.** All charts, graphs, and tables should be large and easy to read.
   - **Position.** All charts, graphs, and tables should be contiguous. If possible, do not split visuals over two pages.

In summary, visuals should aid the client in understanding your material. They should not cloud or distort the information.

Creating a Structure

One of the most important issues in creating effective business decision modeling reports is to know the goal of the report and to create a structure that guides you through the analysis and writing. A common report structure is as follows.

Executive Summary
Introduction—Background
Problem Statement—Purpose
Analysis
Conclusions and Recommendations

EXECUTIVE SUMMARY

The executive summary is the **most critical piece** of the final report. In reality, most busy executives never read beyond this section. Think to yourself how many times you have actually read a report cover to cover; most of us skim the introduction, read the executive summary, and then skip to the conclusions/recommendations.

How much detail should be included in an executive summary? The rule of thumb is the shorter the better. An executive summary is the report in miniature that covers key findings, conclusions, and recommendations. A number of good reference documents on writing executive summaries are listed at the end of this section.

INTRODUCTION—BACKGROUND

The length and the style of the introduction and background section may differ depending on the audience and the problem at hand. This section should be kept to a minimum and should outline the problem and its background as decided on by the client and the report analysts.

PROBLEM STATEMENT—PURPOSE

The statement of purpose, or problem statement, can be included in the introduction but many times is set apart for effect. In addition, this section can provide details and information about definitions and assumptions made in the analysis.

ANALYSIS

This is the heart of the report. The model of how the problem is solved must be presented here along with the "what if," or sensitivity, analysis. Sensitivity analysis will be defined and detailed in Chapter 4. Anyone who is still interested after reading the executive summary will peruse this section, looking for verification and validation of the outcomes seen earlier.

This section must be written very clearly and completely and should include charts, tables, and other graphics. On the other hand, do not overdo it. Excessive use of tables, computer printouts, or mathematical formulas in the body of the report is highly discouraged. Use appendices to house this material and provide proper reference in the body of the report.

CONCLUSIONS AND RECOMMENDATIONS

The recommendation section should sum up what the analysis section and the sensitivity analysis concluded. At a minimum, a restatement of the choice or decision to be made, accompanied by the implications of that choice or decision, must appear. In other words, explain to your client what the best alternatives are, the process to begin exploring those options, and the associated costs, profits, etc. After the conclusions and recommendations section, an appendix can be used to house technical information, computer output, calculations, and/or complete mathematical models.

Executive Summary Example for Surfboard Inc.

The sample document on the right is an executive summary for the Surfboard Inc. model developed earlier in this chapter. The executive summary should be used by students of business decision modeling as a guide for future writing. It must be noted that it is only one example and executive summary style may change, depending on audience and content.

Since the executive summary is the only document presented, it must both explain the problem facing Surfboard Inc. and provide recommendations in a limited amount of space.

EXECUTIVE SUMMARY FOR SURFBOARD INC. BREAK-EVEN ANALYSIS

TO: Eddie
FROM: Business Decision Modeling Consulting Group

Introduction

Surfboard Inc. is seeking a break-even analysis for its North Shore operations. The objective is to find Surfboard Inc.'s break-even point given its cost and pricing structure. We are assuming the firm can sell all surfboards produced.

Current Cost and Pricing Structure

The current cost and pricing structure is summarized in Table 1:

TABLE 1: SURFBOARD MANUFACTURING FIRM COST AND PRICING INFORMATION

Cost category	$ costs	$ price per surfboard
Fixed cost	$100,000	$300
Variable cost per surfboard or average variable cost	$100	

Profit Equation

On the basis of the above information, costs and pricing, a general profit equation can be established. This equation is listed below.

$$\text{Profit} = \$200 \times (\text{number of surfboards}) - \$100{,}000$$

The breakeven point quantity is equal to 500 surfboards. Hence, Surfboard Inc., at the current cost and pricing levels, must produce at least 500 surfboards to break even.

Break-Even Graph

To illustrate this point in relation to other production levels, a break-even graph has been constructed. The graph relates various levels of surfboard sales/production to the resultant levels of profit, revenue, and costs. Figure 1 displays the break-even graph.

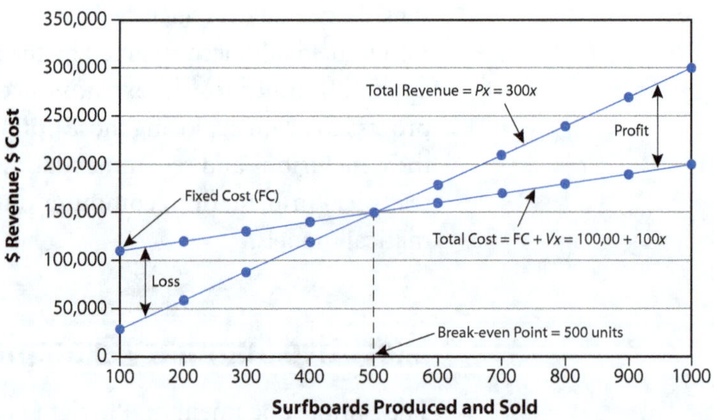

FIGURE 1. Surfboard Inc. Breakeven Graph

Conclusions

Figure 1 illustrates that the break-even point in number of surfboards is equal to 500 surfboards. Surfboard Inc. will incur a loss at sales/production levels of less than 500 surfboards and garner a profit at sales/production levels of greater than 500 surfboards. Total Revenue is defined on the graph as *Px* (price multiplied by quantity) and Total Cost is defined as $FC + Vx$ (fixed cost + variable cost multiplied by units sold).

Optimal Information Area

Bricklin, Dan. "Dan Bricklin's Web Site"
http://bricklin.com/history/sai.htm

Decision Sciences Institute
http://dsi.gsu.edu

Institute for Operations Research and Management Science
http://www.informs.org

Mattessich, Richard. "Early History of the Spreadsheet"
http://www.j-walk.com/history/spreadsh.htm

Power, Daniel. "A Brief History of Spreadsheets"
http://dssresources.com/

Trick, Michael. "Michael Trick's Operations Research Web Site"
http//mat.gsia.cmu.edu

"VisiCalc '79," Dan Bricklin and Bob Frankston, *Creative Computing,* November 1984, vol. 10, pp. 122, 124.

"VisiCalc Production Ends," *PC Magazine,* August 6, 1985. vol. 4, p. 33.

References

Ackoff, Russell L., and Maurice W. Sasieni, *Fundamentals of Operations Research,* New York: John Wiley & Sons, 1968.

Beer, Stafford, *Management Sciences: The Business Use of Operations Research,* New York: Doubleday, 1967.

Hillier, F. S., and G. J. Lieberman, *Operations Research,* 4th ed., San Francisco: Holden-Day, 1987.

Holtz, Herman, *The Consultant's Guide to Proposal Writing: How to Satisfy Your Clients and Double Your Income,* New York: John Wiley and Sons, 1998.

Locker, Kitty, *Business and Administrative Communication,* 4th ed., New York: Irwin/McGraw-Hill, 1997.

Ragsdale, Cliff, *Spreadsheet Modeling and Decision Analysis,* 2nd ed., Cincinnati: South-Western, 1998.

Sant, Tom, *Persuasive Business Proposals: Writing to Win Customers, Clients, and Contracts,* New York: American Management Association, 1992.

Silk, David, *How to Communicate in Business: A Handbook for Engineers,* IEE Management of Technology Series 17, 1995.

Smith, Charles B., *A Guide to Business Research: Developing, Conducting, and Writing Research Projects,* Chicago: Nelson-Hall Publishers, 1991.

Taylor, Bernard, *Introduction to Management Science,* 6th ed., Engelwood Cliffs, NJ: Prentice-Hall, 1999.

PROBLEMS

1. Rick Miles runs a CD-making business. He forecasts demand for his CDs at 5000 for the next year. He charges $20 per CD sold. It costs him $2000 in fixed costs a year to run his business and $2 per CD in variable costs.

   a. What are Rick's revenues?

   b. What are Rick's costs?

   c. Does Rick make a profit?

2. The Scheinbach computer company manufactures computers wholesale. The company's fixed monthly cost is $45,000, and its variable per computer cost is $525. The company sells the computers for $925. Determine the monthly break-even volume for the company.

3. Kathy runs her own computer education business. She needs $4000 a year to pay the leases on the computers she uses. She estimates she will have 400 pupils for the next year. Each pupil pays $200 for the education. However, it costs Kathy $20 to $30 per pupil in supplies and overhead.

   a. What are Kathy's yearly revenues?

   b. What are Kathy's average total costs? What is the range of Kathy's costs?

   c. Does Kathy make a profit? What is the range of Kathy's profit?

4. Wayne owns a shaved ice stand. He sells 700 shaved ice cups per month at $1.50 each, making the total revenue $1050. Each shaved ice costs Wayne $0.50 and he has fixed costs of $750, making his total costs $1100. Therefore, he realizes a loss of $50 a month. Help him determine what his break-even point is.

5. HPU Graduates is a start-up microbrewery in Pahoa, Hawaii. Its fixed costs to produce beer total $8000 per month. The variable cost to produce their beer is $3.00 per case of beer. It sells its beer to one hotel only, and that hotel has said it wants 550 cases this month. What price does HPU need to charge to break even?

6. The VA-TX Company is going to present a new product in Santa Clara, California. In this event, VA-TX will present a seminar with a coffee break. The auditorium's capacity is 500 people. The cost of renting the place is $4000/day, utilities included. Moreover, the cost of the food and drinks is $5 per person. After some other experiences, the company knows that 50% of the audience buys its product, which is priced at $75. Is Santa Clara a profitable place to do this kind of campaign?

7. Eric runs a chiropractic center in Mililani. The annual fixed costs for operating Chiro-Care clinic is $222,000. The variable cost per patient treated is $55. The price billed for each visit is $136. Currently, he has around 2500 visits a year.

   a. Is he making a profit?

   b. He doesn't think he can increase demand, so he is thinking about a cost-cutting measure for his variable costs. What would his variable costs need to be in order for him to break even at 2500 visits a year?

8. John is thinking about getting into the tourism business in Oahu. He will take visitors on a whole-day trip to the main tourist spots on the island in a new van he is planning to buy. He would like to know how many tourists he has to move daily to have a before-taxes profit of $1000 per month so he can save that money. He will work 25 days per month.

   His costs for the new business would be as follows:

   Variable costs per day trip
   - Gasoline: $30
   - Maintenance: $5 (oil, tune-ups, wheels, repairs, etc.)

   Fixed costs
   - Leasing and insurance: $1000 per month
   - Personal expenses: $1000 (the minimum amount he needs for living expenses) per month

   He is planning to charge $45 per visitor for a day trip.

   Using the break-even formula, John will need how many daily travelers in order to achieve a profit of $1000 per month?

9. The Thai Corporation has sales subsidiaries around the world. As a rule of thumb, each new established subsidiary should be able to reach its break-even point during year 2. After 18 months of business activity in Thailand, The Thai Corporation's Thai sales subsidiary generated a sales volume of 200,000 units. Its variable costs are $5 per unit and fixed costs at this level equal $750,000.

   a. In year 2, at a sales price of $17 per unit, how many units does the subsidiary need to sell in order to break even?

   b. Do you think the company will make a profit if last year's sales are a good indicator of future sales?

10. The VA-TX Company has noticed when it advertises, it dramatically increases the amount of customers who buy its product at seminars. With advertising, VA-TX expects the audience to buy the product at a price of $75. The cost of renting a place is $4000/day, utilities included. Moreover, the cost of food and drinks is $5/person. If VA-TX assumes at a minimum it will sell 124 units, what would be the upper bound on advertising dollars (i.e., where would the the company break even?).

11. Bradley is a sales associate for VA-TX. He has suggested that if the company would provide an open bar at the end of the seminar, sales would rise. The open bar would increase the variable cost per customer from $5 to $7.50.

    a. With the same fixed cost structure, how many sales would VA-TX have to make to break even?

    b. How does this compare with the break-even point(s) in Problem 10?

12. Bernie Hsiao runs a lamp-making business. He has two lines of lamps: antler lamps and fishing rod lamps. It costs him $10,000 a year to run his business (labor, materials, and overhead). The estimated demand for antler lamps is anywhere from 100 to 200 units. The estimated demand for fishing rod lamps is 300 to 400 units. He charges $2000 for antler lamps and $200 for fishing rod lamps. However, he incurs $750 in variable costs per antler lamp sold and $30 for each fishing rod lamp sold.

    a. What are Bernie's expected/average revenues from antler lamps? What are Bernie's expected/average revenues from fishing rod lamps? What is the total expected/average revenue Bernie's lamp business could generate? What is the range of total expected/average profit?

    b. What are the expected/average costs associated with the lamp business? Identify the costs associated with antler lamps, fishing rod lamps, and costs associated with both.

    c. Does Bernie make a profit in the case of low estimated demand for each lamp?

    d. Does Bernie make a profit in the case of high estimated demand for each lamp?

    e. If half of the fixed costs are attributable to antler lamps, how much do the antler lamps contribute to this profit? If half the fixed costs are attributable to fishing rod lamps, how much do the fishing rod lamps contribute to this profit?

CHAPTER

2 Introduction to Spreadsheet Modeling

LEARNING *Objectives*

- Understand the process of spreadsheet modeling
- Understand simple spreadsheet concepts (layout, formula bar, active cell, etc.) terminology (cells, text, calculations, etc.), formatting of cells (borders, shading, naming, etc.), and referencing (relative, absolute, etc.)
- Develop skills in creating simple formulas and formatting spreadsheets
- Create a spreadsheet to store and process numerical information
- Learn the basics of the following spreadsheet functions: Goal Seek, Solver, and Curve Fitting

CHAPTER Outline

Business Decision Modeling in Action

Using Spreadsheet Models

Business Decision Modeling throughout the Ages

A Brief History of Spreadsheet Modeling

Business Decision Modeling Behind the Scenes

Spreadsheets in Real Business Situations

Applied Spreadsheet Modeling—Using Basic Functions

- Example 2
- Using MIN Function
- Using IF Function
- Using VLOOKUP Function
- Sensitivity Analysis Using Data Table
- Expected Profit from Demand Probabilities
- Using SUMPRODUCT

Applied Spreadsheet Modeling—Using Solver

- Example 3
- Building the Spreadsheet Model
- Using Excel Solver
- Analysis of Results
- Modification of Constraints and Rerun of Solver

Applied Spreadsheet Modeling—Curve Fitting

- Example 4
- Linear Function
- Power Function
- Exponential Function
- Mean Absolute Percentage Error (MAPE)
- Adding in Solver in Excel

Summary

- Executive Summary Example for Teez's Profit Problem

Case Study—John Woo's Cellular Connections

Interactive Case—Break-Even Analysis at SportsExchange

Summary of Key Excel Terms

Optimal Information Area

References

Problems

Business Decision Modeling in Action

Using Spreadsheet Models

Client Problem

The staff of Schlumberger was confronted with a resource-intensive ordeal during each reporting period. Budget planning posed a resource drain on the accounting staff because of time-intensive manual editing of spreadsheets into various required company formats.

Solution

Beyond Technology (www.beyondtechnology.com) is a widely recognized Microsoft Excel VBA development firm. Beyond Technology develops financial and engineering applications, with special expertise in budget planning, forecasting, investment portfolio analysis, decision support systems, and data modeling. Beyond Technology worked with Schlumberger on a strategy integrating various components of its financial reporting. The first step in the model was developing a planning/project costing model for worldwide budget administration, consolidation, reporting, and analysis. Beyond Technology included a multicurrency break-even model—a vision of the organization's chief controller—to perform "what if" analyses across the company's manufacturing and engineering enterprise. Microsoft VBA functions were used to automate hundreds of time-consuming manual tasks, freeing professional staff to concentrate on the business.

Financial Tools for Negotiation: Examples from PricewaterhouseCoopers

PricewaterhouseCoopers (PWC), at www.pwcglobal.com, is one of the world's largest professional services organizations. The group helps clients to clarify their thinking and strategies through the application of analytical and quantitative techniques. Transaction analytics achieves this by using a variety of techniques, including uncertainty and risk analysis, financial modeling, and systems thinking—a means of mapping the causes and effects of business drivers.

Business Question: How Can We Target Our Customers Individually?

A PWC client wanted to target its existing customers more accurately, building stronger relationships and encouraging brand loyalty, maximizing value from its data. PWC initially developed a spreadsheet-based campaign-planning tool for the client to use and identified a number of new opportunities for the client to build customer profiles. This tool enabled the client to select individual customers for a marketing campaign, drilling down to price sensitivity for individuals, and provided an accurate measure of the financial return for the client.

Business Question: How Can We Evaluate Our Product Options?

PWC built a product strategy decision matrix for the client, which needed to evaluate the different product options available before committing to further development trials. PWC built a decision tree and evaluation matrix to structure the product options, develop criteria to evaluate each option and develop metrics by which to judge the evaluations (including total attractiveness, overall probability of achievement, overall confidence rating, and product utility).

Introduction

Life itself requires one to make countless decisions. What field am I going to concentrate in? Which job offer should I take? Whom am I going to marry? How much should I invest? Making good decisions is a very difficult task. One has to evaluate the numerous courses of action available and choose the best alternative.

In the business world, managers are faced with the same need to make endless qualified decisions. Often managers use spreadsheets as a convenient and useful tool in their analytical toolkit besides experienced guesses to help them make better decisions.

Most spreadsheet models are mathematical formulations.

Spreadsheets accept inputs based on a mathematical relationship with logical assumptions and provide outputs that are insightful to an analytical manager. The power of spreadsheets comes from their flexibility, i.e., the ability to instantly provide the results (output) when one varies the inputs.

By itself, a spreadsheet does not make decisions; it only serves as a tool for managers. Managers have to analyze the decision alternatives before choosing a specific plan for implementation. Models, when properly formulated, can greatly enhance decision making. They also provide structure and quantifiable results, and thus credibility, to the decision-making process.

This is the very essence of using quantitative methods for business decisions.

Background

Most spreadsheet models tend to begin as a mathematical model. Do not be afraid of these terms in the mistaken view that only experts in spreadsheet modeling or higher mathematics can harness the power of spreadsheets for analytical decision making. A simple mathematical model tends to be a quantitative representation or approximation of a real situation. Let's begin with a very well known and well used mathematical model for business modeling—the profit equation:

$$\text{Profit} = \text{revenue} - \text{expenses}$$

The profit equation represents a well-defined functional relationship between revenue and expenses. In simple mathematical terms, profit is a function of revenue and expenses.

$$Y = f(X_1, X_2)$$

where Y represents profit and X_1 and X_2 represent revenue and expenses, respectively.

We could also say that profit *depends* on revenue and expenses. Therefore profit represents a dependent variable Y, whereas revenue and expenses are independent variables X_1 and X_2, respectively.

When modeled properly into a spreadsheet, the revenue and expenses will be the *inputs* to produce the corresponding profit result, which is the *output*.

Functions can be quite complex, involving multiple independent variables as well as intermediate levels of independent variables. The level of expenses could be further dependent on level of activity, as represented, for example, by sales commission for each product sold. Such expenses are known as *variable costs*, in economic terms. Revenue may also depend on unknown variables such as demand.

Not all business problems have a clearly defined functional relationship between the dependent and the independent variables like the profit equation. We will discuss in the next section the different categories of models that can be classified on the basis of the characteristics of the relationship between the variables and characteristics of the values of independent variables.

Categories of Models

DESCRIPTIVE MODELS

The first category of models you are likely to encounter in the business world are called *descriptive models.* Descriptive models simply describe the current situation or system facing the manager. These models tend to have a well-defined relationship between the independent variables (inputs) and the dependent variable (output). Often this translates to a well-defined mathematical formula such as that of a profit equation, where profit is the output. However, the values of the independent variables such as demand are not within the decision maker's control and thus are uncertain. With this type of decision problems, we may use management science techniques such as simulation, as well as queuing, PERT, and inventory models.

Descriptive models describe situations.

For example, you currently manage the Waikiki branch of XYZ convenience stores and you believe long lines at the cash register are deterring potential customers from entering the store and making purchases. The manager wants to build a model that reflects the current situation at the store but that will also be able to improve the current situation if possible. The number of customers entering and making purchases varies and has to be estimated or simulated in order to determine the profit.

PRESCRIPTIVE MODELS

Prescriptive models, on the other hand, prescribe solutions for a manager based on the problem defined. Here the relationship between the independent variables and the dependent variable is well defined and the values of the independent variables are known or are within the decision maker's control. All we need in order to solve the problem is to determine the values of the independent variables (inputs) that will produce the best possible value for the dependent variable (output).

Prescriptive models vary inputs to reach a desired output.

For example, as an operations manager of a bakery, you may know your inventory of flour, butter, and eggs as well as the labor hours available and the rate of production, but you need to find out how many sweet buns you can produce in a day on the basis of this set of known variables. You may wish to find the optimal number of buns to produce in order to maximize profits while having a limited number of resources available. Another example is a typical investor's problem. How should your limited funds be allocated between different investments in order to maximize returns without exceeding a certain level of risk? Overall, a goal of descriptive models is to generate a solution concept early in the process, whereas a goal of prescriptive models is to better understand the requirements before generating a solution.

DETERMINISTIC MODELS

Deterministic means with certainty.

Deterministic models assume all relevant inputs are known with certainty. Perhaps the most common and popular deterministic modeling technique is mathematical programming.

STOCHASTIC/PROBABILISTIC MODELS

Stochastic means involving chance or probability.

Stochastic or probabilistic models, on the other hand, assume that some inputs are not known with certainty. This text will present probabilistic modeling techniques such as decision analysis, simulation, and forecasting.

PREDICTIVE MODELS

Predictive models aim to set up functional relationships between dependent and independent variables.

The final category of decision problems are known as *predictive models,* where the objective is to identify the form of the functional relationship between the dependent variables and the independent variables, as it is unknown. In order to do this, we need to predict how these variables relate to each other, given that the values of the independent variables are known. Several management science techniques such as regression analysis, time series analysis, and discriminant analysis can be used for this purpose.

For example, a marketer believes that the demand for its rejuvenating cream is dependent on price and buyer's age as well as advertising. Here demand is the dependent variable and price, age, and advertising are independent variables. However, the relationship that relates these variables to one another may be unknown. Thus the marketer will have to analyze the relationship, using techniques such as regression analysis of past buying behavior in order to identify the function that relates these variables in a reasonably accurate fashion. Another example is to use historical stock prices to predict the relationship of the current stock price and the underlying index it is traded in.

Models versus Modeling

Good managers learn modeling and not specific models.

It is important to stress that it is not necessary to memorize a particular model to solve real-world problems, but rather to understand the importance of modeling. Modeling is more of a process, where we abstract the essence of a real problem into a model, spreadsheet, or other medium.

Process for Modeling

Why a Process for Modeling?

In general, the problem-solving process is made up of a number of steps including a feedback loop.

The intent in this chapter is to demonstrate a general approach to the model-building process in a spreadsheet environment versus covering specific models. The advantage is for the student to complete this course with the ability to apply the knowledge and practicum of spreadsheet modeling to a wide array of business fields, whether it is in information sciences, marketing, finance, or human resources.

A few general points before delving into the salient points of the problem solving process.

Initially, a process-driven modeling approach forces one to think logically about the problem at hand. In other words, one must consider in a given situation what elements can be controlled and how they are logically related. In a waiting line situation, the number of customers in line is related to the rate at which the cashier serves each customer. Also the probability that potential customers walk away from a purchase is related to the length of waiting time (also quantified as the number of customers waiting in line multiplied by the average service time taken by the cashier).

In addition, you may be unfamiliar with and probably intimidated by the need to conduct spreadsheet modeling for your analysis. This course is taught with the intention of guiding the uninitiated through the basic uses of Excel by way of practical application of the various case studies you and your colleagues will be put through. This chapter will also run through a number of Excel functions that will be useful for a variety of problem-solving applications.

Finally, the problem-solving process that is described in this chapter represents good practice for modelers who are faced with a wide variety of problems rather than a particular problem (Figure 2.1). The steps we describe here will aid you in how you may logically think through the problem at hand and the steps you may need to take to solve and implement it with greater success in the real world. This may seem redundant to a few of you, as you may possess a natural analytical mind-set; however, it is still important to understand how modeling fits into the entire problem-solving process to be an effective modeler.

The Problem-Solving Process

STEP 1: PROBLEM DEFINITION

Normally, those people closest to the business would identify the problem when there exists a disparity between a desired scenario and the actual situation, such as when profits are not as high as anticipated, and the manager wants to understand the underlying cause. Often the manager may have a general idea of the problem but is not able to clearly define it. The analyst or the manager required to model the problem and conduct an analysis has to sort through the information provided

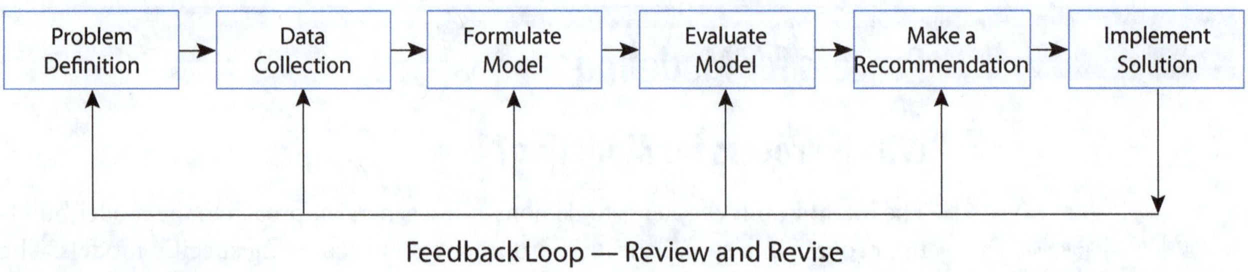

FIGURE 2.1
Problem-Solving Process

and determine the root problem. Identifying the real problem requires insight, investigation, and a certain amount of skepticism.

The result of deriving a proper understanding of the situation at hand would include a clearly defined statement of the problem, the manager's objectives (the dependent variable), and various related parameters (or independent variables). The manager may want to identify what is causing profits to fall, where the objective is to maximize profit. The related parameters could be price, demand, productivity of the sales force, and related expenses.

Remaining objective is very important in modeling.

A major mistake in trying to define a problem is to have a solution in mind based on gut feel or even business instinct. Although it is quite common for managers close to the business to believe their view is quite accurate in this respect, an effective modeler who remains objective at the outset may discover insights overlooked by the manager.

STEP 2: DATA COLLECTION

This stage is not extensively covered, although it is implied, in the rest of the text. Market researchers spend hours collecting data through observation, interviews, surveys, sorting through the organization's historical data, or surfing the Internet. In the chapter on probability, Chapter 3, we show an example of how one may derive a usable function of demand by determining whether demand is normally distributed, from a statement given by the manager. Note that very often the data we collect are at best approximations of actual behavior. For example, it is impossible to accurately predict demand on a daily basis for 365 days of the year. The important thing is to understand what is relevant (i.e., critical factors) and how it affects your problem.

STEP 3: FORMULATE MODEL

Models can be descriptive, prescriptive, deterministic, stochastic, or predictive.

After defining the problem and gathering the necessary data, the manager must formulate a model of the problem. Depending on the objective, the model may be descriptive, prescriptive, or predictive. If a manager is faced with various alternatives, such as to increase the sales force or lower the price, to improve profitability, the model has to be descriptive to compare the results of conducting what-if scenarios for a given situation. On the other hand, a manager who wants to maximize profit while varying the parameters with certain constraints may use a prescriptive model to determine the optimal price or the optimal number of sales people. The model may be a defined mathematical formula, such as the profit equation. The model may be predictive to help define the formula with known variables, such as determining the beta of a stock through a regression analysis of historical stock prices.

After choosing the appropriate modeling technique for the problem, we can use Excel to apply the relevant model. This is when the inputs (or variables) and formulas are entered into the spreadsheet to achieve outputs for the model.

STEP 4: EVALUATE THE MODEL

After model formulation, the model has to be evaluated to determine if the model formulated in step 3 is in fact an accurate representation of the problem. There are two ways to do this. You can enter various known inputs to see if the model accurately depicts the current situation. Alternatively, you can vary the inputs to see if the model generates reasonable results.

Evaluation is completed to ensure the model is accurate.

If the model produces awkward results, the modeler will have to evaluate whether the formula and inputs entered are accurate. If they are, the modeler may have to relook at the model, as a crucial constraint (e.g., labor hours must be less that 50 hours per week) or even a crucial variable (e.g., state law requires any nurse seeing critical care patients to be a registered nurse) may have been overlooked.

Testing the results of the model against known results helps ensure the structural integrity and validity of the model. This step is vital, as it provides feedback to the modeler to modify the model before it is presented to the manager or client.

STEP 5: MAKE A RECOMMENDATION

Given that the spreadsheet model is formulated correctly, the next step is to use the model to analyze the problem it represents and evaluate the alternatives. This may require you to ask several what-if questions and conduct sensitivity analysis. In other cases, if the model is prescriptive, it may provide an optimal solution. Often we make estimations for numerical inputs into a problem; besides providing an optimal solution, sensitivity analysis also provides insights about how the model works.

What-if questions and sensitivity analysis must be part of the recommendations of the model.

Either way, the modeler has to make a recommendation that best meets the organization's objectives. In real-life situations, the modeling team would also have to present and explain their recommendation as well as the workings of the model to the organization.

STEP 6: IMPLEMENTATION AND FEEDBACK

Even if the model is robust and provides an optimal solution, the hardest part is the implementation step. This is because people in general are naturally resistant to change. One way to ensure buy-in and receptivity is for the modeling team to involve the end users from the onset and preferably have them involved in the entire problem-solving process. Besides improving adoptability, this practice would also give modelers a better understanding of the problem and identify bugs in the model early on, reducing the time required to modify the model. To further ensure that the solution will be accepted, the solution/model should be flexible, with user-friendly interfaces.

Implementation may be the most difficult step of the problem-solving process.

This leads us to discuss some basic goals in spreadsheet modeling design in the next section.

Goals in Spreadsheet Design

The primary purpose of spreadsheets is to communicate information to managers. Therefore, the primary design objective in most spreadsheet models is to present the relevant parts of the problem clearly, logically, and in a manner that is simple to comprehend. The output of the spreadsheet model should be correct and consistent.

The primary purpose of spreadsheets is to communicate information to managers.

The model should be constructed such that a manager should be able to retrace the steps followed to generate the different outputs from the model in order to understand the model and verify results. Models therefore should be auditable by a third party and not simply perceived as a black box that receives inputs and spits out results. Often the data and assumptions used are dynamic or are best estimates of a situation. Thus, a well-designed spreadsheet should allow easy modification or enhancement in order to meet dynamic user requirements.

Basic Spreadsheet Modeling Concepts

We will describe some basic spreadsheet modeling concepts so that a beginner may be able to follow the topics and applied examples in the rest of the chapter.

Layout of a Spreadsheet

When you open Excel you will see, from the top, a Ribbon that contains tabs and within those tabs groups of relevant commands. Figure 2.2a displays the basic spreadsheet layout for Excel 2007. Figure 2.2b displays the basic spreadsheet layout for Excel 2010.

An open spreadsheet is displayed with cells labeled as rows in numbers and columns in alphabets. The rows run downward vertically from 1 to 65536 and columns are viewed from left to right from A to IV. The active cell highlighted on the left hand corner, as shown in Figure 2.2a and 2.2b, is referenced as A1. When you enter data in the active cell, it will appear simultaneously in the Formula bar and vice versa.

A standard spreadsheet layout is rows by columns.

A new workbook comes with three sheets indicated by the tabs (labeled Sheet 1, Sheet 2, and Sheet 3) at the bottom of an open workbook. We may use these tabs to

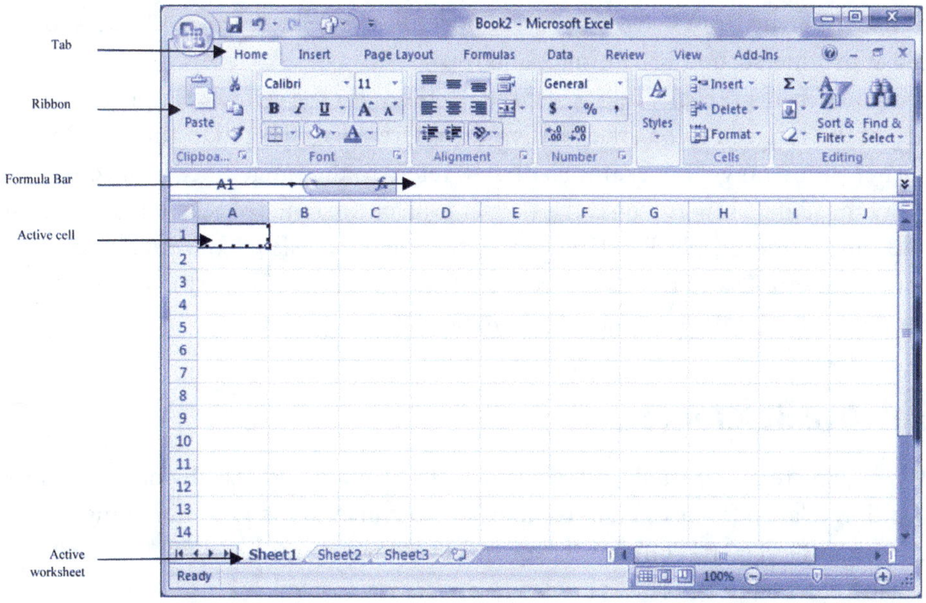

FIGURE 2.2a

Basic Spreadsheet Layout in Excel 2007

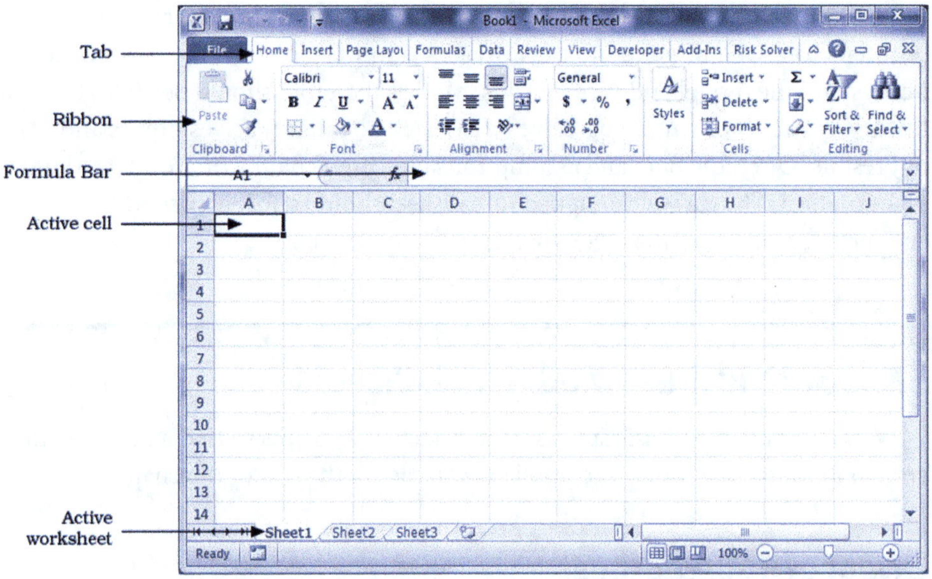

FIGURE 2.2b
Basic Spreadsheet Layout in Excel 2010

toggle between worksheets. We tend not to use all the cells in a single sheet; a complicated model may instead use several worksheets and new sheets may be inserted at the appropriate time. A useful feature of the Excel spreadsheet is the ability to link cells in the same worksheet and across different worksheets. Therefore, when we choose to vary inputs, we will see the effect of these changes within the model, which may span several worksheets (see Figure 2.2a and 2.2b for details).

Reference Cells and Ranges

A reference identifies a cell or a range of cells on a worksheet and tells Microsoft Excel where to look for the values or data you want to use in a formula. With references, you can use data contained in different parts of a worksheet in one formula or use the value from one cell in several formulas. A cell reference A2 refers to the cell at the intersection of column A and row 2.

In a spreadsheet, a reference identifies a cell or range of cells.

To refer to a range of cells, enter the reference for the cell in the upper-left corner of the range, a colon (:), and then the reference to the cell in the lower-right corner of the range. For example, B2:B10 refers to the range of cells in column B row 2 through to row 10. You can also refer to an entire range of cells across columns and rows. For example, B2:D10 refers to the range of cells in column B and row 2 across column D and through to row 10. D:D notation refers to the whole of column D and 2:2 notation refers to the whole of row 2.

To refer to a range of cells use a colon between the beginning cell and ending cell.

Relative References

When you create a formula, references to cells or ranges are usually based on their position relative to the cell that contains the formula. In the preceding range reference example, cell B2 contains the formula =A2; Microsoft Excel finds the value in A2 and enters it in B2. This is known as a *relative reference.*

A relative cell reference in a formula is based on the relative position of the cell that contains the formula and the cell the reference refers to.

Copying Formulas

To copy a formula, select the fill handle and the bottom right hand corner of the cell.

To move or copy a formula, select the cell that contains it and point your cursor to the fill handle at the bottom right corner of the selection. When you point at the fill handle, the pointer changes into a black cross. Left-click and drag the fill handle (see Figure 2.3) to copy the formula into adjacent cells.

When you copy a formula that uses relative references, Excel automatically adjusts the references in the pasted formula to refer to different cells relative to the position of the formula. In the following example, the formula in cell B2, =A2, *which is one cell to the left of B2,* has been copied to cell B3. Excel has adjusted the formula in cell B3 to =A3, which refers to the cell that is *one cell to the left of cell B3.*

On the other hand, when you copy a formula that uses absolute references, the cell references will not be adjusted, but will remain the same.

Absolute References

Absolute references always refer to a specific cell location.

Absolute references are actually cell references that always refer to cells in a specific location. If a dollar sign precedes the letter and/or number, such as $A$1, the column and/or row reference is absolute. You can either type in the $ sign to the cell reference or formula, or use the F4 key on your keyboard to toggle between the absolute, mixed, and relative cell references.

Use absolute references if you don't want Excel to adjust references when you copy a formula to a different cell. Thus, if the formula used in cell B2 was absolute, i.e. =$A$2, the formula copied to cell B3 would remain =$A$2 instead of changing to =A3.

Mixed References

Mixed references can be used to fix a specific column or row.

Excel allows you to not only fix a specific location but also to fix a column or a row. For example, typing $A2 fixes the column A, but the row reference will be adjusted correspondingly. In turn, typing A$2 fixes the row 2 but allows the column A to vary accordingly. An example: if a formula =$A2+B2 were copied to the cell one cell to the right and one cell down, the formula would be =$A3+C3.

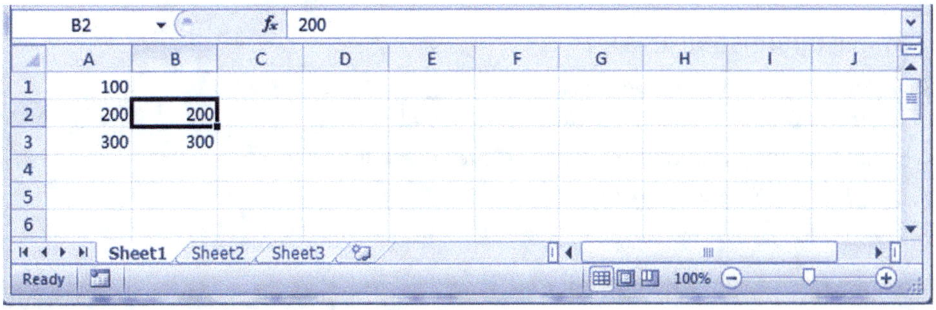

FIGURE 2.3

Fill Handle Example in Excel

Business Decision Modeling throughout the Ages

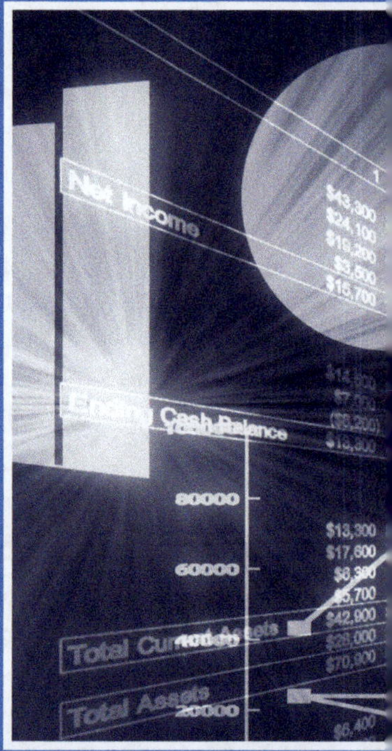

A Brief History of Spreadsheet Modeling

What Is Modeling?

Modeling is the process of building a model to replicate a given situation with the ability to preview, test, analyze, or resolve potential obstacles before the actual is implemented or built. Until a few years ago, analytical modeling was rarely used in business and was viewed as arcane, and perhaps with suspicion, by most managers. Its use and application was limited to an elite few. The advent of cheap, fast computing, however, meant that computational efficiency was no longer a concern for many practical business problems. This created new and exciting opportunities for end-user application.

History of Spreadsheets

VISICALC Computerized or electronic spreadsheets are more recent, and credit for this invention goes to Dan Bricklin and Bob Frankston, who created the software application VisiCalc for Apple II in 1978. Prior to Visicalc, spreadsheet computerization was possible on mainframe computers; however, this was cumbersome and clumsy. VisiCalc was created with the intention of "visualizing the spreadsheet as it was created."

LOTUS 1-2-3 By 1982 there were 18 such spreadsheet programs available in the market. A new product, Lotus 1-2-3, was introduced in 1983. Mitch Kapor, an ex-employee of VisiCorp (the company Bricklin and Frankston founded), developed Lotus 1-2-3, and his spreadsheet program quickly became the new industry spreadsheet standard. By 1985, VisiCalc was removed from the market after being purchased by Lotus. Lotus offered VisiCalc users upgrades to 1-2-3, thereby ensuring Lotus' ability to maintain a dominant market share for almost a decade.

MICROSOFT'S EXCEL But in today's business world, the most widely acceptable spreadsheet program is Microsoft's Excel. Excel was originally written for the 512K Apple Macintoshes in 1985. By 1988, a PC version of Excel was introduced to run under the Windows operating system and was highly successful. Excel is no longer a simple electronic financial spreadsheet; it serves as a data analysis program, a database and presentation program.

Optimal Information Area

D. J. Power's "History of Spreadsheets" website
http://www.dssresources.com/history/sshistory.html

Thomas Grossman's "Spreadsheet Analytics" site (an excellent resource)
http://www.ucalgary.ca/~grossman/resources.htm

Applied Spreadsheet Modeling—Goal Seek

Excel's Goal Seek add-in can be used to solve simple models.

In order to understand the use of spreadsheet modeling, we will run through, step by step, how a spreadsheet model is constructed for a simple profit model and conduct a sensitivity analysis with a data table and chart. We will complete this example by using Goal Seek to identify the break-even level. We will also show the basics of naming cells and using number formats.

Example 1

Teez incorporated sells printed T-shirts of various designs directly to customers at the local market for \$20 per bundle of five T-shirts. The cost of renting the stand for 8 hours is \$100 and Teez pays \$7 an hour to Sam, who sets up and runs the stand every weekend. The cost of producing a T-shirt is \$1.50 per T-shirt. Mr. T, the owner of Teez, believes that, on average, he manages to sell 15 bundles a day. Furthermore, he believes that during the rainy season, the average number of bundles sold is dramatically lowered (sometimes to only five bundles), and during those days his profit is greatly reduced. Mr. T wants to know what quantity he needs to sell to break even and whether he should remain open during the rainy season.

STEP 1: PROBLEM DEFINITION

Teez wants to know the following:

1. How will a change in the quantity sold affect his profit?
2. At what level of sales does he break even?
3. If he estimates sales of five bundles during the rainy season, should he rent the stand?

Mr. T's revenue is determined by the price and quantity of T-shirts sold. His costs include the fixed cost of renting the stand, the hourly cost of hiring Sam, and the number of hours he works, as well as the cost of producing a T-shirt. His profit is determined by deducting total costs from his revenue.

The input variables are:

Price of a bundle of 5 T-shirts = \$20
Quantity sold = 15
Stand rental per day = \$100
Hourly labor rate = \$7; hours worked = 8
Cost per T-shirt in a bundle = \$1.50

The formulas used are:

$$\text{Revenue} = \text{price} \times \text{quantity of T-shirts sold}$$

$$\text{Total cost} = \text{rental} + (\text{hourly labor rate} \times \text{hours worked}) + \text{cost per shirt} \times \text{number of T-shirt bundles}$$

$$\text{Profit} = \text{revenue} - \text{total cost}$$

STEP 2: FORMULATE THE MODEL

Enter the various variables identified earlier. For a more logical presentation of your model, inputs may be grouped and individual cells are named. We first begin with revenue inputs, which consist of the price and the quantity sold (see Figure 2.4a for Excel 2007 and Figure 2.4b for Excel 2010).

Applying Number Format to Cell

Note that after entering 20 in the cell, you may format the input into a dollar format by clicking on the $ shortcut button (indicated by the arrow) in Figure 2.4a for Excel 2007 and Figure 2.4b for Excel 2010.

The $ shortcut button formats cells into dollars and cents.

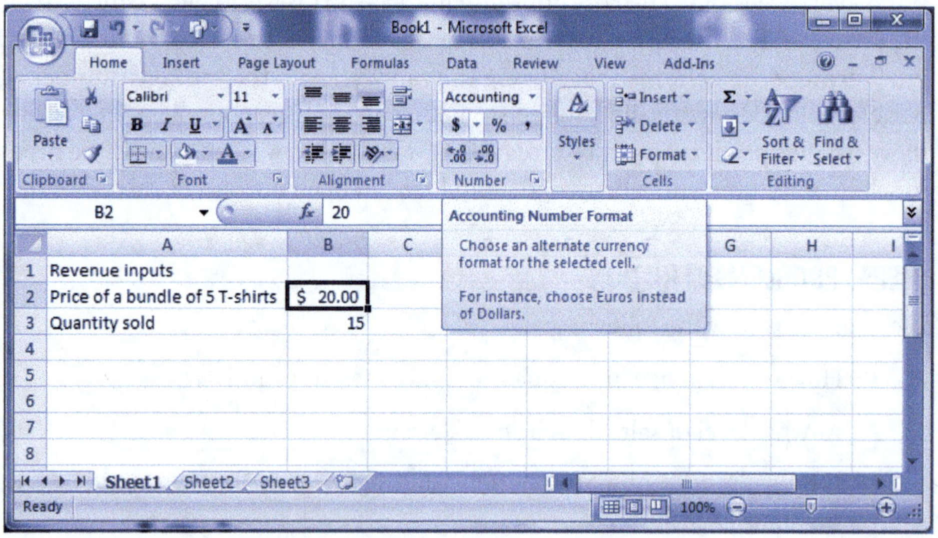

FIGURE 2.4a
Spreadsheet Example for Revenue Calculation 2007

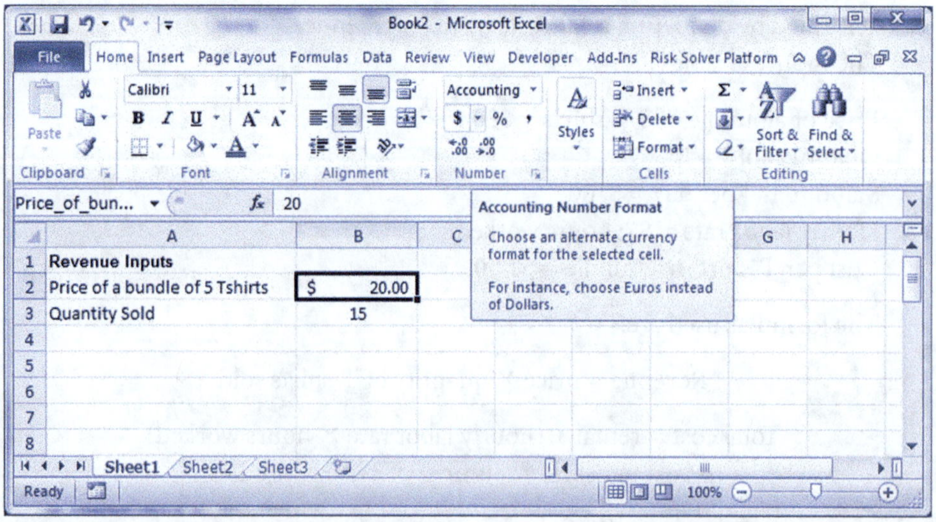

FIGURE 2.4b
Spreadsheet Example for Revenue Calculation 2010

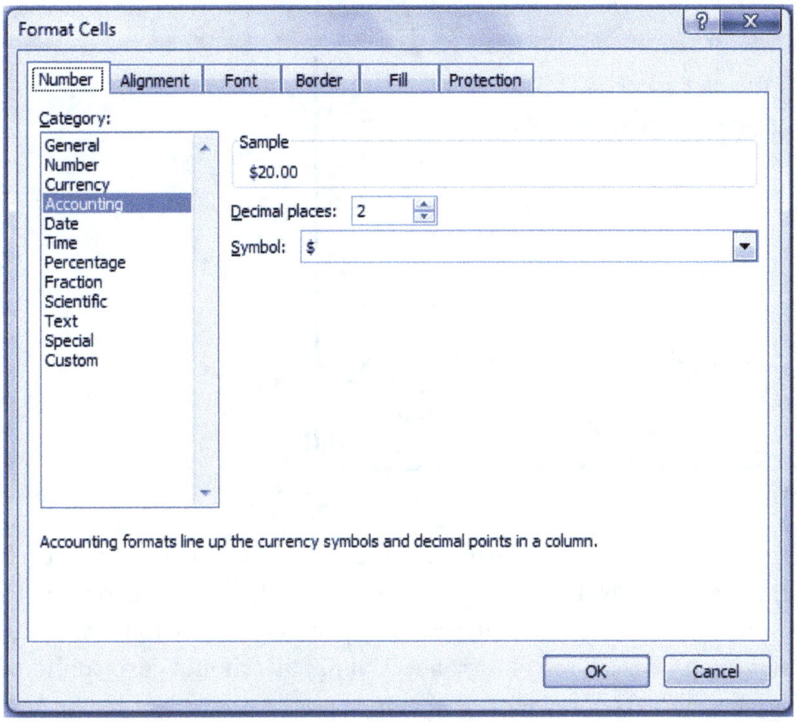

FIGURE 2.5
Example of Number Formatting in Excel

Alternatively you may use the drop-down menu of Format (found on the Menu bar) and point at Cells, after which you will be shown the dialog box in Figure 2.5. You may choose the appropriate format from the left column.

Naming Cells

To name a cell, click on the cell to be named, and then click in the Name box and type in the name of the cell.

Notice that a cell is defined by its location within the columns and rows, In the case of the $20.00 entry, the cell is defined in the spreadsheet as B2, i.e., column B and row 2. Generally it is good practice to name cells that contain formulas or global variables (price, hourly costs, etc.), as it allows the user to more easily identify the concept being modeled within the cells.

To name a cell you have to first click on the cell you wish to name. For the T-shirt example, we wish to name the T-shirt bundle price, cell B2. Therefore, click on cell B2 and then click on the Name box (see Figure 2.6). Type a name for the cell and press Enter. Spaces are unacceptable in a named cell; instead you should use an underscore to indicate a space. For example, the name of B2 should be entered as "Price_of_bundle" instead of "Price of bundle" (see Figure 2.6).

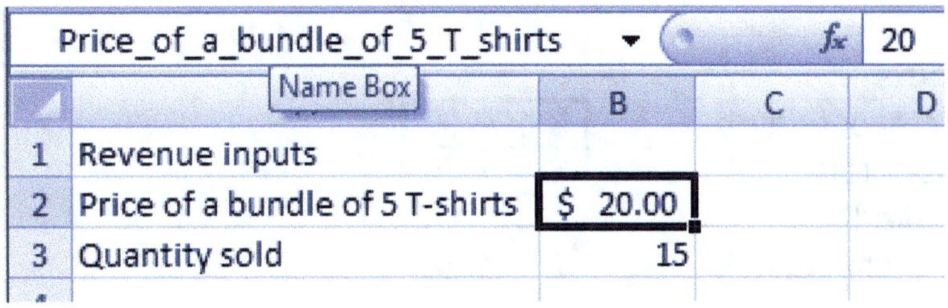

FIGURE 2.6
Example of Naming a Cell in Excel

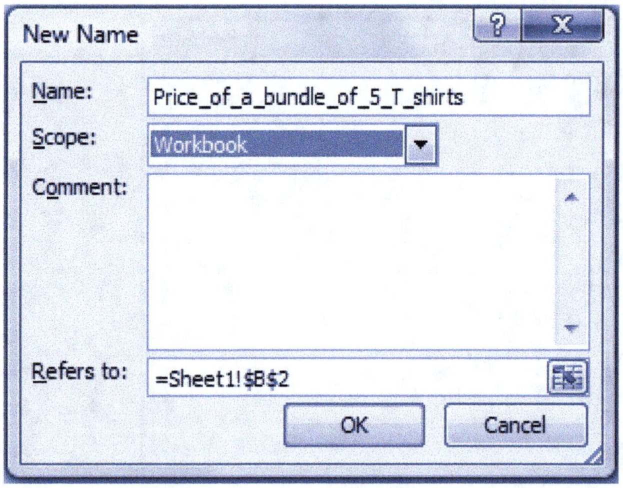

FIGURE 2.7
Defining a Name in Excel

Alternatively, to name a cell, first click on the cell you wish to name. Right click on the cell and choose the Name a Range option. You will see the dialog box in Figure 2.7. You may choose the name suggested or you may choose to rename the cell in a simpler form. The cell refers to =Sheet1!$B$2; this should correspond to the cell you initially clicked on and wished to name.

Continue with naming and formatting the rest of the revenue and cost inputs. The spreadsheet should look similar to Figure 2.8. Again, it is good practice to group inputs and outputs separately.

Next we model the revenue, costs and profits. In the Revenue cell, enter the formula (see Figure 2.9):

=Price_of_bundle_of_5_T_shirts*Quantity_sold

You may manually type in the cell names or first type =, followed by clicking on the cells you need in the formula. Remember to press Enter to complete the formula. If you do type the formula, you have to type the exact names you used for the relevant cells.

In the Total Cost cell, enter the formula:

=Rental_cost+(Hourly_labor_cost*Hours_worked)
+(Cost_per_Tshirt_bundle*Quantity_sold)

Stand_rental_... 100

	A	B
1	**Revenue Inputs**	
2	Price of a bundle of 5 T-shirts	$ 20.00
3	Quantity sold	15
4		
5	**Cost Inputs**	
6	Stand rental per day	$ 100.00
7	Hourly labor rate	$ 7.00
8	Hours worked	8
9	Cost per T-shirt bundle	$ 1.50

FIGURE 2.8
Example of a Formatted Excel Spreadsheet

SUM =Price_of_a_bundle_of_5_T_shirts*Quantity_sold

	A	B	C	D	E
1	**Revenue Inputs**			**Revenue Outputs**	
2	Price of a bundle of 5 T-shirts	$ 20.00		Revenue	=Price_of_
3	Quantity sold	15			
4					
5	**Cost Inputs**			**Cost Ouput**	
6	Stand rental per day	$ 100.00		Total cost	$ 178.50
7	Hourly labor rate	$ 7.00			
8	Hours worked	8		**Profit Output**	
9	Cost per T-shirt bundle	$ 1.50		Profit	$ 121.50

FIGURE 2.9
Example of a Spreadsheet Displaying Revenue

SUM =Stand_rental_per_day+Hourly_labor_rate*Hours_worked+Cost_per_Tshirt_bundle*Quantity_sold

	A	B	C	D	E
1	**Revenue Inputs**			**Revenue Outputs**	
2	Price of a bundle of 5 T-shirts	$ 20.00		Revenue	$ 300.00
3	Quantity sold	15			
4					
5	**Cost Inputs**			**Cost Ouput**	
6	Stand rental per day	$ 100.00		Total cost	=Stand_re
7	Hourly labor rate	$ 7.00			
8	Hours worked	8		**Profit Output**	
9	Cost per T-shirt bundle	$ 1.50		Profit	$ 121.50

FIGURE 2.10
Example of a Spreadsheet for Profit Calculation

and in the Profit cell, enter the formula:

=Revenue–Total_cost

Take note that it is much more efficient to click on the relevant cells to complete the formulas. You will see from our model that for 15 bundles of T-shirts sold, Teez makes a profit of $121.50 (see Figure 2.10).

Creating Data Tables in Excel

To conduct a sensitivity analysis to see how profits vary with the values of quantity sold, we use the Data Table function of Excel (see Figures 2.11 and 2.12).

To start the process, type in cell A12 "Sensitivity analysis of Teez profits," in cell A13 type "Quantity sold," and in cell B13 type "Profit." Then in cell B14, we enter a link to the profit model by clicking on cell E9 or entering =Profit. Next, enter the trial values of the quantity sold that you wish to vary in column A. In this example, we chose values from 5 to 20 bundles. This can be as much or as little as you wish; however, the quantity chosen should be sufficient to reflect the changes in profit in order to conduct a reasonable sensitivity analysis.

The trial values of quantity sold in are entered in cells B15 to B30—values 5 to 20 (see Figure 2.14). Finally, we highlight the entire table range, A14:B30, and click

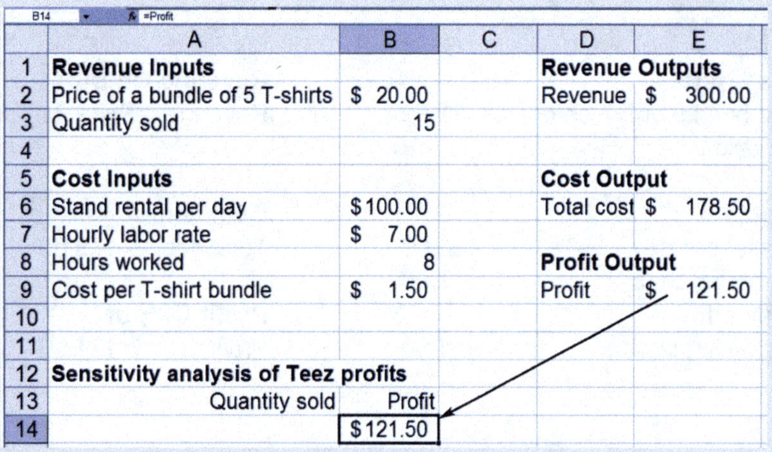

FIGURE 2.11
Example Spreadsheet for Profit Calculation

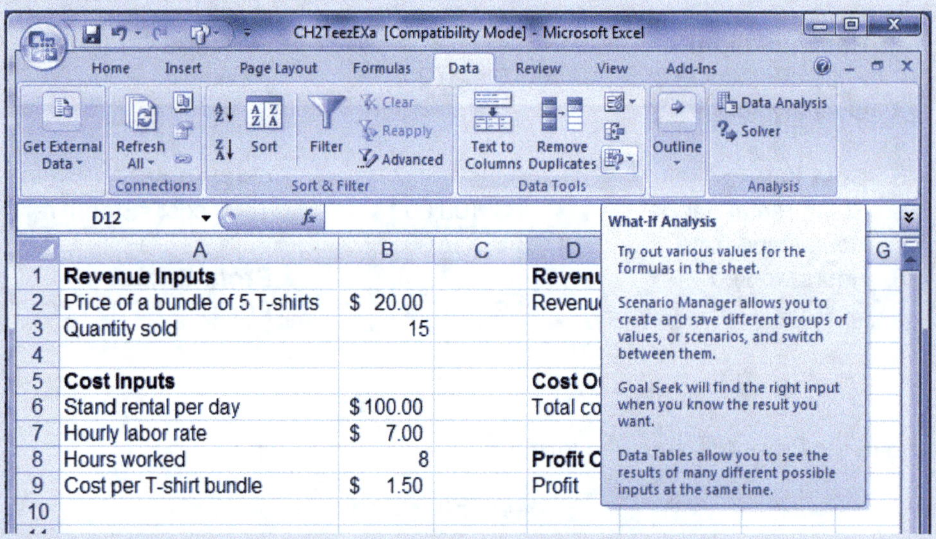

FIGURE 2.12a
What-If Analysis Icon in the Data Tools Menu Excel 2007

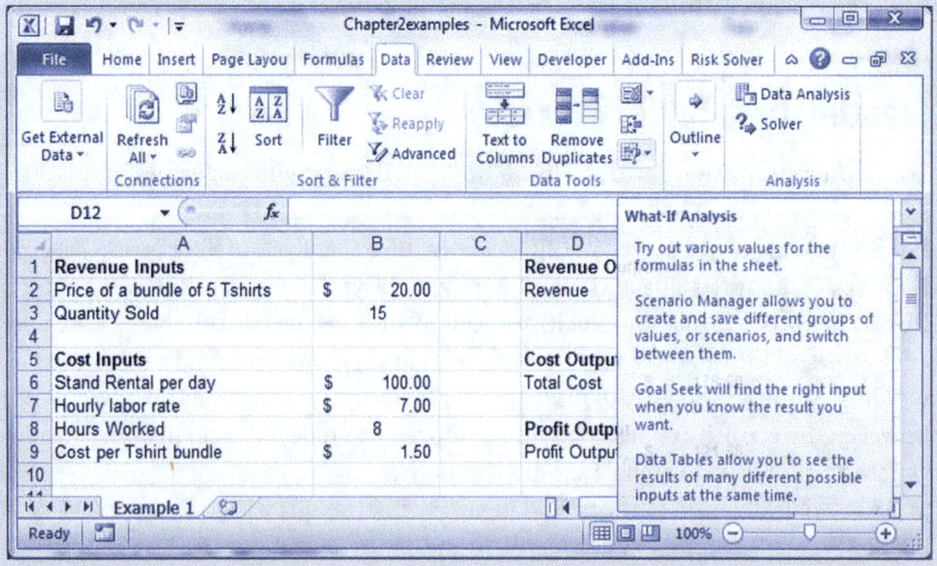

FIGURE 2.12b
What-If Analysis Icon in the Data Tools Menu Excel 2010

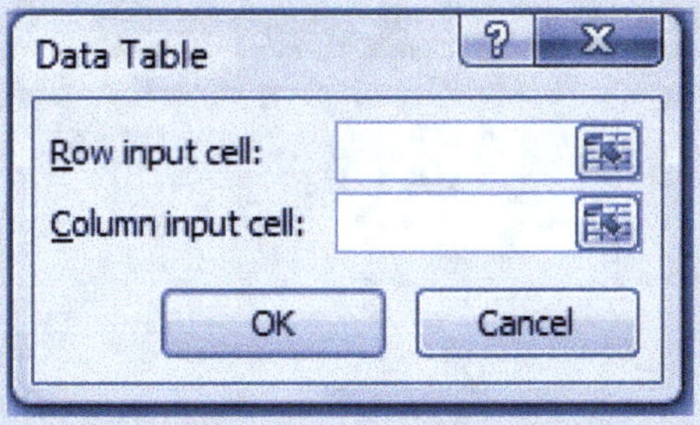

FIGURE 2.13
Data Table Input Menu in Excel

on the What-If Analysis icon in the Data Tools group (see Figure 2.12a and Figure 2.12b). From the What-If Analysis icon select Data Table option to bring up the Table dialog box (see Figure 2.13). Here we fill in Quantity_sold in the column input cell to indicate that only the input quantity sold is listed along a column.

When you click on OK, Excel substitutes each value of quantity sold to provide the corresponding profit values and reports it in the table (see Figure 2.14).

The table results show that Teez would suffer a loss if it sold eight bundles or less and make a profit otherwise. This can be represented graphically by using Excel's Chart function.

Using Excel to Generate PivotTables with One Variable

The following are the steps to generate a PivotTable in Excel. Another example is given that corresponds to a two variable PivotTable.

1. Highlight your data range. Refer to Figure 2.15b for data set.
2. Go to the Insert tab and click on the PivotTable icon on the far left section of the Ribbon in the Tables group (see Figure 2.15a and Figure 2.15b).

B30 {=TABLE(,B3)}

	A	B
12	**Sensitivity Analysis of Teez Profits**	
13	Quantity Sold	Profit
14		$ 121.50
15	5	$ (63.50)
16	6	$ (45.00)
17	7	$ (26.50)
18	8	$ (8.00)
19	9	$ 10.50
20	10	$ 29.00
21	11	$ 47.50
22	12	$ 66.00
23	13	$ 84.50
24	14	$ 103.00
25	15	$ 121.50
26	16	$ 140.00
27	17	$ 158.50
28	18	$ 177.00
29	19	$ 195.50
30	20	$ 214.00
31		

FIGURE 2.14
Data Table Outputs for Profit Sensitivity Analysis

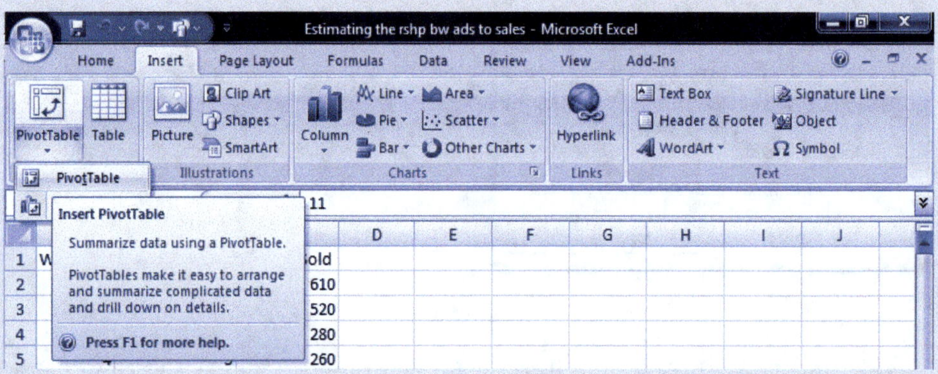

FIGURE 2.15a
Insert Pivot Table Icon in Excel 2007

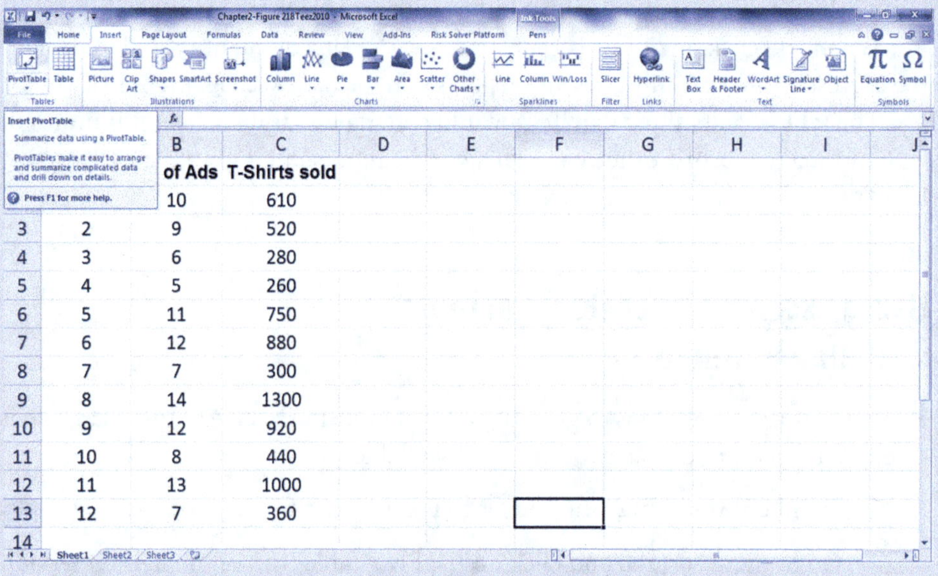

FIGURE 2.15b
Insert Pivot Table Icon in Excel 2010

3. Click the Insert tab, select the PivotTable button from the Tables group, select PivotTable from the list.
4. The Create PivotTable dialog appears (refer to Figure 2.16). Since your data was highlighted the Select a table or range button is clicked and the Table/Range field is filled in. Also, the New Worksheet button is clicked signifying where the PivotTable will be placed. Click on the OK button.
5. After clicking on the OK button a figure resembling Figure 2.17 will appear. This is the PivotTable layout screen.
6. In the new worksheet created you will see that the fields from our source spreadsheet were carried over to the PivotTable Field List.
7. Drag an item such as Number of Ads from the PivotTable Field List down to the Row Labels quadrant. The left side of your Excel spreadsheet should show a row for each Number of Ads value. You should also see a checkmark appear next to Number of Ads (see Figure 2.18).

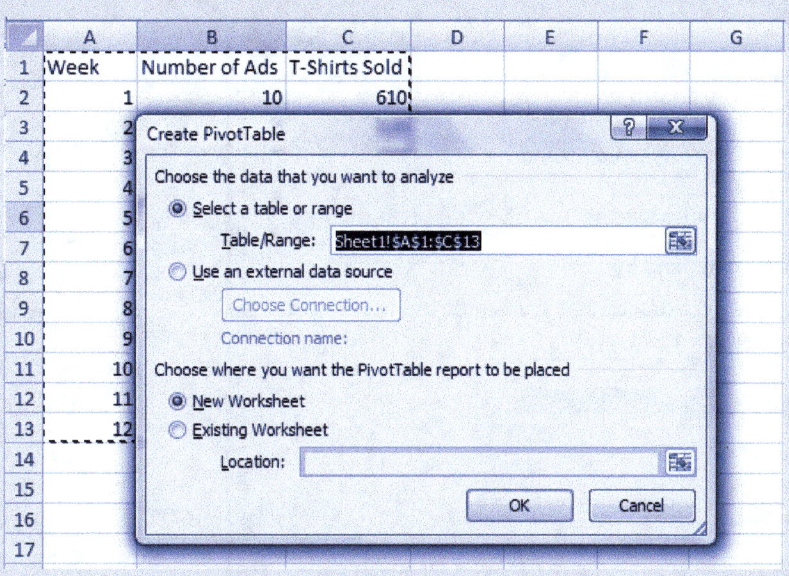

FIGURE 2.16
Create Pivot Dialogue Box in Excel

8. To see the count for each Number of Ads, drag the same field to the Values quadrant (refer to lower right of Figure 2.19).
9. In this case, Excel determines we wanted a Count of Number of Ads. However, if you double-click the entry, Count of Number of Ads, a screen resembling Figure 2.21 will appear. From this Value Field Settings menu you can choose another value field from the Summarize value field by scroll menu.

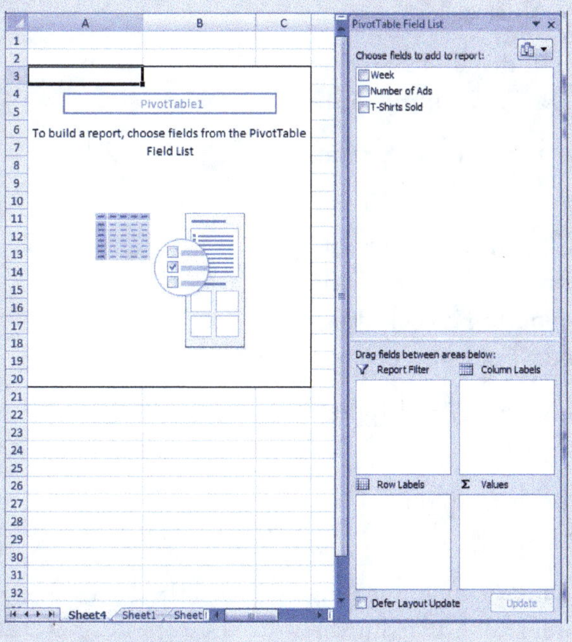

FIGURE 2.17
Pivot Table Layout Screen in Excel

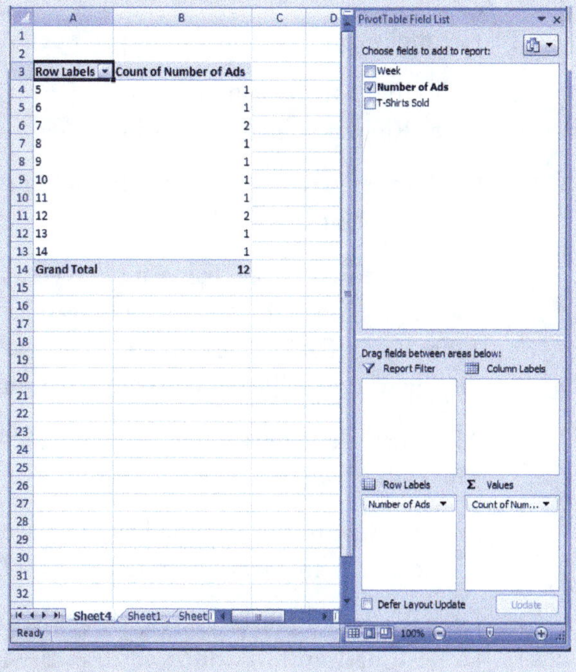

FIGURE 2.18
Pivot Table Field List Screen in Excel

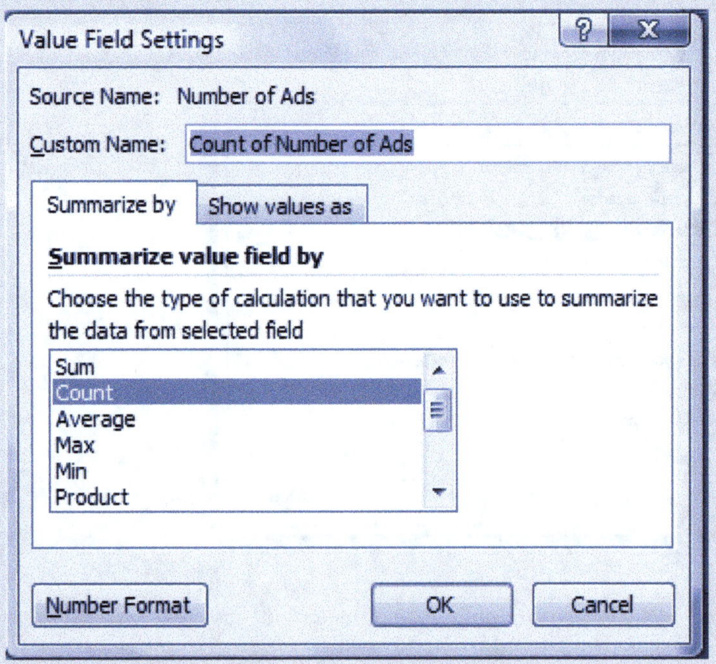

FIGURE 2.19
Pivot Table Value Field Settings Screen in Excel

Using Excel to Generate PivotTables with Two Variables

The following example is the logical extension of the previous PivotTable example. The two variable PivotTable considers Number of Ads and Sum of T-Shirts Sold. These are the steps to obtain the PivotTable output.

1. Highlight your data range after you open the Excel spreadsheet.
2. Go to the Insert tab and click on the PivotTable icon on the far left section of the Ribbon in the Tables group (refer to Figure 2.15a and Figure 2.15b).
3. Click the Insert tab, select the PivotTable button from the Tables group, select PivotTable from the list.
4. The Create PivotTable dialog appears (refer to Figure 2.16). Since your data was highlighted the Select a table or range button is clicked and the Table/Range field is filled in. Also, the New Worksheet button is clicked signifying where the PivotTable will be placed. Click on the OK button.
5. After clicking on the OK button a figure resembling Figure 2.17 will appear. This is the PivotTable layout screen.
6. In the new worksheet created you will see that the fields from our source spreadsheet were carried over to the PivotTable Field List.
7. Drag the item T-Shirts Sold from the PivotTable Field List down to the Row Labels quadrant. In addition, drag the item Number of Ads from the PivotTable Field List down to the Column Labels quadrant. The left side of your Excel spreadsheet should show a row for each T-Shirts Sold category

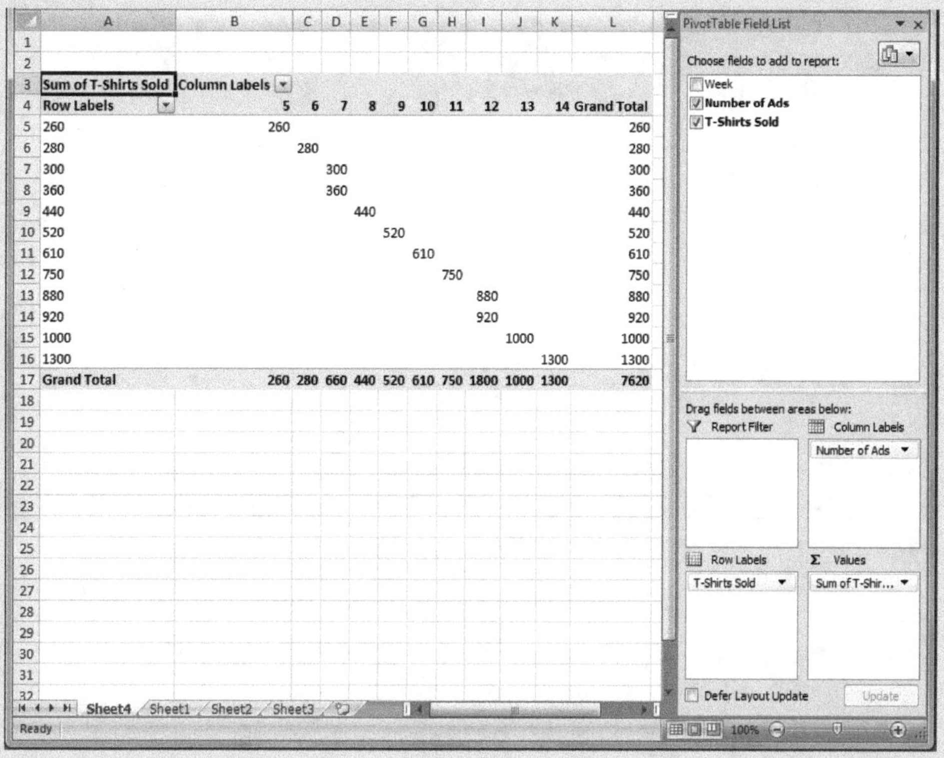

FIGURE 2.20

Two Variable Pivot Table in Excel

and a column for each Number of Ads value. You should also see checkmarks appear next to T-Shirts Sold and Number of Ads.

8. To see the count for each T-Shirts Sold and Number of Ads combination, drag the T-Shirts Sold field to the Values quadrant (see Figure 2.20). Figure 2.20 illustrates what the finished two variable PivotTable looks like.

Creating Charts Using Excel

To create a chart, click on Insert tab on the Menu bar and select from the Charts group; the Scatter option (see Figure 2.21a and Figure 2.21b). At the bottom of the

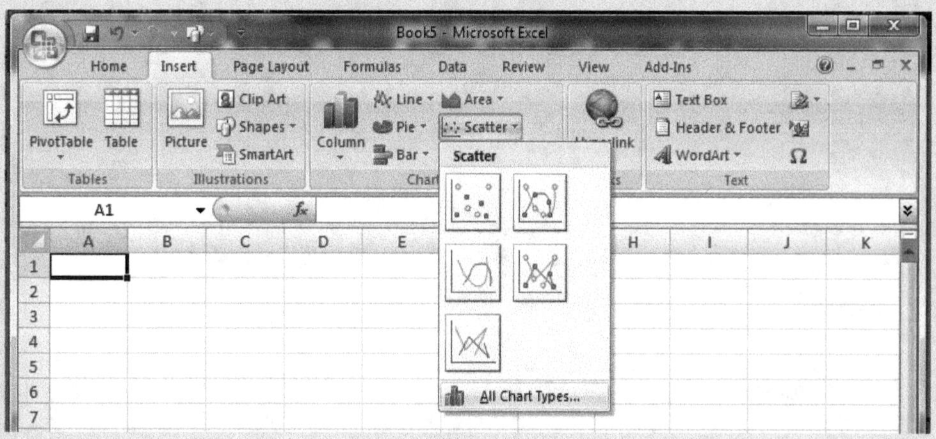

FIGURE 2.21a

Insert Scatter Chart Menu in Excel 2007

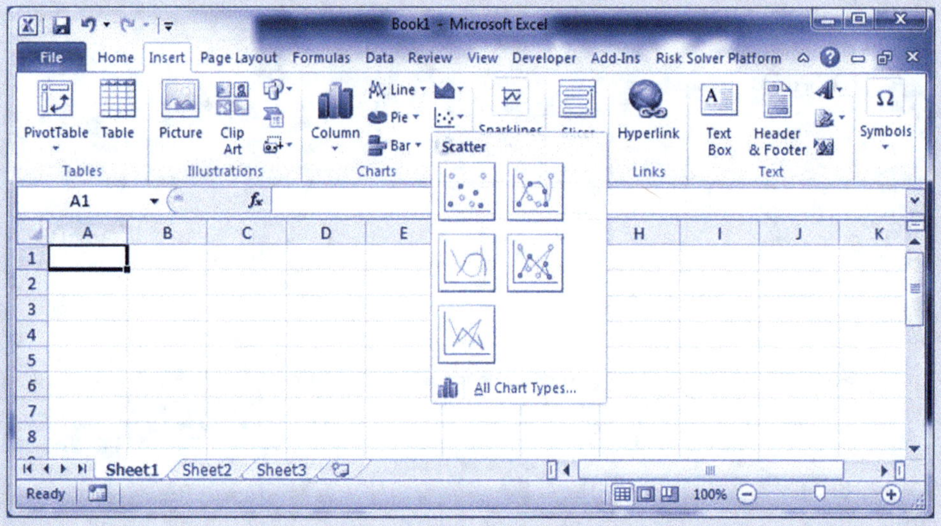

FIGURE 2.21b
Insert Scatter Chart Menu in Excel 2010

Scatter pull-down menu select All Chart Types. A figure resembling Figure 2.22 will appear. Here we choose XY (Scatter) with straight lines and markers (the fourth icon in from the left); this will graph your table in a scatter plot format. Then click on OK button and the graph will appear within your spreadsheet as in Figure 2.23.

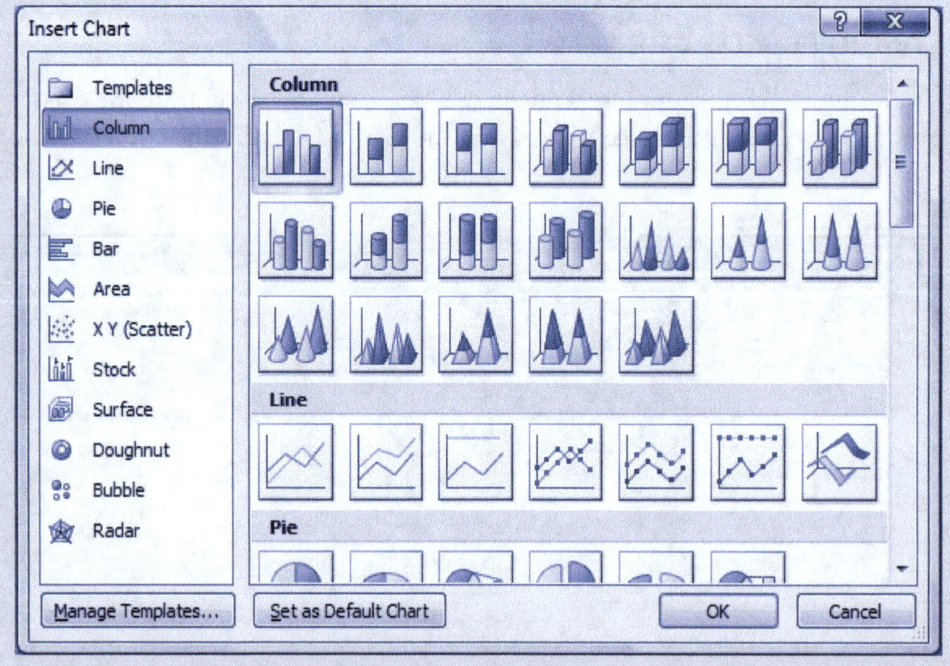

FIGURE 2.22
Insert Chart Menu in Excel

The final data table and the chart, side by side, make it easier for the manager to analyze the results of the data and intuitively understand that profit has a linear relationship with quantity sold. That is, profit increases linearly as more T-shirts are sold. The output is shown in Figure 2.23.

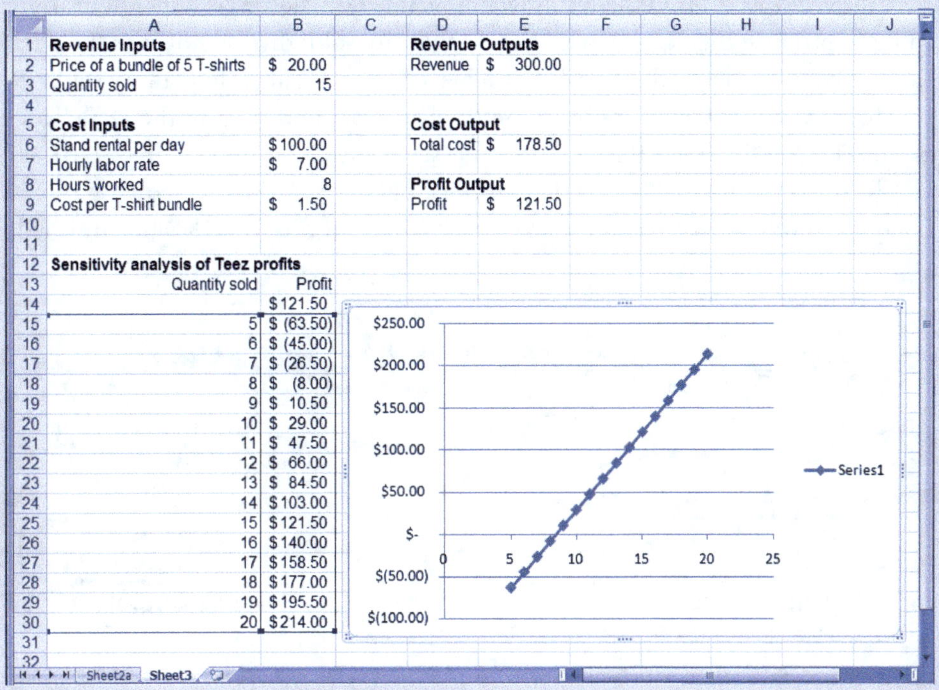

	A	B	C	D	E
1	**Revenue Inputs**			**Revenue Outputs**	
2	Price of a bundle of 5 T-shirts	$ 20.00		Revenue $	300.00
3	Quantity sold	15			
4					
5	**Cost Inputs**			**Cost Output**	
6	Stand rental per day	$ 100.00		Total cost $	178.50
7	Hourly labor rate	$ 7.00			
8	Hours worked	8		**Profit Output**	
9	Cost per T-shirt bundle	$ 1.50		Profit $	121.50
10					
11					
12	**Sensitivity analysis of Teez profits**				
13	Quantity sold	Profit			
14		$ 121.50			
15	5	$ (63.50)			
16	6	$ (45.00)			
17	7	$ (26.50)			
18	8	$ (8.00)			
19	9	$ 10.50			
20	10	$ 29.00			
21	11	$ 47.50			
22	12	$ 66.00			
23	13	$ 84.50			
24	14	$ 103.00			
25	15	$ 121.50			
26	16	$ 140.00			
27	17	$ 158.50			
28	18	$ 177.00			
29	19	$ 195.50			
30	20	$ 214.00			

FIGURE 2.23
Final Chart Output

Sensitivity Analysis

As mentioned, we see from the scatter plot that profit has a linear relationship with the quantity sold. More specifically, we see that with each additional bundle sold, Teez makes $18.50.

From the chart, we see that Mr. T will not make a profit when he sells eight bundles of T-shirts or less. When Mr. T sells 8 bundles he loses $8, but if he sold 9 bundles he would make $10.50. This answers the question as to whether Mr. T should rent a stand if he expects to only sell 5 bundles of T-shirts—obviously not, as he would be losing $63.50. Although it shows the minimum number of T-shirt bundles Teez should sell, it does not quite show the exact breakeven level, i.e., when profit is equal to zero.

Once again, this may be possible with a manual entry of values; nonetheless, Excel has a function called Goal Seek that will automatically compute the exact value for us.

Using Goal Seek in Excel

When you know the desired result of a single formula but not the input value the formula needs to obtain that result, you can use the Goal Seek feature. When goal seeking, Microsoft Excel varies the value in one specific cell until a formula that's dependent on that cell returns the result you want.

Here we wish to find the result where profit = 0. The single dependent input value to produce this result would be the quantity sold; this is known as the decision variable, as the profit value of 0 is achieved by changing cell quantity sold.

To implement Goal Seek, click on the Data tab, and then in the Data Tools group, click on the What-If Analysis menu (see Figure 2.24a and Figure 2.24b).

To implement Goal Seek, click on the Goal Seek option. The dialog box in Figure 2.25 will appear. Fill in the boxes as follows and click on OK when finished.

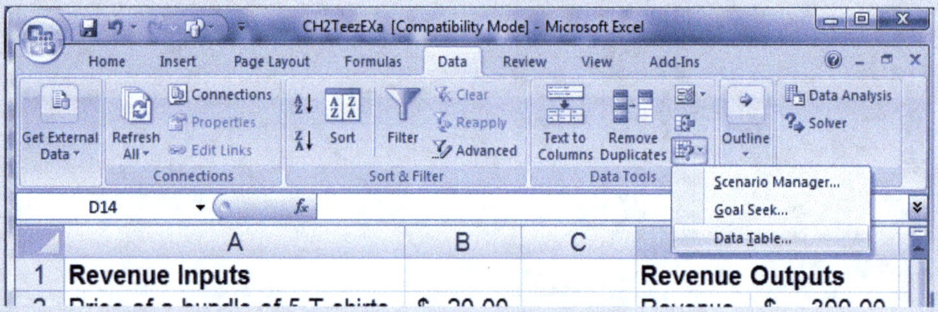

FIGURE 2.24a Location of Goal Seek Menu in Excel 2007

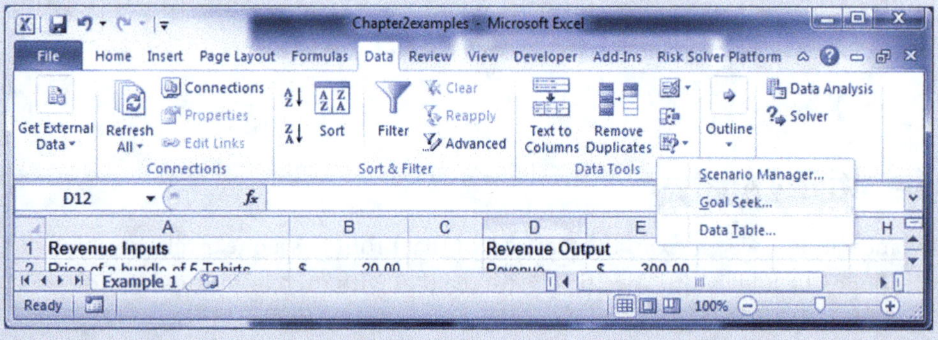

FIGURE 2.24b Location of Goal Seek Menu in Excel 2010

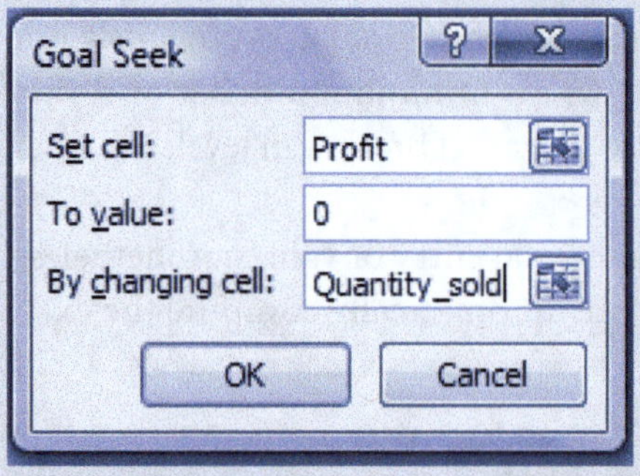

FIGURE 2.25 Goal Seek menu in Excel

1. Move your cursor to the Set cell dialog box and click on the named cell, Profit, in your spreadsheet.
2. Move your cursor to the To value dialog box and enter 0.
3. Move your cursor to the By changing cell dialog box and click on the named cell, Quantity_sold, in your spreadsheet.

Excel will iterate through the possible values in the quantity sold cell to achieve profit = 0. When Excel finds a solution, the Goal Seek Status box will appear (see Figure 2.26).

You will find that on your spreadsheet, the profit value has been changed to 0 and the quantity sold is 8.432432 bundles. Obviously it is currently not possible to sell a fraction of a T-shirt bundle. However, it does show that in order to break even, Teez must sell at least nine bundles, since eight bundles would not cover costs. The final spreadsheet is shown in Figure 2.27.

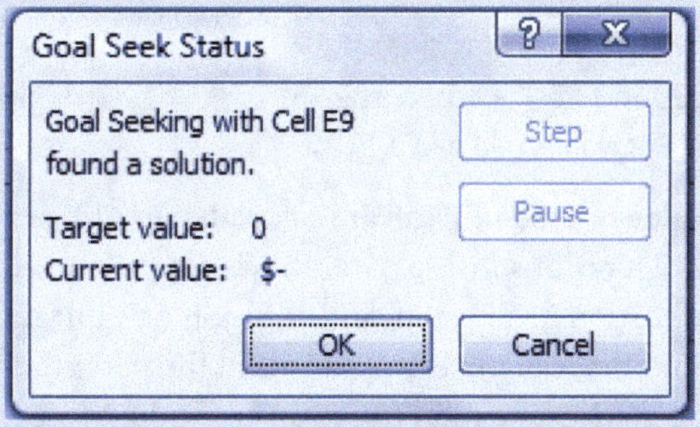

FIGURE 2.26
Goal Seek Status menu in Excel

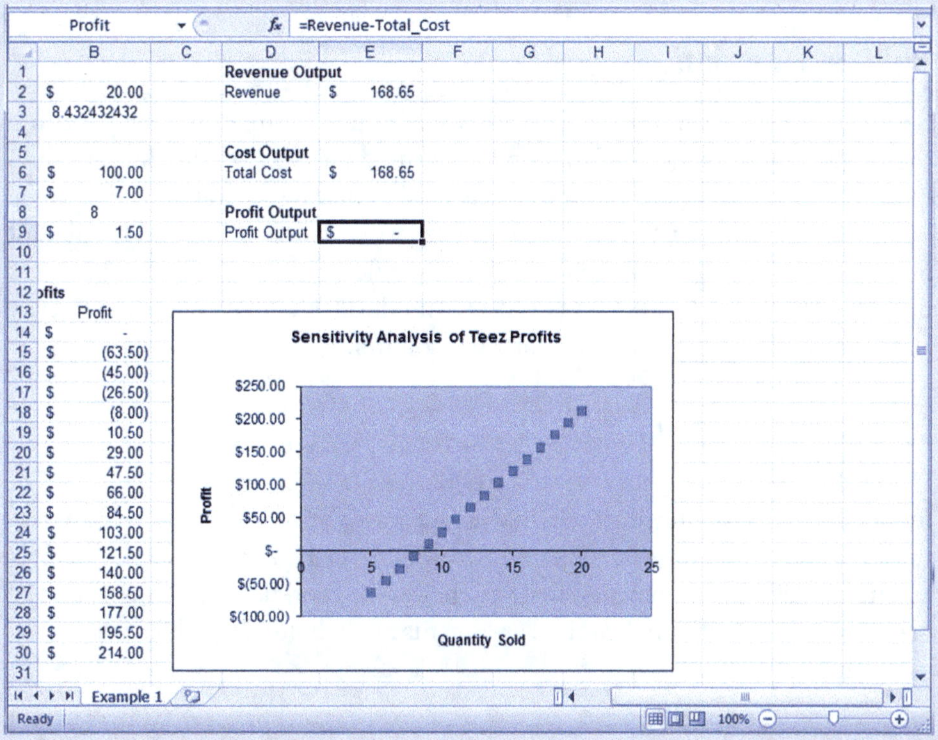

FIGURE 2.27
Final Example Spreadsheet for Teez

Basic Excel Functions

A key advantage of using Excel is the ability to create and use formulas in its spreadsheets. Formulas enable you to quickly perform numeric calculations as we have seen in Example 1. As we mentioned earlier, you may enter a formula in the active cell by first typing the equal sign, = to indicate the beginning of a formula in the cell.

Formulas enable a user to quickly perform numeric calculations in a spreadsheet.

Mathematical Operators

Mathematical operators commonly used in Excel are:

+	for addition
–	for subtraction
*	for multiplication
/	for division
^	for "the power of," e.g., 23 in Excel is typed as 2^3
EXP( )	for exponential, e.g., in Excel is typed as EXP(2)

Commonly used mathematical operators in Excel are +, –, *, etc.

As with basic mathematics, formulas entered in Excel are calculated in order of precedence and not just left to right. Operations inside parentheses are calculated first, followed by exponential, multiplication or division, and addition or subtraction. So the formula =2+3*(2^3) would first calculate 2^3=8 within the parentheses, followed by multiplying with 3, 3*8=24. The final function is to add 2 to 24, 2+24=26.

Built-in Functions

Besides entering formulas, you may use Excel's built-in functions. All functions require an equal sign (=), a function name, and at least one value in the subsequent parentheses. Multiple values for calculation may be separated with commas within the parentheses. We can invoke the Insert Function dialog box by clicking on shortcut key f_x to see all the functions available in Excel (see Figure 2.28). On the left column are the Function categories, and the highlighted category will reveal all the relevant Function names in the right column.

Excel has many built-in functions that can be accessed via the function key, f_x.

SUM(NUMBER1,NUMBER2,...)

Under the Function category we selected Math & Trig and highlighted SUM. The function SUM adds individual cells that are separated by commas within the parentheses. Click OK and the Formula Palette opens (see Figure 2.29). The Formula Palette displays the "arguments" that the chosen function needs (the items that go between the parentheses). Required arguments are in bold; nonbolded arguments are optional.

The SUM function adds individual cells.

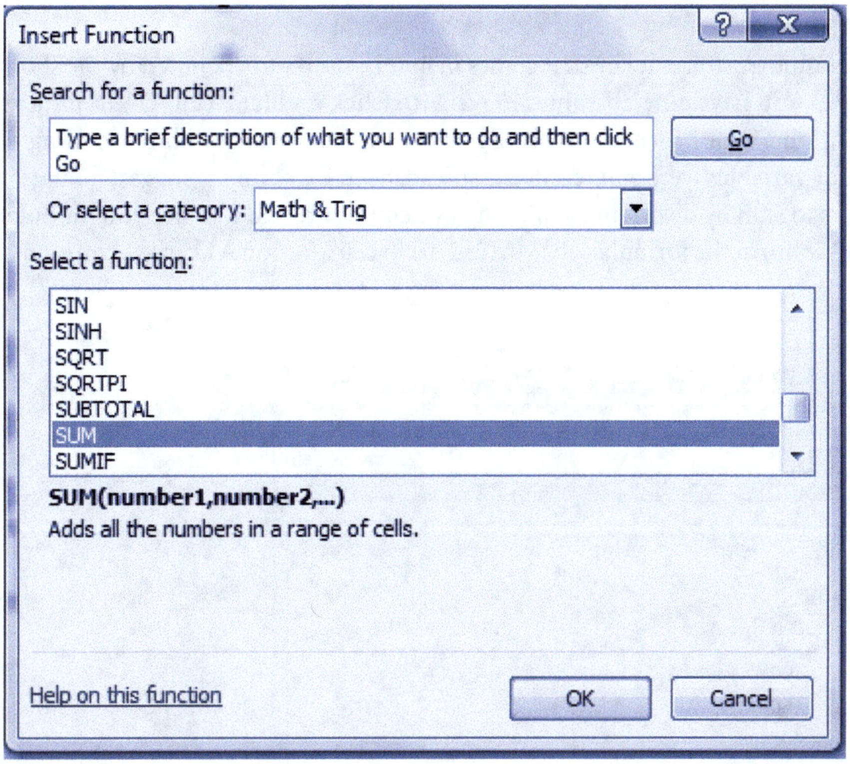

FIGURE 2.28 Paste Function Menu in Excel

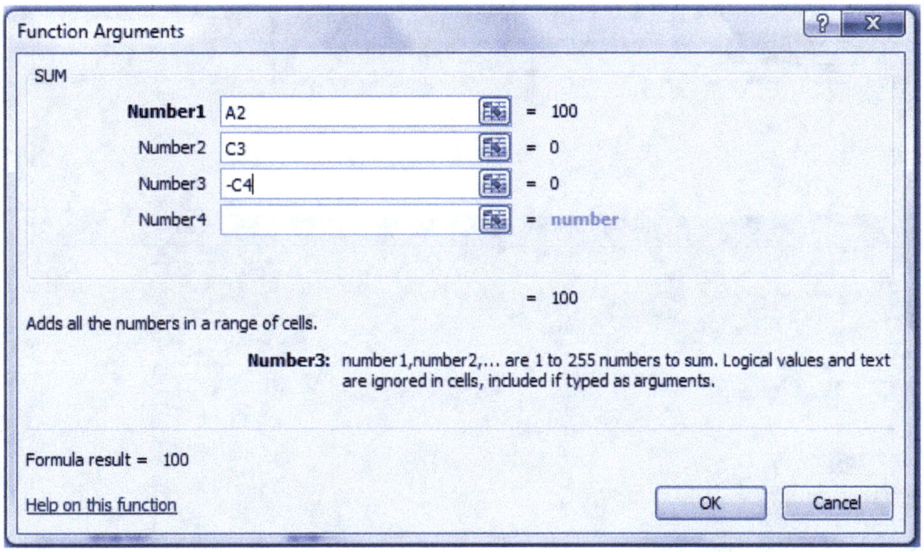

FIGURE 2.29 Formula Palette for SUM Function in Excel

For example, you want to add A2 to C3 and to subtract C4. You may enter the following formula =A2+C3–C4 or you may type directly in the cell =SUM(A2,C3,–C4). With the Formula Palette, you may enter A2 in Number 1 tab to enter the subsequent cells or cell names.

Alternatively, you may wish to add an entire column from A2 through to A10; instead of typing each cell individually, you may use the SUM function with a range reference like =SUM(A2:A10).

AUTOSUM

There is another shortcut key that comes in handy, AutoSum, denoted by the shortcut key Σ. You have entered values in A2:A10. Click on blank cell A11 to indicate the location of your formula, then click on the AutoSum symbol. Depending on how your variables were entered in the spreadsheet, Excel might suggest a range of numbers to sum by displaying a blinking dotted line around it. Once you hit Enter, you will confirm the formula =SUM(A2:A10) in cell location A11 (see Figure 2.30).

The AutoSum function in Excel allows easy summations of designated cells.

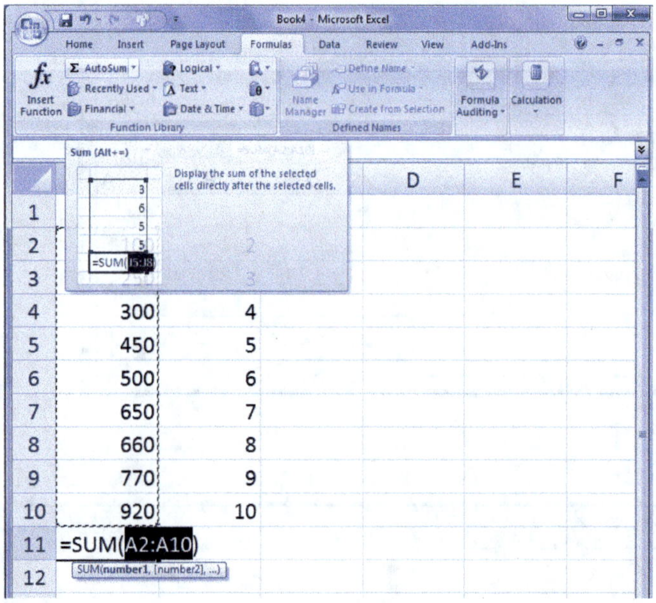

FIGURE 2.30a

Formula Palette for SUM Function in Excel 2007

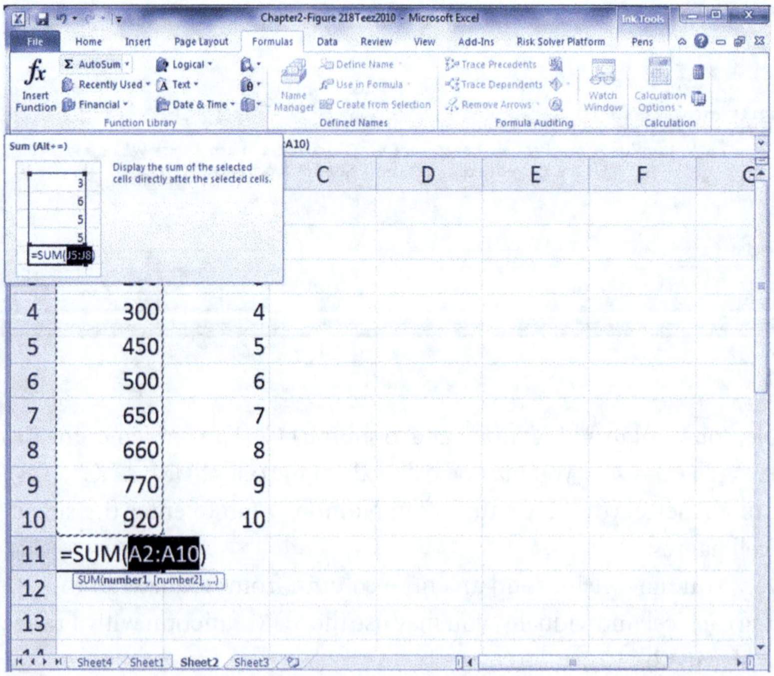

FIGURE 2.30b

Formula Palette for SUM Function in Excel 2010

SUMPRODUCT(ARRAY1,ARRAY2,...)

The SUMPRODUCT function multiplies corresponding values of arrays of the same dimension.

Another variation of the Sum function is SUMPRODUCT; this function multiplies corresponding values of arrays of the same dimension and returns the sum of these products. For example, you wish to multiply the values in column A with values in column B and wish to add all of the results together. You may enter =A2*B2+A3*B3+...+A10*B10 or you can use a much simpler formula with Excel's function =SUMPRODUCT(A2:A10,B2:B10) (see Figure 2.31).

Statistical Functions

AVERAGE

Excel contains a number of common statistical functions.

From the Statistical category, the most commonly used statistical function is *AVERAGE*, also known as the mean. Average totals all the items in a list and divides by the number of items in the list.

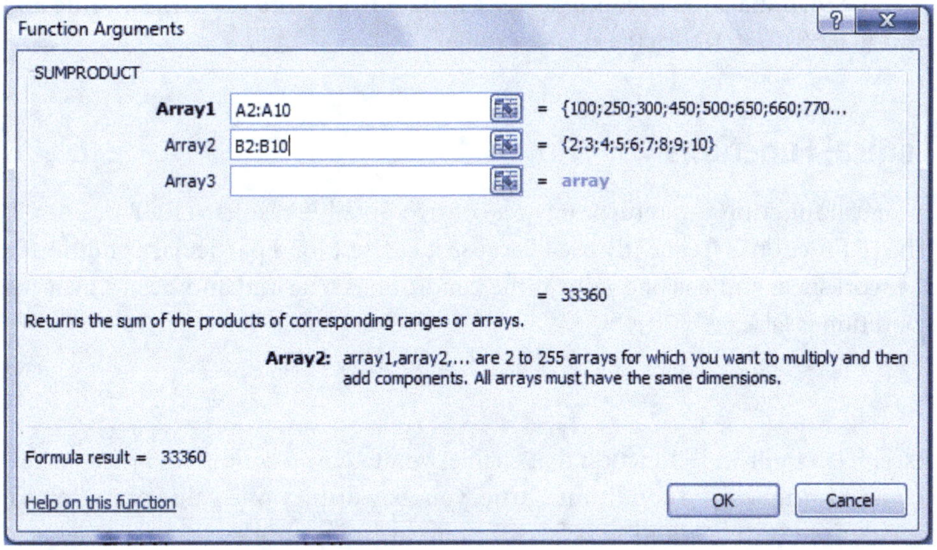

FIGURE 2.31
Formula Palette for SUMPRODUCT Function in Excel

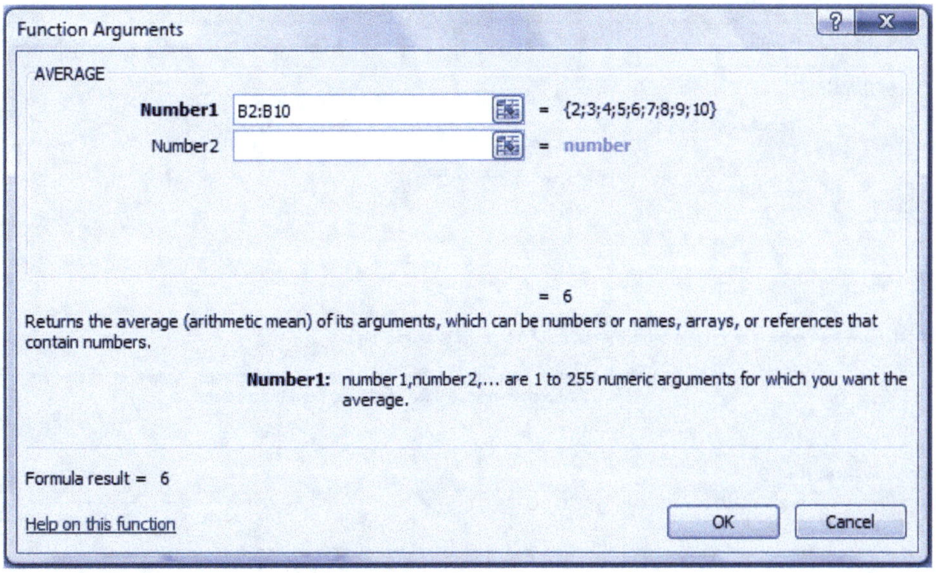

FIGURE 2.32
Formula Palette for AVERAGE Function in Excel

If a cell is blank or contains text, it is ignored and not included in the total or the number of items. The Formula Palette for the AVERAGE function is displayed in Figure 2.32. The formula bar will reflect the formula =Average(B2:B10).

MEDIAN

In statistics the median gives the number in the middle of a set of given numbers. The cell location will indicate the formula =Median(B2:B10). Figure 2.33 displays the formula palette for the MEDIAN function in Excel.

The MEDIAN function in Excel finds the middle number of a group of numbers; that is, half the numbers have values greater than the median and half the numbers have values less than the median.

MIN/MAX FUNCTION

With function Max(number1,number2,...), Excel will return the largest value among the given set of values in a list (see Figure 2.34 for the MAX function and Figure 2.35 for the MIN function). From a list (2,3,4,5,6,7,8,9,10), the maximum value is 10 and the minimum value is 2.

The formula shown would be =MAX(B2:B10) to find the largest value and =MIN(B2:B10) to return the smallest value.

The MIN and MAX functions return the minimum and maximum of a data set.

Logical Functions

A logical function can return only one of two possible results: TRUE or FALSE. The IF function is frequently used because it can test for a particular condition in the worksheet and use one value if the condition is true and another value if the condition is false.

Logical functions in Excel return one of two possible results: TRUE or FALSE.

IF

Excel has a built-in IF function that enables you to create conditional tests on values and formulas. If a condition is true, you may display one value or perform a calculation. If the condition is false, you may display another value or perform

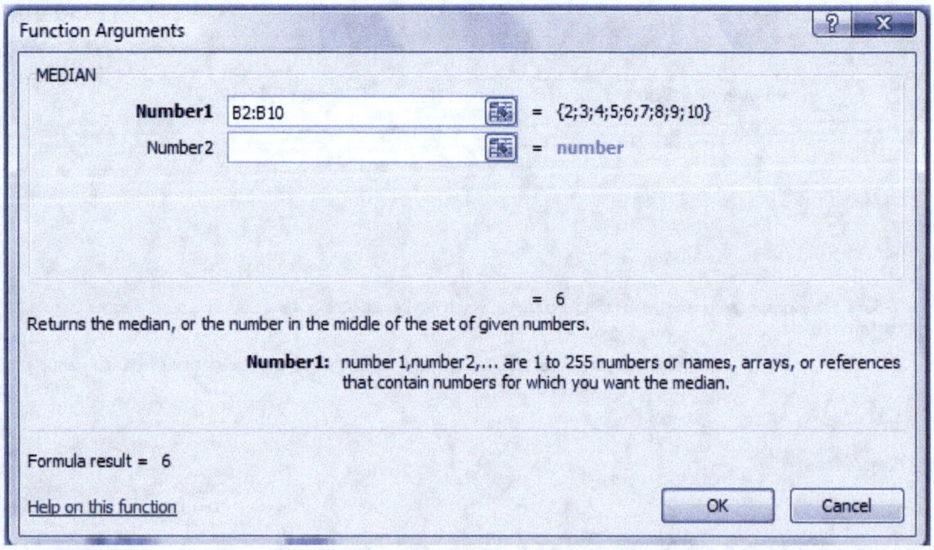

FIGURE 2.33 Formula Palette for MEDIAN Function in Excel

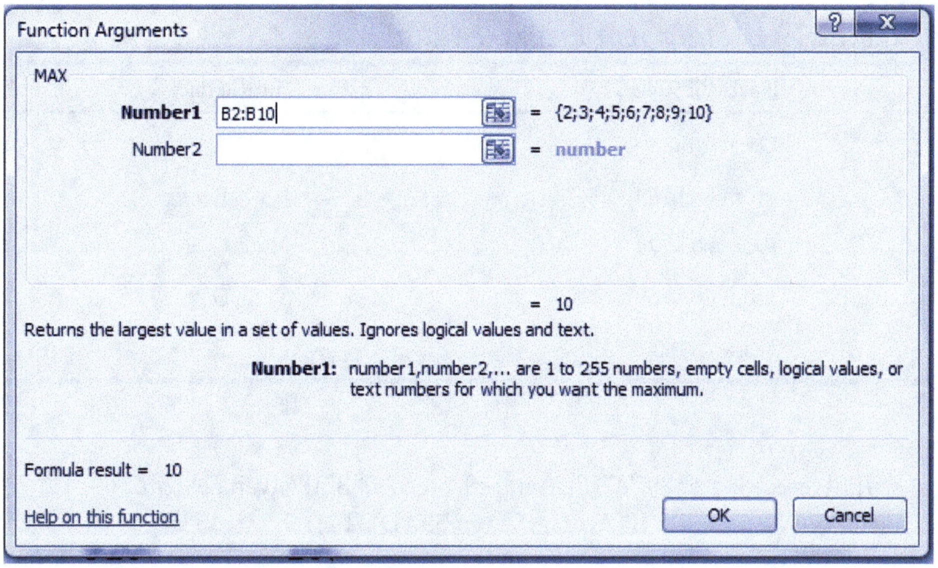

FIGURE 2.34
Formula Palette for MAX function in Excel

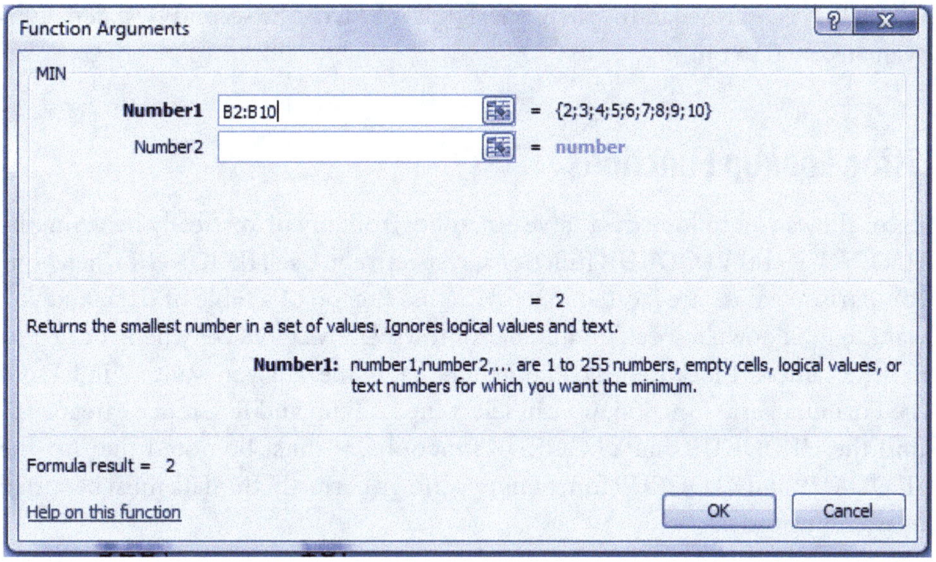

FIGURE 2.35
Formula Palette for MIN function in Excel

The IF function in Excel enables a user to create conditional tests.

another calculation. Thus the syntax of an IF function is different from that of the functions described earlier. Basically, it should follow =IF(logical_test, value_if_true, value_if_false)

The logical test is a condition that has to be met. An example is A2>200 or B2<=150. Note that >= is "equal to or greater than," <= is "equal to or less than," and <> is "not equal to." If the test proves true, if A2 is actually 300, Excel will look at the "value if true" and follow the stated action or return a value (which could also be text). Just include the function to be tested in quotes.

For example, the formula =IF(A2>200, "A", "B") would return A in the cell. The next spreadsheet example will show how this can be applied to a problem. Consider Table 2.1 as an example. You can use the following nested IF function:

TABLE 2.1 *IF Statement Example Data*

IF AVERAGE SCORE IS	THEN RETURN
Greater than 89	A
From 80 to 89	B
From 70 to 79	C
From 60 to 69	D
Less than 60	F

=IF(AverageScore>89,"A",IF(AverageScore>79,"B",IF(AverageScore>69,"C",
IF(AverageScore>59,"D","F"))))

In this function, the second IF statement is also the value_if_false argument to the first IF statement. Similarly, the third IF statement is the value_if_false argument to the second IF statement. For example, if the first logical_test (Average>89) is TRUE, A is returned. If the first logical_test is FALSE, the second IF statement is evaluated, and so on.

Using Lookup Functions

Excel allows you to look up a table either horizontally of vertically by using the HLOOKUP and VLOOKUP functions, respectively. Use HLOOKUP when your comparison values are located in a row across the top of a table of data, and you want to look down a specified number of rows. Use VLOOKUP when your comparison values are located in a column to the left of the data you want to find. From the Formula Paste function, we can select the Lookup and Reference category to find the HLOOKUP and VLOOKUP functions. It must be noted that for the HLOOKUP and VLOOKUP functions to perform correctly, the data must be sorted in ascending order.

HLOOKUP (HORIZONTAL LOOKUP) FUNCTION

To use the HLOOKUP function across an array, we need to first sort through the data in ascending order. Consider Table 2.2 entered in the spreadsheet in this form. A grade with 90 and above will be assigned the letter grade A, a grade between 80 and 89 will be assigned the letter grade B, and so on.

TABLE 2.2 *HLOOKUP Statement Example Data*

89	79	69	59	0
A	B	C	D	F

Sorting Data in Excel

In this table, the data in the first row are in descending order, and we need to sort the data in ascending order. To sort this table of data, highlight the items you wish to sort. Within the Data tab select the Sort option from the Sort & Filter Group (see Figure 2.36a for Excel 2007 and Figure 2.36b for Excel 2010). The Sort dialog box will then appear (see Figure 2.38).

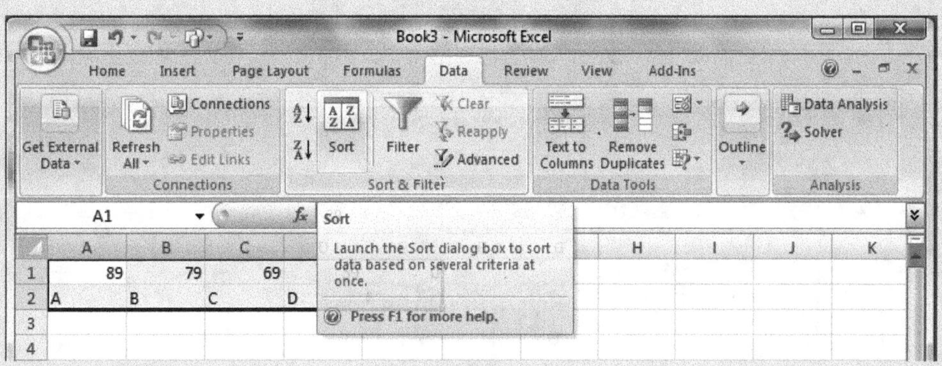

FIGURE 2.36a

Data Tab and Sort & Filter Group in Excel 2007

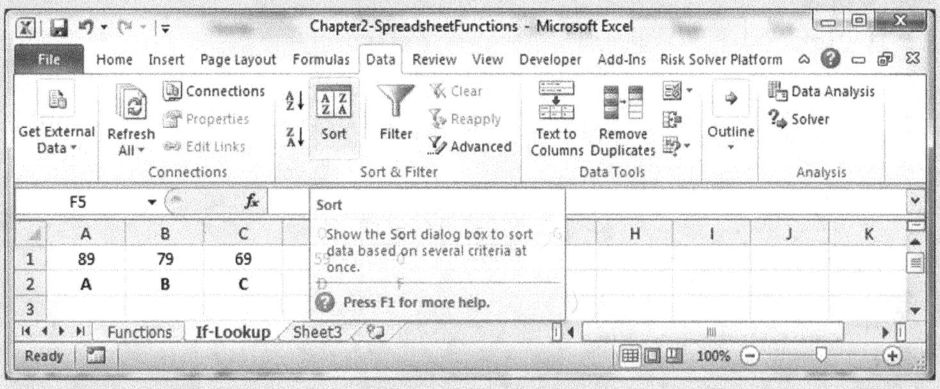

FIGURE 2.36b

Data Tab and Sort & Filter Group in Excel 2010

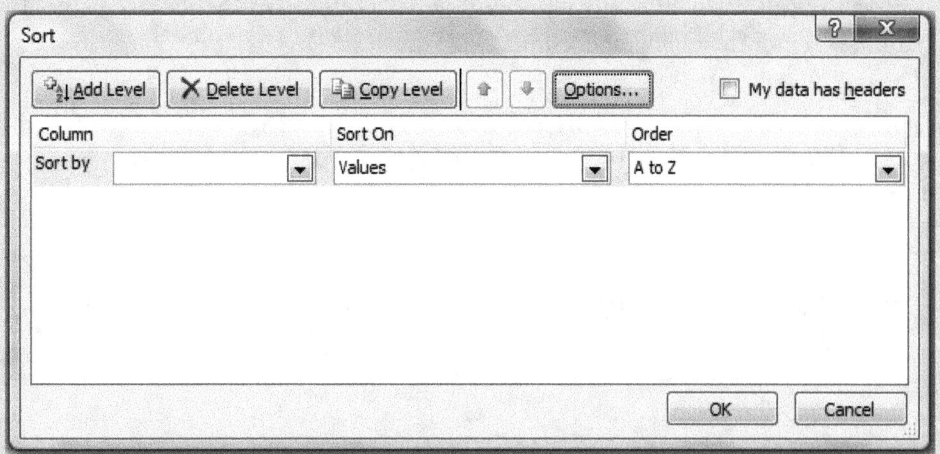

FIGURE 2.37

Data Tab and Sort & Filter Group in Excel

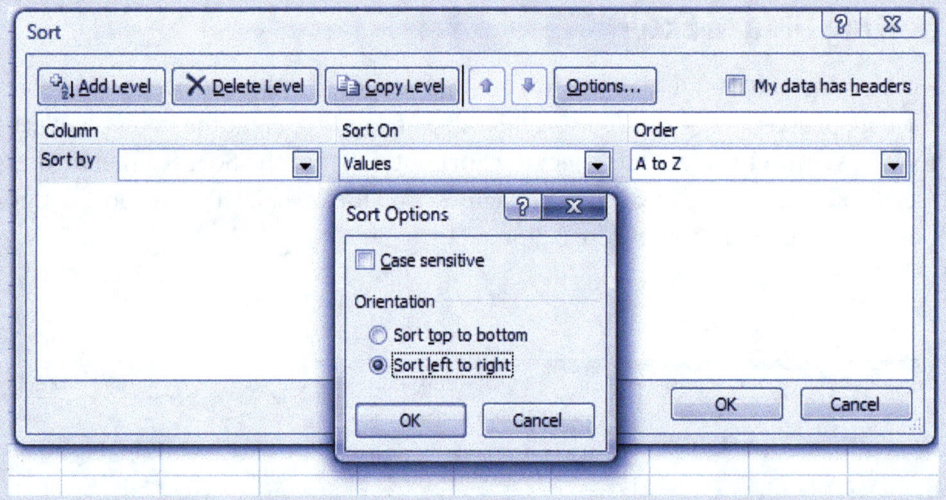

FIGURE 2.38
Sort Options Menu in Excel

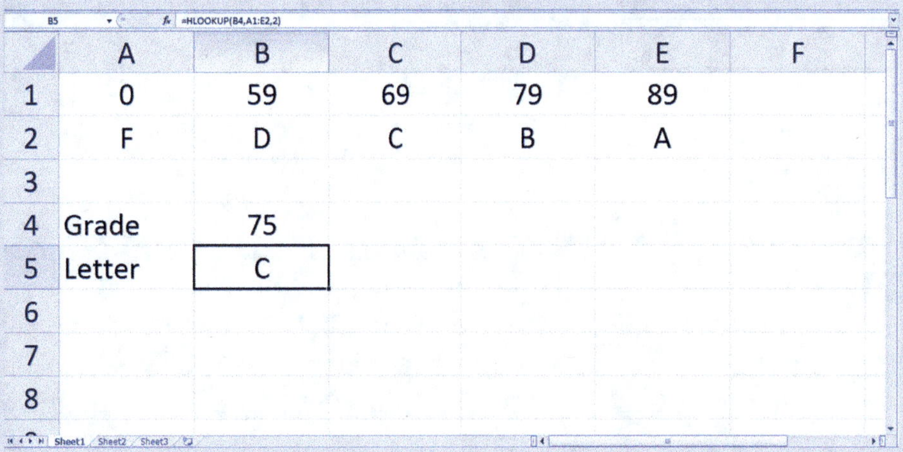

FIGURE 2.39
HLOOKUP Function Example in Excel

Click on Options and select "Sort left to right" (see Figure 2.38). Then click on OK.

The table will be sorted in ascending order from left to right. The sorted table is displayed in Table 2.3.

We use cell B4 to enter the number grade we refer to as the lookup value. In cell B5, we enter the following formula (see Figure 2.39):

=HLOOKUP(B4,$A$1:$D$2,2)

The result returned is the letter grade of C.

TABLE 2.3 *Sorted Data for HLOOKUP Example in Excel*

0	59	69	79	89
F	D	C	B	A

The syntax of HLOOKUP is as follows:

HLOOKUP(lookup_value,table,row_index_num,range_lookup)

The formula we used is

=HLOOKUP(B4,$A$1:$D$2,2)

Thus B4 held our lookup value, while A1:D2 is the table reference where Excel will look up the closest corresponding value and 2 indicates that the value we want returned is found in the second row of the table A1:D2.

The argument range_lookup can take the value True or False. When we type True, Excel will find the closest corresponding to the lookup value. In other words, if an exact match is not found, the next largest value that is less than the lookup value is returned. In this case 75 had no exact match, and the next largest value that is less than 75 was 69, thus Excel returned the value C. When we type False, Excel will find an exact match. Since we did not enter a range lookup value, Excel assumed the value as True.

VLOOKUP (VERTICAL LOOKUP) FUNCTION

VLOOKUP searches for a value in the leftmost column of a table, and then returns a value in the same row from a column you specify in the table. Use VLOOKUP instead of HLOOKUP when your comparison values are located in a column to the left of the data you want to find.

Consider the table of grades in Table 2.4, where the number grade comparison values are on the first column to the left of the letter grade value you wish to find.

TABLE 2.4 *Example Data for VLOOKUP Function*

89	A
79	B
69	C
59	D
0	F

TABLE 2.5 *Sorted Data for VLOOKUP Example in Excel*

0	F
59	D
69	C
79	B
89	A

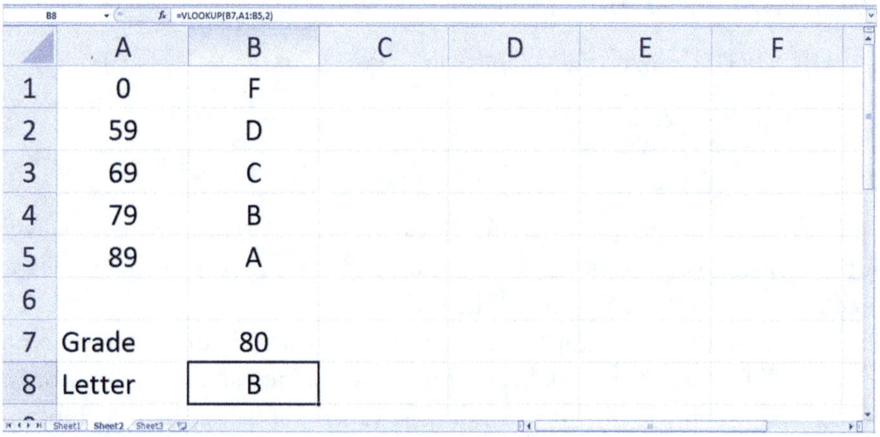

B8 =VLOOKUP(B7,A1:B5,2)

	A	B	C	D	E	F
1	0	F				
2	59	D				
3	69	C				
4	79	B				
5	89	A				
6						
7	Grade	80				
8	Letter	B				

FIGURE 2.40
VLOOKUP Function Example in Excel

However, the values are in descending order, and we should sort the table in ascending order. This time in the Options select “Sort data from top to bottom” to return the format in Table 2.5.

The syntax of VLOOKUP is as follows:

VLOOKUP(lookup_value,table,col_index_num,range_lookup)

The formula we used is

VLOOKUP(B7,$A$1:$B$5,2)

The only difference is the third argument, column index number. In our formula we used 2, as the second column is where the closest or matching value to the lookup value can be found. Figure 2.40 shows the relevant Excel screen.

Applied Spreadsheet Modeling—Using Basic Functions

A further use of functions in Excel is demonstrated here in an extension of the earlier Teez example. The model developed here is considered a descriptive model, where Mr. T wants to use the model to estimate his order quantity from the manufacturer. In the previous example, the price of the T-shirt was fixed. The expected profit is estimated with a set of probabilities of demand.

Example 2

Mr. T of Teez has expanded his operations and now sells his T-shirts in various locations. He intends to maintain the same T-shirt selling price as before; however, as we mentioned, he has to purchase more than 1000 T-shirts to attain the low price of $1.50 from the manufacturer. There are different levels of prices, and the discount table that the manufacturer uses is shown in Table 2.6. With his expanded operation, Mr. T is very uncertain about the demand for his T-shirts; the demand ranges from 20 bundles (100 T-shirts) to 400 bundles (2000 T-shirts) a week. If Mr. T has any left over, he may sell all excess inventory to a discount store for $1 per T-shirt. How many T-shirts should Mr. T order from the manufacturer?

STEP 1: PROBLEM DEFINITION

Mr. T wants to know the following: How many T-shirts should he order to maximize profit on the basis of an uncertain demand and the ability to sell his excess inventory for $1?

STEP 2: FORMULATE MODEL

Revenue comes from selling T-shirts at the regular price to the customers as well as from the sale of leftovers. The regular selling price is $4, while the sale price is $1. If the demand for that week is less than the quantity ordered, the number of units sold at regular price is determined by demand and excess units (quantity ordered – demand) are sold at sale price. If demand exceeds the quantity ordered, revenue would be regular selling price × demand.

To begin, first enter the data inputs we know, the selling price, the sale price, and the arbitrary order quantity and demand.

Using MIN Function

Next we use the MIN function (see Figure 2.41) in a formula to return the number of units sold at regular price in cell B9 (named Sold_reg).

=MIN(Order_quantity,Demand)

TABLE 2.6 *Quantity and Price Discount Data for Teez*

QUANTITY	PRICE DISCOUNT
Less than 100	$3.75
Between 100 and 199	$3.50
Between 200 and 499	$3.25
Between 500 and 799	$3.00
Between 800 and 999	$2.50
1000 and above	$1.50

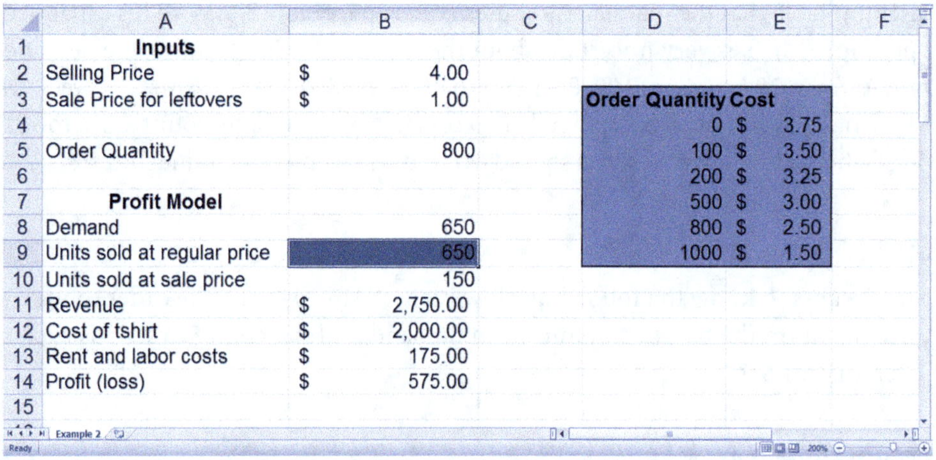

	A		B
1	**Inputs**		
2	Selling Price	$	4.00
3	Sale Price for leftovers	$	1.00
4			
5	Order Quantity		800
6			
7	**Profit Model**		
8	Demand		650
9	Units sold at regular price		650
10	Units sold at sale price		150
11	Revenue	$	2,750.00
12	Cost of tshirt	$	2,000.00
13	Rent and labor costs	$	175.00
14	Profit (loss)	$	575.00
15			

Order Quantity	Cost
0	$ 3.75
100	$ 3.50
200	$ 3.25
500	$ 3.00
800	$ 2.50
1000	$ 1.50

FIGURE 2.41 Teez Spreadsheet Profit Model

This formula returns the lesser of the two arguments. If demand exceeds the quantity ordered, the formula would return the quantity ordered. This follows the logic that the units sold at regular price are limited by the stock on hand.

On the other hand, if demand were less than the quantity ordered, the formula would return demand. Correspondingly, the excess inventory would then be sold at the sale price.

Using IF Function

The formula used to return the number of units sold at sale price in cell B10, which we named Sold_sale, is

=IF(Order_quantity>Demand,Order_quantity–Demand,0)

This formula uses the IF function with the condition that, should the quantity ordered be greater than demand, the formula calculates the excess inventory (value if true). This excess inventory is the number of units sold at sale price. When the condition is violated, such as when demand exceeds the quantity ordered, the formula would return 0 (value if false). This corresponds to the assumption that, with no excess inventory, all T-shirts will be sold at the regular price, thus no leftover T-shirts will be available to be sold at the sale price to the discount store.

With the units of T-shirts sold at regular price and sale price calculated, we can enter the following formula in cell B11 to calculate Teez's revenue.

=Sold_reg*Selling_price+Sold_sale*Sale_price

There is also the issue of quantity discounts. If Mr. T orders only 800 T-shirts, his cost is $2.50 per T-shirt. We need to use a lookup function to return the corresponding cost per T-shirt based on the quantity ordered by Teez. Other costs are fixed, such as rental and labor costs of $175.

Using VLOOKUP Function

The formula used to calculate the cost of T-shirts in cell B11is

=VLOOKUP(Order_quantity,$D$4:$E$9,2)*Order_quantity

We use the order quantity as the lookup value, where the reference table is defined by D4:E9 (color formatted in purple for clarity). The value returned is the corresponding cost per T-shirt according to the order quantity seen in the second column of the table. The resulting cost per T-shirt is multiplied by the order quantity to calculate Teez's total cost of ordering T-shirts.

Profit is simply revenue – cost of T-shirts – other costs. The formula entered in the Profit cell is

=B11–B12–B13

Sensitivity Analysis Using Data Table

Using the same method as in Figure 2.12, create a data table of Teez's profit as Demand (column input) and Quantity ordered (row input) varies. The values from 100 to 1100 are used for both demand and order quantity.

From the data table (see Figure 2.42), we can see that Teez enjoys a healthy profit for higher values of demand and order quantity. In fact, it makes sense to assume that if Mr. T ordered more than 1000 T-shirts, he would make a profit as long as demand remained above 200. But as demand is uncertain, this may not yield the highest expected profit for Teez. This also leads to the next question, "How much more than 1000 T-shirts should Mr. T order?"

Expected Profit with Demand Probabilities

In this example, the quantity ordered is decided by Mr. T and is within his control (the decision variable), while demand is not within his control. On further investi-

Profit (loss) $ 575.00

Data table of profit as a function of order quantity and demand

Order_Quantity	Demand										
$ 575.00	100	200	300	400	500	600	700	800	900	1000	1100
100	$ (125.00)	$ (125.00)	$ (125.00)	$ (125.00)	$ (125.00)	$ (125.00)	$ (125.00)	$ (125.00)	$ (125.00)	$ (125.00)	$ (125.00)
200	$ (325.00)	$ (25.00)	$ (25.00)	$ (25.00)	$ (25.00)	$ (25.00)	$ (25.00)	$ (25.00)	$ (25.00)	$ (25.00)	$ (25.00)
300	$ (550.00)	$ (250.00)	$ 50.00	$ 50.00	$ 50.00	$ 50.00	$ 50.00	$ 50.00	$ 50.00	$ 50.00	$ 50.00
400	$ (775.00)	$ (475.00)	$ (175.00)	$ 125.00	$ 125.00	$ 125.00	$ 125.00	$ 125.00	$ 125.00	$ 125.00	$ 125.00
500	$ (875.00)	$ (575.00)	$ (275.00)	$ 25.00	$ 325.00	$ 325.00	$ 325.00	$ 325.00	$ 325.00	$ 325.00	$ 325.00
600	$ (1,075.00)	$ (775.00)	$ (475.00)	$ (175.00)	$ 125.00	$ 425.00	$ 425.00	$ 425.00	$ 425.00	$ 425.00	$ 425.00
700	$ (1,275.00)	$ (975.00)	$ (675.00)	$ (375.00)	$ (75.00)	$ 225.00	$ 525.00	$ 525.00	$ 525.00	$ 525.00	$ 525.00
800	$ (1,075.00)	$ (775.00)	$ (475.00)	$ (175.00)	$ 125.00	$ 425.00	$ 725.00	$ 1,025.00	$ 1,025.00	$ 1,025.00	$ 1,025.00
900	$ (1,225.00)	$ (925.00)	$ (625.00)	$ (325.00)	$ (25.00)	$ 275.00	$ 575.00	$ 875.00	$ 1,175.00	$ 1,175.00	$ 1,175.00
1000	$ (375.00)	$ (75.00)	$ 225.00	$ 525.00	$ 825.00	$ 1,125.00	$ 1,425.00	$ 1,725.00	$ 2,025.00	$ 2,325.00	$ 2,325.00
1100	$ (425.00)	$ (125.00)	$ 175.00	$ 475.00	$ 775.00	$ 1,075.00	$ 1,375.00	$ 1,675.00	$ 1,975.00	$ 2,275.00	$ 2,575.00

FIGURE 2.42
Data Table Outputs for Teez Sensitivity Analysis

TABLE 2.7 *Demand Probability for Teez Company*

DEMAND	100	200	300	400	500	600	700	800	900	1000	1100
Probability	1%	2%	5%	10%	14%	16%	20%	15%	11%	5%	1%

gation of his sales data, he produced a probability table of demand (see Table 2.7). With these probabilities, we may calculate the order quantity with the highest expected profit and based on the probability of demand.

Using SUMPRODUCT

To calculate the expected profit on the basis of the probabilities in Table 2.7, we enter in cell B37 the formula

=SUMPRODUCT(B20:L20,$B$34:$L$34).

We calculate the expected profit for each order quantity by multiplying the probability of demand with the profit for each row of order quantity that we calculated in the data table earlier. Note how absolute references are used for the probabilities before copying the formula down to cell B47 (see Figure 2.43).

Using the X-Y scatter plot, we achieve the graph that clearly shows that expected profit is highest at $1260 when the order quantity is 1000. This does not mean that Mr. T will be guaranteed to make a profit of $1260; the actual profit will depend on eventual demand. This model is a reasonable way for Mr. T to estimate how much he should order.

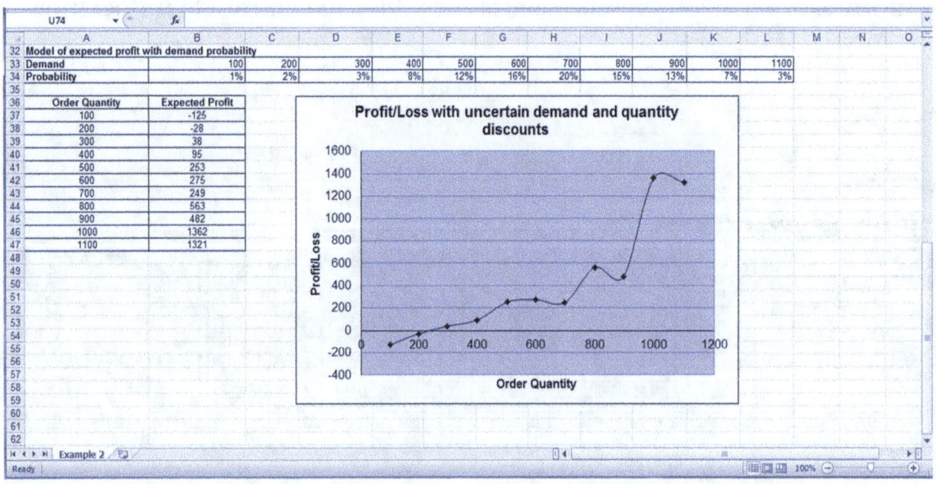

FIGURE 2.43
Expected Profit Calculation for Teez Company

Applied Spreadsheet Modeling— Using Solver

The model developed for a production planning/product mix problem is a prescriptive one. The relationship between variables is well defined and the variables are within the control of the manager. We use Excel's Solver to find the optimal production plan to maximize profits, thus prescribing a solution to the problem.

Example 3

Sweets Bakery is known for its specialty cake and custard pie, and every day there are least 15 customers willing to buy the cakes and 20 willing to buy the pies. The cake is sold for $20 and the custard pie for $18. However, the owner currently has three full-time bakers that she can trust with the recipe, each working 8-hour days. To bake each cake requires a block of butter, 4 eggs, and 2 packets of flour as well as an hour of the baker's time. Each pie requires a block of butter, 12 eggs, and 1 packet of flour, and 45 minutes to bake (0.75 hours). This is shown alongside the cost of each ingredient/input in Table 2.8.

The owner gets a delivery of ingredients fresh daily from the supplier. Her current daily order is shown in Table 2.9.

STEP 1: PROBLEM DEFINITION

The first thing the owner wants to have is a solution that would allow her to adjust her production plan and purchasing decisions based on these parameters. There are several questions she needs to have answered.

1. How many cakes and pies should be produced to maximize profits, based on current inputs.
2. Is production capacity constrained by labor or ingredients?
3. How will production capacity change if input resources are changed?

TABLE 2.8 *Ingredient and Cost Data for Sweets Bakery*

	CAKE	CUSTARD PIE	COST
Butter per block	1	1	$1.00
Egg	4	12	$0.20
Flour per packet	2	1	$3.00
Per hour of labor	1	0.75	$7.00

TABLE 2.9 *Ingredient Delivery Data for Sweets Bakery*

Butter per block	24
Egg	240
Flour per packet	30

STEP 2: MODEL FORMULATE THE MODEL

The decision to be made in this problem is the number of cakes and pies to produce in order to maximize profit. In turn, the actual numbers of cakes and pies to produce are referred to as the decision variables of the problem. Then again, the profitability of Sweets is limited by its production capacity and demand.

To determine the production capacity of Sweets, we have to understand how production is limited by the amount of ingredients and labor used for each cake and pie. The input mix of each product can be described in the form of a closed equation.

One cake = 1 block of butter + 4 eggs + 2 packets of flour + 1 hour of labor
One pie = 1 block of butter + 12 eggs + 1 packet of flour + 0.75 hour of labor

Obviously the multiple of the number of units produced would imply the same multiple of inputs to be used for production. For example, two cakes would use 2 × 1 block of butter + 2 × 4 eggs + 2 × 2 packets of flour + 2 × 1 hour of labor.

However, we are told there is a daily delivery of supplies and three bakers who work 8-hour days. Thus, the supplies and labor available limit production of cakes and pies. This constitutes the input constraints. In the spreadsheet model we have to ensure that inputs used are less than or equal to the inputs available.

Calculation of the profit is fairly straightforward. Because the model limits production capacity to less than or equal to daily demand, we are assuming that all units produced will be sold. Hence, revenue of cakes and pies is determined by the selling price and the number produced. Likewise, cost per item is determined by multiplying the input mix by the number produced of each item and the cost of each input.

Consequently, we may use Excel's Solver to solve for maximum profit, taking into consideration the production capacity and demand constraints.

Building the Spreadsheet Model

Cost inputs and price inputs should be entered first as these are static and values that are given. Enter the matrix of values of the production input mix for both cake and pies (see Figure 2.44).

Subsequently, we formulate the spreadsheet model with the input and the demand constraints (see Figure 2.45). In the section Production Plan we put in arbitrary values of 10 cakes and 10 pies. In cell B23:C23, we enter <= to show the

T39 | f_x

	A	B	C	D	E	F	G	H
1	**Production planning Model for Sweets Bakery**							
2								
3	**Cost Inputs**							
4	Butter	$ 1.00						
5	Egg	$ 0.20						
6	Flour	$ 3.00						
7	Hourly Wage	$ 7.00						
8								
9	**Price inputs**							
10	Price of cake	$ 20.00						
11	Price of pie	$ 18.00						
12								
13	**Production input mix**							
14		**Cake**	**Pie**					
15	Butter	1	1					
16	Egg	4	12					
17	Flour	2	1					
18	Labor (hrs)	1	0.75					
19								

Example 3 | Ready | 160%

FIGURE 2.44
Sweets Bakery Initial Spreadsheet Model

B28 | f_x =SUMPRODUCT($B$22:$C$22,B15:C15)

	A	B	C	D	E	F	G	H
13	**Production input mix**							
14		**Cake**	**Pie**					
15	Butter	1	1					
16	Egg	4	12					
17	Flour	2	1					
18	Labor (hrs)	1	0.75					
19								
20	**Production Plan**							
21		**Cake**	**Pie**					
22	Units produced	10	10					
23		<=	<=					
24	Maximum Sales	15	20					
25								
26	**Input Constraints**							
27		**Used**		**Available**	**Excess**			
28	Butter	20	<=	24	4			
29	Egg	160	<=	240	80			
30	Flour	30	<=	30	0			
31	Labor (hrs)	17.5	<=	24	6.5			

Example 3 | Ready | 160%

FIGURE 2.45
Sweets Bakery Spreadsheet Including Input and Demand

demand constraint in the following line (maximum sales of cake and pie). This symbol does not calculate, but serves to clarify the logic of the model.

We highlighted the cells to show these are the decision variables. Later, we will describe how Solver will vary the values in these cells to determine the maximum profit, given demand and capacity constraints.

The next section shows the input constraints, defined by columns labeled Used, Available, and Excess. In the Used column, under the row of Butter at cell B28, we enter the formula

=SUMPRODUCT($B$22:$C$22,B15:C15)

Notice the use of absolute reference for the units produced, as we then drag to copy this formula to the rest of the input constraints. This formula uses the multiple of each item produced and multiplies it with the butter input (B15:C15) and sums it up to return the total amount of butter used to produce 10 cakes and 10 pies. The other inputs used are calculated the same way.

In the range D28:D31, we enter <= again for clarity purposes to show the input constraints. Under the column Available, we enter the supplies available for daily production. Under the Excess column, we use the IF function to calculate excess supplies at the end of the day after producing 10 cakes and pies. In cell E28, the formula entered is

=IF(D28>B28,D28–B28,0)

Notice the use of relative reference for the units produced, as we then drag to copy this formula to the rest of the input constraints.

Finally, revenue, costs, and profit are formulated for the spreadsheet model (see Figure 2.46). We chose to separate the calculation of revenue, costs, and profits for both the cake and the pie, so that the manager of Sweets can clearly see how each item contributes to the profit calculation.

The formulas are fairly straightforward but we will show one example for the revenue, cost, and profit cells. In the Cake Revenue cell, B35, the formula entered is

=Price_of_cake*Cakes_produced

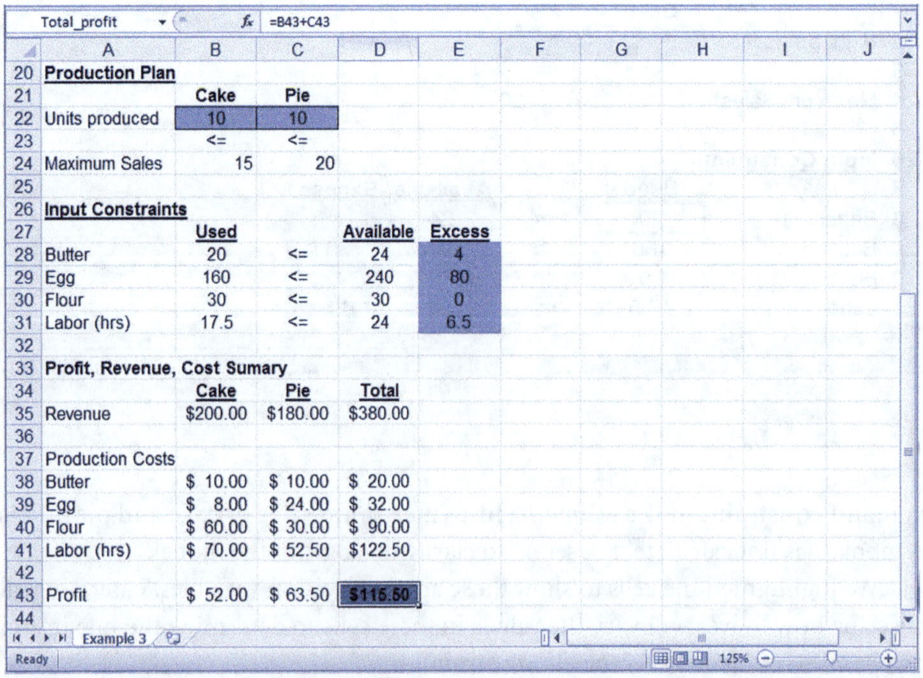

Total_profit | =B43+C43

	A	B	C	D	E
20	Production Plan				
21		Cake	Pie		
22	Units produced	10	10		
23		<=	<=		
24	Maximum Sales	15	20		
25					
26	Input Constraints				
27		Used		Available	Excess
28	Butter	20	<=	24	4
29	Egg	160	<=	240	80
30	Flour	30	<=	30	0
31	Labor (hrs)	17.5	<=	24	6.5
32					
33	Profit, Revenue, Cost Sumary				
34		Cake	Pie	Total	
35	Revenue	$200.00	$180.00	$380.00	
36					
37	Production Costs				
38	Butter	$ 10.00	$ 10.00	$ 20.00	
39	Egg	$ 8.00	$ 24.00	$ 32.00	
40	Flour	$ 60.00	$ 30.00	$ 90.00	
41	Labor (hrs)	$ 70.00	$ 52.50	$122.50	
42					
43	Profit	$ 52.00	$ 63.50	$115.50	
44					

FIGURE 2.46
Sweets Bakery Final Spreadsheet Model

In the input cell B38, the cost cell, the formula entered is

=B4*B15*Cakes_produced

where B4 is the cost of butter, and B15 from the Production Input Mix section is the amount of butter used per cake. In the Cake Profit cell, B43, the formula entered is

=B35–SUM(B38:B41)

The highlighted cell of Total Profit is the target cell representing the cell that Solver will solve for. In this instance, we wish to maximize profit.

Using Excel Solver

Solver is similar to Goal Seek, where Excel will vary input cells to come up with a desired solution. However, with Goal Seek you may change only one input cell, whereas Solver changes multiple input cells. In this chapter, we will not go too

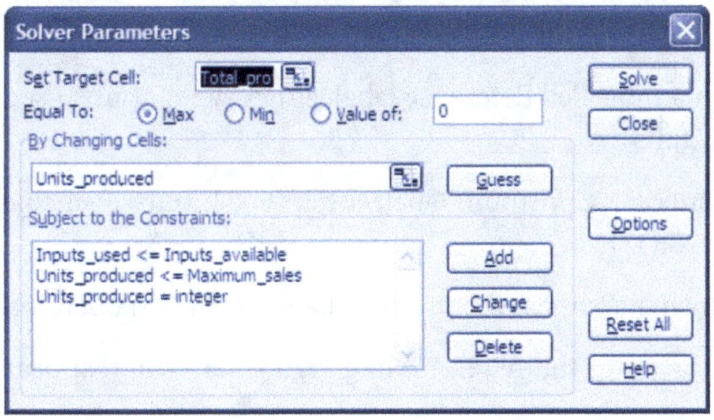

FIGURE 2.47a
Solver Menu in Excel 2007

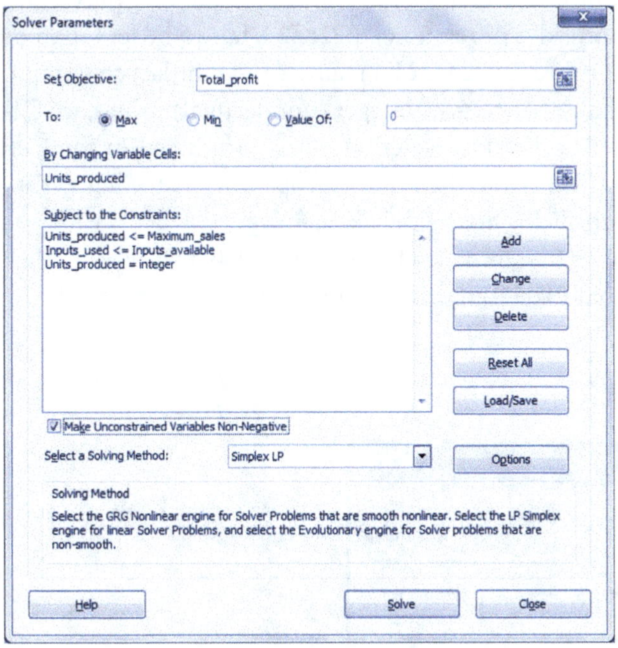

FIGURE 2.47b
Solver Menu in Excel 2010

much in detail about the various uses of Solver, but will demonstrate how simple it is to use to solve a profit maximization problem.

To invoke Solver in Excel, go to the Data tab and within the Analysis group Solver should be listed. If you have not installed Solver in Excel refer to the section entitled "Adding in Solver in Excel" later in this chapter. Refer to Chapter 8, on optimization, for further details on Solver and how to install it and for guidance if you have any other difficulty.

As mentioned, we set cell D43 (named Total_profit) as the target cell and select Max to indicate we wish to maximize Total Profit. In the text box of By Changing Cells, we enter the cells we wish Excel to modify in order to maximize profit. These are the decision variables B22:C22, named Units_produced.

Next, we enter the constraints in the text box of Subject to the Constraints. We do this by clicking on Add to get the following Add Constraint dialog box (see Figure 2.48).

Our first constraint is the input constraint. We know that the Production Mix Inputs Used column has to be less than or equal to the values of the Production Mix Inputs Available column, and we named the ranges as Inputs_used and Inputs_available previously. So we input the constraint as follows:

1. In the box directly under the Cell Reference label, either type Inputs_used or click on the cells B28:B31.
2. In the box directly under the Constraint label, either type Inputs_available or click on the cells D28:D31.
3. In the middle drop-down list choose the <= (less than or equal to) operator.
4. Click on the OK button and a figure resembling Figure 2.47 will reappear on the screen.

To add the next constraint, the demand constraint, we follow the same steps except that we use the name or cell references for units produced and maximum sales. Remember Units_produced, cell reference B22:C22, has to be less than or equal to Maximum_sales, cell reference B24:C24. Finally, we add the last constraint, units produced. To ensure that Solver returns integer (nondecimal) values, we follow the same steps described earlier but we enter Units_produced in the Cell Reference text box and select "int" from the middle drop-down list. Click OK to return to the Solver Parameters dialog box and click on Solve.

Shortly, the following Solver Results dialog box in Figure 2.49 will appear. Click on OK to view the solution that Excel found (see Figure 2.50).

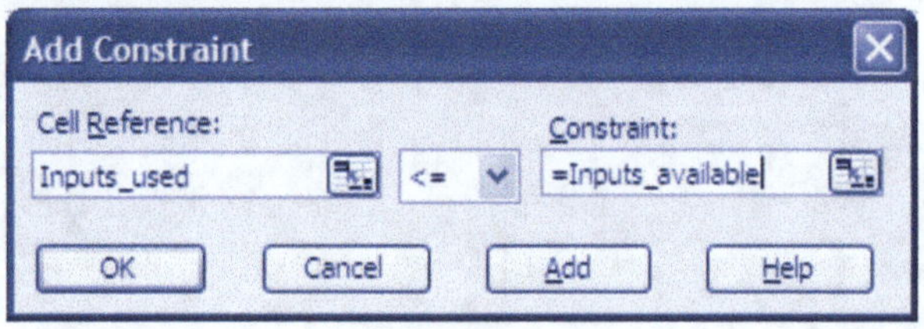

FIGURE 2.48
Solver's Add Constraint Menu

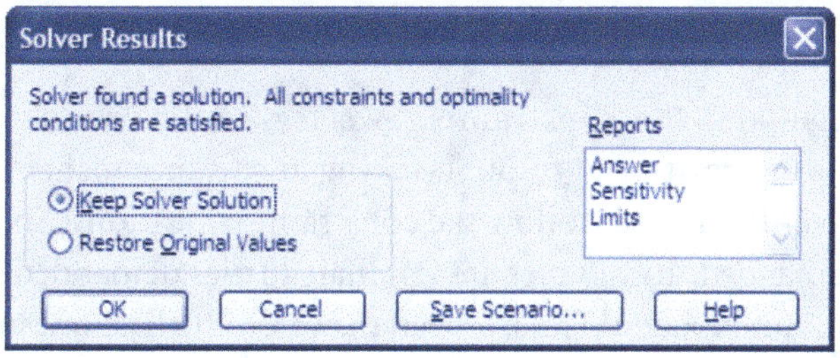

FIGURE 2.49a

Solver Results Menu in Excel 2007

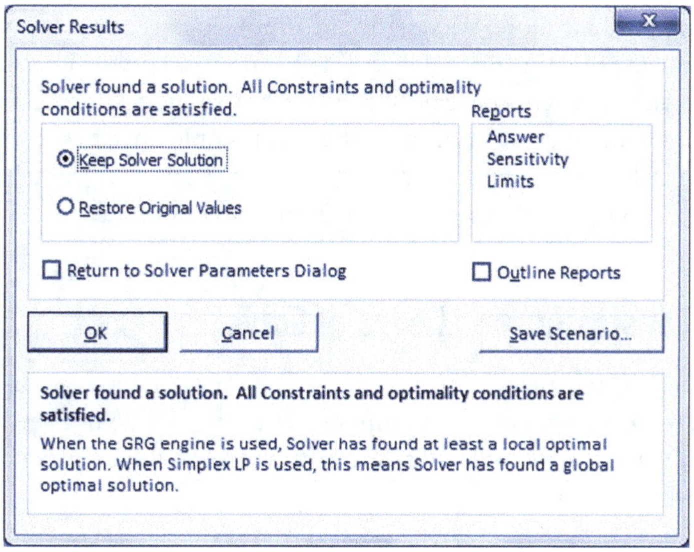

FIGURE 2.49b

Solver Results Menu in Excel 2010

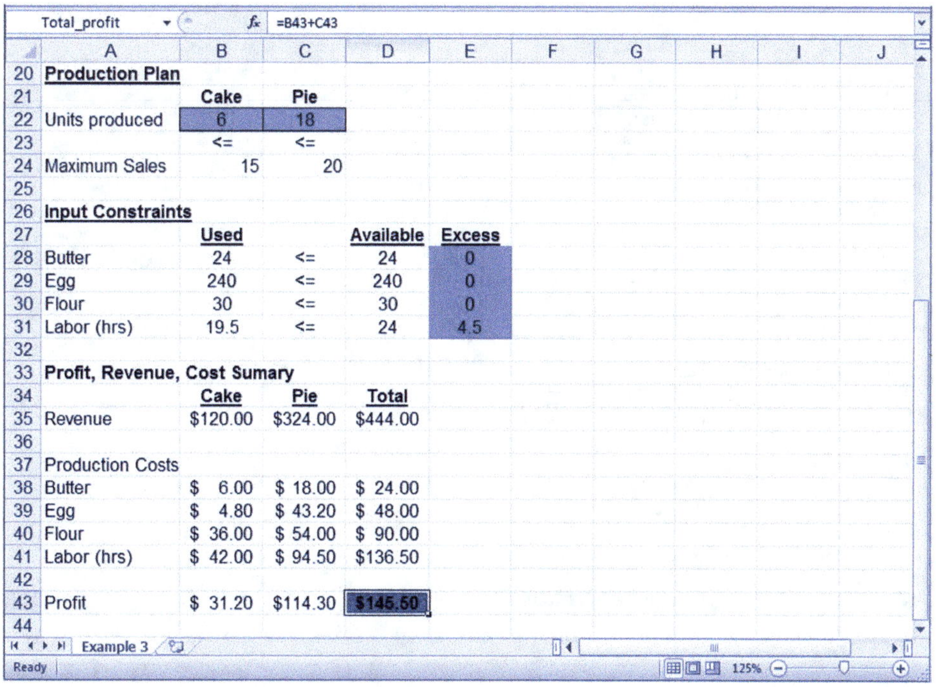

	A	B	C	D	E
20	**Production Plan**				
21		**Cake**	**Pie**		
22	Units produced	6	18		
23		<=	<=		
24	Maximum Sales	15	20		
25					
26	**Input Constraints**				
27		**Used**		**Available**	**Excess**
28	Butter	24	<=	24	0
29	Egg	240	<=	240	0
30	Flour	30	<=	30	0
31	Labor (hrs)	19.5	<=	24	4.5
32					
33	**Profit, Revenue, Cost Sumary**				
34		**Cake**	**Pie**	**Total**	
35	Revenue	$120.00	$324.00	$444.00	
36					
37	Production Costs				
38	Butter	$ 6.00	$ 18.00	$ 24.00	
39	Egg	$ 4.80	$ 43.20	$ 48.00	
40	Flour	$ 36.00	$ 54.00	$ 90.00	
41	Labor (hrs)	$ 42.00	$ 94.50	$136.50	
42					
43	Profit	$ 31.20	$114.30	$145.50	
44					

FIGURE 2.50

Sweets Bakery Final Spreadsheet Output

Analysis of Results

On the basis of the objective and the constraints, Sweets should produce 6 cakes and 18 pies to achieve a profit of $145.50. Looking at the spreadsheet (Figure 2.50), we see that Solver did indeed follow the constraint conditions. Six cakes are less than 15 cakes demanded, and 18 pies are less than 20 pies demanded. The input constraints are also not violated. Thus, Solver answered the first question as to how much Sweets may produce to maximize profit based on its limited resources. Specifically, $145.50 profit with 6 cakes and 18 pies.

Since demand exceeds Sweet's production capacity, we need to analyze how or why Sweets is unable to produce more. We refer to the Input Constraints section and the answer is clear in the Excess column. Observe in Figure 2.50 that the Excess column indicates that all ingredients have been used in the production process, but bakers are left idle for 4.5 hours. This implies the bakers could have baked at least 4 more cakes if they had sufficient ingredients! In other words, the production capacity of Sweets is constrained by its supply of ingredients and not labor.

Modification of Constraints and Rerun of Solver

Sweets could then modify (increase or decrease) the inputs for available ingredients and/or labor and rerun Solver. The second time Solver is run, you do not need to reset the target, changing cells or constraints. Excel remembers all of these settings and saves them when you save the file.

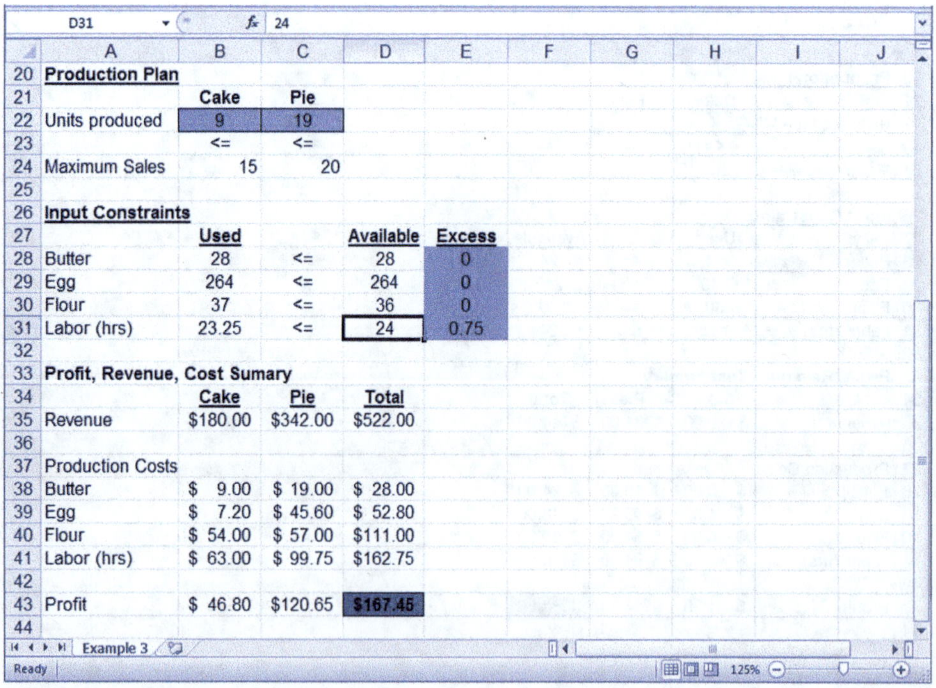

	A	B	C	D	E
20	Production Plan				
21		Cake	Pie		
22	Units produced	9	19		
23		<=	<=		
24	Maximum Sales	15	20		
25					
26	Input Constraints				
27		Used		Available	Excess
28	Butter	28	<=	28	0
29	Egg	264	<=	264	0
30	Flour	37	<=	36	0
31	Labor (hrs)	23.25	<=	24	0.75
32					
33	Profit, Revenue, Cost Sumary				
34		Cake	Pie	Total	
35	Revenue	$180.00	$342.00	$522.00	
36					
37	Production Costs				
38	Butter	$ 9.00	$ 19.00	$ 28.00	
39	Egg	$ 7.20	$ 45.60	$ 52.80	
40	Flour	$ 54.00	$ 57.00	$111.00	
41	Labor (hrs)	$ 63.00	$ 99.75	$162.75	
42					
43	Profit	$ 46.80	$120.65	$167.45	
44					

FIGURE 2.51 Sweets Bakery Modified Spreadsheet Output

Total_profit fx =B43+C43

	A	B	C	D	E
20	Production Plan				
21		Cake	Pie		
22	Units produced	9	20		
23		<=	<=		
24	Maximum Sales	15	20		
25					
26	Input Constraints				
27		Used		Available	Excess
28	Butter	29	<=	29	0
29	Egg	276	<=	276	0
30	Flour	38	<=	36	0
31	Labor (hrs)	24	<=	24	0
32					
33	Profit, Revenue, Cost Sumary				
34		Cake	Pie	Total	
35	Revenue	$180.00	$360.00	$540.00	
36					
37	Production Costs				
38	Butter	$ 9.00	$ 20.00	$ 29.00	
39	Egg	$ 7.20	$ 48.00	$ 55.20	
40	Flour	$ 54.00	$ 60.00	$114.00	
41	Labor (hrs)	$ 63.00	$105.00	$168.00	
42					
43	Profit	$ 46.80	$127.00	$173.80	
44					

Example 3

FIGURE 2.52
Sweets Bakery Modified Spreadsheet Output

To demonstrate how changing input resources will affect the solution, we add to our available resources 4 blocks of butter, 24 eggs, and 8 packets of flour. Total ingredient resources now include 28 blocks of butter, 264 eggs, and 38 packets of flour. The results are in Figure 2.51. Profit is now $167.45, units produced have increased to 9 cakes and 19 pies, with 1 excess packet of flour and 0.75 hours of excess labor.

We know that a pie could be made by using the leftover 1 packet of flour and 0.75 hours of labor if we could obtain a block of butter and a dozen eggs. The problem can be modified again by simply adding one more block of butter and 12 eggs. The results of the Solver rerun are displayed in Figure 2.52.

As seen in Figure 2.52, Sweets should produce 9 cakes and 20 pies to maximize profit. In order to do so, Sweets has to increase its daily order of supplies to 29 blocks of butter, 276 eggs, and 38 packets of flour.

Applied Spreadsheet Modeling—Curve Fitting

This example shows how we may estimate the relationship between advertising and sales by using curve functions, given historical sales data. In other words, the model developed is a predictive one. We briefly explain the properties of three trend lines that can be used to fit into a scatter plot.

Example 4

Teez Company began a radio advertising campaign to promote its T-shirts. As expected, Mr. T noticed sales figures had improved since the radio ads began airing. But Mr. T wanted to know how effective this campaign has been, so he wrote down his weekly sales as well as the number of ads run during that week. The data are shown in Table 2.10.

STEP 1: PROBLEM DEFINITION

Mr. T wants to know how sensitive his sales are to the radio ads; that is, he wants to know how much his advertising campaign has been helping sales. In this case we are assuming that other factors such as price or weather are not significant factors.

TABLE 2.10 *Teez Ad and T-Shirt Sales Data*

WEEK	NUMBER OF ADS	T-SHIRTS SOLD
1	10	610
2	9	520
3	6	280
4	5	260
5	11	750
6	12	880
7	7	300
8	14	1300
9	12	920
10	8	440
11	13	1000
12	7	360

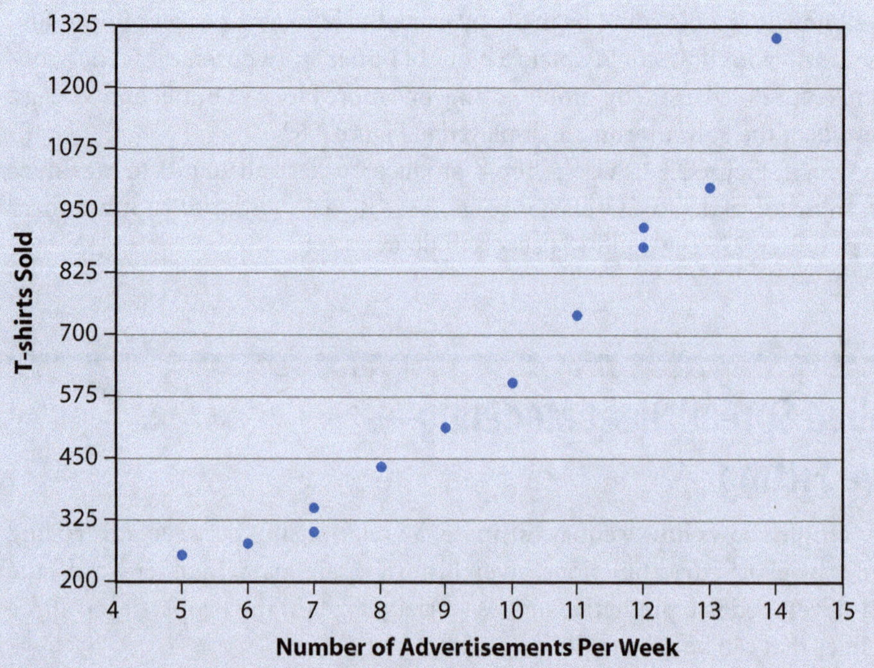

FIGURE 2.53 Graph of Teez Ads and T-shirt Sales

Business Decision Modeling Behind the Scenes

Spreadsheets in Real Business Situations

Introduction

Decision Models (www.decisionmodels.com) provides comprehensive consultancy and modeling services based on Microsoft Excel. Decision Models has worked with Federal Express in Europe. Two major FedEx projects are the Price Rate Development Tool and a series of European route planning models.

Price Rate Development Tool

The Price Rate Development Tool is an Excel VBA add-in that links to a number of server databases and templates (Excel, Access, and Informix). The tool has an additional Excel menu that provides an easy-to-use set of commands and forms to allow the user to perform a wide range of pricing tasks. The tool can generate an Excel workbook on the user's PC with the following functions:

Rate upload/download and comparison
New rate development
Discount matrix and rates development
Impact analysis pivot table
Multicurrency rate comparison and conversion

All the standard, familiar Excel functions can be used on the generated workbook. The tool has been designed to increase the user's productivity and reduce errors by automating routine calculations and administrative tasks, so that the user can concentrate on developing the optimum pricing strategies.

Design and Development of Opportunity Sizing and Service Take-up Forecasting Model

Another example is a model developed for Inmarsat's planned fourth-generation broadband satellite network. The model integrates research by RS Consulting, providing telephone and face-to-face interview results, demographic data, and Delphi Forecasting results. The Excel model develops worldwide 10-year volume forecasts of mobile data communication traffic and satellite service take-up, segmented by international and geographic region, economic development level, industry and product. The model factors in cellular rollout and development, price sensitivity, and channel, technology and regulatory rollout.

To maximize flexibility and future proofing, the model is dynamically generated from sets of relational tables. In addition to the standard Excel facilities, the model generator provides alternate and delta case handling, what-if audit trail maintenance, and pivot table generation.

STEP 2: BUILDING THE MODEL IN EXCEL

The independent variable *x* in this problem is the number of advertisements that Mr. T places on the radio each week. The dependent variable *y* is the T-shirts sold during the corresponding week. In this situation we can use the help of Excel's Charting and Trendline functions to identify the relationship (function) between the variables. In other words, this is a predictive model, as the final relationship would allow us to predict how the number of ads we place affects sales.

Using the chart function (see the section entitled Creating Charts in Excel, Chapter 2), we create an *x*-*y* scatter plot of a chart with sales on the *y* axis and number of ads on the *x* axis. Figure 2.54 shows clearly that sales increase as the number of ads increases.

After creating the chart, right click on the data points within the graph and select from the menu Add Trendline. The Format Trendline dialog box, as shown in Figure 2.55, will appear. You can choose any of the six types of trend lines, but we will focus on three: Linear, Power, and Exponential. These lines have basic equations linking the dependent variable *y* to the independent *x* with *a* and *b* as constants. To display the equation of the trendline as well as the associated R-squared value, click on the appropriate check boxes at the bottom of the Format Trendline menu (see Figure 2.55).

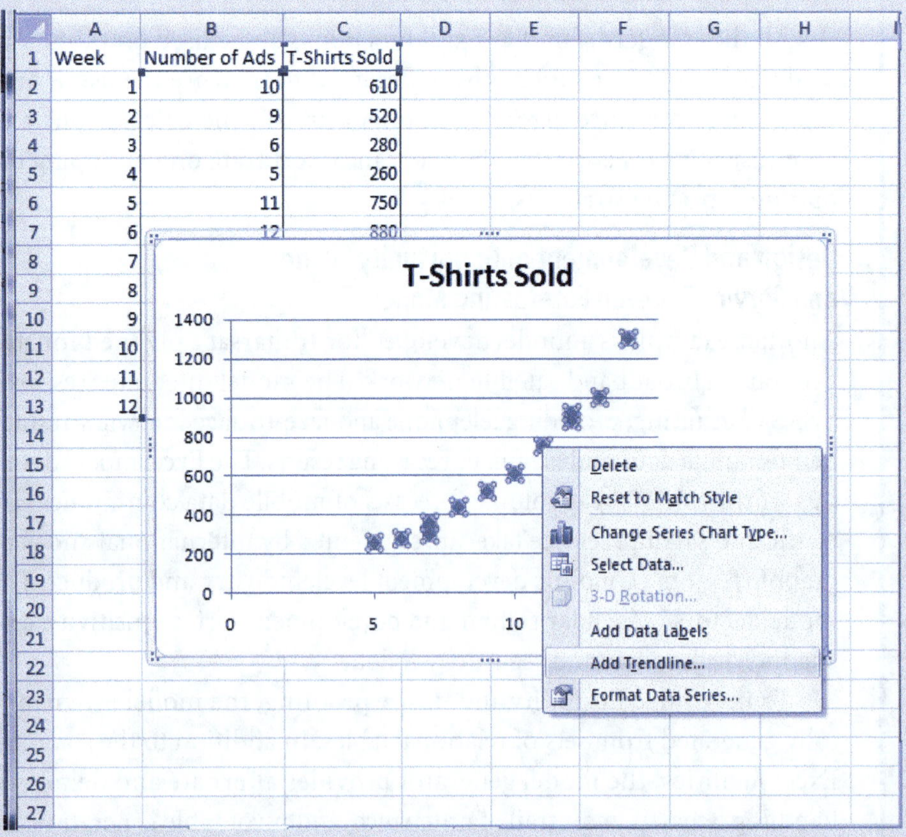

FIGURE 2.54
Graph of Teez Ads and T-shirt Sales

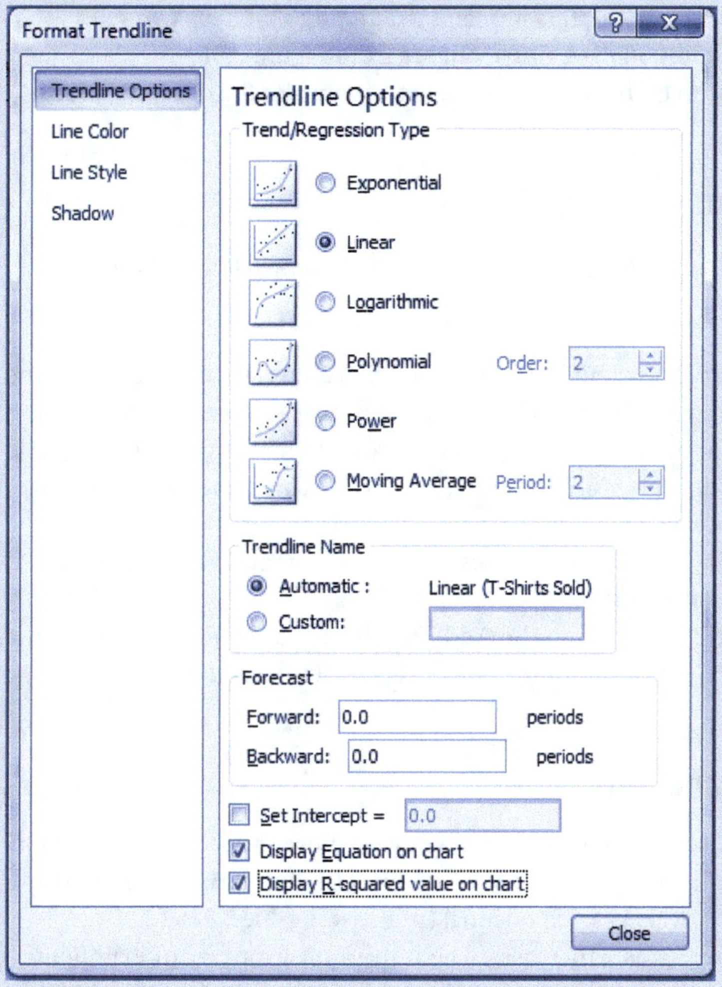

FIGURE 2.55
Format Trendline Menu in Excel

Linear Function

The linear function, used as a predictor, is defined by the general equation

$$\hat{y} = a + bx$$

Standard nomenclature is to refer to the left side of the equation as "y-hat" or the predicted value. A "hat," or caret (^), over the y is used to distinguish it from the original data values (the y) values. On a graph, this is a straight line, where a is the intercept and b is the slope. When and $a = 0$, then $y = x$. This means that when x changes by 1, y will also change by 1. Thus, b is also the multiple of x.

From Add Trendline, we select Linear. Then in the same dialog box, we select the Options tab and tick Display equation on the chart. The linear trend line will appear on the chart with the best-fitting linear line and the corresponding equation. Teez's best-fitting line to estimate the function is

$$\hat{y} = -421 + 111.16x$$

If we accept this function, this model is predicting that Teez will sell 111.16 T-shirts with each additional ad. As we can see from Figure 2.56, using a straight line does not appear to fit the data very well. Let us consider the other functions.

Power Function

The Power function, used as a predictor, is defined by the general equation

$$\hat{y} = ax^b$$

The power curve is determined by exponent b. In a special case when $b = 1$, the function becomes a straight line. If $b > 1$, y increases at an increasing rate as x increases. The important property of power curves is that when x changes by 1%, y changes by approximately b%. In this case, $b = 1.6331$. This means when x changes by 1%, y will increase by 1.6331%.

Note also that if $0 < b < 1$, y increases at a decreasing rate as x increases; and if $b < 0$, y decreases as x increases.

This time, select Power from the Add Trendline dialog box. The trendline shown in Figure 2.57 is the best-fitting power curve with the equation.

Exponential Function

The exponential function also represents a curve whose shape is determined by exponent b. The general equation for the exponential function, when used as a predictor, is $\hat{y} = ae^{bx}$, where e is exponential (numerical value 2.7182...).

If $b > 0$, y increases as x increases. The important property of exponential curves is that when x changes by 1 unit, y changes by approximately $100 \times b$%. In

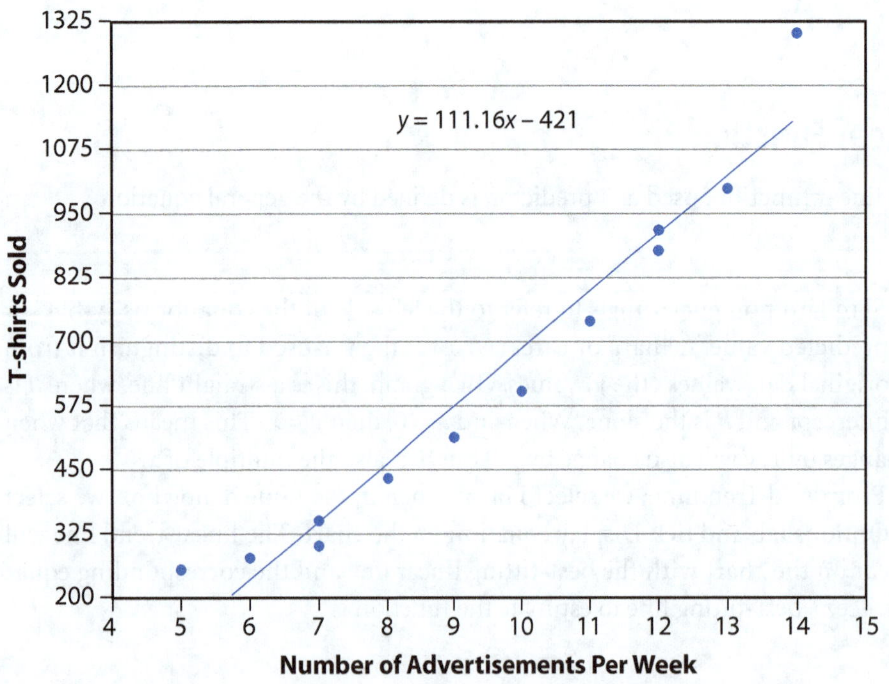

FIGURE 2.56 Linear Relationship for Teez Sales and Advertisements

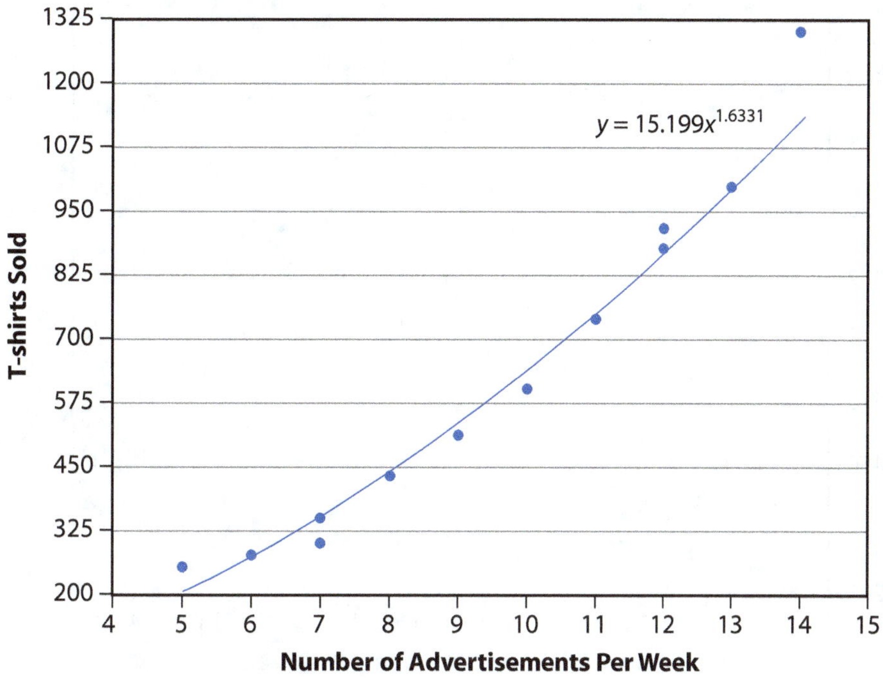

FIGURE 2.57

Power Relationship for Teez Sales and Advertisements

this case, $b = 0.1854$. This means that when x changes by 1 unit, y will increase by 18.54%. Note that if $b < 0$, y decreases as x increases. Selecting the Exponential function, we get the best-fitting curve, see Figure 2.58, and the following equation:

$$\hat{y} = 95.466e^{0.1854x}$$

Mean Absolute Percentage Error (MAPE)

But which one of these functions best reflects the relationship between the number of ads to sales? We have to determine the curve function that will predict, with the least average error (with most accuracy), the actual data set. So we calculate the average percentage error between the observed sales and the predicted sales figure (as predicted by the respective curve function) for each row of data. This is known as the mean absolute percentage error (MAPE). The curve function with the lowest MAPE predicts the actual sales figures with the least amount of error.

$$\text{APE} = \frac{|\text{actual sales} - \text{predicted sales}|}{\text{observed sales}}$$

$$\text{MAPE} = \frac{\sum_{i=1}^{n}\left(\frac{|\text{actual Sales} - \text{predicted sales}|}{\text{observed sales}}\right)_i}{n}$$

We have to use each function's equation indicated on the charts to calculate the predicted sales figures for each of the last 12 weeks' data based on the given number of ads aired. Therefore, for each function we have the inputs of a and b.

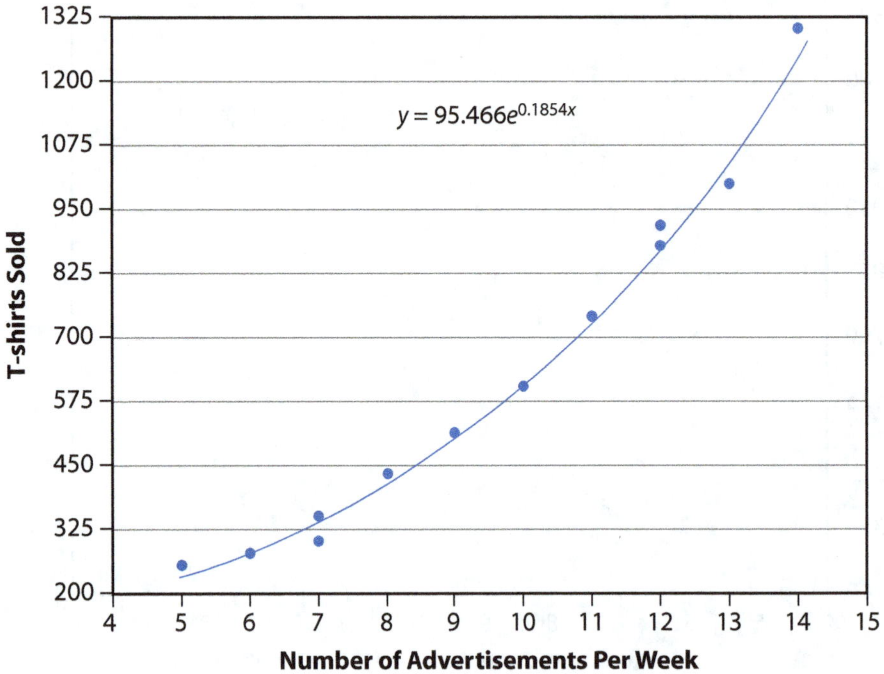

FIGURE 2.58
Natural Logarithmic Relationship for Teez Sales and Advertisements

Name the following inputs for each function: Linear will have linear_a and linear_b. Power will have power_a and power_b. Exponential will have exp_a and exp_b. Recall each function will predict the sales figure *y*, where variable *x* is the number of ads.

Next build a table of predicted results for each best-fitting function. Following the equation of the linear function, we enter in cell E5 the formula =intercept_a+slope_b*B5. For subsequent results the formula advances the *x* value from B5 through to B16. Figure 2.59 displays the spreadsheet model for Teez curve fitting model.

To calculate the predicted sales results from the best-fitting power function in cell F5, we enter the power equation according to the formula

=power_a*B5^power_b

Recall the power function equation is $y = ax^b$.

To calculate the predicted sales results from the best-fitting exponential function in cell G5, we enter the exponential equation according to the formula =exp_a*EXP(exp_b*B5). Here EXP( ), returns the exponential of the values within the parentheses.

Next, the table is extended to calculate the average percentage error (APE) for each function, using the appropriate equation given earlier. The formula you should enter for the linear function is

=ABS(C5–E5)/C5

Move your cursor close to the bottom right corner of the active cell H5 until it changes from a white cross to a black cross. Click and drag to highlight the cells you wish to copy the formula to. Excel will automatically copy the formula into the

SUM =Intercept_a+Slope_b*B5

	A	B	C	D	E	F	G	H	I	J
1	Estimating the relationship between advertising and t-shirt sale									
2										
3		Observed data set				Predicted		Absolute Percentage Error		
4	Week	No of Ads	T-Shirts sold		Linear	Power	Exponential	Linear	Power	Exponential
5	1	10	610		e_b*B5	653.00	609.58	13.21%	7.05%	0.07%
6	2	9	520		579.44	549.78	506.42	11.43%	5.73%	2.61%
7	3	6	280		245.96	283.54	290.37	12.16%	1.26%	3.71%
8	4	5	260		134.80	210.52	241.23	48.15%	19.03%	7.22%
9	5	11	750		801.76	762.98	733.75	6.90%	1.73%	2.17%
10	6	12	880		912.92	879.48	883.22	3.74%	0.06%	0.37%
11	7	7	300		357.12	364.71	349.52	19.04%	21.57%	16.51%
12	8	14	1300		1135.24	1131.25	1279.69	12.67%	12.98%	1.56%
13	9	12	920		912.92	879.48	883.22	0.77%	4.40%	4.00%
14	10	8	440		468.28	453.58	420.72	6.43%	3.09%	4.38%
15	11	13	1000		1024.08	1002.30	1063.13	2.41%	0.23%	6.31%
16	12	7	360		357.12	364.71	349.52	0.80%	1.31%	2.91%
17							MAPE--->	11.48%	6.54%	4.32%
18	Inputs for each function									
19										
20	Linear									
21	Intercept a	-421								
22	slope b	111.16								
23	Power									
24	power a	15.199								
25	power b	1.6331								
26	Exponential									
27	exp a	95.466								
28	exp b	0.1854								
29										

Example 4

FIGURE 2.59

Spreadsheet Curve-fitting Model for Teez

blank cells with the corresponding predicted and observed data of each row of weeks. You will see in H6 that the formula will be copied as =ABS(C6–E6)/C6.

You may also use absolute referencing, since column C remains unchanged. The formula may be edited to =ABS($C5–E5)/$C5 (see Figure 2.60).

Once the weekly APE's are calculated, you can average the results to find the mean average percentage error (MAPE) of each function. In cell H17:J17, the formula is =AVERAGE(H5:H16).

Since the exponential function yields the lowest MAPE, 4.32%, it is obvious that the exponential function would predict the most accurate sales results given the number of ads. In comparison with the earlier charts, it also appears as if more of the data set lies near or on the trend line than the other function lines.

H5 =ABS(C5-E5)/C5

	B	C	D	E	F	G	H	I	J
2									
3	ved data set				Predicted		Absolute Percentage Error		
4	No of Ads	T-Shirts sold		Linear	Power	Exponential	Linear	Power	Exponential
5	10	610		690.60	653.00	609.58	13.21%	7.05%	0.07%
6	9	520		579.44	549.78	506.42	11.43%	5.73%	2.61%
7	6	280		245.96	283.54	290.37	12.16%	1.26%	3.71%
8	5	260		134.80	210.52	241.23	48.15%	19.03%	7.22%
9	11	750		801.76	762.98	733.75	6.90%	1.73%	2.17%
10	12	880		912.92	879.48	883.22	3.74%	0.06%	0.37%
11	7	300		357.12	364.71	349.52	19.04%	21.57%	16.51%
12	14	1300		1135.24	1131.25	1279.69	12.67%	12.98%	1.56%
13	12	920		912.92	879.48	883.22	0.77%	4.40%	4.00%
14	8	440		468.28	453.58	420.72	6.43%	3.09%	4.38%
15	13	1000		1024.08	1002.30	1063.13	2.41%	0.23%	6.31%
16	7	360		357.12	364.71	349.52	0.80%	1.31%	2.91%
17						MAPE--->	11.48%	6.54%	4.32%
18	unction								
19									

Example 4

FIGURE 2.60

Spreadsheet Curve-fitting Model for Teez

Adding in Solver in Excel

Excel includes an add-in called Solver. It is accessed in the Data tab, Analysis Group and is labeled Solver (see Figure 2.61). Steps in setting up Solver in Excel 2007 if it is not already loaded in the Data tab, Analysis Group are as follows:

1. Click on the Office button and select the Excel Options button at the bottom of the screen (see Figure 2.61a for Excel 2007 and Figure 2.61b for Excel 2010).
2. Within the Excel Options window click on the Add-Ins option on the left. A screen that resembles Figure 2.62 will appear.
3. Select Excel Add-Ins from the Add-Ins menu and then click on the Go button.
4. The Add-Ins menu to appear (see Figure 2.63) and click on the check box for Solver, then click OK.

Once this has been completed, the Solver option in the Analysis group under the Data tab will appear.

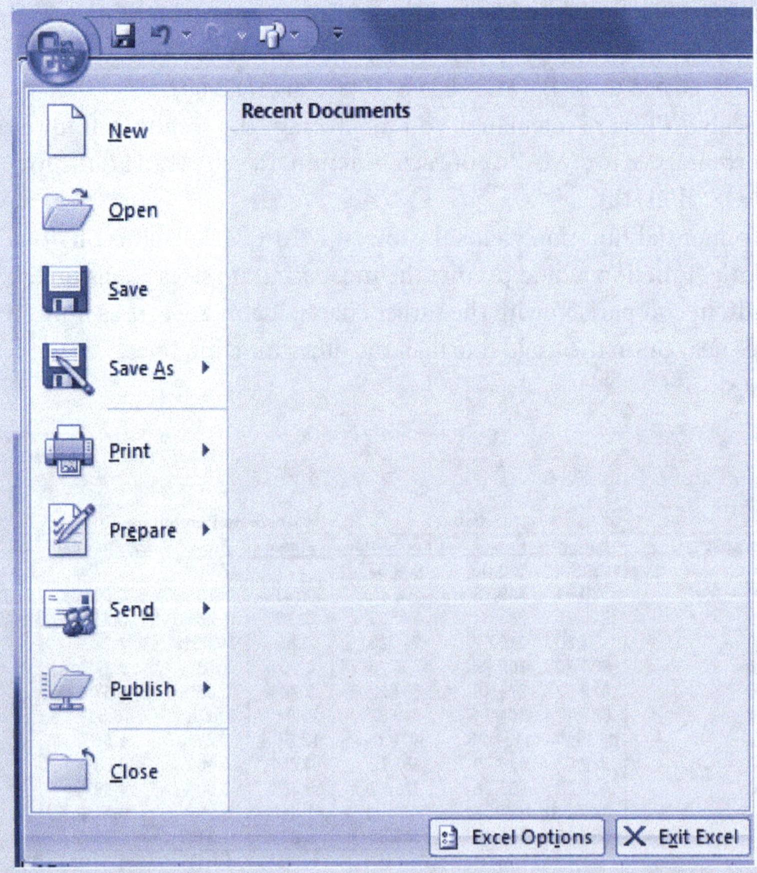

FIGURE 2.61a
Office Button in Excel 2007

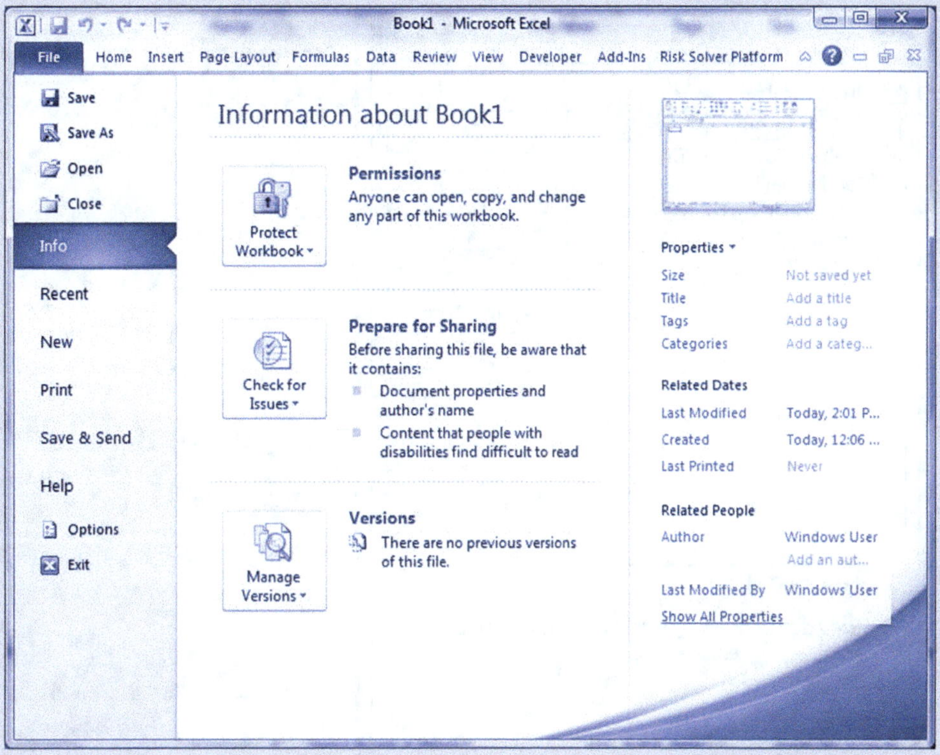

FIGURE 2.61b
Office Button in Excel 2010

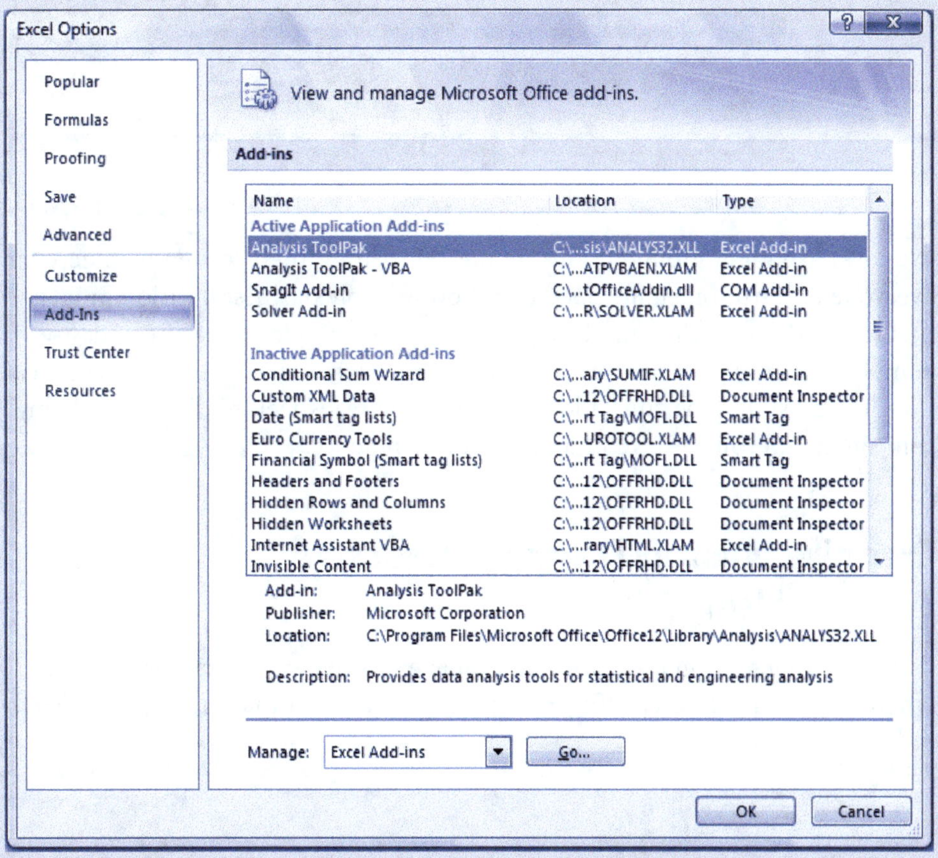

FIGURE 2.62
Add-ins Menu in the Excel Options Window

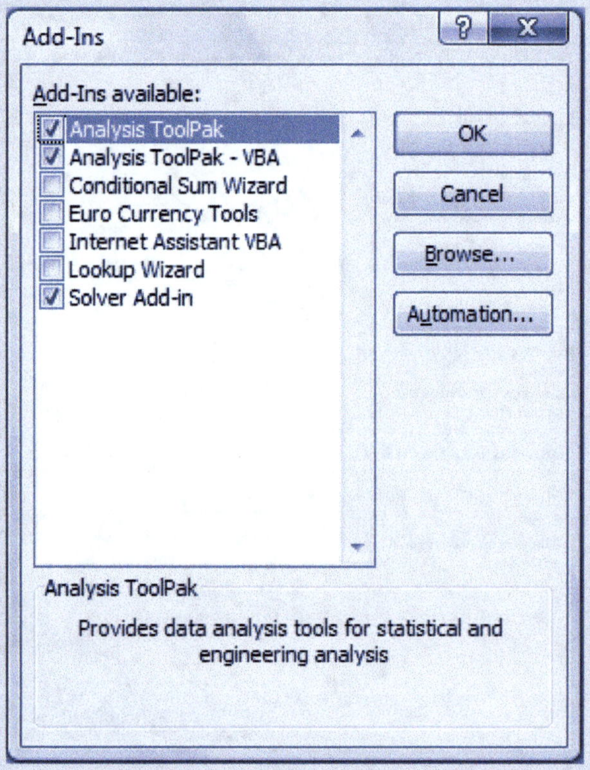

FIGURE 2.63
Add-ins Menu Excel

Summary

We covered a lot of ground in this chapter. Hopefully, there was enough here for everyone to learn something new about how to apply business decision modeling methods into spreadsheet modeling. To some, the examples shown here may seem complicated at first glance, but take yourself through each of the examples and at the end you should be quite adept at building spreadsheet models. As with anything in life, all you need is a little patience and practice.

Executive Summary Example for Teez's Profit Problem

The following section presents an example executive summary for Example 2, where we discuss Teez's profit problem with quantity discounts and uncertain demand.

EXECUTIVE SUMMARY FOR TEEZ PROFIT PROBLEM WITH QUANTITY DISCOUNTS AND UNCERTAIN DEMAND

TO: Stephanie Leung
FROM: Cua Consulting

Problem Identification

Teez Corporation has to make a purchasing decision in order to maximize its profit. The purchase price is dependent on the quantity ordered and the quantity to order is dependent on the expected demand. Given the discount schedule and demand probability, Teez has to decide the quantity of T-shirts to order.

Modeling the Problem

A spreadsheet model was developed to clearly demonstrate the relationships between discount price, order quantity, and expected demand to profitability.

First, revenue is obtained from selling T-shirts at the regular price as well as from selling the leftover T-shirts at the sale price. The cost of a T-shirt depends on the quantity ordered and follows a discount schedule.

$$\text{Revenue} = (\text{demand} \times \text{regular price}) + (\text{leftover} \times \text{sale price})$$
$$\text{Total cost} = \text{other costs} + (\text{price of quantity } j \times \text{quantity } j)$$

Cua Consulting constructed a profit/loss graph based on historical sales records to ascertain the demand pattern and the likelihood of demand for T-shirts. The profit or loss is first tabulated with varying order quantities. The results are shown in graphical form in Figure 1.

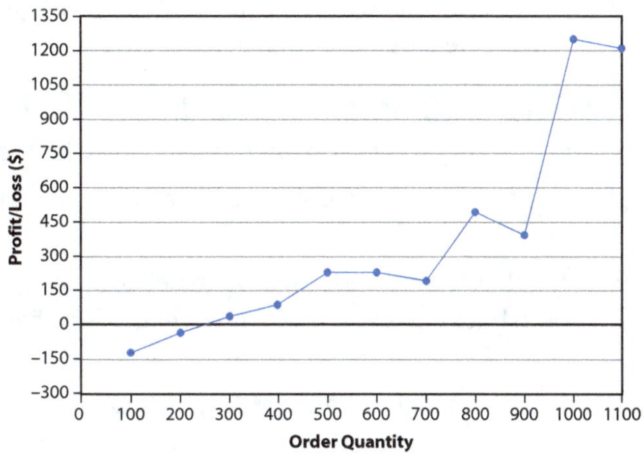

FIGURE 1. Profit/loss Graph for Teez Company

It must be noted that the profit/loss scenarios presented in Figure 1 are based on historical sales demand records. If drastic changes occur in the marketplace for Teez's shirts, then this information must be incorporated into the model and the graph redrawn.

Conclusions

On the basis of historical demand patterns, Teez Corporation should order 1000 T-shirts every month in order to maximize profit. If Teez wishes to order less than 1000, the next best range of order quantities are between 800 and 1000. Teez should not order less than 270 T-shirts, as this would result in a loss for the company. If demand patterns (as well as price or discounts) should change, Teez Company may modify the data in the model developed by Cua Consulting to review the best order quantity.

CASE STUDY

John Woo's Cellular Connections

Background

John Woo runs a small advertising firm. He employs 10 sales agents who need individual cellular phone service at all times. He is trying to decide which cell phone package to purchase.

John's Concerns

John has noticed that some plans tend to "low-ball" on the monthly fee but then stick the customer with big per minute charges when the free minutes are used up. John was wary of plans like this because if his employees used a lot of minutes the per minute fees swamped any saving obtained in the low monthly fees.

On the other hand, some plans "low-balled" the "per minute" charges but stuck users with a high monthly fee. These plans appealed to customers who knew they would use large amounts of minutes, but John felt uncertain about if the higher monthly fees were worth the lower "per minute" charges.

Plan Options

He has narrowed his options down to two plans; however, he is uncertain about which plan to select. Each employee uses about the same amount of airtime a month. John wants a plan that meets his current needs but will also be advantageous as his needs grow.

The "regular" plan charges a fixed fee of $55 per month for 2000 minutes of airtime plus $0.15 per minute for any time over 2000 minutes. The "executive" plan charges a fixed fee of $75 per month for 1000 minutes of airtime plus $0.09 per minute over 1000 minutes.

Spreadsheet Modeling and Discussion Questions

Construct an Excel spreadsheet model with graphs to assist John with the following questions:

1. If John expects his sales agents to use the phone for 50 hours per month, which plan should he select?
2. Perform an analysis based on the idea that John believes his agents' average use will be 50 hours per month but knows that they will never use less than 40 hours or more than 60 hours per month.
3. How does the decision change if the agents' usage habits change and they now use the phone on average 65 hours a month, but will never use more than 85 hours or less than 50 hours a month?

INTERACTIVE CASE

Break-Even Analysis at SportsExchange

Facility Comparison at SportsExchange

SportsExchange is a regional refurbisher of sporting goods equipment. It specializes in upgrading football equipment that it receives from high schools and colleges. Processes used by SportsExchange include sewing pants and jerseys, replacing pads, repairing and painting helmets, and replacing laces, snaps, and elastic in pants.

The most expensive process for SportsExchange is painting helmets. Regulations that control worker safety and environmental emissions mandate a paint room that manages fumes effectively. In order to continue in its lucrative business, SportsExchange is required to invest in a new state-of-the-art painting facility. SportsExchange has identified three manufacturers of turnkey spray booths. The fixed and variable costs associated with each of the three alternatives are presented in Table 1 below:

TABLE 1: COSTS ASSOCIATED WITH SPORTSEXCHANGE'S THREE PAINTING ALTERNATIVES

Alternative	Fixed cost	Variable cost
A: Enviro-Spray	\$500,000	\$0.148
B: Spray Center	\$207,500	\$1.321
C: Crystal Coat	\$265,000	\$0.910

Analysis

SportsExchange believes it will need to refinish 200,000 helmets. What is the total cost for each of the alternatives for refinishing that quantity of helmets? Which alternative appears to be the best choice (i.e., lowest total cost)? What alternative appears to the best choice if quantity to refinish increases to 320,000 helmets?

The cost accountants at SportsExchange may have made an error in calculating the fixed costs associated with the Spray Center alternative. They now believe that the fixed costs for the Spray Center alternative should be \$150,000. If SportsExchange expects to refinish 200,000 helmets, which alternative looks the best now? What happens to the relative attractiveness of the Crystal Coat alternative as Spray Center's fixed costs decrease to \$150,000?

In addition, the cost accountants have revealed that their estimate for Crystal Coat's variable cost may be too low. However, they don't know how by much they are off and would like to know how sensitive Crystal Coat is to changes in variable costs, specifically increases in variable costs. Give the cost accountants some assistance here by increasing Crystal Coat's variable costs and describe the changes that occur relative to the other alternatives.

Summary of Key Excel Terms

TERMS	EXPLANATION	EXCEL
Auditing toolbar	Useful for checking which cells are related to other cells through formulas	Use Tools/Customize menu item, select Formula Auditing from Toolbars tab
Cell comments	Useful for documenting contents of the cell	Right-click on cell, select Insert Comment menu item
Cell comments	Useful for documenting contents of the cell	Right-click on cell, select Insert Comment menu item
Efficient copying	Shortcut for copying a formula to a range	Select range, enter formula, and press Ctrl-Enter
Efficient selection	Useful for selecting a large rectangular range	Pressing Shift key, click on upper left and bottom right cells of range
fx button	Useful for getting help on Excel functions	On Standard toolbar (by default)
Goal Seek	Solves one equation in one unknown	Use Tools/Goal Seek menu item
HLOOKUP function	Useful for finding a particular value on the basis of a comparison	=HLOOKUP(*valueToCompare, lookup Table, columnToReturn*)
IF function	Useful for implementing logic	=IF(*condition, resultIfFrue, resultIfFalse*)
NPV function	Calculates NPV of a stream of cash flows starting in year 1	=NPV(*discount Rate, cashFlow*)
One-way data table	Shows how one or more outputs vary as a single input varies	Use Data/Table menu item
Pasting range names	Provides a list of all range names in the current workbook	Use Insert/Name/Paste menu item
Range names	Useful for making formulas more meaningful	Type name in Name box, or use Insert/Name/Define menu item
Relative, absolute cell addresses	Useful for copying formulas; absolute row or column stays fixed, relative row or column "moves"	Al (relative), $Al or A$l ,(mixed), Al (absolute); press F4 to cycle through possibilities
Splitting screen	Useful for separating the screen horizontally and/or vertically	Use screen splitters at top and right of scrollbars
SUMPRODUCT Function	Calculates the sum of products of values in two (or more) similar-sized ranges	=SUMPRODUCT(*rangel, range2*)
Two-way data table	Shows how a single output varies as two inputs vary	Use Data/Table menu item
VLOOKUP function	Useful for finding a particular value based on a comparison	=VLOOKUP (*valueToCompare, lookup Table, columnToReturn*)

Optimal Information Area

Models in Business Decision Making
http://personal.bellsouth.net/lig/b/u/burrus01/ModelsinBusDecision.htm

Decision Support Models
http://www.intelligententerprise.com/010216/decision1_1.shtml?bi%7Cbusintel

PWC Global Business Dynamics Division
http://www.pwcglobal.com/uk/eng/about/svcs/bd/index.html

Decision Support Resources, a repository of resources relating to Decision Support
http://www.dssresources.com

OR/MS Today
http://www.lionhrtpub.com/ORMS.shtml

Frontline Systems, sample solutions using Solver
http://www.solver.com/solutions.htm

Excel Spreadsheets for Financial Modeling, including derivatives
http://members.attcanada.ca/~johnjaz/spreadsheets.htm

References

Camm, J. D., and J. R. Evans, *Management Science: Modeling, Analysis, and Interpretation,* Cincinnati: South-Western, 1996.

Leon, L., Z. Przasnyski, and K. C. Seal, "Spreadsheets and OR/MS models: An End-User Perspective," *Interfaces,* vol. 26, no. 2, 1996, pp. 92–104.

Ragsdale, Cliff, *Spreadsheet Modeling and Decision Analysis W/Excel,* Thomson Learning, 2000.

Winston, W., and C. Albright, *Practical Management Science: Spreadsheet Modeling and Applications,* Duxbury Press.

PROBLEMS

1. Create a simple spreadsheet to balance your checkbook. Include rows for money in and money out, columns for each month, and sums at the bottom of each column and row.

2. Jennifer can earn 4% on any money she saves in her credit union account. She wants to know how much she will accumulate over 5 years if she starts with $100. Build a spreadsheet that displays this information. Use the simple equation principle*(1+interest rate) to calculate the yearly totals in Excel or another spreadsheet application. Does Excel or another spreadsheet application have a function that does this calculation automatically? If so, use the function and compare your answers.

3. Schalpfer Inc. is trying to determine whether to give a $15 rebate, to cut the price to $8, or to have no price change on a software networking product. Currently, 40,000 units of the product are sold each week for $45. The variable cost of the product is $6. The most likely case appears to be that a $15 rebate will increase sales 35% and about two-thirds of all people will claim the rebate. For the price cut, the most likely case is that sales will increase 25%.

   a. Given all other assumptions, use Excel to create a model that describes all the scenarios given.

   b. Holding all assumptions constant except the rebate claim rate, at what rebate claim rate would the rebate and price cut be equally desirable?

   c. Is the no price change scenario a good choice? When?

4. Samantha and Sabrina are opening a soda stand. They believe the fixed cost per week of running the stand is $50.00. Their best guess is that they can sell 300 sodas per week at $0.75 per soda. The variable cost of obtaining a can of soda is $0.20.

   a. Given her other assumptions, and using Excel, find the level of sales volume that will enable them to break even.

   b. Given her other assumptions, draw a break-even graph and discuss how a change in sales volume affects profit.

   c. From the graph in (b) discuss how changes in sales volume and variable cost jointly affect profit.

5. Ralph knows the information in the following table about processing times of claim forms at the clearinghouse he works at. He notices that as more claim forms are processed the processing time per form decreases.

UNIT	PROCESSING TIME HOURS
1	18
5	10.72
9	8.87
18	7.10
27	6.23
36	5.68

a. Fit a linear curve to the data using Excel or another spreadsheet application.

b. Fit a power curve to the data using Excel or another spreadsheet application.

c. Fit an exponential curve to the data.

d. Which curve fits best?

e. Use your answer from (d) to predict the 40th unit's processing time.

6. Copy the information from the following table into a spreadsheet. Multiply the two columns together by using a spreadsheet function such as * or the product command in Excel.

COLUMN A	COLUMN B
11	11
22	22
33	33
44	44
55	55
66	66

7. Graph the numbers presented in the table in Problem 6 and your answer to Problem 4. Compare the graphs. Are the graphs similar or different? Why would they be similar or different?

8. You are thinking of opening a copy shop. It costs $8000 to rent a copier for a year. It costs $0.023 per copy to operate the copier. Other fixed costs of running the store amount to $600 per month. You charge an average of $0.12 per copy. You are open 365 days per year. Each copier can make up to 150,000 copies per year.

a. Using Excel, construct a two-way profit table (number of copiers on the left running top to bottom and daily demand on the top running from left to right) for 1 to 5 copiers rented and daily demands of 1000, 1500, 2000, and 2500 copies per day. That is, compute annual profit for each of these combinations of copiers rented and daily demand.

b. Given that you rent three copiers, what daily demand for copies will allow you to break even? Draw a break-even graph to show this break-even relationship.

9. Eve Brown is trying to save for her retirement. She believes she can earn 12% on average each year on her retirement fund. Assume that at the beginning of each of the next 40 years, Eve will allocate x dollars to her retirement fund. If at the beginning of a year Eve has y dollars in her fund, by the end of the year, it will grow to $1.12y$ dollars.

a. Using Excel, develop a spreadsheet model to find out how much Eve should allocate to her retirement fund each year to ensure that she will have $1 million at the end of 40 years.

b. Are there any key factors that are being ignored in our analysis of the amount saved for retirement?

10. Chipper Payroll Services knows the demand for its services during the current year is around 50,000 worker hours and with current operations covers all customer demand (i.e., Chipper's capacity currently is 50,000 worker-hours). Chipper is planning on a 5% growth rate each year. Chipper's current office space and staff will eventually outgrow demand. Expanding the office space and staff depends mostly on the hours that will be worked total in the facility. If we let x = total worker-hours, Chipper will incur a one-time cost of 15x$ to expand [i.e., if Chipper goes from 50,000 worker-hour capacity to 70,000 worker-hour capacity, it will incur a cost of $15 × (70,000 – 50,000) = $300,000]. Chipper needs to expand its current space and staff, since any new business will be lost to its competitors if it cannot accommodate the new customers. Each customer serviced incurs a variable cost of $3.00 per worker-hour. It also costs Chipper $6.00 per worker-hour of capacity per year (i.e., if Chipper has 70,000 worker hours total then Chipper incurs $6 × 70,0000 = $420,000 per year in costs). Chipper garners $25 per worker hour from its customers. Construct an Excel spreadsheet model to determine what the projected revenue, costs, and potential profits would be over the next 10 years based on the current capacity, 50,000 worker-hours, an expansion to 70,000 worker-hours, and an expansion to 90,000 worker-hours.

CHAPTER

4 Decision Analysis: Building the Structure for Solving the Problem

LEARNING *Objectives*

- Understand the components of decision analysis
- Understand the types of decision environments managers face
- Understand how probability assessments impact the decision making process
- Conduct sensitivity analysis within the decision making process
- Develop decision trees to aid in the decision making process
- Use Excel to solve decision problems

CHAPTER *Outline*

Business Decision Modeling in Action

How Legal Decision Makers Use Decision Models

Business Decision Modeling throughout the Ages

A Brief History of Decision Making

Business Decision Modeling Behind the Scenes

The Story of John von Neumann

Decision Analysis: Building the Structure for Solving the Problem
- Importance and Relevance of Decision Analysis and Theory
- Linking Probability and Statistics to Decision Making
- Framing the Decision Problem

Components of a Decision-Making Problem
- States of Nature
- Decision Alternatives
- Outcomes
- Outcomes versus Payoffs
- Payoff Tables

Decision-Making Criteria without Probability Assessments
- Spreadsheet Solution for Payoff Table Decision Problem
- Steve's Mutual Fund Decision Problem
- Maximax Criterion
- Maximin Criterion
- Minimax Regret
- Management Science Definition of Regret
- Economics Definition of Regret—Opportunity Cost
- Marketing Definition of Regret—Buyer's Remorse
- Psychological Definition of Regret—Cognitive Dissonance
- Minimax Regret Criterion Process
- Regret as a Measure of Risk
- Equal Likelihood Criterion—LaPlace and Simple Weighted Averages
- Hurwicz Criterion
- Summary of Decision Criteria Results

Decision-Making Criteria with Probability Assessments
- Expected Value of Perfect Information
- Confusion over Multiple "Good" Choices
- Three Areas of Sensitivity Analysis

Sensitivity Analysis
- Step 1: Establish a Dominant Decision
- Step 2: Examine the Trade-offs between Dominant Decisions
- Step 3: Define and Quantify the Risk
- Importance of Sensitivity Analysis
- Sensitivity Analysis: Steve's Mutual Fund Example
- "What If" Analysis
- How to Construct a Sensitivity Graph in Excel
- Establish Dominance
- Risk Defined and Quantified by Regret
- The Risk-Return Trade-off

Modeling, Decision Trees, and Influence Diagrams
- Definition of Modeling

Business Decision Modeling in Action

How Legal Decision Makers Use Decision Models

Containing Litigation Costs: The Use of Decision Models in Litigation

An increasing number of companies and their lawyers have turned to decision structures such as decision trees and influence diagrams to help them make better decisions in litigation management and settlement. The results have been lower transaction costs and better outcomes.

Litigators first identify the factual and legal uncertainties in a case—the "issues"—and then proceed, through fact discovery, legal research, and the use of experts, to cope with these uncertainties. Driving this costly process is the assumption that it will culminate in a trial, at which time a judge and jury will resolve the legal and factual issues.

The reality, though, is that more than 90% of all cases end up being resolved through settlement rather than trial.

Decision trees and influence diagrams can be enormously helpful in allocating resources before trial. They can effectively demonstrate the cost-effectiveness of forgoing the additional research or discovery, thereby saving the client time and money. Decision trees and influence diagrams make it possible to perform the analyses needed to maximize opportunities for early settlement and reduced transaction costs while fully addressing the need to be prepared for trial.

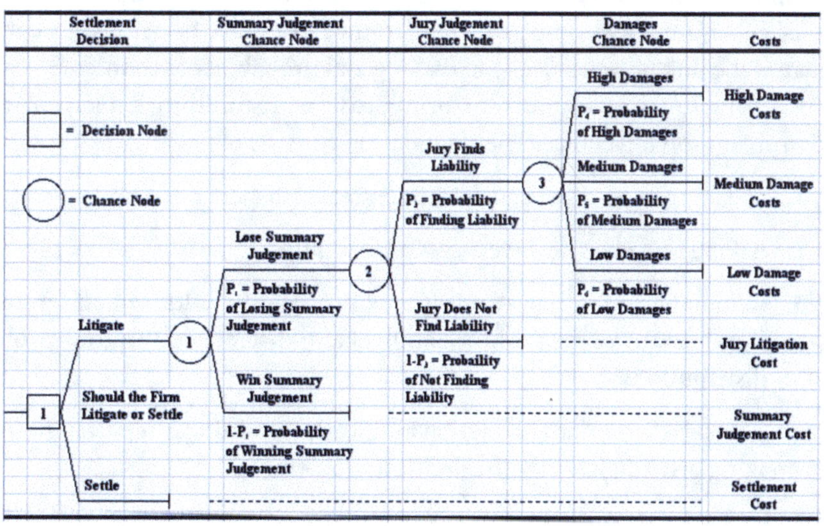

Decision Tree for Litigation Example

Decision Analysis: Building the Structure for Solving the Problem

In Chapter 2, the importance of describing data sets in terms of central tendency and measures of dispersion was discussed. Simple statistics, like mean, median, range, and standard deviation, were defined and described. Chapter 3 developed probability theory and the rules of probability along with the addition and multiplication formulas.

Importance and Relevance of Decision Analysis and Theory

The importance of managers' painting the full picture of data sets by using both measures of central tendency and measures of dispersion was developed. Managers do this by linking simple statistics with a mental and graphical picture of real-life data sets. This chapter will build up from the foundation that probability and statistics set down in the preceding chapters.

Managers must link simple statistics with a mental and graphical picture of data sets.

Linking Probability and Statistics to Decision Making

Linking probability and statistics to decision making is a goal of this chapter. Chapter 3 taught us to use the language of probability properly. A main rhetorical question was asked regarding how individuals assess probabilities as decision makers. Managers must think about how assessing probabilities will help them in becoming more effective and efficient problem solvers. Most managers do not consciously go around assessing probabilities; they just make decisions. One may ask: Where is the link between decision making and probability assessment?

A strong foundation must be formed, as we are building a decision-making and problem solving edifice. That foundation consists of

1. Speaking in terms of central tendency and dispersion
2. Asking ourselves how we assess probabilities
3. Remembering the laws and rules of probability (addition and multiplication laws, three rules of probability) and discrete continuous probability distributions

Good decision makers create a link from the world of probability to the world of decision making.

A manager starts with this foundation and works toward the next step in the decision-making process: framing the decision problem.

Framing the Decision Problem

A manager must think about building up an edifice and putting a structure, literally a framework, around decision-making problems. Students must ask themselves an important question, "How do I make decisions and what is the process I

Critical Reasoning and Judgment Question

Take a moment and ask yourself the following question about decision making, "How do I make decisions and what is the process I go through as I choose one alternative over another?" Managers make decisions all the time, and this text is not here to tell a student of business decision modeling exactly how or what is the best way to make decisions. It would be folly to attempt to do this in one class or text.

Managers must develop their own decision-making process or rational methodology for solving problems. All of us understand that individuals make decisions all the time: we chose to come to class, read the text, when and where to eat lunch, when to wake up, when to go to bed.

The techniques individuals use to make these decisions obviously play an important role in everyday life. Decisions made regarding situations in business and government, or choice of college and career, for example, may also deal with a tremendous amount of uncertainty.

Components of a Decision-Making Problem

A number of structures will be presented throughout the next few chapters. The next sections will discuss one basic structure to build from. Bear in mind that it is simplistic and is just one way to structure a decision-making problem.

Decision analysis problems generally have three distinct components:

Decision problems have three components: states, decisions, and outcomes.

1. States of nature
2. Decisions alternatives
3. Outcomes

States of Nature

States of nature can be defined as events that may occur in the future. As managers, we rarely have control over the states associated with a decision-making problem. In fact, the decision maker is generally uncertain which state of nature will occur.

A good example of uncertain states of nature is the weather report. The information provided by the weather forecaster may give us some insight into tomorrow's weather, but the chance of rain or no rain is uncertain. In turn, as business decision makers, we have no control over the possibility of rain and therefore must plan accordingly if that weather will adversely affect our day-to-day operations (running an amusement parks, farming, etc.).

However, as decision makers we do have control over one item. The ultimate decision that is made is the purview of the decision maker. For the rain/no rain example, the decision may be to carry an umbrella or not to carry an umbrella.

Decision Alternatives

Decision alternatives are the second component in a decision analysis problem. At times decisions are also referred to as *alternatives.* As stated earlier, the decision maker has ultimate control over the decision made or the alternative chosen.

Decision makers have ultimate control over which decision alternative they choose.

For example, the decisions a business decision maker could make regarding an outdoor promotional event could be as follows: rent and set up a tent or do not rent and set up a tent.

Renting and setting up the tent or not renting and setting up the tent incurs certain consequences. Take for example this scenario: the weather forecaster believes it will rain tomorrow; we concur and so we decide to rent and set up the tent. Remember, weather forecasters just provide advice; they are not clairvoyant. This leads directly into the definition and discussion of outcomes.

Outcomes

The third component of a decision analysis problem is outcomes. An outcome is defined as the combination of a state and a decision. For our rain example, we chose to rent and set up the tent and it did happen to rain; therefore, the outcome is that the umbrella came in handy and we stayed dry. However, there exist four possible outcomes for the rain example. Table 4.1 lists the possible outcomes.

Outcomes are the resultant combination of a state of nature and a decision alternative.

Outcomes versus Payoffs

Outcomes are generally referred to as payoffs and are given in monetary units.

It should be noted that outcomes are also referred to as payoffs. Pure decision analysts and economists generally refer to the combination of states and decisions as an outcome. However, managers tend to use the term payoffs.

Payoffs are typically expressed in monetary terms such as profits, revenues, or costs. The outcomes from the rain example could be turned into payoffs by equating getting wet with the cost of dry cleaning your clothes after the fact.

The term payoff is used because it directly links the combination of states and decisions to a monetary result. The authors will use the term payoff from this point on in the text.

Critical Reasoning and Judgment Question

Every decision problem has states, decisions, and outcomes/payoffs. Think about a recent decision you made and try to identify the states, decisions, and outcomes/payoffs associated with the problem. Were the states easy to describe? Were the outcomes/payoffs easily quantified?

Payoff Tables

The layout of Table 4.1 allows the decision maker to see all the possible outcomes but does not organize the three components of a decision-making problem very well.

Payoff tables are a means to organize states, decisions, and payoffs.

Traditional decision analysis uses what is called a payoff table to organize states, decision alternatives, and outcomes. Table 4.2 displays the payoff table for the rain example.

TABLE 4.1 *Possible Outcomes for Rain Example*

DECISION ALTERNATIVE	STATE	OUTCOME
Rent and set up tent	Rain	Stay dry and promotional items are not adversely affected
Rent and set up tent for nothing	No rain	Incurred cost of renting and setting up tent
Do not rent and set up tent	Rain	Get wet and promotional items are spoiled
Do not rent and set up tent	No rain	No worries—dry at no additional costs

The payoffs listed in Table 4.2 are situations rather than monetary amounts associated with the combination of a state and a decision alternative. However, one could quickly assign monetary amounts to the situations listed above.

At times these monetary amounts may be negative, or considered costs. For example, costs of not carrying the umbrella if it does not rain could be zero, while one cost of carrying the umbrella if it does rain could be the cost of the umbrella itself.

As students of business decision modeling you may be inclined to ask the question "What is the probability of it raining?" This is a good question to ask because the resulting answer to the question may help the decision maker choose a better course of action or save time and money.

However, the probability of a state occurring is not always readily available and decision makers may have a difficult time assigning probabilities to events. Decision making without probability assessments will be discussed next.

Critical Reasoning and Judgment Question

Managers make numerous decisions each day. However, not all those decisions are made by using probability assessments. Are there decisions you make each day without the use of probability assessments? How about where you are going for lunch?

TABLE 4.2 *Payoff Table for Rain Example*

	STATES OF NATURE	
DECISION ALTERNATIVES	RAIN	NO RAIN
Rent and set up tent	Stay dry and promotional items are not adversely affected	Incurred cost of renting and setting up tent for nothing
Do not rent and set up tent	Get wet and promotional items are spoiled	No worries—dry at no additional costs

A Brief History of Decision Making

Business Decision Modeling throughout the Ages

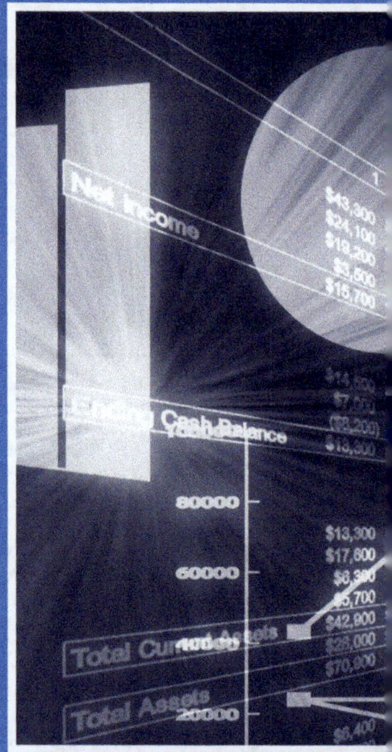

History of Decision Making

Historically, decision techniques have focused on outcome prediction, not decision process or technique. Take a look at the progression and remember that the way we make decisions today may come from decisions made in the past.

Soothsayers, Astrologers, and Fortune Tellers

- Elders consulted for alternatives and probability of success.
- Alexander the Great consulted oracles and fortune tellers.
- The Oracle at Delphi was famous and became hugely popular.

The Romans, The Babylonians, the Chinese and the Use of Hard Data

- Romans also had oracles but relied heavily on "hard" data—Haruspicists examined animal entrails to predict the future (we might say they used their gut feelings).
- The Babylonians used the Talmud to deal with decisions on division of wealth; indirectly this document led to the understanding of cooperative games.
- The Chinese developed I Ching around 3000 BC. People asked I Ching for the prognosis of a given decision; an answer detailing potential risks and opportunities resulted.

The 1700s and 1800s

- Ben Franklin is credited with the "balance sheet" approach to decision making.
- Playfair, in 1786, used the perspective ratios of height and width of graphs depicting government debt to imply skyrocketing national debt due to the British government's borrowing to support the various colonial wars of that century. Sound familiar?
- In the late 1800s, the neoclassical revolution in economics elevated mathematical utility theory and axiomatic methods of mathematics began to permeate decision theory; famous participants include Ramsey, de Finetti, Alt, and Frisch.

Infinity and Beyond

- The 1960s and 1970s brought database systems and the cliché of "let's crunch the numbers."
- The 1990s introduced faster desktop and laptop computers and new software algorithms, and we began to see decision analysis tools available for our personal use.
- And what does the new century bring? I'll let you decide....

Optimal Information Area

Peter L. Bernstein, *Against the Gods: The Remarkable Story of Risk,* New York: John Wiley & Sons, 1996.

Decision-Making Criteria without Probability Assessments

Decision making without probabilities is generally referred to as nonprobabilistic.

Decision-making that does not involve uncertainty is fairly simple. Without uncertainty, we tend to have limited choices or just one choice and simple outcomes. Many of life's basic choices are this simple, or the process used in making the choice is fundamentally an unconscious one, involuntary, or a learned response.

Decision makers use decision-making criteria when determining which alternatives to choose. When information regarding the probability of a state is limited or not available, decision makers use what are referred to as *nonprobabilistic criteria.* The following sections will detail three of these criteria: the maximax, the maximin, and the minimax regret.

Spreadsheet Solution for Payoff Table Decision Problem

This section details the use of Excel spreadsheets to illustrate three nonprobabilistic criteria— a maximax, maximin, and minimax regret—and also demonstrates the Hurwicz decision criteria. A step-by-step creation of a graph to illustrate the three areas of sensitivity is developed.

Critical Reasoning and Judgment Question

Take a moment and think to yourself, "Do I know people who make decisions regularly, using the maximax criterion?" Maybe you are the type of decision maker who uses the maximax criterion to make decisions. Can you think of professions that use this type of criterion? How about gamblers? High-risk derivatives or commodities traders?

Steve's Mutual Fund Decision Problem

Steve has a decision to make. He wishes to invest in one of the three mutual funds offered in the market. Table 4.3 displays the three decisions, the states of nature, the associated payoffs, and the probability of each state of nature to occur.

The payoffs are yearly percentage returns. Take the information in Table 4.3 and input it into an Excel spreadsheet to obtain the results displayed in Figure 4.1.

TABLE 4.3 *Steve's Mutual fund Payoff Table*

	STATES OF NATURE	
MUTUAL FUND	GOOD ECONOMIC CONDITIONS	BAD ECONOMIC CONDITIONS
Stock fund, aggressive growth	20%	–8%
Index fund, moderate S&P 500	12%	2%
Bond fund, conservative U.S. Treasury	6%	4%
Probability of states of nature	40%	60%

	A	B	C
1	**Steve's Mutual Fund Decision**		
2	**Payoff Table**		
3		**State of Nature**	
4		**Good**	**Bad**
5	**Mutual Fund**	**Economic Condition**	**Economic Condition**
6	**Stock Fund**	20%	-8%
7	**Aggressive Growth**		
8			
9	**Index Fund**	12%	2%
10	**Moderate S&P 500**		
11			
12	**Bond Fund**	6%	4%
13	**Conservative U.S. Treasury**		
14			

FIGURE 4.1
Excel Spreadsheet for Steve's Mutual Fund Payoff

Maximax Criterion

The maximax criterion is defined as the criterion where a decision maker selects the decision that will result in the maximum of the maximum payoffs. A decision maker who chooses to use this criterion is looking for the best of the best. It could be said that a decision maker using maximax is optimistic (believes the best will always occur). It could also be said that the decision maker using maximax is willing to accept more risk.

The maximax decision criterion chooses the best of the best payoffs.

A spreadsheet solution using the maximax decision criterion is shown in Figure 4.2. The payoff table with appropriate headings is placed in cells A4 through cell C13. The Excel formulas that provide the calculations and an optimal solution recommendation are:

Cell D6 Compute the maximum payoff
= MAX(B6 : C6)
(Repeat formula for cells D9 and D12)

Cell E6 Determine which decision alternative is recommended
= IF(D6 = MAX($D$6, $D$9, $D$12), A6, "")
(Repeat formula for cells E9 and E12)

If the maximum payoff in cell D6 is equal to the best payoff in cells D6, the fund's name will be displayed in E6; otherwise, this cell will be left blank. As Figure 4.2 shows, the maximax criterion recommends the aggressive growth stock fund decision alternative with a best payoff of 20%.

Maximin Criterion

The maximin criterion is defined as the criterion where a decision maker selects the decision that will result in the maximum of the minimum payoffs. In other words, the decision maker is looking for the best of the worst. It could be said that a decision maker using maximin is pessimistic (believes the worst will always

The maximin decision criterion chooses the best of the worst payoffs.

	A	B	C	D	E
1	**Steve's Mutual Fund Decision**				
2	**Maximax Decision Criterion**				
3		State of Nature			
4		Good	Bad	Maximum	Recommended
5	Mutual Fund	Economic Condition	Economic Condition	Payoff	Decision
6	Stock Fund	20%	-8%	20%	Stock Fund
7	Aggressive Growth				
8					
9	Index Fund	12%	2%	12%	
10	Moderate S&P 500				
11					
12	Bond Fund	6%	4%	6%	
13	Conservative U.S. Treasury				
14					

FIGURE 4.2
Excel Spreadsheet for Maximax Decision

occur). A maximin decision maker could also be categorized as risk averse or not willing to accept more risk.

A spreadsheet solution using the maximin decision criterion is shown in Figure 4.3. The payoff table with appropriate headings is placed in cells A4 through C13. The Excel formulas that provide the calculations and optimal solution recommendation are:

Cell D6 Compute the minimum payoff
= MIN(B6 : C6)
(Repeat formula for cells D9 and D12)

Cell E6 Determine which decision alternative is recommended
= IF(D6 = MAX($D$6, $D$9, $D$12), A6, “”)
(Repeat formula for cells E9 and E12)

The only difference between the spreadsheets in Figures 4.2 and 4.3 is that the maximin criterion finds the minimum payoff in each decision alternative.

Critical Reasoning and Judgment Question

Take a moment and think to yourself, “Do I know people who make decisions regularly, using the maximin criterion?” Maybe you are the type of decision maker who uses the maximin criterion to make decisions. Can you think of a group of people who use this type of criterion? How about those individuals who lived through the Great Depression in the United States?

	A	B	C	D	E
1	**Steve's Mutual Fund Decision**				
2	**Maximin Decision Criterion**				
3		State of Nature			
4		Good	Bad	Minimum	Recommended
5	Mutual Fund	Economic Condition	Economic Condition	Payoff	Decision
6	Stock Fund	20%	-8%	-8%	
7	Aggressive Growth				
8					
9	Index Fund	12%	2%	2%	
10	Moderate S&P 500				
11					
12	Bond Fund	6%	4%	4%	Bond Fund
13	Conservative U.S. Treasury				
14					

FIGURE 4.3
Excel Spreadsheet for Maximin Decision Criterion

Notice the formulas in E6, E9, and E12 remain the same. This is because Steve is still looking for the maximum result in column D. With the appropriate changes, the spreadsheet in Figure 4.3 shows that the maximin criterion recommends the Conservative U.S. Treasury Bond Fund decision alternative with the best payoff value of 4%.

Minimax Regret

The minimax regret criterion is defined as the criterion where a decision maker selects the decision that will result in the minimum regret. Before this criterion is detailed, the measure of regret must be defined.

The minimax regret criterion chooses the decision that results in the minimum regret.

Management Science Definition of Regret

Management scientists define regret as the difference between the payoff from the best decision and all the other decision payoffs. Students of business decision modeling must keep in mind that management science is not the only discipline to define regret. Economics and marketing both have similar concepts of regret.

Management science defines regret as the difference between the best decision and all other decisions for a particular state.

Economics Definition of Regret—Opportunity Cost

Economists use the words *opportunity cost* to define or refer to regret. Opportunity cost is the value of the next best alternative, or opportunity, that was given up by choosing the best alternative. For example, by choosing to spend your money on beer and pizzas you give up the opportunity to invest that money in a retirement account. Your opportunity cost is the choice you gave up.

Economists refer to opportunity costs when speaking about regret.

Regret, as defined by management science, is akin to the concept of opportunity cost in economics. In management science, regret is the quantifiable amount a decision maker gives up to choose a different alternative.

Marketing Definition of Regret—Buyer's Remorse

The concept of regret is manifested in consumers by what marketers call buyer's remorse. Marketers describe the feeling consumers experience when they purchase an item and then feel as if they could have gotten a better deal on another item. At times this is also referred to as *postdecision doubt.*

Marketers refer to regret as buyer's remorse.

Buyer's remorse can also manifest itself in consumers when they make a decision and then regret making that decision after the fact. Buyer's remorse occurs with some frequency in buying a home. Some homebuyers have a sense of letdown after deciding to purchase a home.

Real estate brokers attribute this feeling to the fact that a home is a very large purchase, not in terms of just dollars, but in the sense of status, ego, and commitment. A homebuyer, after making the final decision, may look around and feel a sense of regret, believing that better deals existed and were missed.

Psychologists refer to regret as cognitive dissonance.

Psychological Definition of Regret—Cognitive Dissonance

According to cognitive dissonance theory, there is a tendency for individuals to seek consistency among their beliefs and choices. Cognitive dissonance theory applies to all situations involving attitude formation and change. It is especially relevant to managers in the decision making and problem solving process.

Consider someone who is going to purchase an expensive car but discovers that it is not comfortable on long drives. The driver believes that an expensive car should be comfortable. Cognitive dissonance exists, since the belief that an expensive car should be a comfortable car on long drives is violated.

In general, decision makers will alter their beliefs instead of removing the conflicting attitude or behavior. The buyers of the expensive but uncomfortable car may convince themselves that the car will be used only for short trips, thereby eliminating the conflict in beliefs.

The term cognitive dissonance has also been adopted by the marketing discipline. Many advertising campaigns attempt to eliminate cognitive dissonance or buyer's remorse by focusing on product strengths or developing new nonconflicting attitudes toward the product.

Critical Reasoning and Judgment Question

As a decision maker have you ever felt regret? Have you ever thought about the opportunity costs of choosing one item over another? As a consumer have you ever felt buyer's remorse? Should decision makers rely on minimizing regret as the criterion to make decisions or solve problems? Do you make choices based on minimizing regret, opportunity costs, or buyer's remorse?

Minimax Regret Criterion Process

A decision maker who chooses to use this criterion is looking to minimize the measure of regret. Regret has been defined as the difference between the payoff from the best decision and all the other decision payoffs. Therefore, the first step in the minimax regret criterion is to determine regret .

A spreadsheet solution using the minimax regret decision criterion is shown in Figure 4.4. The payoff table with appropriate headings is placed in cells A4 through C13. The Excel formulas that provide the calculations and optimal solution recommendation are:.

Cell B19 Compute the amount of regret
= MAX($B$6, $B$9, $B$12) – B6
(Repeat formula for cell B22 and B25)

Cell C19 Compute the amount of regret
= MAX($C$6, $C$9, $C$12) – C6
(Repeat formula for cell C22 and C25)

Cell D19 Compute the maximum regret
= MAX(B19 : C19)
(Repeat formula for cell D22 and D25)

Cell E19 Determine which decision alternative is recommended
= IF(D19 = MIN($D$19, $D$22, $D$25), A19, " ")

In Figure 4.4, Steve first calculates the amount of regret under each economic condition by subtracting each return figure from the largest figure in the appropriate economic condition. Steve then finds the maximum regret for each fund in column D. Continuing, Steve then finds the minimum regret in the Maximum Regret column, and thus accomplished the minimax regret decision. We can see from Figure 4.4 that the moderate S&P 500 index fund offers the least amount of regret.

Regret as a Measure of Risk

Measures of dispersion were linked to measures of risk earlier in Chapter 2. Regret can also be used as a means to define and quantify risk. The definition of regret has been established in the minimax regret example. Regret is usually presented in terms of units.

It is important to remember that regret is not something tangible. In the previous example, Steve did not lose $11 by choosing the S&P 500 index fund. He will experience the least amount of regret by choosing the S&P 500 index fund. As was detailed in the sections preceding the minimax regret example, regret can be thought of as an opportunity cost, or a feeling of buyer's remorse, or a psychological feeling of cognitive dissonance.

Regret is used as a measure of risk to give decision makers a sense of what the other alternatives have to offer. Sometimes regret is called upside or downside risk. The concept of upside and downside risk will be detailed in the section "Sensitivity Analysis," below.

Equal Likelihood Criterion—LaPlace and Simple Weighted Averages

The equal likelihood criterion is akin to an expected value when all states are weighted equally, i.e., are a simple mean.

The concept of expected values was introduced in Chapter 3. Expected values are commonly referred to as *weighted averages.* In other words, each event has a weight

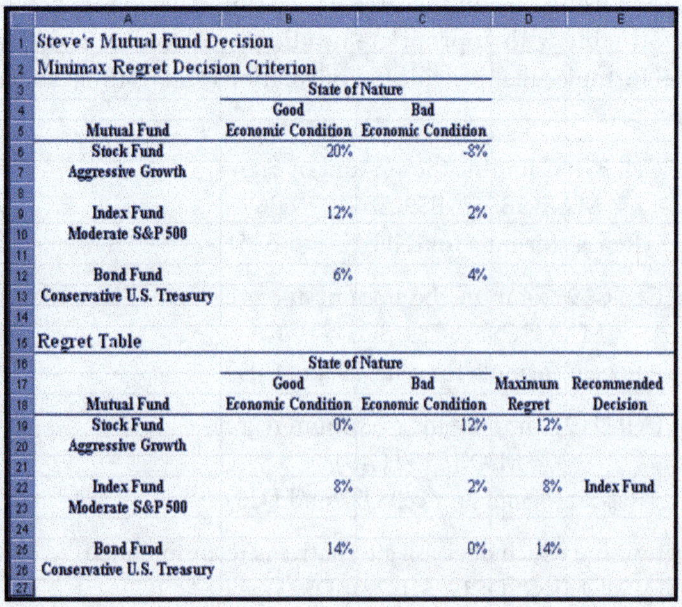

Steve's Mutual Fund Decision

Minimax Regret Decision Criterion

	State of Nature	
	Good	Bad
Mutual Fund	Economic Condition	Economic Condition
Stock Fund Aggressive Growth	20%	-8%
Index Fund Moderate S&P 500	12%	2%
Bond Fund Conservative U.S. Treasury	6%	4%

Regret Table

	State of Nature			
	Good	Bad	Maximum	Recommended
Mutual Fund	Economic Condition	Economic Condition	Regret	Decision
Stock Fund Aggressive Growth	0%	12%	12%	
Index Fund Moderate S&P 500	8%	2%	8%	Index Fund
Bond Fund Conservative U.S. Treasury	14%	0%	14%	

FIGURE 4.4

Excel Spreadsheet for Minimax Decision Criterion

> **Critical Reasoning and Judgment Question**
>
> Have you ever used a weighted average before? More than likely you have. At times information on the likelihood of states is not available or time is limited to assess state probabilities, so in many cases a simple weighted average, or simple mean, is used. When managers use a simple mean, they are assigning equal probabilities to all states. When do you use a simple mean to calculate central tendency?

or a probability assessment associated with it. The equal likelihood criterion also weights each state of nature. As the name implies, all events are weighted equally.

The equal likelihood criterion is also referred to as the LaPlace criterion, named for the mathematician Pierre Simon LaPlace. By assigning equal weights to the events in the event space, the decision maker is assuming that the states of nature are also equally likely to occur. This approach is akin to summing the payoffs for each decision and dividing by the number of payoffs summed. In other words, taking a simple mean or an expected value where all the p (x)'s are equal. For Steve's mutual fund example, we find the equal likelihood payoffs to be 6% for aggressive stock, 7% for the index fund, and 5% for the bond fund, therefore the index fund is chosen.

Hurwicz Criterion

The Hurwicz criterion weights the best and worst payoffs according to the decision maker's optimism about that state occurring.

The Hurwicz criterion is said to be a compromise of the maximax and maximin criterion. The three criteria combined complete the entire spectrum of expected outcomes. The maximax criterion relays the best of the best outcomes, the maximin criterion details the best of the worst outcomes, while the Hurwicz criterion covers every outcome in between.

The Hurwicz criterion uses a coefficient of optimism to weight the best and worst payoff for each decision. This coefficient of optimism is referred to as *alpha* in standard decision analysis nomenclature. The idea of payoffs is not a new one. Chapter 3 introduced the concept of expected value.

The Hurwicz criterion is the same concept as expected value but referred to by a different name. The general equation for expected value is a weighted average or the sum of a set of unique probabilities (or weights) multiplied by the corresponding payoffs. The equal likelihood criterion is a specific case of the expected value where all the alphas, or weights, are equal.

The payoff table with appropriate headings is placed in cells A3 through C14. The Excel formulas that provide the calculations and optimal solution recommendation are:

Cell D6 Compute the payoff
= B6*$B$14 + C6*$C$14
(Repeat formula for cells D9 and D12)

Cell E6 Determine which decision alternative is recommended
= IF(D6 = Max($D$6, $D$9, $D$12), A6, "")
(Repeat formula for cells E9 and E12)

Given alpha equal to 0.4, Figure 4.5 displays, for the mutual fund example, the Hurwicz criterion. For example, in the mutual fund scenario, alpha 0.4 would be applied to the good economic conditions state. In this example, good economic conditions and bad economic conditions are mutually exclusive events and, consequently,

	A	B	C	D	E
1	**Steve's Mutual Fund Decision**				
2	**Hurwicz Decision Criterion: Alpha = .40**				
3		State of Nature			
4		Good	Bad		Recommended
5	Mutual Fund	Economic Condition	Economic Condition	Payoff	Decision
6	Stock Fund	20%	-8%	3.2%	
7	Aggressive Growth				
8					
9	Index Fund	12%	2%	6.0%	Index Fund
10	Moderate S&P 500				
11					
12	Bond Fund	6%	4%	4.8%	
13	Conservative U.S. Treasury				
14	*Probability of States*	*40%*	*60%*		
15					

FIGURE 4.5
Excel Spreadsheet for the Hurwicz Decision Criterion

according to the rules of probability, the coefficient or weight applied to the bad economic conditions state is 1 alpha, or 0.6. For situations with more than two states of nature, the same procedure is followed by using just the best and worst payoffs for each decision alternative.

In Figure 4.5, we first calculated the payoff by multiplying the return figures of each fund under both economic conditions against their appropriate probabilities of occurrence. Furthermore, if the maximum payoff in column D is equal to the best payoff of a fund, the fund's name will appear in column E indicating that fund is the optimal recommended decision. In using the Hurwicz decision criterion, we can see that the moderate S&P 500 index fund offers the optimal payoff of 6.0%.

Critical Reasoning and Judgment Question

As a decision maker, ask yourself "How do I assess probabilities of the occurrence of certain states?" Do you see the similarity when a manager guesses and applies the same probability to all states and uses the equal likelihood criterion? Can we apply the same principles of central tendency and dispersion to the Hurwicz criterion and decision-making processes?

Summary of Decision Criteria Results

Table 4.4 displays the final mutual fund example decision choices for each decision criterion. It can be seen from Table 4.4 that no one mutual fund alternative dominates the decision criteria. Depending on the decision criteria, the stock, index, or bond fund could be the best choice.

TABLE 4.4 *Summary of Final Mutual Fund Example Choices*

DECISION CRITERION	MAXIMAX	MAXIMIN	MINIMAX REGRET	EQUAL LIKELIHOOD	HURWICZALPHA = 0.40
Fund to choose	Stock fund	Bond fund	Index fund	Index fund	Index fund

Critical Reasoning and Judgment Question

Faced with numerous optimal or "good" choices how does a manager make the right choice? Is there a process that a person uses when faced with multiple conflicting "good" choices? Are there a set of standard analyses that a manager can follow that will assist in the decision making process?

Strict dominance cannot be established for the mutual fund example. Dominance is the first area a manager should analyze in the decision making process. The principle of dominance will be defined and discussed later in this chapter.

From these results, it seems that a manager has a dilemma. Unless a manager can assess the probability of the states exactly (i.e., predict the future) or has a very optimistic or pessimistic risk profile, there will be multiple optimal choices. In fact, there seems to be some sort of interactions or trade-offs between the three choices.

Decision-Making Criteria with Probability Assessments

A more common occurrence in business decision modeling problems is decision making under uncertainty or decision making relying on probability assessments. Given Steve's payoff table with probability assessments for all states of nature, the expected value of his decision alternatives can be calculated. From Chapter 3, recall that the expected value calculation is

$$E(x) = \sum_{i=1}^{n} x_i p(x_i)$$

For Steve's mutual fund example problem, let's attach a probability of the good economic conditions happening as 0.6, and therefore the probability of the bad economic conditions happening would be 0.4. The expected value of each decision alternative is then calculated as follows:

$$E(\text{stock fund}) = 20\% \times 0.6 + (-8\%) \times 0.4 = 8.8\%$$

$$E(\text{index fund}) = 12\% \times 0.6 + 2\% \times 0.4 = 8.0\%$$

$$E(\text{bond fund}) = 6\% \times 0.6 + 4\% \times 0.4 = 5.2\%$$

Thus, according to the expected value criterion, Steve would chose the stock fund, since it garners the maximum expected value.

Expected Value of Perfect Information

Now let's suppose that Steve has a good friend who is a prominent economist and has given Steve some insight into the future state of the economy. Steve's economist friend claims that he can tell with certainty whether the future economic conditions will be good or bad. This information would change Steve's decision problem from one under uncertainty to one under certainty. This information would help Steve make a better choice and garner a better return.

However, Steve's friend wants a cut of the action. Specifically, he wants a couple of percentage points, 2 points, of return for his efforts. In other words, if Steve would garner an 8% return, 2 of those percentage points would go to Steve's friend, leaving Steve with a net 6% return. Is it worth it to Steve to pay this fee? Is 2 percentage points fair, or what do you think it might be worth to Steve? To answer these questions we need to calculate the expected value of perfect information (EVPI).

If Steve's friend were able to determine which state of nature would occur, then they would know exactly what alternative to choose to maximize returns. Since the payoffs under this perfect information will increase, this knowledge has value. Therefore, we need to determine the value of this information. The expected value of perfect information is defined as the difference between the payoff under certainty and the payoff under risk.

$$\text{EVPI} = \text{expected value under certainty} - \text{maximum expected value}$$

To find the EVPI we must compute the expected value under certainty. The expected value under certainty is the expected return if the decision maker has perfect information before each decision has to be made.

In calculating this value, the decision maker chooses the best alternative for each state of nature and multiplies its payoff by the probability of occurrence of that state of nature. For Steve's example, we will use 0.6 as the probability of good economic conditions (the same probabilities used to calculate expected value earlier), and expected value under certainty is then calculated as follows:

$$\text{Expected value under certainty} = 20\% \times 0.6 + 4\% \times 0.4 = 13.6\%$$

The 20% is the best payoff under the good economic conditions and the 4% is the best payoff under bad economic conditions. Therefore, the expected value of perfect information is, for the expected value under certainty and maximum expected value calculations,

$$\begin{aligned}\text{EVPI} &= \text{expected value under certainty} - \text{maximum expected value}\\ &= 13.6\% - 8.8\% = 4.8\%\end{aligned}$$

In other words, the most Steve would be willing to pay for the perfect information is 4.8 percentage points.

If Steve's friend is asking for 2 percentage points then Steve would come out ahead by at least 2.8 percentage points. So it appears that taking his friend's advice is worth it. This conclusion is based on the assumption that the probability of good economic conditions occurring will be 0.6. If the probability assessment of good economic conditions changes, then the expected value of information will change.

Confusion over Multiple "Good" Choices

Obtaining multiple conflicting "good" choices is often confusing to students of business decision modeling as well as real-world managers. This confusion over choices is actually common when people are attempting to solve complex problems. Part of the confusion is linked to the belief that the decision analysis process will lead managers and/or students to one ultimate correct choice.

Sensitivity analysis assists managers when faced with multiple conflicting choices.

The decision analysis process should lead a decision maker to a set of "good" choices and subsequently produce a more robust picture of the entire problem. The tool to assist decision makers to produce a more robust picture is sensitivity analysis.

Three Areas of Sensitivity Analysis

The principles of dominance, trade-offs, and risks are commonly used in solving decision problems. If dominance cannot be established, multiple optimal choices arise. Multiple optimal choices lead to trade-offs between those choices and a need to analyze the risk involved with one choice compared to another. In sum, when faced with multiple optimal choices, managers must complete analysis with regard to three areas:

Sensitivity analysis is characterized by three areas: dominance, trade-offs, and risk.

- Dominance
- Trade-offs
- Risks

The principles of dominance, trade-off analysis, and risk analysis can be grouped together into a standard set of analyses. This standard set of analyses is referred to as sensitivity analysis. Sensitivity analysis and the three areas of analysis are detailed next.

Sensitivity Analysis

Managers can sort out all possible scenarios and make a more effective and efficient decision by using sensitivity analysis.

The sensitivity analysis process assists managers faced with multiple conflicting "good" choices. Sensitivity analysis includes analysis in three areas: dominance, trade-offs, and risks. The three areas could be referred to as a three-step approach to building a more robust understanding of the decision-making problem. The three areas, or steps, are detailed next followed by an application to the mutual fund payoff table example.

Step 1: Establish a Dominant Decision

In general, dominance is established on the basis of maximizing expected value.

Given that a decision maker wishes to maximize expected value, an alternative that always returns the highest expected value would be considered the dominant choice. However, in many problems there is not one dominant decision. In other words, the decision that maximizes expected value may change, depending on the decision maker's probability assessments of the states.

When strict dominance cannot be established, trade-offs among the alternatives will occur. Trade-off analysis is the second step of analyzing a decision problem.

Step 2: Examine the Trade-offs between Dominant Decisions

If strict dominance can not be established, trade-offs between the alternatives must exist. Trade-offs are akin to the break-even analysis detailed in Chapter 1. A trade-off is defined as the point where the expected value of two or more alternatives is equal. On the leading edge of this trade-off point, one alternative dominates, while on the lagging edge of the trade-off point another alternative dominates.

Trade-off analysis gives the decision maker a means to judge how much will be given up by choosing one alternative over another.

In break-even analysis, the trade-off is the point where costs are equal to revenues. On the leading edge of the break-even point, costs dominate revenues (i.e., revenues are not covering fixed costs, resulting in losses). In turn, on the lagging edge of the break-even point, revenues dominate costs (i.e., revenues cover fixed costs, resulting in profits).

Trade-off analysis gives the decision maker a means to judge how much will be given up by choosing one alternative over another.

Step 3: Define and Quantify the Risk

The author believes that, as managers assess probabilities of states occurring, they are actually assessing a measure of risk.

Risk must be defined and then quantified for each decision-making problem. Risk can be defined in a number of different ways. Table 4.5 lists the ways in which this text has defined risk. A manager may employ all of these definitions and methods of quantification when making complex decisions.

Risk can be defined and quantified by a number of criteria: range, regret, and/or standard deviation.

Each method carries with it certain advantages and inadequacies. However, a manager must define and quantify risk in order to fully analyze a decision-making problem.

Importance of Sensitivity Analysis

It is the manager's job, when solving complex problems, to complete the three steps of sensitivity analysis before coming to a conclusion. Some refer to sensitivity analysis as *what if analysis* or *scenario analysis.* These terms are synonymous with sensitivity analysis.

TABLE 4.5 *Definitions and Quantifications of Risk*

RISK MEASUREMENT	RELATION OF MEASUREMENT	DEFINITION OF MEASUREMENT
Range	Larger ranges relate to higher relative risk	Difference of high versus low of a data set
Regret	Regret is not a monetary amount, but a feeling of loss	Buyer's remorse or opportunity costs (i.e., minimax regret criterion)
Standard deviation	Relatively higher standard deviations mean relatively higher risk	$SD^{*} = \sqrt{\frac{\Sigma(x-\mu)^2}{n-1}}$ $SD^{\dagger} = \sqrt{\Sigma(x-E(x))^2\,p(x)}$

*Use with raw data.

† Use when a probability distribution is given.

> ### Critical Reasoning and Judgment Question
>
> At times sensitivity analysis is referred to as "what if" analysis. In fact, the term what if analysis has become the standard nomenclature with the proliferation of the spreadsheet as a decision support tool. Have you ever conducted a what if or sensitivity analysis on a decision problem? I would bet you have, especially when final exam time rolls around.

It is important to note that, while sensitivity analysis may be the most critical and meaningful aspect of the decision making process, it often tends to be the most underutilized. It could be said that a problem is only half-solved if a manager does not include a formal sensitivity analysis. The next section will detail the three steps of sensitivity analysis with regard to the mutual fund investment example.

Sensitivity Analysis: Steve's Mutual Fund Example

Now that Steve has computed the results of the maximax, maximin, minimax regret, and Hurwicz decision criteria, he is faced with a difficult decision because there is not one dominant decision.

This section will detail a sensitivity analysis, which offers Steve a deeper understanding and will assist him in making a better decision on which mutual fund to invest in.

"What If" Analysis

At times sensitivity analysis is referred to as what if analysis. In other words, "What if something changes, does our recommended decision change?" Figure 4.6 shows an adequate method to analyze the outcomes for the expected value criterion. In addition, the information contained in Figure 4.6 can be graphed to reveal a much clearer picture of what is really happening as alpha changes.

	A	B	C	D
1	Steve's Mutual Fund Decision Problem			
2	Payoff Table			
3		State of Nature		
4		Good	Bad	
5	Mutual Fund	Economic Conditions	Economic Conditions	
6	Stock Fund	20%	-8%	
7	Aggressive Growth			
8				
9	Index Fund	12%	2%	
10	Moderate S&P 500			
11				
12	Bond und			
13	Conservative U.S. Treasury	6%	4%	
14				
15	Expected Value Criterion			
16			Expected Payoff Values	
17		Aggressive Growth	Moderate S&P 500	Conservative U.S. Treasury
18	p(Good Economic Conditions)	Stock Fund	Index Fund	Bond Fund
19	0	-8.00%	2.00%	4.00%
20	0.1	-5.20%	3.00%	4.20%
21	0.2	-2.40%	4.00%	4.40%
22	0.3	0.40%	5.00%	4.60%
23	0.4	3.20%	6.00%	4.80%
24	0.5	6.00%	7.00%	5.00%
25	0.6	8.80%	8.00%	5.20%
26	0.7	11.60%	9.00%	5.40%
27	0.8	14.40%	10.00%	5.60%
28	0.9	17.20%	11.00%	5.80%
29	1	20.00%	12.00%	6.00%
30				

FIGURE 4.6
Sensitivity Analysis Data Calculations

Figure 4.6 uses different alphas, ranging from 0.0 to 1.0 and shows the payoff potential for each fund. The following Excel commands produce the information in Figure 4.6.

Cell B19 Compute the payoff figure for the aggressive growth stock fund
= $B$6*A19 + $C$6*(1 - A19)
(Repeat formula for cells B20 through B29)

Cell C19 Compute the payoff figure for the moderate S&P 500 index fund
= $B$9*A19 + $C$9*(1 - A19)
(Repeat formula for cells C20 through C29)

Cell D19 Compute the payoff figure for the aggressive growth stock fund
= $B$12*A19 + $C$12*(1 - A19)
(Repeat formula for cells D20 through D29)

The essence of sensitivity analysis is to paint a more robust picture of the dominance, tradeoffs, and risks among the alternatives.

Steve has now computed all the possible combinations on the occurrence of the state of nature. Since Steve is more visual than mathematical, he decides to convert the tabular display into a graphical display. A detailed walk-through on creating a sensitivity graph in Excel is next.

How to Construct a Sensitivity Graph in Excel

This section is a step-by-step tutorial on converting tabular data into a graphical form. This should prove useful to any student who is unfamiliar with Excel 2007. Figure 4.7 shows the construction of the graph from the data in Figure 4.6. The steps are:

1. Highlight cells B18 through D29.
2. Click on Insert tab on the Menu bar and select from the Charts group, the Scatter option (see Figure 4.8a for Excel 2007 and Figure 4.8b for Excel 2010).
3. Click on the option at the bottom of the Scatter pull-down menu, select All Chart Types. A figure resembling Figure 4.9 will appear.
4. Choose XY (Scatter) with straight lines and markers (the fourth icon in from the left); this will graph your table in a scatter plot format.
5. Click on OK button and the graph will appear within your spreadsheet as in Figure 4.7a for Excel 2007 and Figure 4.7b for Excel 2010.
6. To format the graphs axis in Excel 2007, position the cursor over the axis to format and right click. An options menu resembling Figure 4.10 will appear.
7. Click on the format axis option and a figure resembling Figure 4.11 will appear. Use this menu to modify the axis options. Another method to accomplish this task is to click on the Layout tab and use the Axes group to complete modifications (see Figure 4.12a for Excel 2007 and Figure 4.12b for Excel 2010).

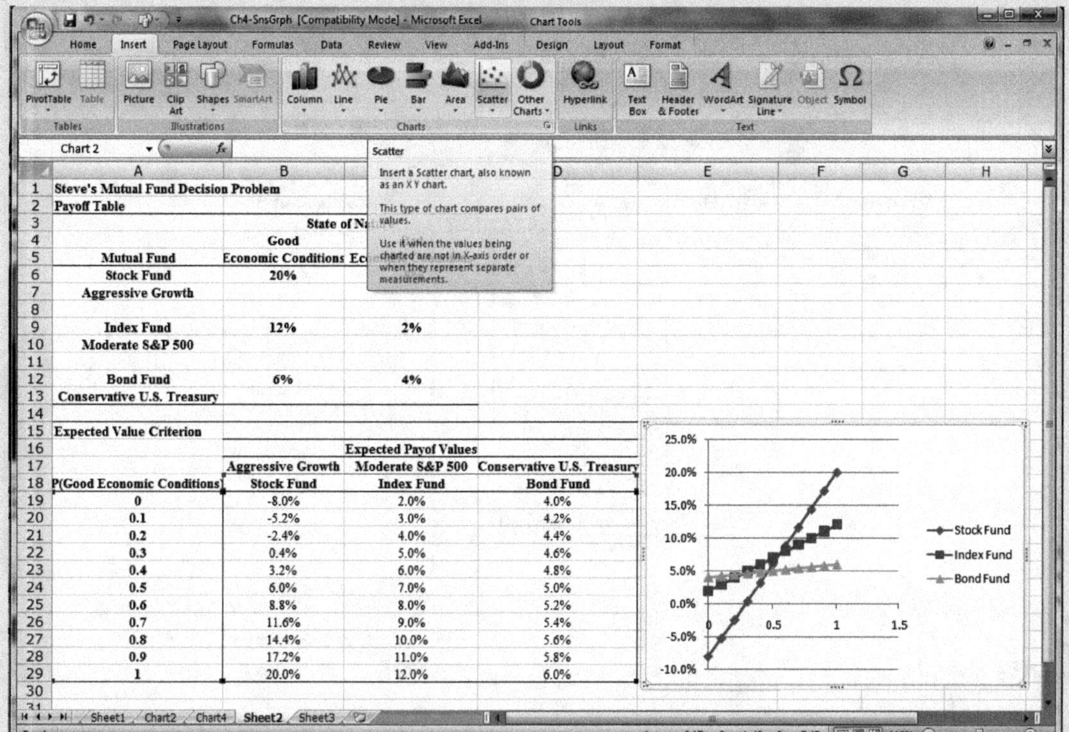

FIGURE 4.7a

Final Chart Output in Excel 2007

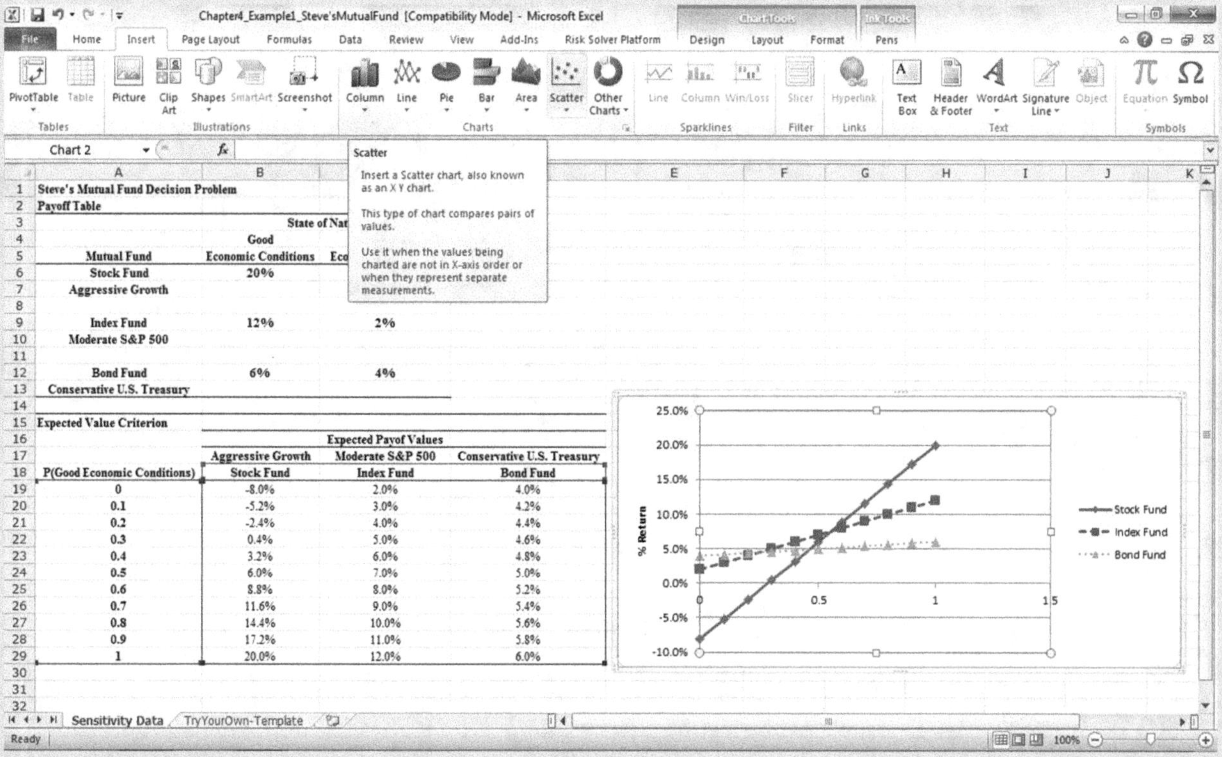

FIGURE 4.7b

Final Chart Output in Excel 2010

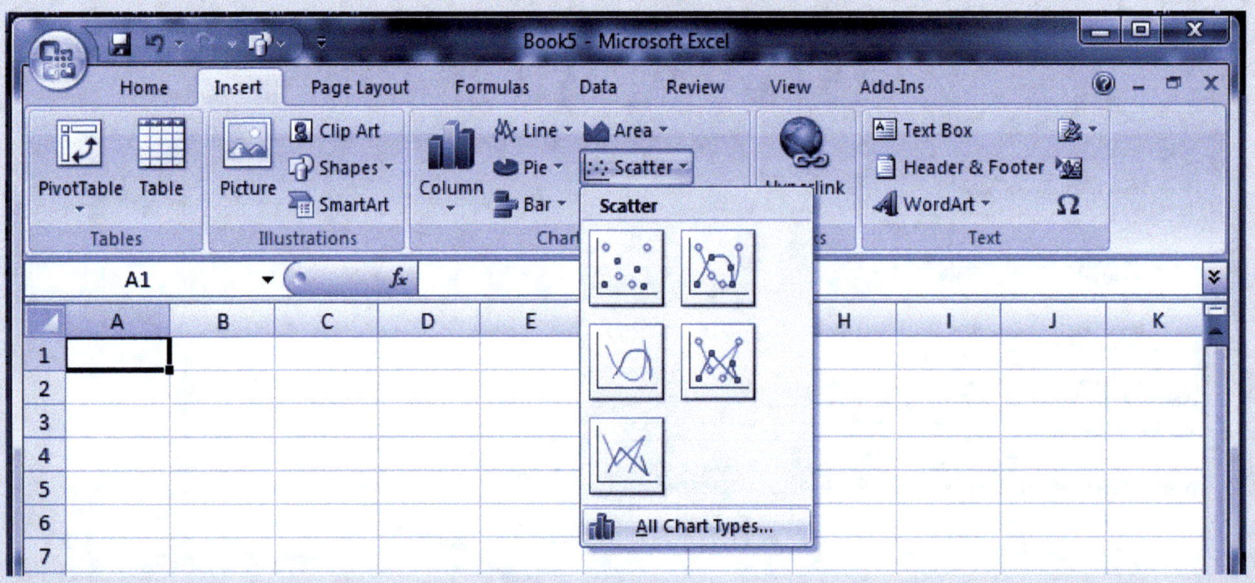

FIGURE 4.8a

Scatter Chart Menu in Excel 2007

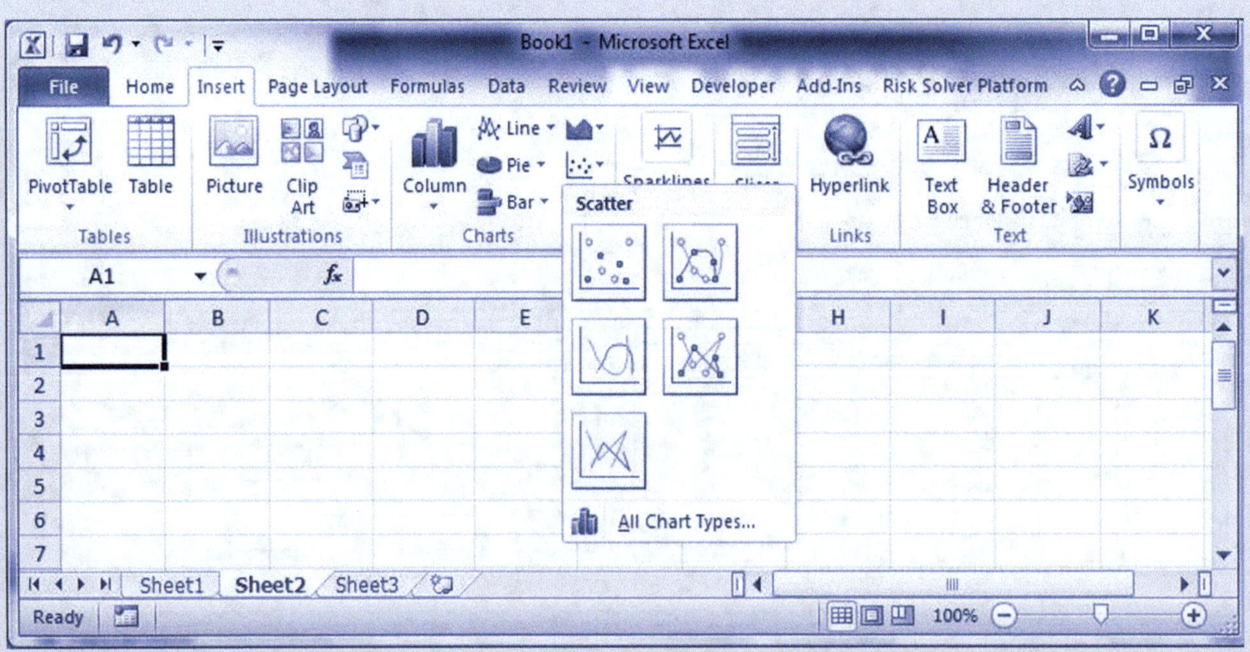

FIGURE 4.8b

Scatter Chart Menu in Excel 2010

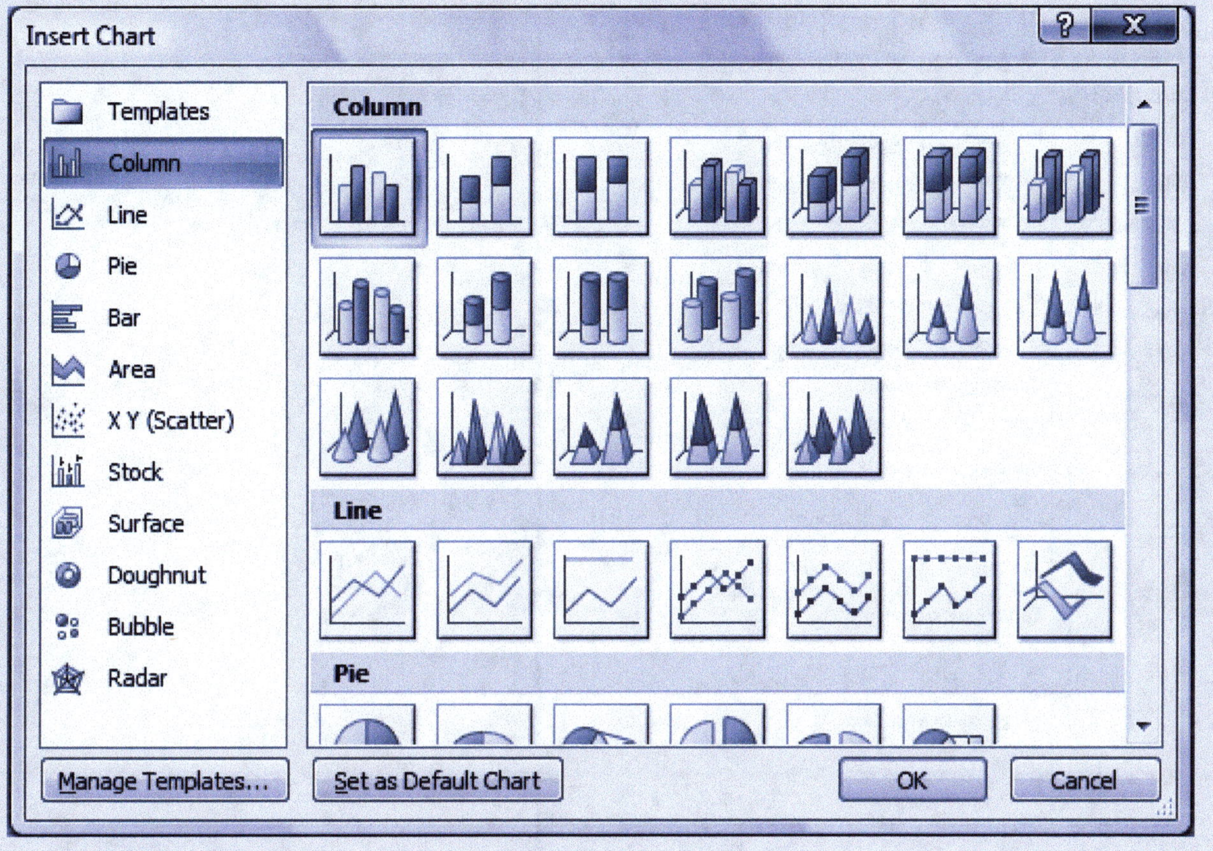

FIGURE 4.9
Insert Chart Menu in Excel

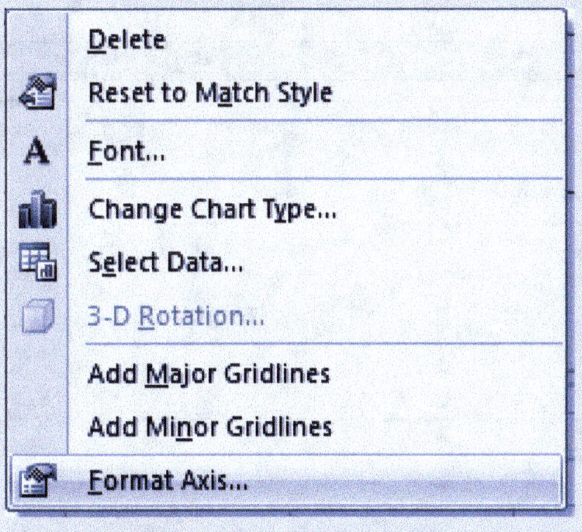

FIGURE 4.10
Format Axis Option After Right Click in Excel

8. To move the graph in Excel 2007, right click anywhere on the graph itself. A figure resembling Figure 4.13 will appear. Click on the Move Chart option and a screen resembling Figure 4.14 will appear. From this menu, choose where you wan the graph to be placed.

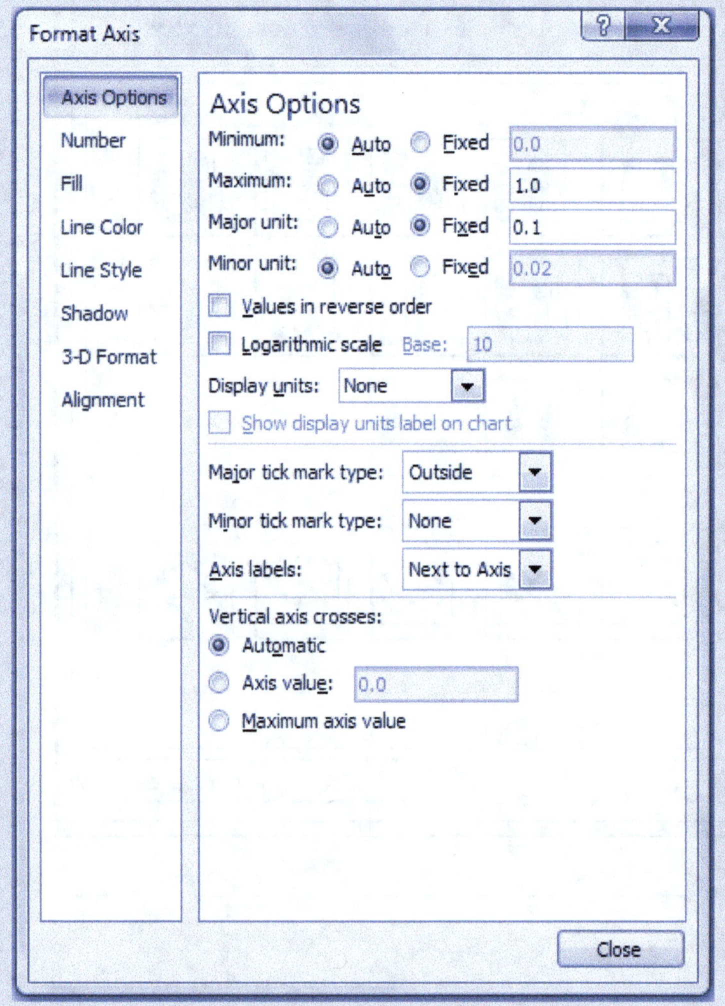

FIGURE 4.11

Format Axis Menu in Excel

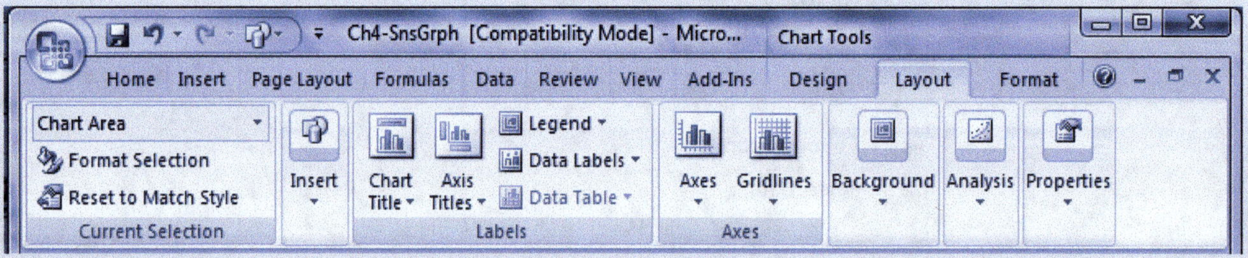

FIGURE 4.12a

Layout Tab for Modifying Graphs in Excel 2007

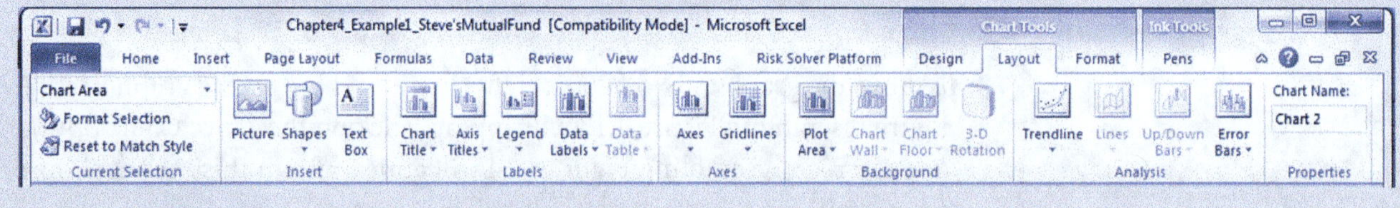

FIGURE 4.12b

Layout Tab for Modifying Graphs in Excel 2010

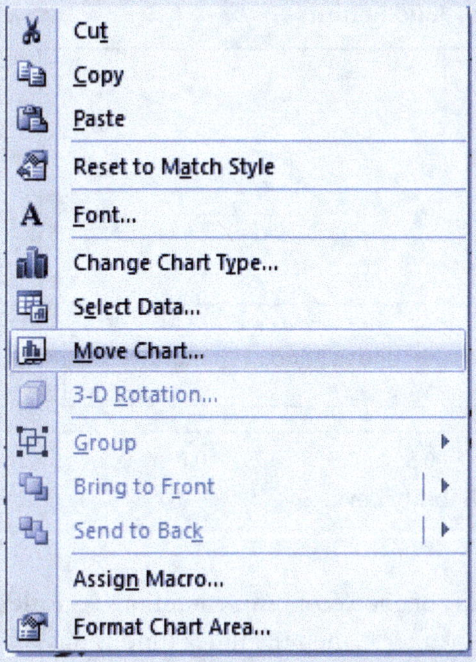

FIGURE 4.13
Move Chart Option for Modifying Graphs in Excel

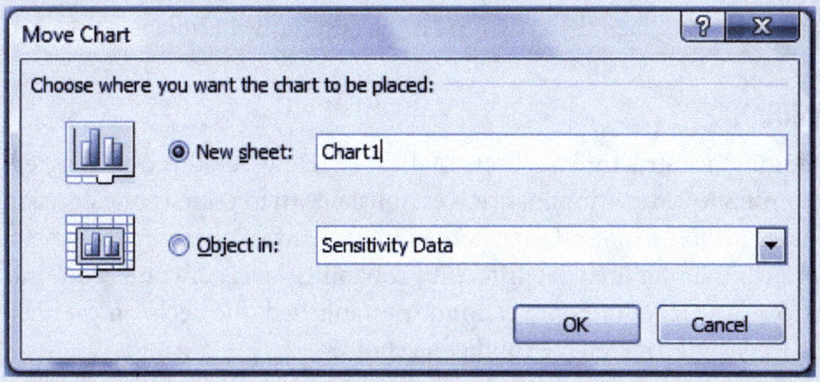

FIGURE 4.14
Move Chart Dialogue Box for Modifying Graphs in Excel

Analyzing the Sensitivity Graph

Figure 4.15 reveals some very interesting information about the mutual fund example. The sensitivity graph in itself illustrates the three areas of sensitivity analysis: dominance, trade-offs, and risk. Let's review the three steps of sensitivity analysis with regard to Figure 4.15.

Establish Dominance

The dark lines juxtaposed on the graph represent the dominant decisions for Steve's mutual fund example. The graph is telling the decision maker the following:

1. If your assessment of the probability of good economic conditions is less than about 25%, then the bond fund is the best fund alternative.

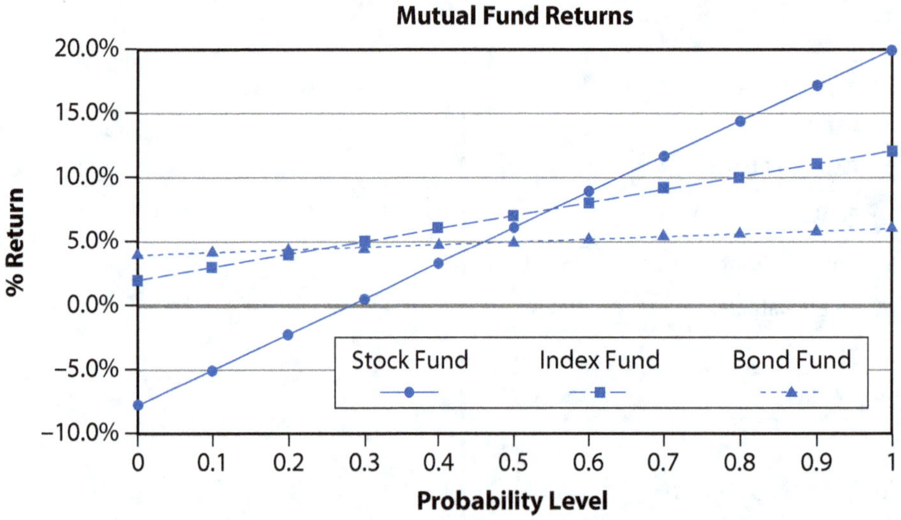

FIGURE 4.15
Excel Output for Mutual Fund Sensitivity Analysis

2. If your assessment of the probability of good economic conditions is greater than about 25% but not greater then 55%, then the index fund is the best fund alternative.

3. If your assessment of the probability of good economic conditions is greater than about 55%, then the stock fund is the best fund alternative.

STRICT DOMINANCE

Overall, a dominance structure has been established. However, this dominance is not strict dominance. Strict dominance is established when there is one decision that dominates in all situations. In the mutual fund example, there are three decision alternatives that dominate at different probability levels of good economic conditions. Since strict dominance cannot be established, the decision problem will contain trade-offs between the conflicting choices.

If strict dominance can be established, there is one decision that is better than all others.

TRADE-OFF ANALYSIS

Let's assume a manager is clairvoyant and knows whether or not good economic conditions will occur. The decision, then, would be very simple. A manager with this clairvoyant edge would only look at the right hand or left hand side of the graph to make a decision. As we all know, no manager is clairvoyant. Therefore, the point at which the two dominant choices cross is very important.

The point at which the two dominant choices intersect is referred to as the *trade-off point.* The exact value of the trade-off point can be calculated, but is not of overall importance to the manager. The most important issue is the identification and acknowledgment of the trade-off point.

There are several trade-offs involved with the three mutual funds. It is Steve's understanding that, should he yearn for a more profitable return, he would have to take on more risk from the aggressive growth stock fund (represented by the steep slope of the line), moderate risk with the moderate S&P 500 index fund, and the least risk with the conservative U.S. Treasury Bond fund. Thus, in order for Steve to make his decision, Steve should really think about his risk tolerance level.

DEFINING AND QUANTIFYING RISK

Risk must be defined by the decision maker and used to evaluate the choices in comparison to each other.

Risk must be defined and quantified when a manager is faced with trade-offs associated with numerous "good" alternatives. At the trade-off point, the alternatives look equally desirable. Subsequently, the risk associated with each of the alternatives may be the only way to differentiate the alternatives.

For the mutual fund example, risk is defined by using the measures of range and regret. Risk will not be defined by standard deviation, because of the small payoff sample size. Standard deviation will be used to define and quantify risk in Chapter 5, Simulation Modeling.

RISK DEFINED AND QUANTIFIED BY RANGE

From Figure 4.15 it can be seen that the lines associated with the different fund alternatives have different slopes. The stock fund tends to have a much steeper slope than the index and bond funds do. In this case, the slope of the line is related directly to range.

Range is defined as the difference between the highest value and the lowest value in the data set. Larger measurements of range mean the highest and lowest values in the data set are farther apart. As a line becomes steeper, the difference between the high and low values is greater. Hence, steeper slope, like larger values of range, translates into higher relative risk.

Table 4.6 contains the range calculations for the mutual fund example. From the table it is seen that the stock fund has the highest range and could be considered to have the highest relative risk. Refer back to Figure 4.15 and relate the range measurements to the slope of each line.

If Steve has assessed the probability of good economic conditions to be around the tradeoff point, 0.55, the range definition of risk could assist the decision-making process. An investor who is optimistic or who is more risky may choose the stock fund because of the higher payoff in the best scenario. Conversely, an investor who is less optimistic or less risky may choose one of the other two fund alternatives.

Risk Defined and Quantified by Regret

If Steve chooses to invest in the index fund, the payoff received will be moderate compared to the Stock Fund but greater than the Bond Fund most of the time. Steve could say he might have less regret by investing in the index fund when comparing it to the highs and lows of the other funds. In fact, it has been shown that the index fund is the choice that minimizes regret. Table 4.7 contains the minimax regret calculations for the mutual fund example.

TABLE 4.6 *Range calculations for Mutual fund Example*

FUND	RANGE
Stock	28
Index	10
Bond	2

TABLE 4.7 *Minimax Regret Calculations for Mutual fund Example*

FUND	MINIMAX REGRET
Stock	12
Index	8
Bond	14

However, if Steve chooses the index fund in order to minimize regret, something is given up. Steve may actually feel some measure of regret by choosing the index fund. Specifically, he will lose the ability to receive higher payoffs from the stock fund or more stable payoffs from the bond fund.

The Risk-Return Trade-off

A manager must analyze a problem with regard to measures of central tendency and dispersion in order to make an informed decision. In the words of decision analysis, a manager must analyze each decision problem with regard to return (i.e., expected values) and risk (i.e., range or regret). Only after analyzing the risk-return trade-offs can a decision be made.

Modeling cannot tell a manager what the best decision is; it can only provide a framework to compare the different alternatives.

Each of us must analyze complex decision problems in terms of return and risk. As students of business decision modeling and future managers, we must integrate sensitivity analysis into the problem-solving process while developing critical reasoning and judgment skills with regard to the risk/return trade-off.

In sum, this book cannot tell decision makers exactly what decisions will be the best when they are faced with complex problems. It is a guide to assist in developing a rational methodology for solving problems. Overall, the text provides a process for becoming a more effective and efficient problem solver.

Modeling, Decision Trees, and Influence Diagrams

Definition of Modeling

A decision model can be defined as any quantitative or logical abstraction of reality that is created and used to help decision makers solve a problem. A model consists of states, decisions, payoffs, a structure to frame those decision components, and the definition and quantification of objectives the decision maker wishes to investigate.

Why Model?

A manager creates a model to assist in the decision-making process. Models assist managers in two ways. First, in building a model and structuring a decision problem, a manager can respond to increased levels of complexity that cannot be grasped and/or resolved by analyzing the individual pieces of a problem.

Models are created to assist in the decision-making process.

Second, a model, with computer support, can keep track of many details and rapidly perform all necessary computations and sensitivity analysis. This allows a manager to devote attention to judgments about the individual details and composite results produced by the model.

Five Main Reasons for Modeling

Five main reasons are detailed in this chapter. They encompass the major themes of modeling.

NECESSITY

Models are built from necessity. They are done when simpler approaches are not adequate. Models are not a goal in themselves even though they can be engaging and, at times, almost supplant the decision at hand in our attention. However, managers require the assistance that models can efficiently give. Learning to model requires adapting one's language in order to communicate the model and its results effectively.

BETTER DECISIONS

There are numerous advantages to modeling, but five reasons—necessity, better decisions, insight, intuition, and aiding in the presentation—are central to the theme of modeling.

It could be said that a model has helped a decision maker if a better decision is reached. In general, the decision is better because the model has allowed a sensitivity analysis. Sensitivity analysis, as presented in Chapter 4, allows for the study of the outcomes of interest as different assumptions are methodically varied, the effect of uncertain factors on the surety of results, and which assumptions affect the outcomes the most. The decision can include the interaction of influences over a much longer period of time so that the decision does not just respond to the most obvious short-term considerations.

INSIGHT

A model gives the decision maker insight into a subject. The model allows a manager to explore the dominance of alternatives, the trade-offs among the factors that enter into those alternatives, and the risk associated with one alternative compared to another. Modeling equips a manager with the ability to break a problem into pieces and put it back together, offering insight along the way, that otherwise might have been overlooked.

INTUITION

Overall, complex systems behave nonintuitively. Modeling gives a manager insight into these nonintuitive behaviors that come from time lags between actions and responses, from interactions, and from the damping of one influence by another. The model provides intuition about the whole, starting with intuition about the parts.

The model tells you which uncertainties in your knowledge matter. In general, a decision maker may be working with incomplete understanding and incomplete data. Some of this uncertainty may not affect the decision choice; however, the model analysis reveals which pieces of information are of the most importance. If time and money allow, a manager will know which areas to study more to improve the quality of the decision; i.e., intuition has been achieved.

AID TO PRESENTATIONS

A model is an aid to the final presentation of the results. The presentation to the client uses the structure inherent in the model to explain those final results. The model illustrates the problem as compactly as possible. In general, clients need to see a physical structure in order to fully understand the problem and the alternatives presented.

Structuring Decision Problems

Earlier in this chapter the components of a decision problem were identified and defined. In addition, a simple structure, called a *payoff table,* was presented to aid in the decision-making process. As a student of business decision modeling, you will quickly find out that payoff tables, although straightforward and helpful, are inadequate for more complex problems.

Payoff tables are an example of a very simple model.

Payoff tables are just one way to structure problems. What kind of structure is needed for these more complex problems? How should one proceed in modeling complex decision problems? The decision modeling process consists of three fundamental steps:

1. Identifying and defining the variables and outcomes of interest
2. Organizing the variables and outcomes into a logical framework
3. Verification and refinement of the framework

Each of these steps will be detailed next.

Identifying and Defining Variables and Outcomes of Interest

The decision maker must first identify the variables that affect the decision. Once these variables are identified, they must be defined and the initial parameters, or bounds, set on their values. Outcomes of interest may be identified at the same time or after variables are established. Let's turn back to Chapter 1 and use a break-even example.

Identifying the variables that impact the decision is the first step in modeling.

- A manager must define the variables that affect the decision problem. For example, how many units do I need to produce to break even?
- The variables that are needed are fixed costs, variable costs, and price charged.
- The outcome of interest for the manager is the break-even point.
- The links between fixed cost, variable cost, and price charged are fairly straightforward and a basic mathematical equation or framework already exists for this decision problem.

Organizing Variables and Outcomes into a Logical Framework

Modeling gives a decision maker a means to structure a decision problem.

Payoff tables were introduced as a means to organize states, decisions, and payoffs. Payoff tables are one means to structure or put a physical framework around a decision problem. However, as was mentioned earlier, payoff tables become inadequate fairly quickly when a manager is faced with complex problems. Two additional means of framing a decision problem are introduced here: decision trees and influence diagrams.

Each of the approaches has different advantages for framing complex decision problems. Decision trees work extremely well for multistage decision problems while influence diagrams structure problems needing additional interactions and/or feedback. In fact, the two structures complement each other.

Verification and Refinement of the Framework

Models must be refined and the structure verified in order to proceed with further analysis.

Once a manager has identified and defined the variables and outcomes of interest and framed the problem, verification and refinement of the model or framework must be completed. This follows closely the review and iterate step in the business decision modeling process from Chapter 1.

A manager must be clear on what variables affect the outcomes of interest, what the basic parameters of those variables and outcomes are, and how to measure the outcomes. In addition, the overall structure should be analyzed. A manager need not lose sight the forest for the trees by choosing a framework that accommodates all the details but is too unruly or complex as a whole. One goal of putting structure to decision problems is to provide the client with a visual package to aid in the understanding and analysis of the situation.

Take, for example, the mutual fund decision problem. A payoff table appeared to work well for Steve's simple decision regarding mutual fund to choose. However, the payoff table framework soon becomes inadequate when additional variables are introduced. A review and refinement of the decision structure would be in order. The next section presents the concepts of decision trees and influence diagrams.

Decision Trees

Decision trees contain three types of symbols: square decision nodes, round chance nodes, and straight-line branches.

A decision tree is a graphical representation of a decision problem. Decision trees are another method to structure a problem. The decision tree framework consists of nodes and branches.

Decision Nodes, Chance Nodes, and Decision Trees

A decision tree contains two types of nodes, decision nodes and chance nodes, and branches, defined as follows:

A **decision node**, defined by a square, denotes when a decision maker must make a choice or a decision.

A **chance node**, defined by a circle, represents an event or state of nature that can occur in the future.

A decision maker can use a decision tree to structure a problem and compute expected values.

A **branch**, defined by a line, represents decision alternatives and/or states of nature, and links decisions and/or states.

In using a decision tree, a manager computes expected values at each chance node and makes a choice or decision on the basis of those expected values at decision nodes.

Decision trees provide a visual representation of the states, decisions, and outcomes of a sequential decision problem. Decision trees provide a framework for problems that payoff tables are unable to illustrate.

Building Decision Trees

To frame a problem by using a decision tree, the components of the problem must be identified and defined. Recall that the components of any decision-making problem are as follows: states, decisions, and payoffs. Let's use Steve's mutual fund problem example as the decision problem of interest. Figure 4.16 displays the payoff table for the mutual fund example.

From the information given in the payoff table, a decision tree can be built. First, let's relate the components of the decision problem to the graphical components of decision trees.

From any payoff table, a decision tree can be built.

Obviously, the three decisions match up with the decision node component. A common starting place for most decision trees is a decision node. For the mutual fund payoff table, three decisions emanate from the initial decision node as decision branches.

At the end of each of the decision branches, a chance node is placed. From each chance node two branches depicting the two states—good economic conditions and bad economic conditions—emerge. At the end of these chance branches the payoffs associated with each decision/state combination are listed. Figure 4.17 displays the corresponding decision tree.

For the mutual fund example, only one decision and one set of chance nodes are needed. The decision tree structure allows for any combination of decision and

	A	B	C
1	**Steve's Mutual Fund Decision**		
2	**Payoff Table**		
3		**State of Nature**	
4		**Good**	**Bad**
5	**Mutual Fund**	**Economic Condition**	**Economic Condition**
6	**Stock Fund**	20%	-8%
7	**Aggressive Growth**		
8			
9	**Index Fund**	12%	2%
10	**Moderate S&P 500**		
11			
12	**Bond Fund**	6%	4%
13	**Conservative U.S. Treasury**		
14			

FIGURE 4.16
Payoff Table for Steve's Mutual Fund Example

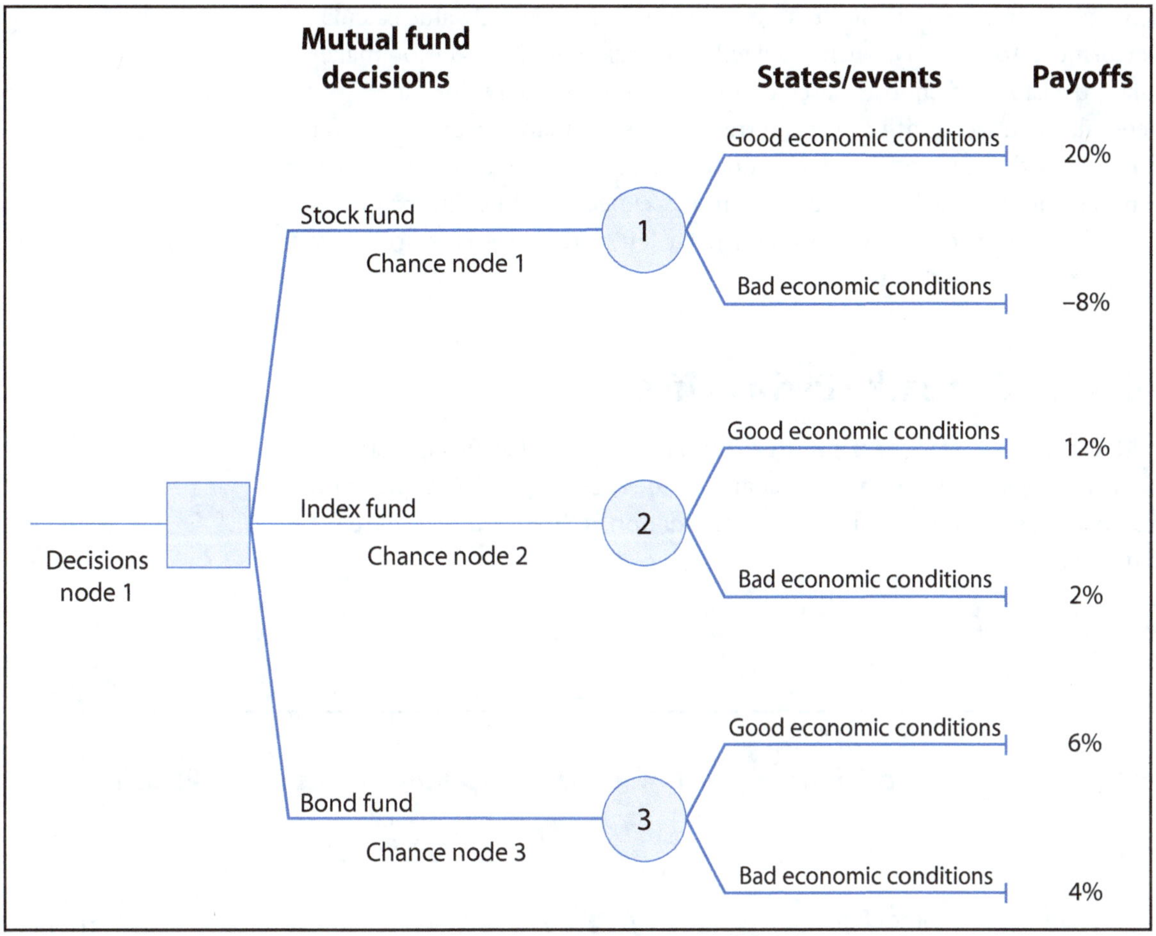

FIGURE 4.17

Decision Tree for Mutual Fund Example

chance nodes. The next section will briefly discuss the concept of folding back the tree. The application of decision trees to multiple sequential decision making will be detailed later in this chapter.

Folding Back the Tree: Calculating Expected Values

Folding back the tree refers to the process of calculating expected values at chance nodes.

One goal of a decision tree is to calculate the expected value of the tree, or perform a process called *folding back the tree.* This process is based on a set of rules for decision trees. When analyzing a decision tree a decision maker may encounter decision nodes or chance nodes.

Two rules govern decision trees regarding these nodes:

1. At a chance node, a decision maker computes an expected value based on the payoffs and probabilities given.
2. When faced with a decision node, a decision maker must make a decision. The criterion used to make the decision is to maximize the expected value of the various alternatives in question.

When a decision maker encounters a chance node an expected value calculation is performed. Accordingly, when faced with a decision node, a decision maker must make a decision and chooses based on maximizing expected value.

In general, when faced with a decision tree, a decision analyst begins at the far right of the tree with the payoffs, at chance nodes calculates expected values, and at decision nodes chooses the decision that maximizes expected value. This process is followed until the decision analyst reaches the far left of the tree. This process is referred to as folding back the tree.

Example of Folding Back a Decision Tree

Figure 4.18 displays the tree for the mutual fund example under the equal likelihood scenario. Expected values for the chance nodes are shown on the tree and will be calculated; in addition, a final recommendation is displayed on the tree at the final decision node.

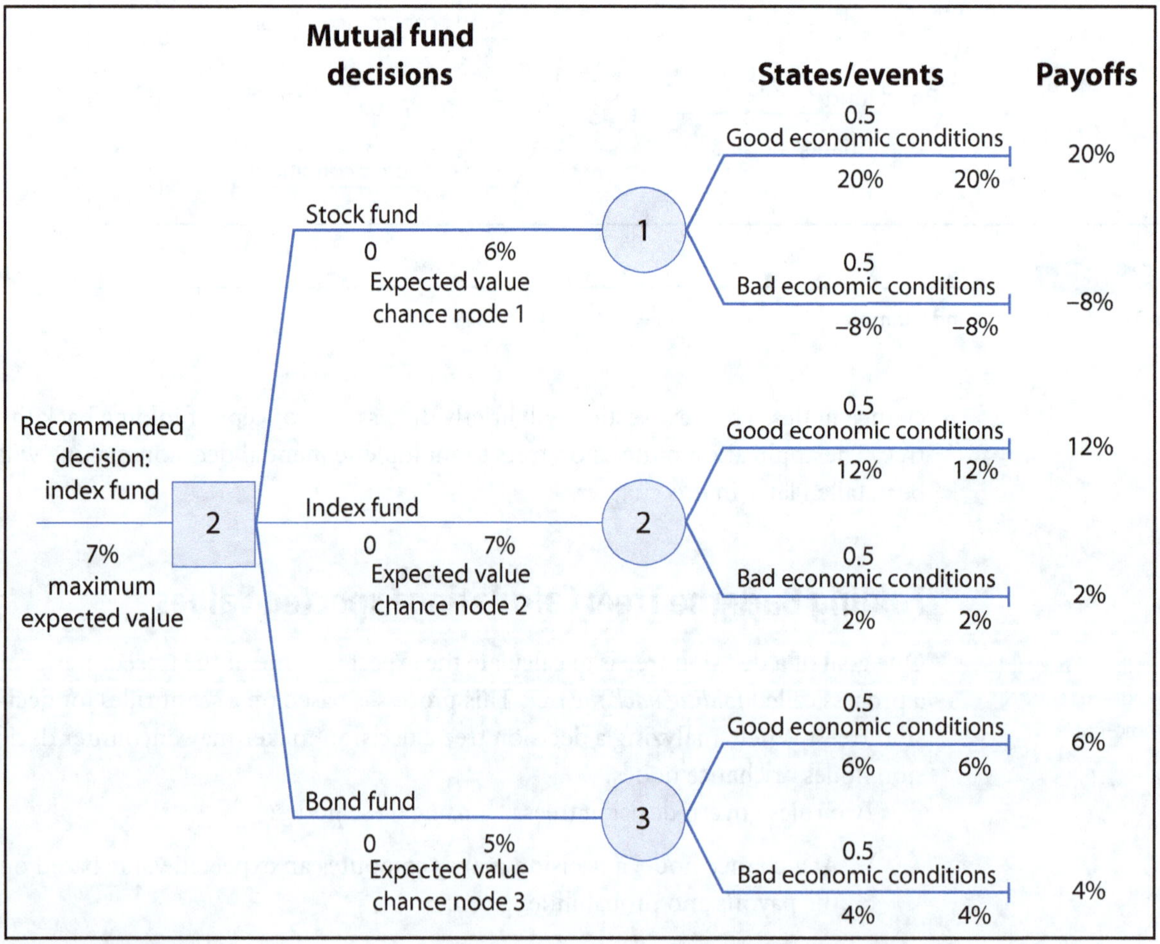

FIGURE 4.18

Mutual Fund Example Decision Tree

TABLE 4.8 *Mutual fund Decision Tree Expected Values*

MUTUAL FUND	EXPECTED VALUE, $\alpha = 0.5$
Stock fund	6%
Index fund	7%
Bond fund	5%

According to the rules set down in the previous section, expected values are calculated at chance nodes 1, 2, and 3. The calculations are as follows:

Folding back the tree is akin to finding the weighted average of the branches at each chance node of a decision tree.

Chance node1: $E(1) = 20\% \times 0.5 + (-8\%) \times 0.5 = 6\%$

Chance node 2: $E(2) = 12\% \times 0.5 + 2\% \times 0.5 = 7\%$

Chance node 3: $E(3) = 6\% \times 0.5 + 4\% \times 0.5 = 5\%$

Subsequently, at the far-left decision node, the expected values are compared and the mutual fund with the highest expected value is chosen. Table 4.8 displays the three expected values and highlights the index fund as the final recommendation made at the far-left decision node.

In summary, the process of folding back a decision tree consists of calculating expected values at chance nodes and making decisions at decision nodes based on maximizing expected values. Therefore, in the mutual fund example, when the decision maker's assessment of the occurrence of good economic conditions state is 0.5, the index fund will be the recommendation.

In sum, when a decision maker is confronted with a chance node an expected value must be calculated; subsequently, when confronted with a decision node, the decision maker must make a choice based on maximizing expected value.

Multistage Decision Trees

Decision trees generally begin with a decision node, but a decision maker does not always have to follow this rule.

In general, decision trees begin with a decision node. However, it is possible to begin a decision tree with a chance node. In addition, the decision tree structure allows for any number and combination of decision nodes and chance nodes.

For example, if Steve wishes to make another decision after witnessing bad economic conditions, he may want to switch to Fund B; the decision tree structure allows this very easily. In addition, Steve knows that there is a chance of a corporate scandal if he is invested in the stock fund.

Multistage decision trees depict events and decisions that occur one after another or in a sequential manner.

To accommodate these additional decisions and states, the original decision tree must be augmented. Figure 4.19 displays the modified decision tree including these added decisions and states.

From Figure 4.19 it is obvious that any order, combination, and/or number of decision and chance nodes is possible. This makes the decision tree framework very robust for structuring decision problems with multistage decisions and states.

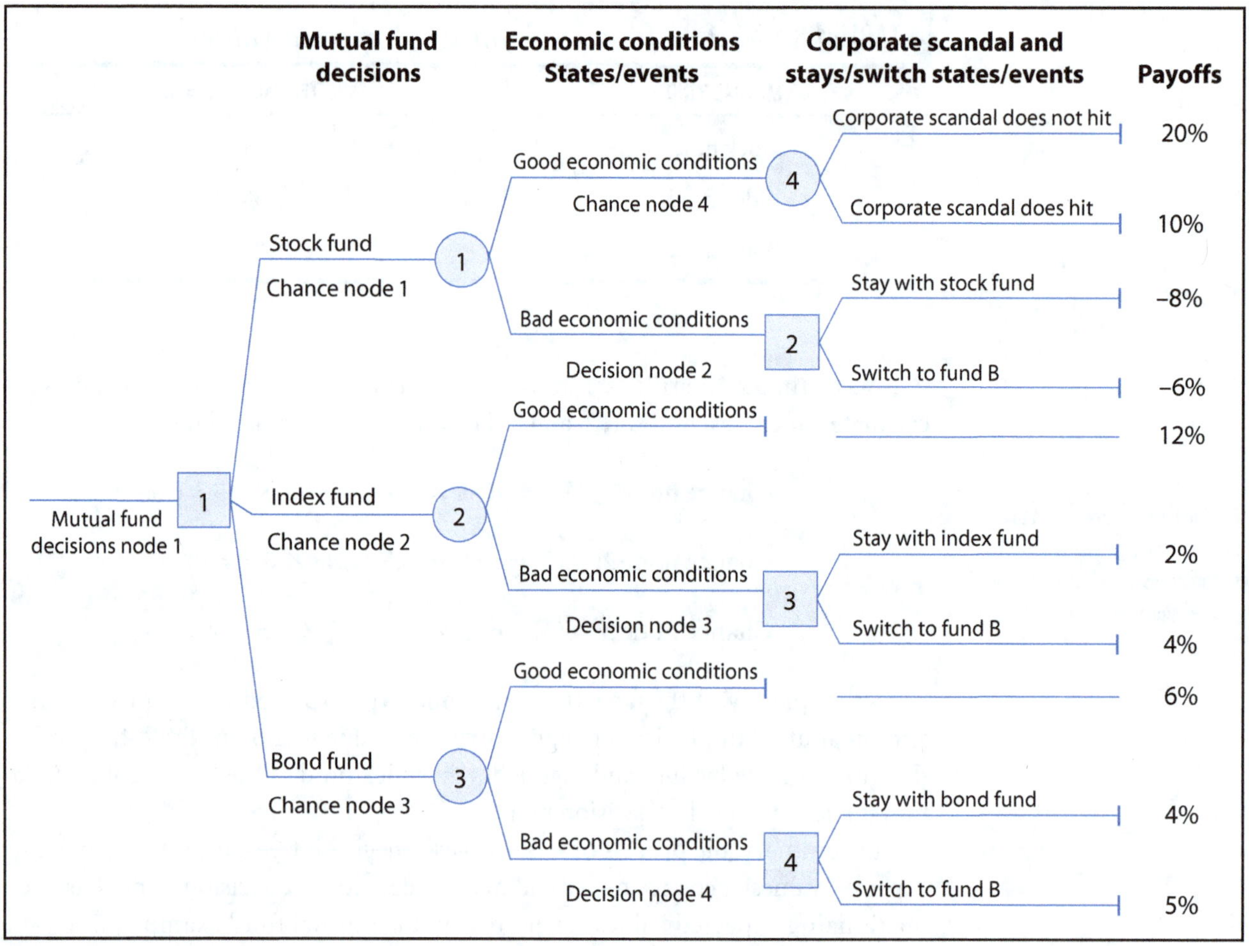

FIGURE 4.19
Multistage Decision Tree Example

Inadequacies of Decision Tree Structures

Although decision trees provide a more robust structure for framing decision problems, there may be times when a decision maker is faced with a problem that does not exactly fit the tree format. In fact, the basic tree format does not incorporate feedback well. In addition, the tree structure becomes large as the number of decision and chance nodes grows. To ameliorate these inadequacies, another decision structure is introduced—the influence diagram.

One inadequacy of decision trees is the lack of a feedback loop.

Influence Diagrams

Influence diagrams are tools for structuring a model design from a set of defined variables. Having identified and defined the variables of a model, we next decide how these variables relate to one another.

An influence diagram displays all the model variables and indicates the direction and type of influence from one variable to another.

Influence Diagram Symbols

Influence diagrams consist of three types of symbols: square decision variables, round intermediate variables, and oval attribute or outcome variables.

A rectangle in an influence diagram represents a decision variable, a circle is an intermediate variable, and an oval (or ellipse) signifies an attribute or an outcome of interest. Figure 4.20 depicts these symbols.

Figure 4.21 depicts a number of simple influence diagrams characterizing the different types of variables, influence, and random or nonrandom nature.

Influence Diagrams and Depicting Influence

Arrows connect related variables in an influence diagram. An arrow indicates the direction of influence. The arrow indicates that the value of the influencing variable is set first and is used in determining the level of any variable that it influences.

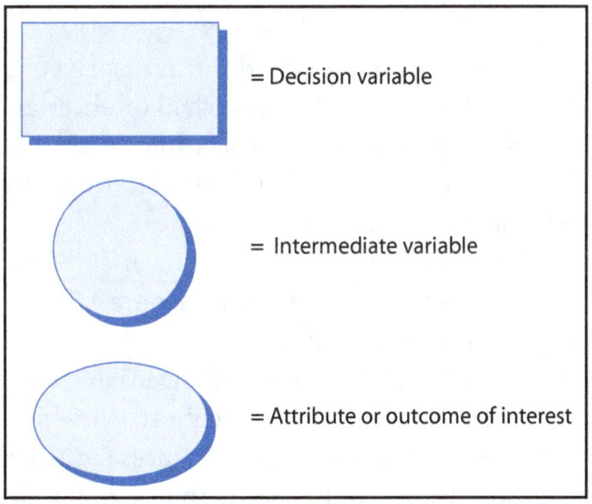

FIGURE 4.20
Influence Diagram Symbols

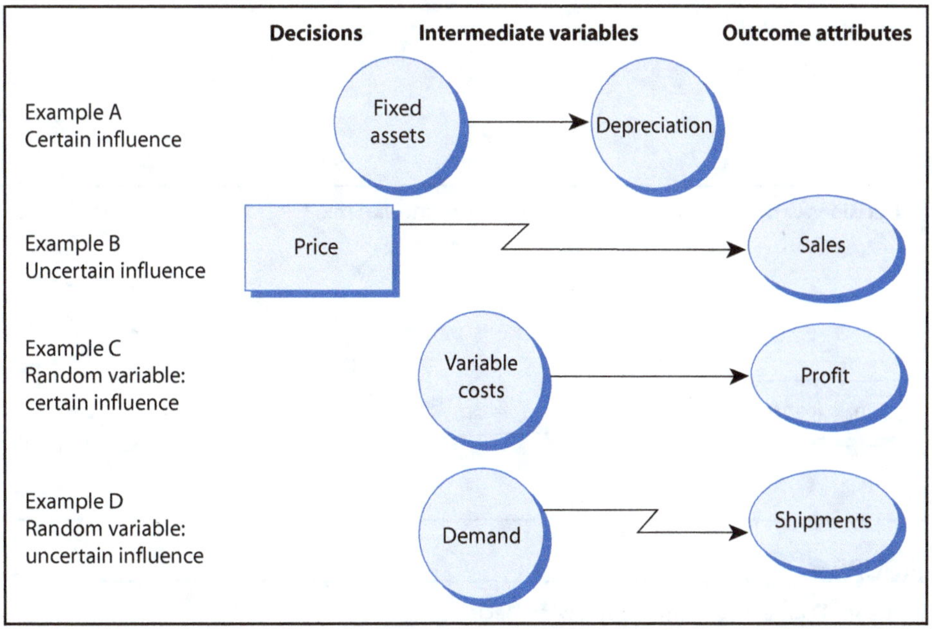

FIGURE 4.21
Examples of Simple Influence Diagrams

Three types of influence arrows are used in an influence diagram. A single straight arrow, as displayed in Figure 4.21 Example A, indicates certain influence. An arrow that resembles a lightning bolt, as displayed in Figure 4.21 Example B, stands for an uncertain influence.

Three types of influence are used in influence diagrams: a single straight arrow, a single kinked arrow, or a double arrow.

Looking at Example A, we see the level of fixed assets has certain influence on the amount of depreciation. If fixed assets increase, then without question, depreciation will increase. This is indicated by the single straight arrow.

In contrast, Example B of Figure 4.22, price, a decision variable, will affect sales, in this case an outcome attribute. But the influence is uncertain. That is, if price is changed upward, we would expect sales to be lower (recall economics and simple supply and demand), but we are unsure by how much. Actually, if we did know this we would have a measure of the price elasticity of the item being sold. This uncertainty is represented by an arrow with a lightning bolt look to it.

Arrows connect related variables and indicate direction of influence.

Random Variables

A variable and its influence may also be exogenous, or random, as displayed in Figure 4.21 Examples C and D. Random variables can impart certain or uncertain influence. However, by definition, random variables have no decision variables as direct or indirect predecessors in the influence diagram structure. In this case, *predecessor* refers to the influence relationship, not necessarily in time.

Any variable influenced by a random variable is also a random variable. Any random variable will be noted with a tilde (~) above the variable. Figure 4.22 displays an influence diagram for a simple borrowing decision.

Variables that are random are represented by a tilde (~) above the respective variable.

Figure 4.22 shows a decision variable at the left. This decision variable indicates which loan is taken. This choice influences the down payment needed, which, in turn, influences the buyer's cash position. The decision also influences the actual percentage rate on the loan. This example has two outcome attributes: the applicant's cash remaining and the actual percentage rate on the loan.

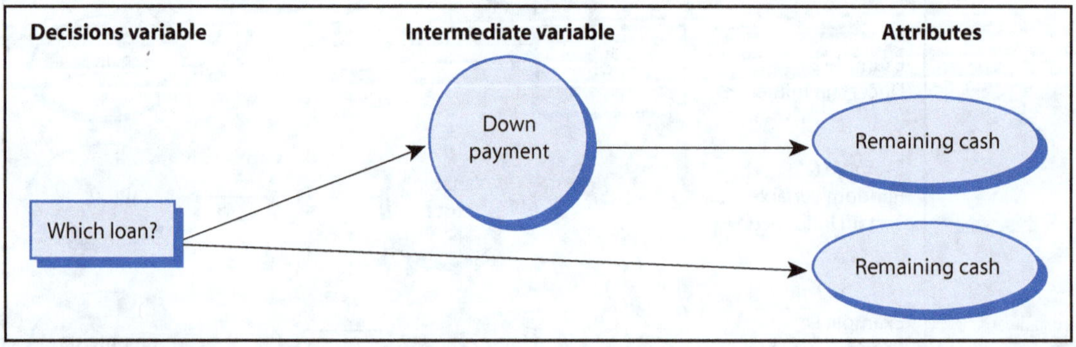

FIGURE 4.22

Influence Diagram for Simple Borrowing Decision

Order, Precedence, and/or Influence Diagram Structure

Variables in an influence diagram can appear in virtually any order.

Influence relationships have been described that relate decision variables to intermediate variables or to outcome attributes. Influence relationships may also relate intermediate variables to outcome attributes or they may simply relate one intermediate variable to another.

Variables may appear in virtually any precedence order in the influence diagram. This is in contrast to a decision tree, where the structure of the problem tends to flow from left to right. In fact, outcome attributes or intermediate variables resulting from one set of decision variables may themselves influence other decisions.

Figure 4.23 displays an influence diagram having two decisions. First, an undergraduate student decides on the level of effort to put into an academic career. An outcome of this level of effort is the grades the student receives. But grades may in turn influence the decision made by a graduate admissions committee whether to admit the student into a particular graduate program. This decision in turn influences the career path that the student pursues.

Two-Way and Loop Influence

Influence diagrams differ from decision trees in that they allow two-way and loop influence.

Relationships that contain two-way influence are also possible. However, it should be cautioned that if the variables are treated as random variables, two-way influences become so complex that the solution goes beyond the scope of this text. Two-way relationships between random variables do appear in econometric models and are treated in texts on econometric model building.

The following example using interest expense and debt levels illustrates a two-way dependency. This relationship would be expressed in a line model by two simultaneous equations.

The equations might be as follows:

$$\text{Interest expense} = 0.08(\text{debt level})$$

$$\text{Debt level} = 10{,}000 + \text{Interest expense}$$

Figure 4.24a displays the influence diagram associated with the debt level and interest expense example.

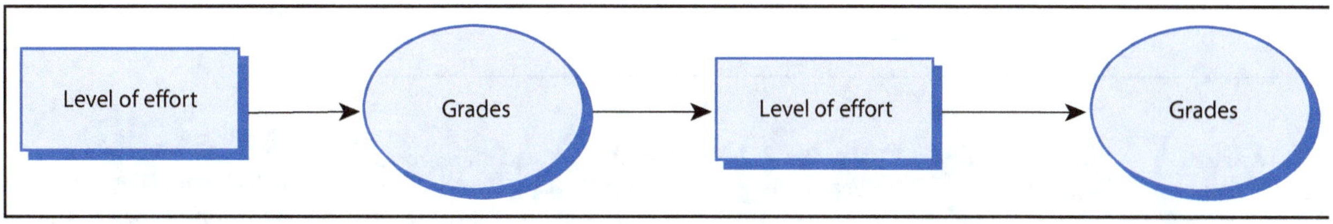

FIGURE 4.23

Student's Influence Diagram

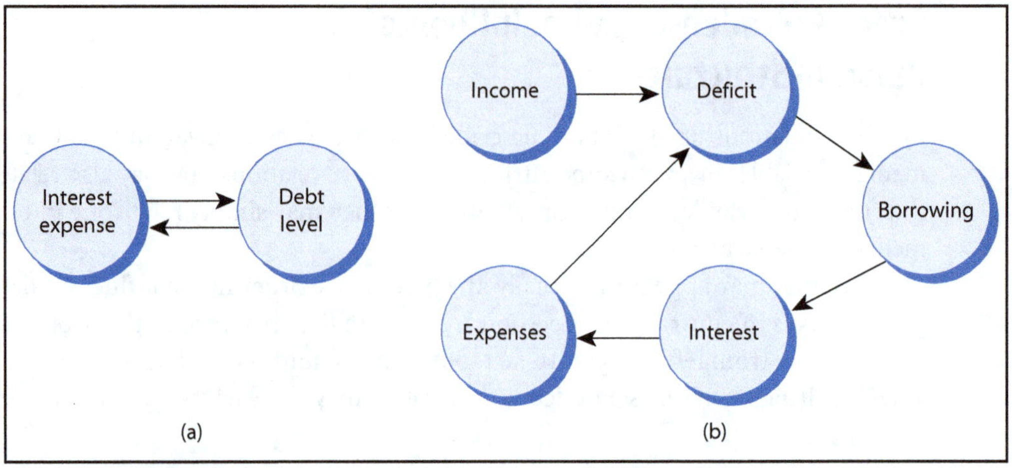

FIGURE 4.24
(a) Two-way Influence Diagram and (b) Loop Influence Diagram

The concept of an influence loop is created when the arrows go in both directions. A loop involving many variables without using two-way influences can also be created. Figure 4.24b depicts an example where both income and expenses affect the deficit, which, in turn, affects borrowings. This, in turn, affects expenses through interest expense.

An influence loop is created when influence arrows go in both directions between variables.

One reason for drawing an influence diagram prior to constructing the mathematical model is to detect loops such as this. Any time such a loop exists, simultaneous equations are needed in the model and special instructions may be required to enable the model to run.

Influence Diagrams to Measure Time

Influence diagrams can also be constructed to measure the effect of variables in different time periods. Figure 4.25a illustrates an influence diagram of the relationships between assets and depreciation in different time periods. The assets in year *n* determine the depreciation in year *n*, which in turn affects the assets in year $n + 1$. This case does not involve a loop, since assets in year *n* and year $n + 1$ are really separate variables.

Influence diagrams can also be constructed to measure the effect of variables in different time periods.

Rather than create separate variables for each time period, which may result in a large, cluttered influence diagram, the modeler may instead use subscript

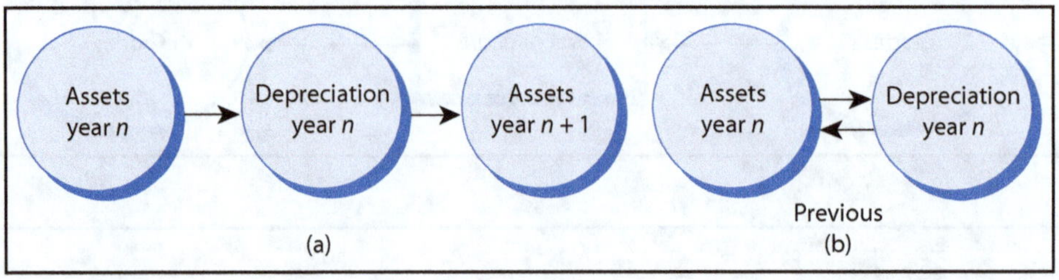

FIGURE 4.25
(a) Influence Diagram Measuring Time; (b) The Same Relationship with Subscript Notation to Show Time Variation

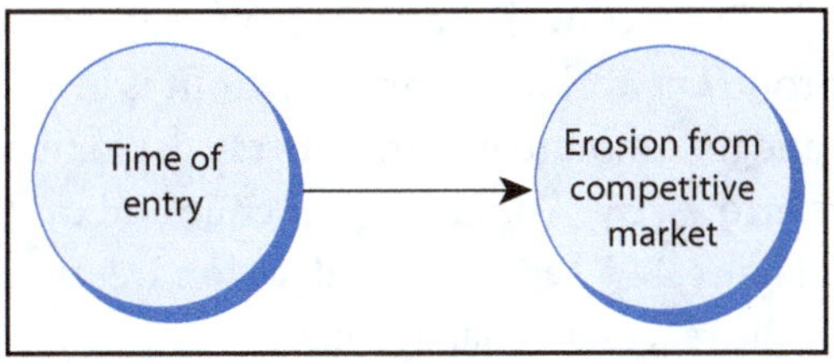

FIGURE 4.26
Sales Erosion Influence Diagram

notation to show time variation. If a variable, e.g., assets, is influenced by the previous value of another variable, e.g., depreciation, this may be indicated by using a notation system, such as the subscript "Previous," on the arrow. Figure 4.25b is such a way of writing the general relationship in Figure 4.25a.

To show the effects of time in an influence diagram, a modeler may use subscript variables.

At times modelers use a separate variable to depict the effects of time. For example, Figure 4.26 depicts the effects of the introduction of a new product into a market. One of the variables is sales erosion of the new product that would result from the future entry of a competitive product. The magnitude of that erosion may depend on when competitors introduce their product.

Building the Influence Diagram Structure

Managers are faced with large, complex problems that require large complex models.

As a manager, you will be faced with large, complex problems that require large, complex models. In designing large models, it is not advisable to attempt to write down the entire model in one step. Outline the parts of the model first, then proceed to flesh out the details. Begin with the two ends of the problem and the simplest decisions and outcomes, then work to fill in the linkage between them.

Coyle (1977) proposes six possible justifications for an influence between variables: conservation considerations (mass balance), direction observation, instructions (or policy statements) of a system, accepted theory, hypothesis or assumption, and statistical evidence. A manager should think of the justification that may be appropriate when documenting influence, not only to avoid modeling erroneous influences but also to be able to understand what the influence is.

Putting It All Together: A Real Estate Influence Diagram

The rental price on apartment units is a variable that a manager decides on. Profits are the final outcome of interest. The development of a complete set of relationships is necessary to link the price decision to the profit outcome.

It is easy to see that the decision variable, price, will affect occupancy. In turn, occupancy affects revenue, and finally profit. Or working in reverse, profit is influenced by cash flow from the rental units and the amount of money invested. Linking the appropriate variables with influence arrows, e.g., connecting revenue and cash flow, completes the influence diagram. Figure 4.27 represents a decision tree and the corresponding influence diagram for the real estate management example.

Converting a Decision Tree to an Influence Diagram

It is possible to structure the problem using a decision tree and then convert the tree to an influence diagram. It is always possible to convert a decision tree into an influence diagram. This is accomplished by including the variables at the nodes of the decision tree in the diagram and by adding arrows flowing between them in the same direction as the tree opens up.

It is possible to structure a problem by using a decision tree and then converting the tree to an influence diagram. However, the converse may not be true.

Even though an influence diagram can be created for any decision tree, the converse is not true. Not every influence diagram created can be turned into a decision tree. Decision trees cannot accommodate feedback loops in their structure. There are a number of differences between influence diagrams and decision trees. A comparison of the two decision structures is next.

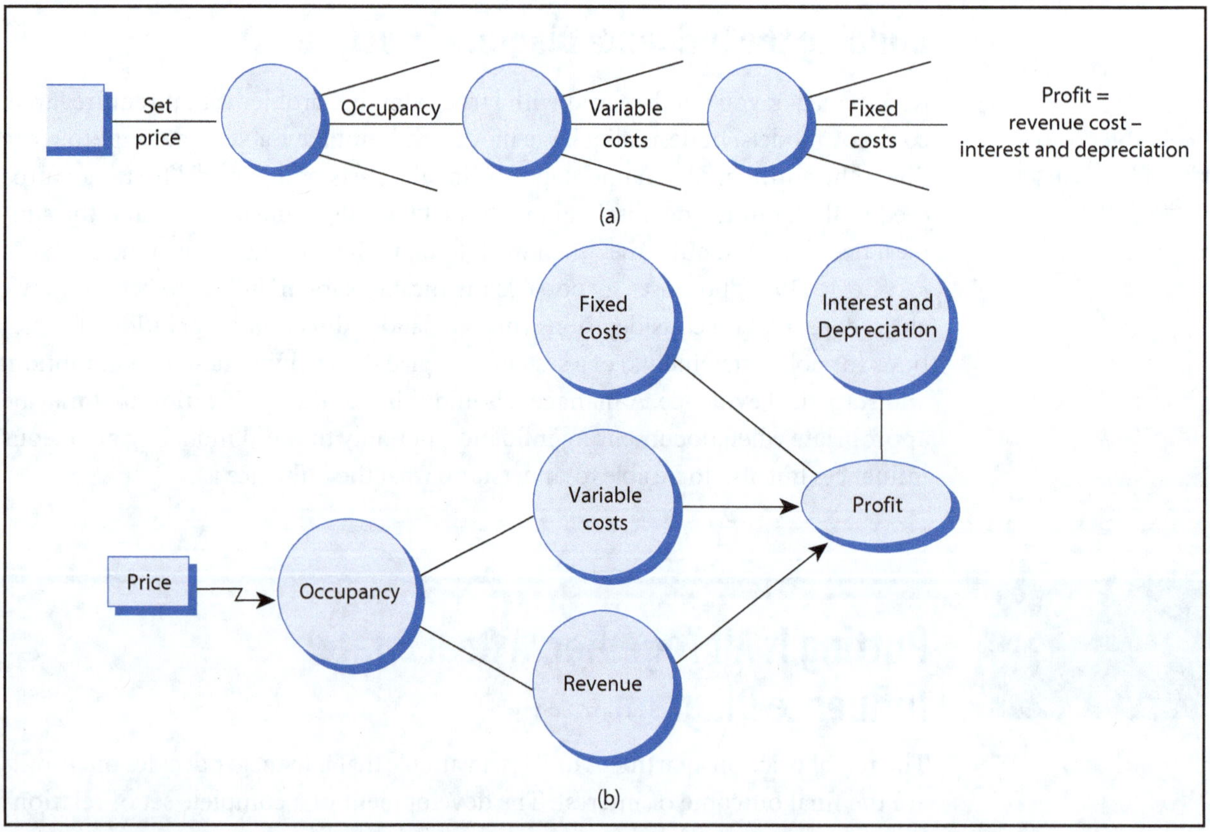

FIGURE 4.27

Real Estate Management (a) Decision Tree and (b) Influence Diagram

Influence Diagrams and Decision Trees: A Comparison

Influence diagrams have flexibility, which decision trees do not. Decision trees are sequential in nature. Variables to the right are implicitly influenced by variables to their left. This is seen in Figure 4.27a, where the fixed cost node must be inserted before or after variable cost. The placement of the fixed cost node may suggest influence over variable cost or vice versa. However, as is explicit in simple financial models, fixed cost generally does not influence variable cost nor does variable cost influence fixed cost.

Influence diagrams show relationships more concisely and accurately than decision trees and indicate a wider range of intricate relationships. These points are demonstrated in the subsequent influence diagram in Figure 4.27b. The influence diagram clearly illustrates that variable and fixed costs are unrelated.

In addition, the influence diagram reveals that revenue is influenced directly by price and also indirectly influenced by price through occupancy. Decision trees do not have the ability to portray these links. Numerous predecessors having any structure of relationships among them may influence variables in an influence diagram.

Advantages of Influence Diagrams and Areas of Consideration

In general, influence diagrams accommodate and accomplish a number of items more effectively and efficiently than decision trees. These areas are summarized as follows:

Advantages of influence diagrams: They are a general decision structuring device, expandable, and simple to build and use.

1. Influence diagrams are more general tools for structuring models than decision trees.
2. Influence diagrams are expandable; variables can be broken down into finer points or variables.
3. Influence diagrams are simple to initiate and easy to modify.

Although influence diagrams appear to be simple enough tools, first-time modelers often encounter pitfalls during development. The following areas should be noted to prevent misuse and overuse:

Influence diagrams are not: flow charts, precedence charts, or hierarchical structures.

1. An influence diagram is not:
   a. A flow chart; it does not indicate things such as "units shipped from point A to point B."
   b. A precedence chart, such as might be used in PERT planning. An arrow does not mean "must be followed by."
   c. A representation of hierarchical structure, as in an organizational chart. An arrow does not mean "is an element of."
2. Think of variables as levels of some quantity and arrows as effects of variables on each other, but make it clear what higher or lower levels mean.
3. Divide variables into two or more variables only when more detailed expression is needed for clarity.
4. If (and only if) an influence arrow needs more explanation, insert another variable.

The Completed Real Estate Influence Diagram

Figure 4.28 displays the completed influence diagram of a real estate investment model that is to be used in evaluating new apartment-building projects. The company faces three decisions in any new project: (1) whether to take it on, (2) how big a building to build (or whether to expand a purchased building), and (3) what to charge for rent.

Two uncertain influences are included in the diagram: the price-occupancy relationship and market demand. Fixed costs and variable costs are treated as random variables. Two attributes, amount invested and net present value (NPV), are the outcomes of interest. Amount invested is linked to NPV by the fact that larger investments should bring larger returns, or NPV. The general model for the real estate

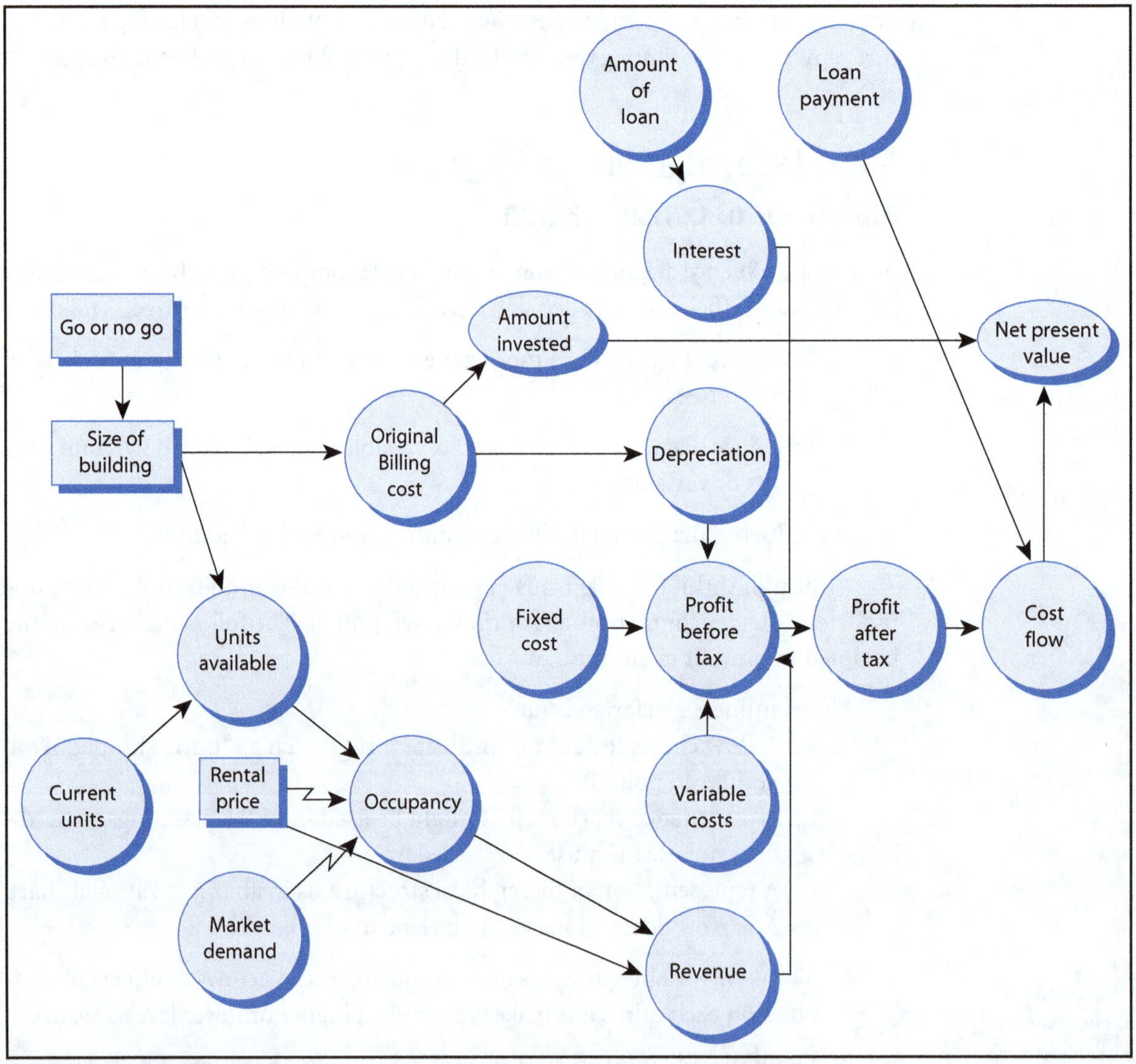

FIGURE 4.28

Loading and Accessing TreePlan in Excel 2003

investment problem is described adequately by the influence diagram. However, two additional steps are necessary to generate the model from the diagram.

1. Mathematical forms of relationship (functions) that apply to each arrow in the diagram must be constructed. The functions for most of the arrows would be the same for all projects considered (for example, the same form of depreciation rule would be applied to each project). A quick perusal of a real estate investment text would supply most of the answers to the functional relationships depicted in the influence diagram.
2. Specific numbers must be supplied to these functions, e.g., the prevailing interest rate. Specific numbers may vary from case to case or project to project. The influence diagram is flexible enough to handle these variations.

Using TreePlan to Develop Decision Trees in Excel

TreePlan is an add-in to Excel spreadsheets that greatly simplifies the process of constructing decision trees. Excel does have sufficient resources to develop decision trees without using an add-in software package like TreePlan, but the process is difficult and slow. This section describes and explains how to access, install, and use TreePlan in conjunction with Excel.

Loading and Accessing TreePlan in Excel

TreePlan is an add-in to Excel spreadsheets that greatly simplifies the process of constructing decision trees. Excel does have sufficient resources to develop decision trees without using an add-in software package like TreePlan, but the process is difficult and slow. This section describes and explains how to access and install TreePlan in conjunction with Excel.

Since TreePlan is an add-in for Excel, the first step in using TreePlan is loading the software via Excel's Add-Ins menu. You must copy the Excel add-in file, TreePlan.xla, onto your hard disk drive. To add in TreePlan, it is necessary to click on the Office button and select the Excel Options button at the bottom of the screen (see Figure 4.29a for Excel 2007 and Figure 2.29b for Excel 2010). This action brings up the Excel Options window and within this window click on the Add-Ins option on the left. A screen that resembles Figure 4.30 will appear. In the Add-Ins menu go to the Manage drop down box at the bottom of the screen (refer to the bottom middle of Figure 4.30), select Excel Add-Ins from the menu, and then click on the Go button. This will prompt the Add-Ins menu to appear (see Figure 4.31). TreePlan should be listed in the Add-Ins menu in Figure 4.31. If TreePlan does not appear in the Add-Ins menu, click browse in the Add-Ins menu (Figure 4.31), locate where you saved the TreePlan.xla file on your computer, and then click OK in the Browse menu. Click on the check box that is labeled TreePlan and then click OK. Once this has been completed, the TreePlan option in the Menu Commands group under the Add-Ins tab will appear (see Figure 4.32a for Excel 2007 and Figure 3.23b for Excel 2010).

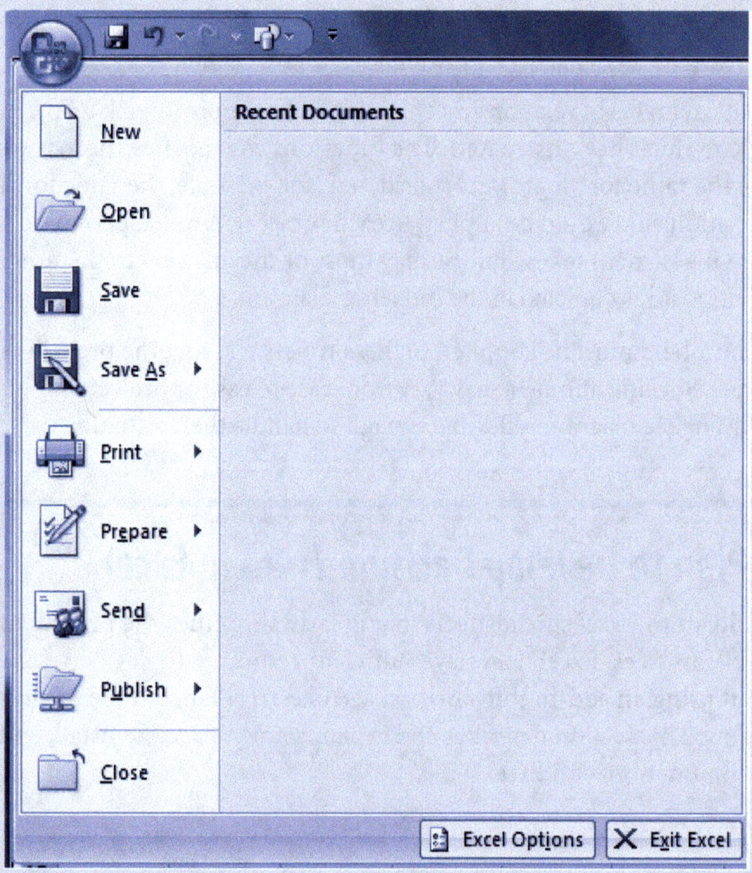

FIGURE 4.29a
Excel 2007 Office Button Menu

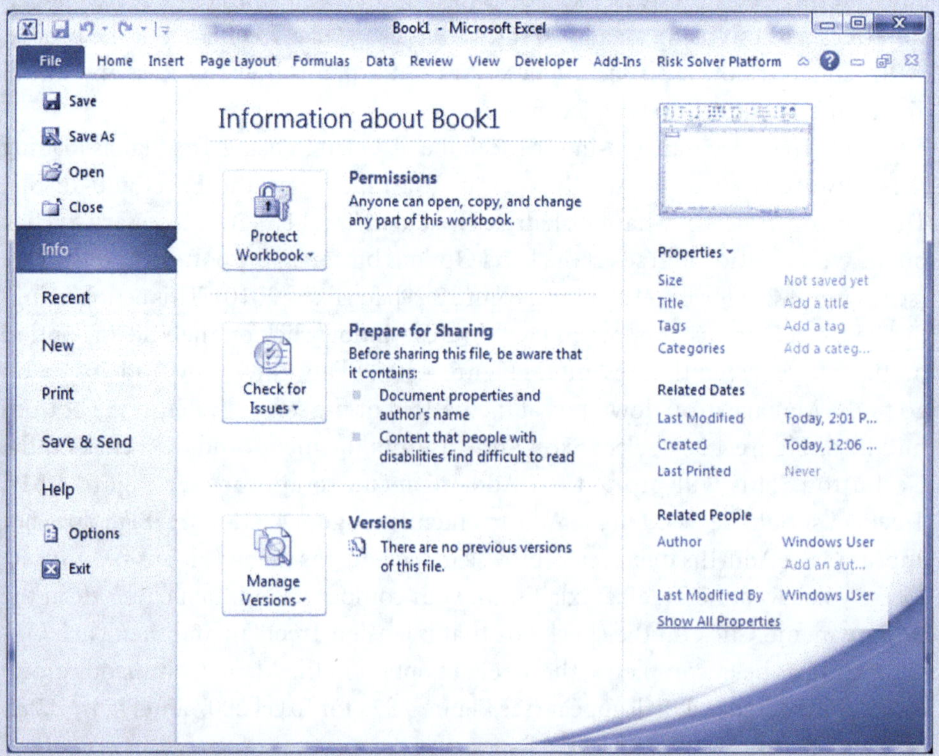

FIGURE 4.29b
Excel 2010 Office File Menu

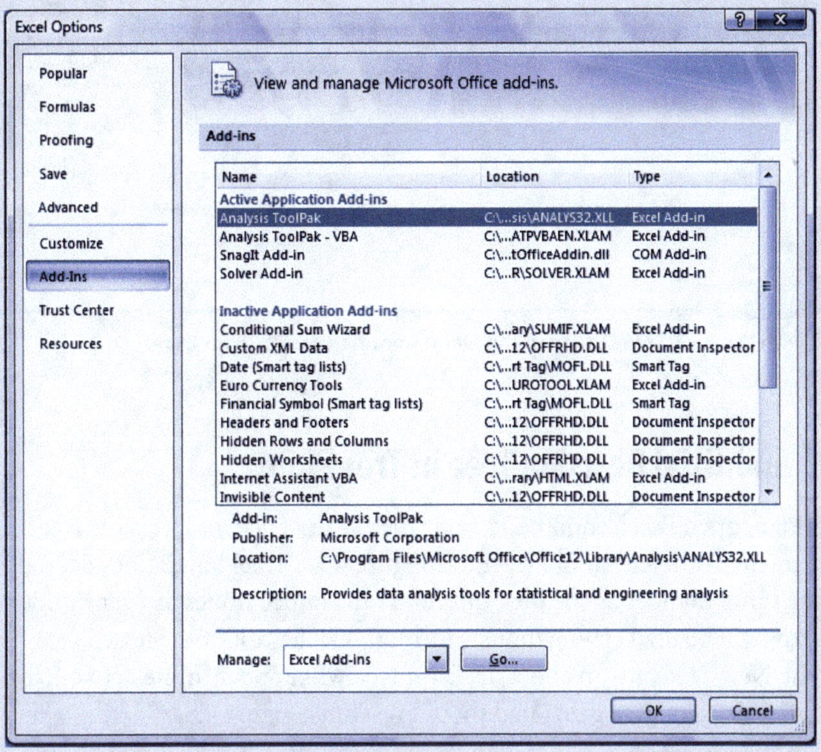

FIGURE 4.30
Excel Options Menu Add-ins Screen

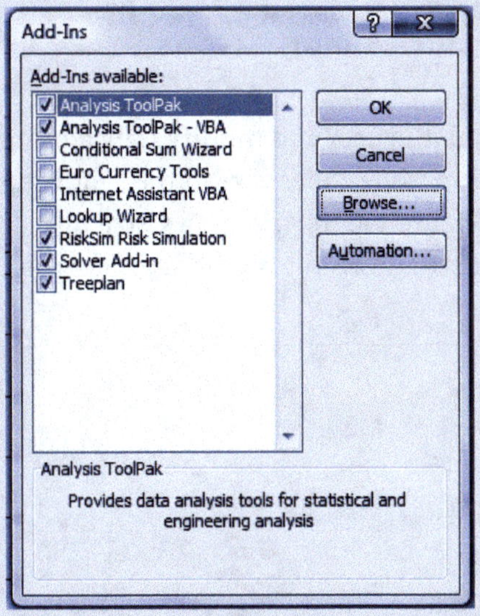

FIGURE 4.31
Excel Add-ins Menu with Treeplan Selected

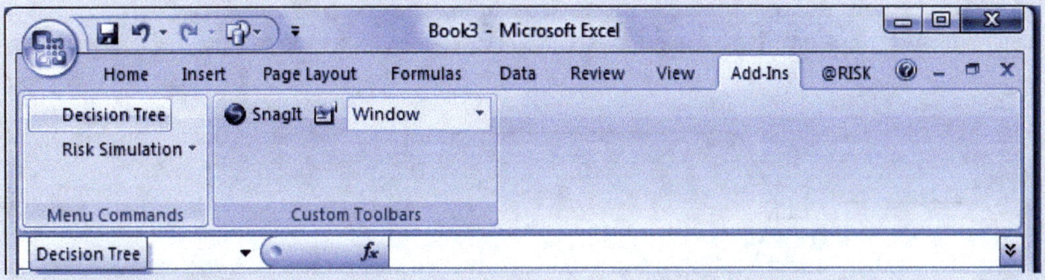

FIGURE 4.32a
Add-ins Tab with Decision Tree Option in the Menu Commands Group for Excel 2007

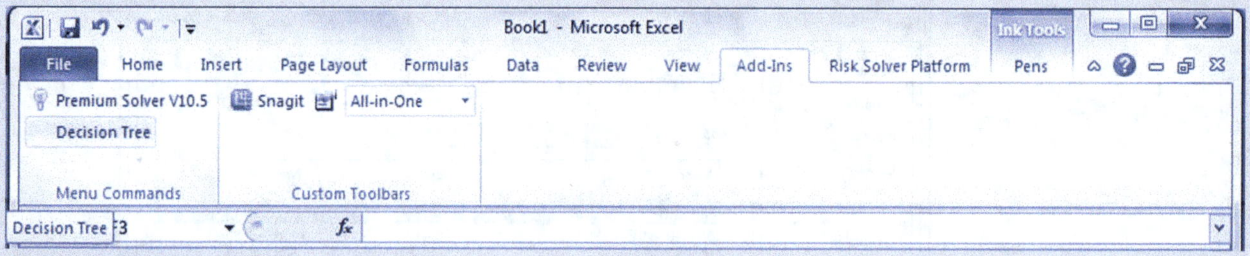

FIGURE 4.32b
Add-ins Tab with Decision Tree Option in the Menu Commands Group for Excel 2010

Creating an Initial Decision Tree in TreePlan

To use TreePlan, open Excel, choose the Tools menu, and click on Decision Tree . . . menu. The menu displayed should resemble Figure 4.33. TreePlan defines decision nodes in the same manner as the text, but refers to chance nodes as event nodes. The two terms will be used synonymously throughout the rest of the text.

Click the New Tree button and a decision tree will appear in the active Excel worksheet. The decision tree generated should resemble Figure 4.34.

Adding, Changing, and/or Modifying a Decision Tree in TreePlan

Once the initial tree has been created in Excel, the user can modify it by adding branches, chance nodes, or additional decision nodes. Please read the following note regarding data input into TreePlan and refer to Figure 4.35 for a visual display of the concept. The next section details the instructions for modifying a decision tree in TreePlan.

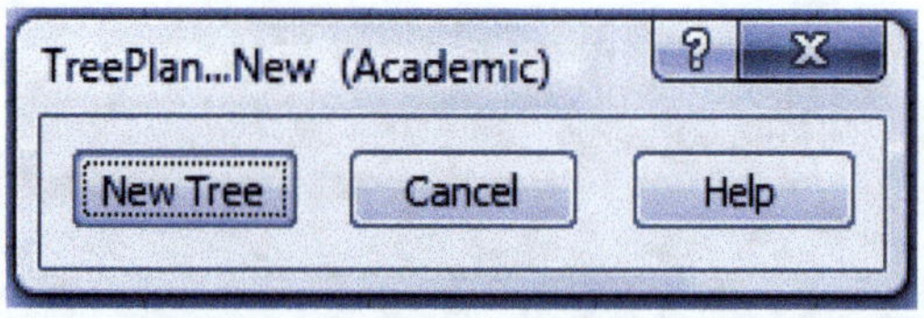

FIGURE 4.33
Initial Treeplan Menu in Excel

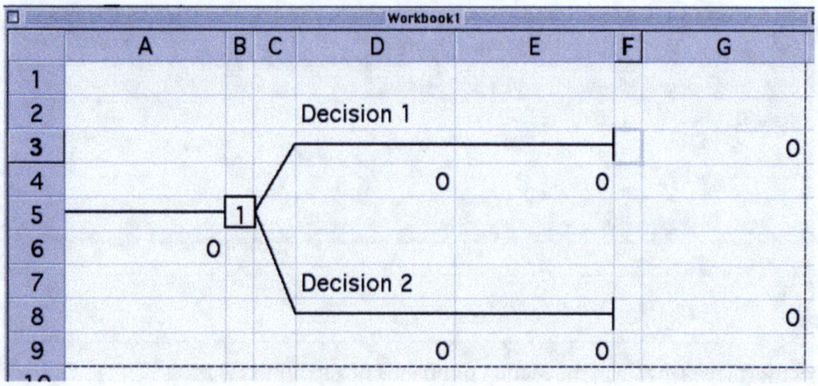

FIGURE 4.34
Initial Decision Tree

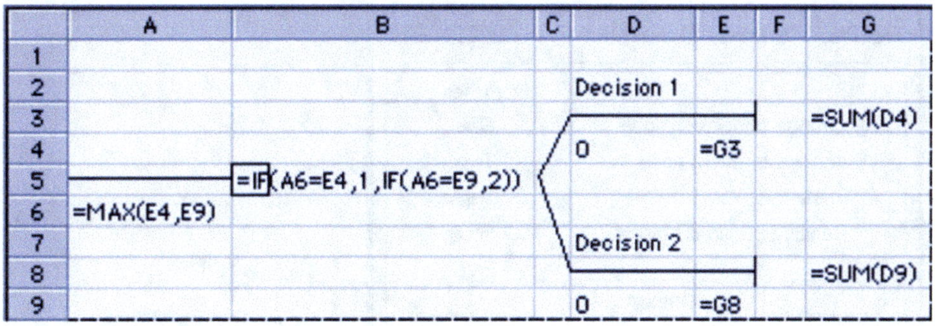

FIGURE 4.35
Treeplan Formula Example

Note: Do not type cells that contain formulas. This invalidates the tree and consequent tree calculations.

ADDING CHANCE NODES

1. To add a chance node in TreePlan, place the cursor at the end of a branch at the T intersection, or terminal node. The placement of the cursor should resemble that in Figure 4.36.
2. After placing the cursor, click on the Tools menu and chose the Decision Tree option.
3. A dialog box resembling Figure 4.37 will appear.
4. Chose the option you wish to perform. For example, in Figure 4.38 the cursor is at the end of a terminal node and an event node is to be added. Therefore, click on the Change to event node button and click OK.
5. The tree in your workbook should resemble Figure 4.39 after this procedure is finished.

MODIFYING DECISION NODES

1. To modify a decision node in TreePlan, place the cursor on the decision node you wish to modify.
2. Chose the Decision Tree . . . option from the Tools menu. A menu resembling Figure 4.39 should appear.

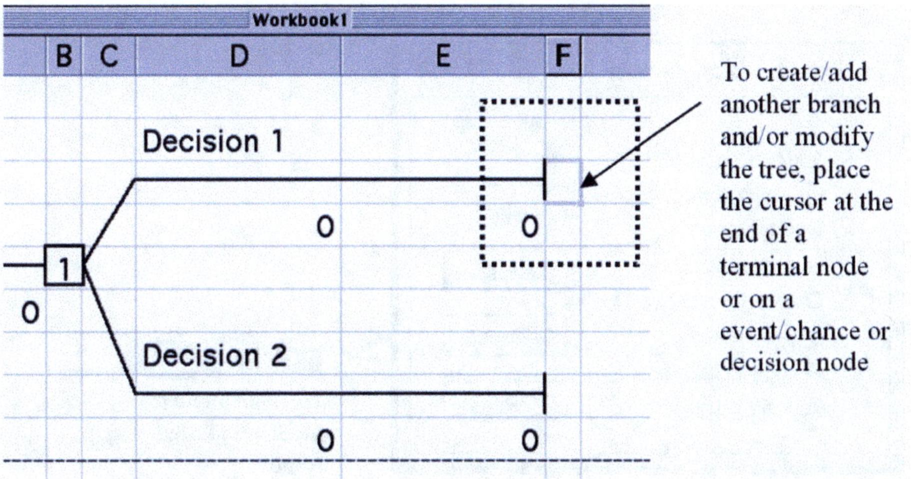

FIGURE 4.36
Cursor Placement for Modifying Trees in TreePlan

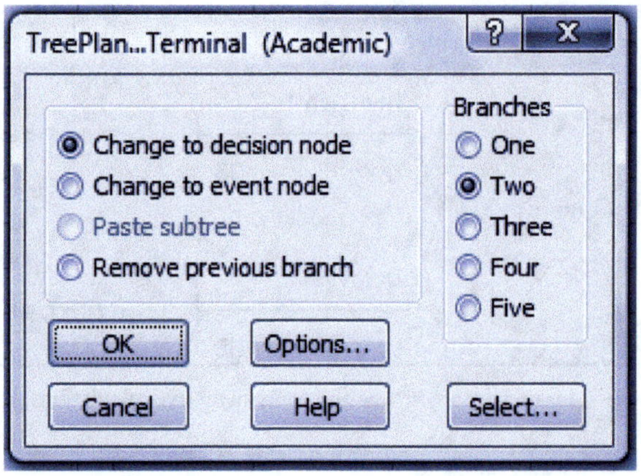

FIGURE 4.37
TreePlan Add/Change/Modify Dialog Box

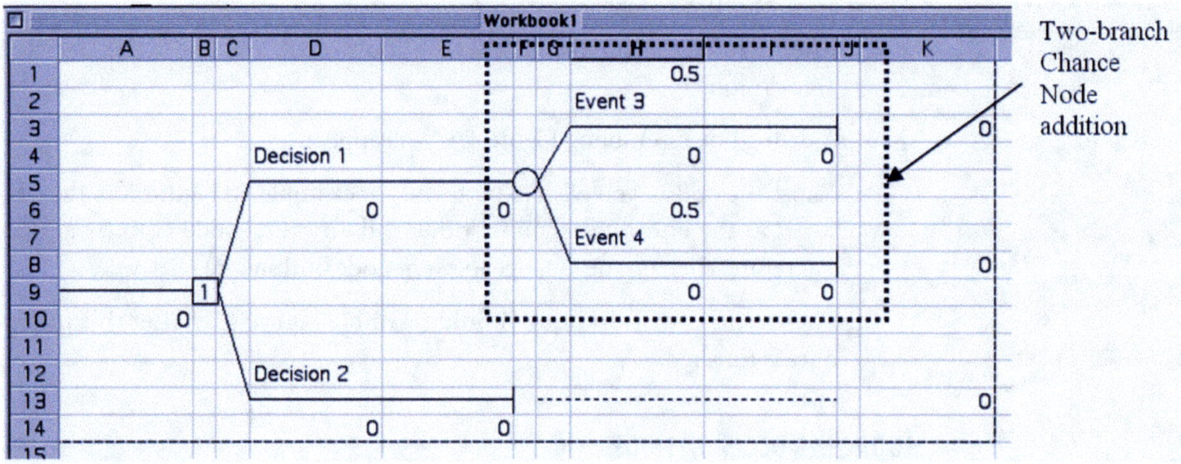

FIGURE 4.38
Decision Tree with Chance Node Added

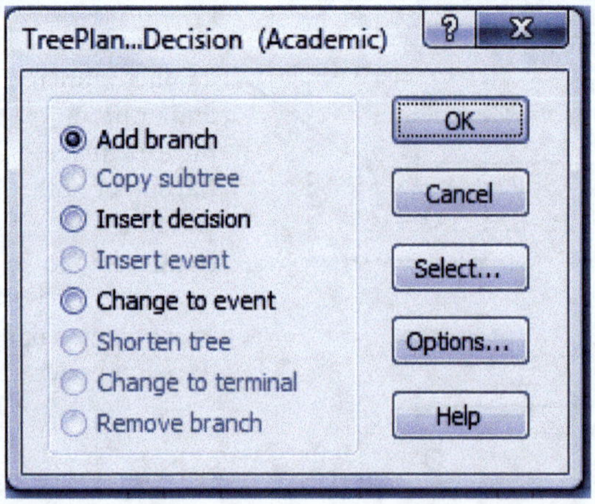

FIGURE 4.39
TreePlan Menu for Modifying an Existing Node

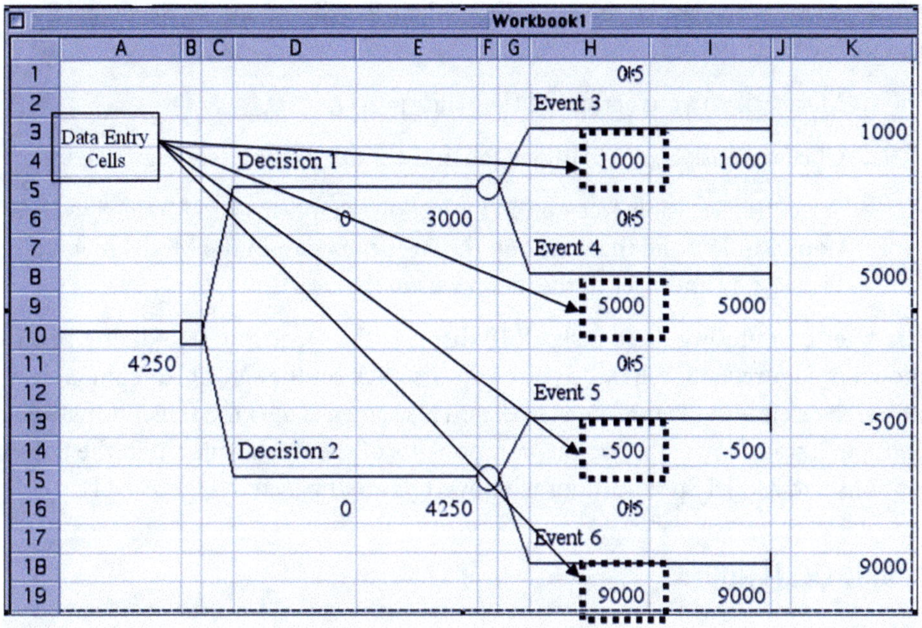

FIGURE 4.40
Example Tree Depicting Data Entry Areas

3. From the menu in Figure 4.39, chose the instruction you wish to have TreePlan perform.
4. The same procedure can be used to modify chance nodes.

These commands for adding chance nodes and/or modifying decision nodes can be combined to create detailed sequential decision trees. A few items must be taken note of whenever you are developing a decision trees in TreePlan:

- As a previous note cautions, **do not type in the cells** that contain formulas in TreePlan. Figure 4.40 displays a generic two-decision, two-state decision tree. Dashed boxes mark the cells where data should be entered and asterisks mark the cells where probabilities should be entered.
- It is acceptable to enter data into any of the cells containing a probability (refer to the asterisked numbers in Figure 4.40). However, the user must keep in mind the rules of probability. **If the sum of the event probabilities does not add to 1.0, TreePlan will return an error.**
- **It is easier to go forward building a tree than to undo hastily made branches or nodes.** Draw the tree on paper first and then proceed in TreePlan.

Creating Decision Trees with Risk Solver Platform

The Excel add-in Risk Solver Platform (RSP) includes a tool that assists in creating and analyzing decision trees. The next section illustrates how to use this tool to develop tree models.

To create a decision tree using Risk Solver Platform, open a new workbook and follow these steps:

1. Make cell A1 your active cell (i.e., click in A1).
2. Click the Risk Solver Platform tab in the Excel Ribbon (see Figure 4.41)
3. Select the Decision Tree option in the Solver Options and Model Specifications window and then click on the large plus sign in the Model menu (see Figure 4.42 and refer to the menu within the oval).

After completing these tasks, RSP displays the Decision Tree dialog box as shown in Figure 4.43. When this box appears click on the OK button and a decision tree resembling Figure 4.44 appears. This screen is also the screen for adding nodes to a tree. Notice the various components of the tree displayed in the Solver Options and Model Specifications window (refer to the oval in Figure 4.44).

ADDING EVENT NODES

1. To add a event or decision node, first you must decide where you wish to add a node and which type of node you wish to add. For this example, we will add an event node to the first branch in the tree, Decision 1. In general, the process is the same for either type of node.

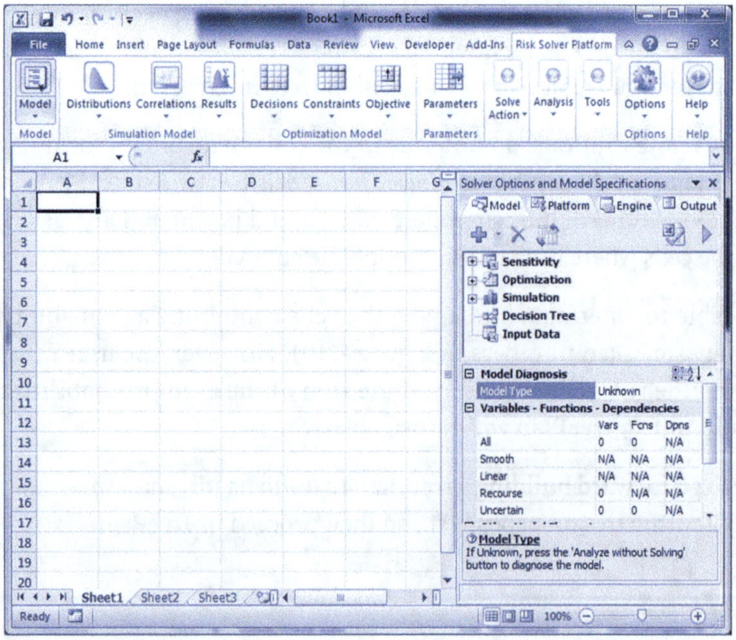

FIGURE 4.41

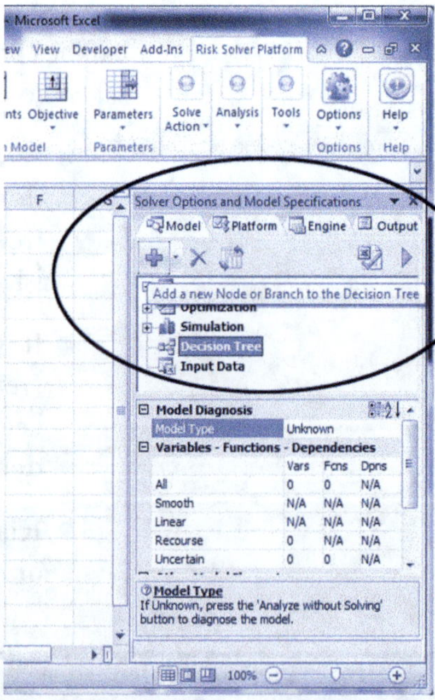

FIGURE 4.42

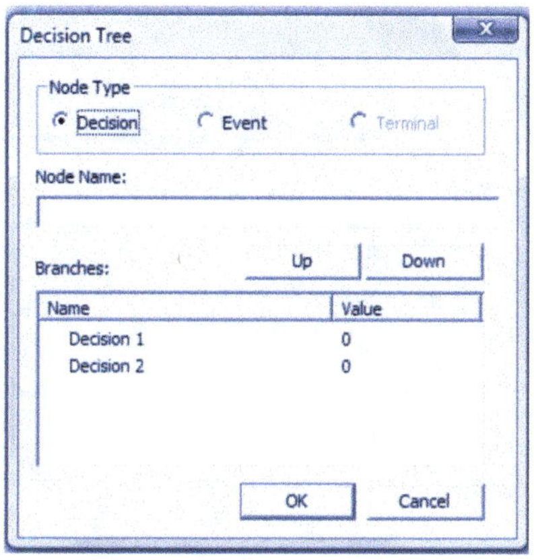

FIGURE 4.43

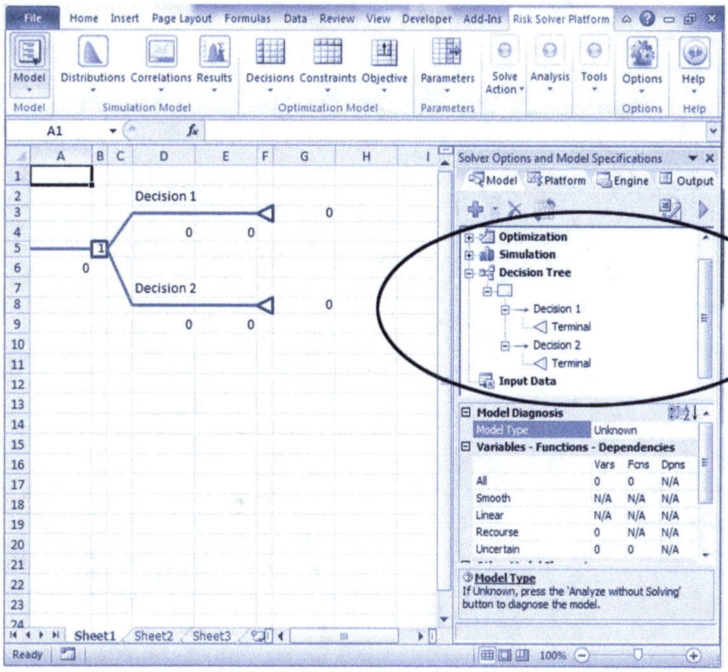

FIGURE 4.44

2. Chose the cell (in this case cell F3) associated with the terminal node for Decision Node 1 (see Figure 4.45 and the cell within the oval).
3. Click on the large plus sign in the Model menu within the Solver Options and Model Specifications window. Figure 4.43 reappears. As previously state this is also the menu for adding event and/or decision nodes.
4. Click Event and then the OK button. An event node with two events is now displayed (see Figure 4.46).

MODIFYING NODES

1. To change an existing node, double click on the node description in the in the Model menu within the Solver Options and Model Specifications window. Figure 4.43 reappears and now you can change the node to another type if you wish.
2. To delete a node and its corresponding branches, click on the mode description in in the Model menu within the Solver Options and Model Specifications window and click the large X in the Model menu.

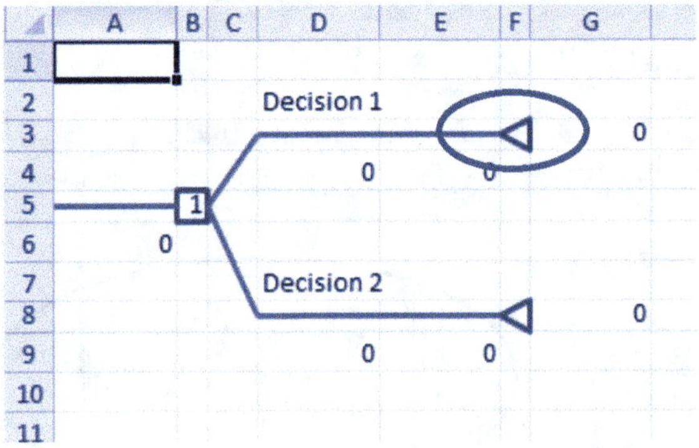

FIGURE 4.45

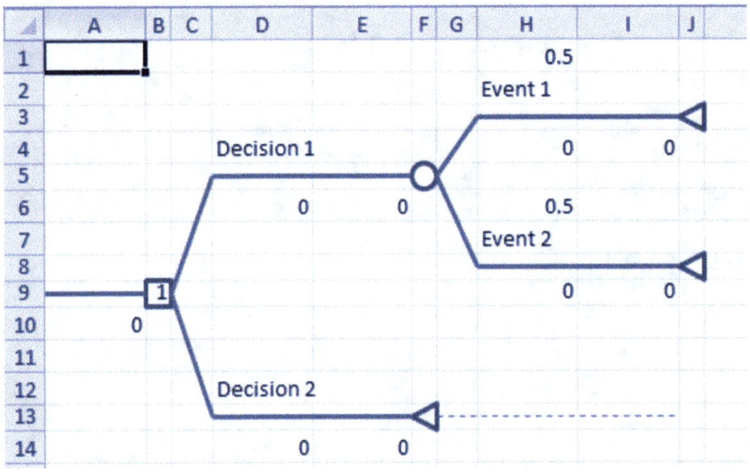

FIGURE 4.46

ADDING NAMES, VALUES, AND PROBABILITIES

These commands for adding chance nodes and/or modifying decision nodes can be combined to create detailed sequential decision trees. A few items must be taken note of whenever you are developing a decision trees in RSP:

- As a previous note cautions, do not type in the cells that contain formulas in RSP. Figure 4.47 displays a generic two-decision, two-state decision tree. Ovals mark the cells where data should be entered and dashed arrows mark the cells where probabilities should be entered.
- It is acceptable to enter data into any of the cells containing a probability (refer to the numbers denoted by dashed arrows in Figure 4.47). However, the user must keep in mind the rules of probability. If the sum of the event probabilities does not add to 1.0, RSP will return an error.
- It is easier to go forward building a tree than to undo hastily made branches or nodes. Draw the tree on paper first and then proceed in RSP.

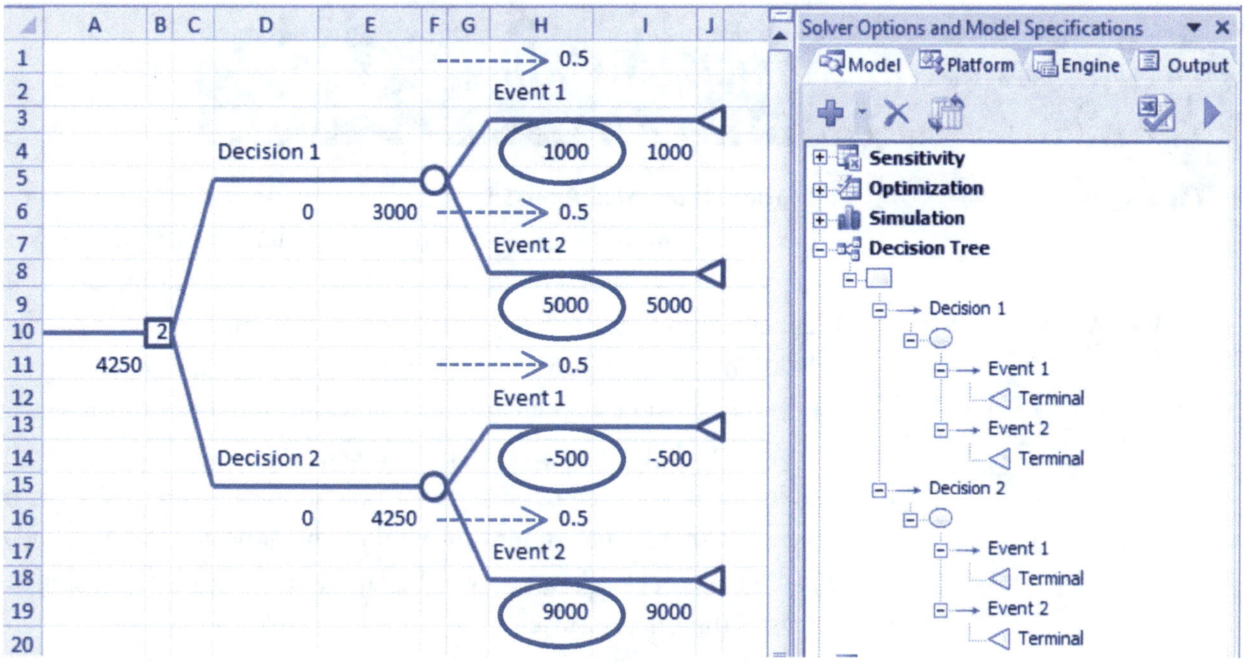

FIGURE 4.47

Summary

This chapter illustrates how decision analysis can be used to structure and analyze decisions involving numerous and conflicting alternatives. A rational methodology has been put forth for a manager to become a more effective and efficient problem solver. The goal of decision analysis is to identify the best alternative in the face of uncertain or risky future conditions.

Three types of criteria were presented for making decisions not based on probability assessments: the maximax, the maximin, and the minimax regret. The concept of expected values and the Hurwicz criterion were linked with the issue of probability assessment and decision analysis. Three areas of sensitivity analysis were explored and the idea was presented that the decision analysis framework and sensitivity analysis provide a manager with a rational method to compare and ultimately make a choice.

A completed decision tree and/or influence diagram expresses the structure of a formal model. They provide participants in the modeling process a means of communication. They also serve as the framework for expressing more specifically the exact nature of relationships.

The following example executive summary illustrates the application of the concepts discussed in this chapter.

Business Decision Modeling Behind the Scenes

The Story of John von Neumann

The Father of Decision Analysis

John von Neumann (1903–1957), often considered to be the father of decision analysis, was a child prodigy born into a banking family in Budapest, Hungary. At the age of 6, von Neumann was able to divide eight-digit numbers in his head. From the age of 13 he showed a pronounced interest in mathematics, which was fostered by his teachers at the Lutheran High School of Budapest. After graduation from high school, von Neumann studied chemistry for 2 years in Berlin and for 2 years in Zurich, but spent much of his time with mathematicians, taking a Ph.D. in mathematics at the University of Budapest not long after receiving his chemistry diploma at Zurich.

Mathematician, Economist, and Physicist

Von Neumann lectured at Berlin from 1926 to 1929 and at Hamburg from 1929 to 1930. In 1930 von Neumann became a visiting lecturer at Princeton University, being appointed professor there in 1931. He became one of the original six mathematics professors in 1933 at the newly founded Institute for Advanced Study in Princeton, a position he kept for the remainder of his life.

Von Neumann's brilliant work in mathematics also carried him into theoretical economics and technology as well as theoretical physics—areas where he was able to make vital contributions not only to science but also to the welfare of his adopted country. His work in quantum mechanics gave him a profound knowledge concerning the application of nuclear energy to military and peacetime uses, enabling him to occupy an important place in the scientific councils of the nation.

Developer of Atomic Bomb and Advisor to the Atomic Energy Commission

During the Second World War, he played a major role among the Los Alamos group of scientists who developed the atomic bomb. After the war he served on the advisory committee of the Atomic Energy Commission and on the commission itself from 1954 until his death.

Optimal Information Area

http://mondrian.princeton.edu/CampusWWW/Companion/von_neumann_john.html

http://ei.cs.vt.edu/~history/VonNeumann.html

EXECUTIVE SUMMARY FOR STEVE'S MUTUAL FUND DECISION

TO: Steve Puryear
FROM: Steve's Consulting Group

Problem Identification

Steve is faced with a dilemma in deciding which mutual fund to invest his money in. Each of the three funds' potential returns is forecasted according to two possible future economic conditions, good and bad at 40% and 60% respectively. Steve assumes that the forecasted returns for the funds are accurate and he bases his decision on the figures given.

Modeling the Problem

To avoid rash decision making, Steve decides to conduct a series of quantitative method decision analyses to resolve his dilemma. The methods that Steve employs are the maximax, maximin, minimax regret, and Hurwicz decision criteria.

By simply using the different decision criteria analysis, Steve simply cannot make a decisive decision since all three funds appear superior in one criterion to another. Thus, Steve decides to conduct a sensitivity analysis using the Hurwicz criterion by using a range of possible alpha level ranging from 0.00 to 1.00. The results are shown in graphical format below. This section details three areas of sensitivity analysis for Steve's decision problem.

TABLE 1: PAYOFF TABLE DECISION CRITERIA

Fund	Maximax	Maximin	Minimax regret	Hurwicz
Stock fund	20.00%			
Index fund			6.00%	6.00%
Bond index		4.00%		

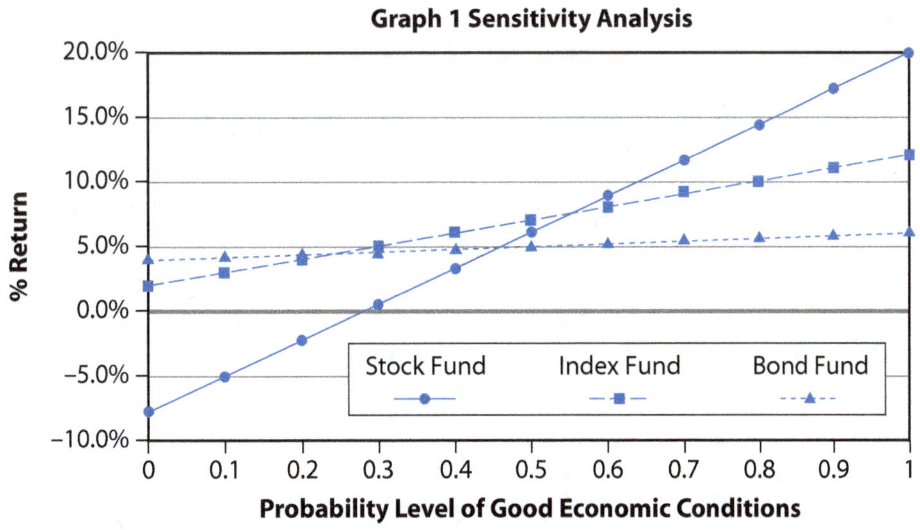

GRAPH 1. Sensitivity Analysis

(continues)

EXECUTIVE SUMMARY FOR STEVE'S MUTUAL FUND DECISION (CONTINUED)

Dominance

No dominant solution was identified by the previous analysis. Therefore, Graph 1 displays a sensitivity analysis for Steve's decision. It is apparent from the graph that each of the decisions is dominant at some level of economic conditions. The Bond Fund is dominant for approximately the first quarter of the graph, while the Index Fund is dominant over approximately the second quarter of the graph. The Stock Fund then dominates roughly the second half of the graph.

Trade-offs

After conducting the sensitivity analysis, Steve can see that there are several trade-offs. Trade-offs occur between each of Steve's decisions, specifically where the various funds cross each other on the sensitivity graph (e.g., at around 25% and 55%).

Sensitivity Analysis: Dominance, Trade-offs, and Risks

Graph 1 shows where the various funds cross each other (i.e., at around 25% and 55%).

Risk

Considering the difficulty in accurately predicting future economic conditions, we recommend that Steve consider the risk of each investment. Risk can be defined and quantified by range (i.e., high value–low value). The stock fund exhibits the largest risk (range = 28) followed by the index fund (range = 10), with the bond fund having the lowest risk (range = 2).

Conclusions and Action Items

With Steve being a very conservative investor, we recommend he invest in the bond fund where return will range between 4.00 and 6.00%. For Steve, the other two funds are simply too volatile; their return fluctuates too much and they are more risky.

CASE STUDY

Ibañez Produce

Background

Mike Ibañez had a big decision to make. He had inherited his family's vegetable business. Ibañez Produce grew, harvested, packaged, and sold produce. Mike was concerned because a large storm was approaching and he had to make a decision regarding his lettuce crop.

Ibañez Produce had around 10,000 acres in cultivation and lettuce made up around 25% of the total crop value. Mike's concern was that the storm might bring severe winds and dust. Rain was not a major concern, but high winds and blowing dust wreaked havoc on the lettuce crop. The high winds generally tear apart the lettuce and the dust renders the crop almost unsalvageable.

The Solution

From his father's records, he had read that if he applied water combined with standard wax a residue would form on the lettuce and the crop could be saved. He knew that if the storm did come he could lose the whole crop if it was not protected. However, he didn't know how much the solution would cost him or how much he should pay.

The Outcomes

Mike knew that the storm had about a 50/50 chance of hitting. He also knew that if the storm did not hit and he did protect his crops the residue left might cause problems during harvest. After conversing with his Co-op Extension officer, he had surmised that the probability of the residue causing problems was around 30%. If this problem did occur, Mike would get only 80% of his normal crop.

Mike usually sold his lettuce with a $0.15 margin per pound. Normally the crop was around 800,000 pounds. If he did not protect his crop and the storm hit, he maybe could salvage 10% of the lettuce. However, if he did protect and the storm did hit, there was no guarantee that 100% of the crop would be saved.

In fact, from the information the Co-op Extension officer had provided, there was around a 60% chance that he would lose part of his crop even if he did take protective measures and the storm hit. He surmised that three scenarios could occur in this case: a 90% salvage rate, a 75% salvage rate, and a 50% salvage rate. Mike thought these three scenarios had equal probability.

Mike's Decision Problem

Mike also knew that if he harvested right now he could make $0.05 margin per pound on the total crop of lettuce. Overall operating costs were about the same in any situation. Mike needs to know if he should protect his crop and a starting point on what he should pay. Help Mike with his dilemma.

Discussion Questions

1. What is Mike's expected gross revenue if he harvests now? What is his gross expected revenue if he does nothing and waits out the storm? What are the risks in choosing to harvest now or in waiting out the storm?
2. Is it a good idea for Mike to protect his crop? Why? What is the maximum that Mike should pay for the protection?

Optimal Information Area

Lexicon of Decision Analysis
http://faculty.fuqua.duke.edu/daweb/lexicon.htm

References

Bayes, T., "An Essay towards solving a problem in the doctrine of chances," *Phil. Trans. Royal Society,* vol. 53 (1763), pp. 370–418.

Bazerman, Max, and Margaret Neale, *Negotiating Rationally,* New York: Free Press, 1992.

French, Simon, *Decision Theory: An Introduction to the Mathematics of Rationality,* London: John Wiley & Sons, 1986.

Hogarth, Robin M., *Judgment and Choice,* 2nd ed., New York: John Wiley & Sons, 1987.

Howard, Ronald A., and James Matheson (eds.), *The Principles and Applications of Decision Analysis* (2 volumes). Palo Alto, CA: Strategic Decisions Group, 1983.

Daniel Kahneman, Paul Slovic, and Amos Tversky (1982) *Judgment under Uncertainty: Heuristics and Biases.* Cambridge: Cambridge University Press.

Keeney, Ralph, *Value-Focused Thinking: A Path to Creative Decision Making,* Cambridge, MA: Harvard University Press, 1992.

Lindley, Dennis V., *Making Decisions,* 2nd ed., New York: John Wiley & Sons, 1985. (This is a classic by a founder in the field. Professor Lindley explains difficult concepts well. The problems tend to be somewhat abstract.)

Miller, G. A., The Magical Number Seven Plus or Minus Two: Some Limits on Our Capacity for Processing Information, *Psychological Review,* vol. 63 (1956), pp. 81–97.

Morgan, M. Granger, and Max Henrion, *Uncertainty: A Guide to Dealing with Uncertainty in Quantitative Risk and Policy Analysis,* Cambridge, England: Cambridge University Press.

von Neumann, J., and O. Morgenstern, *Theory of Games and Economic Behaviour,* Princeton, NJ: Princeton University Press, 1944.

Raiffa, Howard, *Decision Analysis,* Reading, MA: Addison-Wesley, 1968.

PROBLEMS

1. Mr. Merrill Lynch is planning on investing in stocks. He is considering three different types stocks, ABC, DEF, and XYZ to choose from under two possible states, good and bad. As a result of favorable stock market conditions, there is a 0.75 probability of good and 0.25 probability of bad state. The table below indicates the profits and losses of investing in the following three stocks under the given states—good and bad.

STOCKS	GOOD (0.75)	BAD (0.25)
ABC	\$75,000	\$45,000
DEF	\$90,000	–\$30,000
XYZ	\$35,000	\$15,000

Using Excel, set up a spreadsheet to find the best decision using:

a. Maximax

b. Maximin

c. Equal likelihood

d. Expected value

2. Etsuko needs to decide between two choices stock investments—IBN and Microsopht. The return for each investment given two future economic conditions is shown in the following payoff table. Set up an Excel spreadsheet to determine what probability for each market condition would make her investment choice even between IBN and Microsopht.

DECISION	BOOM	STEADY
IBN	\$6,000	\$1,500
Microsopht	\$100,000	–\$40,000

3. SellsLotsOfStuff.com, a small online retailer, is considering buying a firewall for its website. The cost of the firewall is \$10,000. There is an 85% chance that the site will not be hackerattacked during the life of the firewall, a 10% chance of a minor attack occurring resulting in \$25,000 in damage, and a 5% chance of a major attack occurring resulting in \$125,000 in damage. Construct an Excel spreadsheet to:

a. Compute the expected cost for each decision and select the best one strictly on the basis of expected cost.

b. Discuss the risks involved with basing the decision strictly on expected cost.

4. A company is planning to start a manufacturing unit. The success of the manufacturing unit depends on the ability of the company to obtain patent approval on a product. The company can invest to receive patents from the U.S. government. If the company is successful in its patent application, it can make \$60,000. If it doesn't receive the patent, the company will make \$5,000. Or the company can fund a caucus for election 2000; if it is accepted then the company can make \$50,000, or else it

loses $20,000. Or if the company goes for an awareness campaign, it can make $25,000, but if it is not successful, then the return will be only $10,000. Probability of success is 0.6 and of failure is 0.4. Construct an Excel spreadsheet to find the best decision using the following:

a. Maximax

b. Maximin

c. Equal likelihood

d. Expected value

e. Create a sensitivity graph comparing the different alternatives as the probability of success changes.

5. John has to determine which stock he should invest in: stock A or stock B. The economic conditions, good and poor, will determine the profit and loss from his investment. Construct an Excel spreadsheet to compute the expected value for each decision and select the best one.

DECISION	GOOD (0.6)	POOR (0.4)
Stock A	$12,000	–$3,000
Stock B	$3,500	$3,000

Using the spreadsheet find the best decision for the following:

a. Maximax

b. Maximin

c. Equal likelihood

d. Expected value

e. What does the probability of good have to be to make the two decisions equally attractive with regard to expected value?

6. Etsuko, who is an HPU student, is wondering whether she should purchase HMSA health insurance or not for next year. Construct an Excel spreadsheet to compute the expected value to determine whether she should purchase HMSA or not. Is one option riskier than the other? Explain.

DECISION	NO ACCIDENT (0.99)	ACCIDENT (0.01)
Purchase HMSA	$416	$416
Do not purchase HMSA	$0	$50,000

7. A machine shop owner is attempting to decide whether to purchase a new drill press, a lathe, or a grinder. The return from each will be determined by whether the company succeeds in getting a government military contract. The profit or loss from each purchase and the probabilities associated with each contract outcomes are shown in the following payoff table. Construct an Excel spreadsheet to:

a. Compute the expected value for each purchase and select the best one.

b. Decide if one purchase more risky than another. Explain.

PURCHASE	CONTRACT (0.7)	NO CONTRACT (0.3)
Drill press	$40,000	–$8,000
Lathe	$20,000	$4,000
Grinder	$12,000	$10,000

8. A farmer needs to decide which crops to grow this year. According to his Farmer's Almanac, there is a 0.45 probability that the weather will be good this year and a 0.55 probability that it will be bad. The following table is given. Construct an Excel spreadsheet to:

a. Determine which crop he should grow this year if he wants to maximize expected value.

b. Create a sensitivity graph comparing the different alternatives as the probability of success changes.

PURCHASE	GOOD (0.45)	BAD (0.55)
Soy	$100,000	–$30,000
Corn	$80,000	–$10,000
Potatoes	$90,000	–$2,000

9. ABC can sell surfboards or body boards. The revenues of selling and producing surfboards or body boards depend on how the waves are during this season. If the waves, on average, are bigger than 5 feet, producing and selling surfboards will result in sales of $4,000,000, while producing and selling body boards will lead to sales of $1,500,000. If the waves are smaller than 5 feet, surfboards will result in sales of $1,000,000 and body boards will result in sales of $3,500,000. According to the latest forecast for the 3-month period, there is a 60% chance of getting waves bigger than 5 feet on average.

Create a payoff table in Excel and use it to find the following:

a. Maximax

b. Maximin

c. Equal likelihood

d. Expected value

e. Create a sensitivity graph comparing the different alternatives as the probability of success changes.

10. Rob's three brothers offer to buy his mint-condition Yugo. They each offer different payment plans. Each brother has an interesting situation that might make him completely default on the payment plan.

Ryan will buy the Yugo outright for $1,500 cash. There is a 0.20 probability that his cash is counterfeit and worthless.

Ronald will pay $1,000 outright in noncounterfeit money and pay $500 at the end of the year for the next 2 years. There is a 0.30 probability that Ronald will go bankrupt by the end of the year and never pay Rob any more than the original $1,000.

Ray will pay no money down but will pay $500 at the end of the year for 5 years. There is a 0.40 probability that Ray will flee the country to Mexico at the end of the third year.

Construct an Excel spreadsheet to analyze Rob's offers. On the basis of expected value what is the best choice for Rob? What is the risk associated with this choice?

11. A computer company is contemplating whether to buy a new server, router, or phone system. The return from each will be determined by whether the company gets picked for a contract. The probability that the company will get the contract is 70%, and the probability that the company doesn't get the contract is 30%. Construct an Excel spreadsheet to determine the equipment that will give the best-expected returns.

PURCHASE	CONTRACT (0.7)	NO CONTRACT (0.3)
Server	$70,000	–$10,000
Router	$90,000	–$15,000
Phone system	$60,000	–$2,000

12. Kristine is helping her cousin Logan (5 years old) develop his business spirit. He can sell either lemonade or coffee at his corner stand. If it is a sunny day, Logan will sell 55 glasses of lemonade and 12 cups of coffee. If it is an overcast day, Logan will sell 10 glasses of lemonade and 12 cups of coffee. If it is a rainy day, Logan will sell 0 glasses of lemonade and 40 cups of coffee. Both of the beverages sell for $0.50. The weather forecast calls for 40% chance of rain, 40% chance of sun, and 20% chance of overcast.

   a. In Excel, develop a payoff table for the above situation.

   b. Using the spreadsheet, find the following:
      i. Maximax
      ii. Maximin
      iii. Equal likelihood

   c. Using the spreadsheet, create a sensitivity graph comparing the different alternatives as the probability of success changes.

13. Ricardo and sons are planning to invest in advertising to sell three of their products. There are three different outcomes: A sells the most, B sells the most, or C sells the most. Two possible states exist, good and bad. The table below indicates the profits and losses of investing in the advertising of the three products under given states—good and bad. Construct an Excel spreadsheet to answer the following:

   a. Determine which product they should invest in this year based on maximizing expected value.

   b. Create a sensitivity graph comparing the different alternatives as the probability of Good changes.

PRODUCT	GOOD (0.6)	BAD (0.4)
A	$5.0 million	$0 million
B	$2.5 million	$2.5 million
C	$7.5 million	–$2.5 million

14. A new small manufacturing company, which produces toys, has to decide whether it wants to distribute its product through a wholesale distributor, go directly to department stores, or open its own store. The table below shows the revenue results for each decision. Construct an Excel spreadsheet to answer the following:

a. What is the probability value of good economic conditions that will make distributing through a wholesaler or direct sales equal? What is the probability value to equate wholesaler and own store?

b. Create a sensitivity graph comparing the different alternatives as the probability of good economic conditions changes.

DISTRIBUTION NETWORK	GOOD ECONOMIC CONDITIONS	NOT-SO-GOOD ECONOMIC CONDITIONS
Wholesale	$75.0 million	$60 million
Direct	$82.5 million	$12.5 million
Own store	$177.5 million	–$112.5 million

15. Tech and A&M are in the fourth quarter of their annual football game. A&M has the ball, and it is third down and 10 yards to go on their own 30. A&M's offensive coordinator is trying to determine what play to call to get the necessary 10 yards. A screen pass has an 85% chance of being completed, and if completed, has a 20% chance of gaining 20 yards, a 30% chance of gaining 10 yards, and a 50% chance of gaining 5 yards. A slant pass has a 60% chance of being completed, and if completed has a 30% chance of gaining 20 yards, a 40% chance of gaining 12 yards, and a 30% chance of gaining 8 yards. A bomb has a 20% chance of being completed, and if completed has a 20% chance of gaining 40 yards, a 20% chance of gaining 50 yards, and a 60% chance of gaining 70 yards. A&M receives no yards if the pass is incomplete.

a. Using TreePlan, create a decision tree for this problem, computing the expected yardage under each scenario.

b. Which decision should A&M make if they want to maximize expected total yards?

c. Which decision should they make if they want to maximize their chance for a first down (>10 yards)?

16. The profit level for a router manufacturer using three different plants 1, 2, and 3 and the demand level A, B, and C, is given by the following table ($000). Construct an Excel spreadsheet to answer the following:

a. For the information in the table, what decision would be made by using the maximax criterion?

b. For the information in the table, what decision would be made by using the maximin criterion?

c. For the information in the table, what decision would be made using the minimax regret criterion?

d. Using the information in the table and TreePlan, draw a decision tree for the problem. Be sure to carefully label the branches of the tree and provide the value at each node.

	DEMAND		
PLANT	A	B	C
1	200	350	600
2	250	350	540
3	300	375	490

17. A couple has just purchased a second home to remodel into a bed and breakfast. The table below contains their expected profit ($000s) the first year, depending on how many rooms they choose to remodel and demand. Construct an Excel spreadsheet to answer the following:

a. For the information in the table, what decision would be made if the maximax criterion is used?

b. For the information in the table, what decision would be made if the maximin criterion is used?

c. For the information in the table, what decision would be made if the minimax regret criterion is used?

d. For the information in the table, what decision would be made if the equal likelihood criterion is used?

e. For the information in the table, what decision would be made if the Hurwicz criterion is used with alpha = 0.75?

f. For the information in the table, what is the expected value of each alternative? What is the best decision?

g. Using the information in the table and TreePlan, draw a decision tree for the problem. Be sure to carefully label the branches of the tree and provide the value at each node.

	DEMAND		
ALTERNATIVE	LOW (0.30)	MODERATE (0.50)	HEAVY (0.20)
5 rooms	15	20	25
10 rooms	10	35	50
15 rooms	5	50	75

18. Legal Services of Kinston is going to increase its capacity to provide free legal advice but must decide whether to do so by hiring another full-time attorney or by using part-time attorneys. The table below shows the expected costs of the two options for three possible demand levels.

	STATES OF NATURE		
ALTERNATIVE	LOW DEMAND	MEDIUM DEMAND	HIGH DEMAND
Hire full time	$300	$500	$700
Hire part time	$0	$350	$1,000
Probabilities	0.25	0.45	0.30

a. Using Excel, calculate the expected value of each alternative.

b. What should Legal Services do?

19. Chad Holmes has been thinking about starting his own independent gasoline station. Chad's problem is to decide how large his station should be. The annual returns will depend on both the size of the station and a number of marketing factors related to the oil industry and demand for gasoline. After a careful analysis, Chad developed the following table:

SIZE OF FIRST STATION	GOOD MARKET ($)	MODERATE MARKET ($)	POOR MARKET ($)
Small	55,000	25,000	10,000
Medium	85,000	35,000	–20,000
Large	150,000	35,000	–40,000
Very large	350,000	25,000	–160,000

a. Using Excel, determine the maximax decision.

b. Using Excel, determine the maximin decision.

c. Using Excel, determine the equally likely decision.

20. The following table displays the sales levels for different scenarios for a bakery. Construct an Excel spreadsheet to answer the following:

a. For the data in the table, what is the expected value of profit for each level of inventory (i.e., 10, 11, 12, and 13 dozen)?

b. For the data in the table, what decision would be made using the Hurwicz criterion (with alpha = 0.3)?

c. On the basis of expected value, what level of inventory would you tell the bakery to hold and why? How does this differ from your recommendation in part e?

	SALES LEVEL			
	10 DOZEN	11 DOZEN	12 DOZEN	13 DOZEN
	PROBABILITY			
INVENTORY LEVEL	0.10	0.20	0.40	0.30
10 dozen	$3,000	$3,000	$3,000	$3,000
11 dozen	$2,970	$3,300	$3,300	$3,300
12 dozen	$2,940	$3,270	$3,600	$3,600
13 dozen	$2,910	$3,240	$3,570	$3,900

21. A T-shirt salesperson at a Lynyrd Skynyrd concert tour created a table of conditional values for the various alternatives (stocking decision) and states of nature (size of crowd):

	STATES OF NATURE (DEMAND)		
DECISION ALTERNATIVES	HEAVY	AVERAGE	LIGHT
Larger stock	$24,000	$10,000	–$2,000
Average stock	$16,000	$8,000	$6,000
Smaller stock	$8,000	$6,000	$4,000

The probabilities associated with the states of nature are 0.35 for a heavy demand, 0.45 for an average demand, and 0.20 for a light demand.

a. Using Excel, determine the alternative that provides the greatest expected value.

b. Using Excel, compute the expected value of perfect information (EVPI).

22. The Dandy Don Specialty Co. is considering a new consumer product. Managers believe that there is a probability of 0.45 that the Jim Dandy Co. will come out with a competitive product. If Dandy Don adds an assembly line for the product and Jim Dandy Co. does not follow with a competitive product, Dandy Don's expected profit is $60,000; if Dandy Don adds an assembly line and Jim Dandy follows suit, Dandy

Don still expects $12,000 profit. If Dandy Don builds a new plant addition and Jim Dandy does not produce a competitive product, Dandy Don expects a profit of $650,000; if Jim Dandy does compete for this market, Dandy Don expects a loss of $200,000.

a. Using Excel, develop a payoff table for Dandy Don's decision problem.

b. Using Excel, determine the expected value of each decision.

c. Using Excel, compute the expected value of perfect information.

23. James Bernard, head of leasing at New Braunfels Inc., has to decide whether to build a new state-of the-art processing facility. If the new facility works, the company could realize a profit of $200,000. If it fails, New Braunfels could lose $150,000. At this time, he estimates a 60% chance that the new process will fail. The other option is to build a pilot plant and then decide whether to build a company-wide facility. The pilot plant would cost $10,000 to build. James estimates a 50-50 chance that the pilot plant will work. If the pilot plant works, there is a 90% probability that the complete plant, if it is built, will also work. If the pilot plant does not work, there is only a 20% chance that the complete project (if it is constructed) will work. James faces a dilemma. Should he build the plant? Should he build the pilot project and then make a decision? Help James by analyzing this problem:

a. Create a decision tree, using TreePlan.

b. What recommendation, based on expected value, would you give James?

24. Daryll Miller, president of Seacresst Industries, is considering whether to build a manufacturing plant in the Ozarks. Her prospective revenues for the plant are summarized in the following table:

ALTERNATIVES	FAVORABLE MARKET	UNFAVORABLE MARKET
Build large plant	$400,000	$300,000
Build small plant	$80,000	$80,000
Don't build	$0	$0
Market probabilities	0.33	0.67

a. Construct a decision tree using TreePlan.

b. Determine the best strategy, using expected value.

c. What is the expected value of perfect information (EVPI) and how would it help Daryll make a decision?

25. Jennifer Coggburn buys forms from two suppliers. Supplier A's overall nondefect rate is 90% (i.e., 90% of the time no forms are defective, whereas 10% of the time there are defects). Supplier B's overall nondefect rate is 85% (i.e., 85% of the time no forms are defective, whereas 15% of the time there are defects). The quality of the forms, when forms are defective, from each of the suppliers is indicated in the following table:

PERCENT DEFECTIVE	PROBABILITY FOR SUPPLIER A	PROBABILITY FOR SUPPLIER B
1%	0.70	0.30
2%	0.15	0.45
3%	0.15	0.25

For example, if a batch of forms is defective, the probability that the batch is 1% defective from supplier A is 0.70. Because Jennifer orders 10,000 forms per order, this would mean that there is a 0.7 probability of getting 100 defective forms out of the 10,000 forms if supplier A is used to fill the order. A defective form can be used for other purposes within Jennifer's own department, but it costs her $0.50 per form in internal handling charges to do so. Although the quality of supplier B is lower, it will sell an order of 10,000 forms for $37 less than supplier A.

a. Develop a decision tree, using TreePlan.

b. Which supplier should Jennifer use if she bases her choice on the expected value criterion? (Hint: Jennifer is looking for the least expensive solution.)

CHAPTER

5 Simulation Modeling

LEARNING *Objectives*

- Understand what basic simulation and spreadsheet simulation is
- Understand how simulation can affect and how it can benefit managers
- Develop random number intervals and use them to generate outcomes
- Explain the advantages and disadvantages of simulation
- Develop spreadsheet simulation models for a wide variety of business problems, such as profit/loss generation, queuing, and waiting lines
- Use a commercially available simulation package, such as @Risk or Risk Solver Platform

CHAPTER *Outline*

Business Decision Modeling in Action

The Super Flush Simulation

Business Decision Modeling throughout the Ages

Monte Carlo Simulation

Business Decision Modeling Behind the Scenes

The Major Players and the Story Behind the Development of Monte Carlo Simulation

Simulation Modeling
- Background
- Computer Spreadsheet Simulation
- What Is Simulation? And Why Are We Using It?
- Real-World Simulation Examples

Simulation Affecting Managers
- Types of Data
- Numerical Data—Discrete versus Continuous
- Simulation and the Link to Earlier Chapters
- Simulation, Spreadsheet Modeling, and Model Verification and Validity
- Simulation Verification
- Model Validity

Random Number Generation
- Random Number Generation Techniques
- Developing Random Number Generation Techniques
- Generating Random Numbers by Spreadsheets

Simulation and Currency Exchange Rates
- Cumulative Probability Distributions and Random Number Intervals
- Generating Random Numbers and Simulating Currency Values
- Excel Spreadsheet Simulation of Currency Value Example

Simulation of a Queuing System
- Single Server Waiting Line System
- Where Customers Come From—The Calling Population
- The Order in Which Customers Are Served—The Queue Discipline
- How Often Customers Arrive at the Queue—The Arrival Rate
- How Fast Customers Are Served—The Service Time

Lunch Wagon Simulation Example: Arrivals and Profit Determination
- Customer Spending Habits
- Origination of Probability Distributions
- Random Number and Normal Probability Generation
- Computing Relevant Simulation Statistics and Distributions
- Lunch Wagon Waiting Line Simulation
- Interarrival Times
- Customer Service Times
- Simulation's Real Payoff—The Sensitivity/What-If Analysis

@Risk Tutorial

- Running @Risk in Excel
- What @Risk Will Do for the Modeler
- User Responsibilities
- Getting Started
- Input Cells
- The Triangular Distribution
- The Normal Distribution
- Output Cells
- Summary of Inputs and Outputs
- @Risk Window
- Running a Risk Analysis
- Simulation Data Button
- Simulation Sensitivities Button
- Simulation Scenarios Button

Graphing the Results in @Risk

- Graphing: Understanding the Data More Clearly
- Using @Risk to Create a Histogram of NPV
- Using @Risk to Create a Smooth Bell-Shaped Curve of NPV
- Using @Risk to Create a Cumulative Distribution Graph of NPV
- Cumulative Distribution Outline Graph
- Summary Output Graphs
- Interpretation of the Summary Graph
- Sensitivity Analysis and the Tornado Diagram
- Graphing in Excel
- @Risk Example with Multiple Decision Alternatives
- Structure of Project 2
- Input Cells for Project 2
- Output Cells
- Running the Simulation
- Interpreting the Results
- Dominance
- Trade-offs
- Risk Analysis

Getting Started with RSP and the XYZ Corporation Model

- Input Cells
- Simulation Modeling
- The Normal Distribution
- Output Cells

Business Decision Modeling in Action

The Super Flush Simulation

Simulation at a Major American Football Stadium

A very interesting simulation took place in the summer of 1998 at the Baltimore Ravens' new football stadium in Northern Maryland. The simulation consisted of 600 football fans flushing the stadium's toilets.

Flushing Toilets? Simulation? Is This for Real?

Hundreds of Baltimore Ravens fans requested passes to participate in a choreographed "Super Flush." The idea behind the test was to simulate halftime conditions in games when fans race for the restrooms. Although rigorous design and planning had gone into the plumbing systems for the stadium, and the system's designers had simulated peak usage conditions with a computer simulation model, the engineers staged the practice run to help detect any major overflows or underflows.

Emcee of the Super Flush

The Baltimore Ravens invited VIPs and even hired an emcee to preside over the simulated plumbing event. The flushes were conducted in waves, with groups of 300 people trying the toilets on the east side of the stadium first, followed by another test on the west side 40 minutes later.

Super Flush Results

It was concluded that the plumbing system at the stadium was ready to go, as everything went smoothly at the Super Flush. The question that needs to be asked with regard to the principles of simulation is: "Were there enough flushes and were those flushes randomly generated?" The author will leave the students of business to decide, but just think to yourself next time you are at the game: Have these restrooms passed the Super Flush simulation test?

Reference

"'Super Flush' passes test," *USA Today*, July 16, 1998.

Simulation Modeling

This chapter focuses on a different business decision modeling technique than has been studied so far in the text. All the previous concepts and techniques presented do play a role in simulation. Some of the earlier topics presented solution approaches that were more or less analytical and were based on mathematical models. However, problems arise that cannot be fully examined by using only these analytical methods.

Background

Simulation modeling can be used to analyze problems in a different light. Simulation has been a technique used by scientists for many years. Much of the training done in the military or in the development of industrial age inventions is simulation. Modern day simulation is a technique that allows inputs to a model to vary and measures the outcomes of various model outputs. Computer simulation allows for numerous replications of inputs to develop a broad idea of what the output characteristics are.

Computer Spreadsheet Simulation

Simulation allows a problem solver to manipulate a process or system and observe how the process or system reacts to changes in the underlying assumptions.

Why replicate a current process or system with an off-line or outside-of-real-life process or system? There are many processes in everyday life that we are interested in replicating. For example, all of society would benefit from the replication of certain surgical processes to hone surgeons' skills without the risk of actually cutting into a person, or military leaders might gain insight from replicating troop movements before an operation took place.

Simulators do exist, and they operate on the same principle as replication. We use simulators to train pilots and even surgeons. Simulations are used to predict weather characteristics. Simulation models of worldwide weather patterns exist for which much hope is expressed but which can't be utilized yet because of the inadequacies of the current generation of computers. However, with the advent of desktop computers and advanced software, much of the simulation effort has turned to computer spreadsheet models.

This text focuses on computer spreadsheet simulation. The chapter covers the concept of random number generation, use of spreadsheets in simulation modeling, and Monte Carlo simulation, and presents a tutorial on simulation model building and the use of the software package Crystal Ball.

What Is Simulation? And Why Are We Using It?

Simulation is a powerful tool to help managers make better decisions.

Simulation is a powerful business decision modeling tool to help managers make better decisions. Many studies have revealed that simulation is one of the most often used tools in academia, business decision modeling, and the business world. Simulation is also in use in much of the real world around us.

It is used in the design process, for example. Automobiles, airplanes, ships, hair dryers, etc. can be designed on a computer, and then, using simulations, one can predict what the performance characteristics will be and how the product will really work and react under simulated real-life conditions.

Real-World Simulation Examples

We see the effect of simulation in the auto industry, where sedans tend to look alike, the jellybean look, some say, because simulations show this shape saves the most fuel as a car moves through air. Today we see airplanes with unusual wing and tail configurations because simulations show advantages to these. It is much more efficient and effective to try given configurations out through simulation without actually building a prototype until one is confident of the design.

An especially talented group of experts over a period of years has developed a highly promising simulated model of the human heart. When in use, it will allow surgeons to simulate different operations to repair defects and predict the results. Artificial heart design should also make quantum leaps. A group of brilliant scientists is spending years of hard work in New Mexico trying to simulate the process of evolution. In the military, simulation is used to model combat strategies in exercises called war games.

Simulation Affecting Managers

Simulation is widely used in the business world to model waiting lines, inventory, stock and commodity pricing, consumer behavior and marketing, and election results. You must look very hard to find a more universally applicable technique. Simulation has considerable utility in modeling both highly complex phenomena and phenomena that are less complex.

Simulation is widely used by business problem solvers to model waiting lines, inventory, stock and commodity pricing, consumer behavior, etc.

Types of Data

This chapter will discuss two types of data important to simulation models: categorical and numerical. Categorical data is sometimes referred to as *qualitative* data; whereas numerical data is referred to as *quantitative.* The basic distinction between the two is whether any arithmetic will be done on the data. It makes sense to do arithmetic on numerical data. Although we are interested in categorical data, this chapter focuses on the analysis of numerical data from simulation models.

Numerical Data—Discrete versus Continuous

Discrete data arise from observations that can take only certain numerical values, usually counts such as the number of quarterly earnings reports submitted or the number of machines on an assembly line. Continuous data are numerical data that theoretically can be measured in infinitely small units. For example, although profit and loss is usually analyzed to two decimal places, it is considered continuous since profit or loss can be any positive or negative number. The interval measurement scale is intended for continuous data. Sometimes continuous data are given discrete values at certain thresholds; for example, growth rate of quarterly gross domestic product (GDP) is a discrete value, but GDP itself is a continuous quantity; in these situations it is reasonable to treat discrete values as continuous. Remember that information is lost when continuous data are recorded only in ranges, and the statistical analysis of continuous data is more powerful than that of categorical data.

Simulation and the Link to Earlier Chapters

In becoming more effective and efficient problem solvers, managers must remember what was set forth in the earlier chapters of the text. The concepts of central tendency, dispersion, probability theory, decision structures and criteria, and spreadsheet modeling will all be incorporated in simulation modeling.

Simulation, Spreadsheet Modeling, and Model Verification and Validity

Simulation modeling is akin to spreadsheet "what if" analysis. This chapter examines spreadsheet simulation modeling.

Chapters 2 and 4 spoke about the concept of modeling, especially the concept of spreadsheet modeling. The major payoff of modeling and building decision structures such as decision trees and influence diagrams is the sensitivity analysis that results. Simulation modeling leads to the same end. Asking "what if" questions and interpreting the outcome after your model has run is one of the main strengths of simulation. It is also very important to make sure your model can be verified and that it is valid.

Simulation Verification

Validation of a simulation model must be completed.

By verification we mean making sure the computer or spreadsheet program used in the model is not flawed. This requires checking and rechecking the work, perhaps writing it in different languages to see if similar results occur and perhaps asking independent experts to review the work.

Model Validity

Verification of a simulation model must be completed.

A simulation is valid when it models what it is supposed to model. After working long hours on a simulation and viewing results that are aesthetically pleasing, it is easy to be seduced into believing the results while losing sight of the fact that the model misses the point.

A few years ago, an American city was just about to invest nearly 2 billion dollars on a limited rapid transit system that simulations indicated would be cost-effective. An astute member of the city council insisted on talking to other cities that had experience with such systems and discovered many systems to be less than cost–effective, and the plans were scrapped.

In building and validating a simulation model it is important to talk to workers closest to the action, to contrast and compare other models and the experience of other experts, utilize whatever data is available to identify trends for what-if analysis, and keep an open mind.

Random Number Generation

Before any computer spreadsheet models are considered, the concept of random number generation must be developed. Random number generation is an integral step in the simulation process. As a preliminary step we need to gain some understanding of random numbers and how to assign them to a probability distribution before a simulation model can be built.

Random number generation is an integral step in the simulation process.

As an example of a random number, suppose you are asked to fill 100 blanks with a random sequence of integers. Figure 5.1 displays 100 blanks filled in with 100 random numbers from 0 to 1.

Random Number Generation Techniques

Could you free-associate and produce a stream of random numbers? Could anybody? You are invited to try to do this and to find objective tests to see if you succeed. The fact is that humans are not good at this. We tend to favor some numbers at the expense of others, and most people fail to adequately represent successions of the same number.

Think of techniques you might use to fill in the blanks in a manner that would produce a true random set of numbers. What we mean by random is that each of the 10 integers is equally likely to appear on each of the blanks. What occurs before or after a given blank must have no bearing on that blank, and the method of choice must make it equally likely that any of the 10 possible integers appear.

Generating random numbers is not a trivial exercise, but is essential to creating and running simulation models.

0.9942	0.0496	0.3057	0.6575	0.9925	0.2069	0.9823	0.9806	0.6048	0.4372
0.8404	0.7913	0.5677	0.8781	0.8946	0.8086	0.8491	0.7477	0.1354	0.3631
0.5802	0.5688	0.4429	0.2226	0.4355	0.5429	0.5921	0.8076	0.6965	0.9331
0.0990	0.9123	0.5915	0.2238	0.2096	0.6906	0.8170	0.2597	0.8688	0.1824
0.9465	0.0369	0.0687	0.3290	0.1670	0.6268	0.6186	0.2945	0.7551	0.6961
0.1406	0.7184	0.7062	0.0430	0.4858	0.0296	0.2596	0.7634	0.0849	0.6920
0.7281	0.6495	0.7857	0.8361	0.1568	0.3220	0.7856	0.2879	0.4204	0.8502
0.5849	0.8281	0.1902	0.6128	0.0653	0.1296	0.5037	0.2226	0.5428	0.8857
0.9117	0.2474	0.1067	0.4460	0.4225	0.0012	0.1263	0.8703	0.4066	0.1990
0.6702	0.2026	0.7418	0.4543	0.0579	0.7455	0.5190	0.8237	0.6961	0.3235

FIGURE 5.1
Random Number Example

Business Decision Modeling throughout the Ages

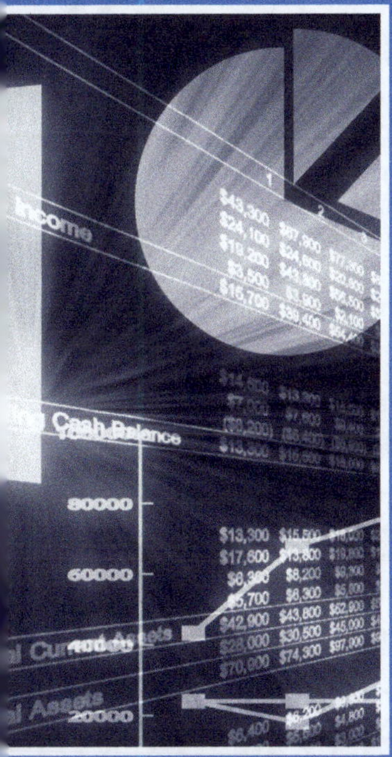

Monte Carlo Simulation

What Is Monte Carlo Simulation?

The term *Monte Carlo* refers to a group of methods in which physical or mathematical problems are simulated by using randomly generated numbers. Monte Carlo methods have been used for centuries, but only in the past several decades has the technique gained the status of a full-fledged numerical method capable of addressing the most complex applications.

Some of the applications of Monte Carlo simulation statistical techniques can be found in nuclear reactor design, radiation cancer therapy, econometrics, stock index forecasting, and oil well exploration. As is evident, the range of application varies enormously.

Background of Monte Carlo Terminology

The term Monte Carlo was not coined until 1944, during the development of the atomic bomb under the Manhattan Project. The work involved a direct simulation of the probabilistic problems concerned with random neutron diffusion in fissile material.

The term Monte Carlo was used because of the simulation technique's similarity to the statistical simulation of a game of chance and also because the capital of Monaco, at that time, was the center for gambling and similar pursuits.

Use of Monte Carlo Simulation Method

In the early 1970s, the newly developing theory of computational complexity provided a more precise and persuasive rationale for employing the Monte Carlo method. The theory identified a class of problems for which the time to evaluate the exact solution to a problem within the class grew at an exponential rate, and the results of several studies conducted by mathematicians and scientists make it evident that the Monte Carlo method has lived up to its potential by being able to solve complex problems.

Optimal Information Area

Sabri Pllana's History of Monte Carlo Method
http://www.geocities.com/CollegePark/Quad/2435/

Contingency Analysis Monte Carlo Simulation Glossary
http://www.contingencyanalysis.com/glossarymontecarlosimulation.htm

Computational Science Education Project Introduction to Monte Carlo Methods
http://csep1.phy.ornl.gov/mc/node1.html

Developing Random Number Generation Techniques

Developing random number generators is not a trivial exercise. As you read these words, some of the world's greatest mathematicians are trying to find better ways to generate random numbers. (One promising technique is to measure the radiation emanating from a "lava lamp" type device.)

Although random number generation from lava lamps is interesting, for our purposes, random numbers can be found in tables or by using calculators or computer spreadsheets that have algorithms built into them that produce number streams sufficiently random for all but the most sophisticated research.

Generating Random Numbers by Spreadsheets

At this point you should make sure you can generate such numbers with a spreadsheet. This section explains how it is done.

Business decision modeling is the application of a scientific approach to solving management problems.

To generate random numbers in an Excel spreadsheet, go to a cell and type

=rand( )

in the formula bar for the cell and move to another cell. If you want a column or row of random numbers, highlight the cell with a random number, place the crosshair of the cursor on the lower right corner of that cell, and drag the cursor across the cells you want to show random numbers. A detailed section on how to generate random numbers in an Excel spreadsheet is provided later in this chapter.

The "=rand( )" function in Excel generates random numbers.

Random numbers can be generated via a spreadsheet program such as Excel or with a spreadsheet add-in such as Crystal Ball.

Simulation and Currency Exchange Rates

Imagine you are planning to start selling some of your products abroad in the near future. You are interested in exchanging your U.S. dollars for the currency of the country you are trading with (e.g., country X). You could take a look on the Internet and find what the current exchange rate is and base your calculations for U.S. dollar conversion on that rate. However, if you exchange your dollars now for the other currency, the rate of exchange may be different by the time you finish the deal. If the currency value (X/$) appreciates you will have lost out on some extra money, but if the currency value (X/$) depreciates you will have protected yourself against a drop in how much your dollar could buy. No one knows exactly what the future rate will be but history gives some clue. In all, you would like to know on average what your outcome would be. Consider Table 5.1 as an example.

Table 5.1 describes what can happen to the currency value (column 1), the historical frequency over the last 200 days of the event (second column), and finally the historical frequencies converted to a probability distribution (column 3).

TABLE 5.1 *Currency Exchange Rate Information*

EVENT (X/$)	HISTORICAL FREQUENCY OVER LAST 200 DAYS (DAYS)	PROBABILITY OF OCCURRENCE
Currency value stays neutral	24	24/200 = 0.12
Currency value of $ appreciates (i.e., X/$ rate rises)	90	90/200 = 0.45
Currency value of $ depreciates (i.e., X/$ rate falls)	86	86/200 = 0.43

Cumulative Probability Distributions and Random Number Intervals

For the sake of simplicity, let's define the outcomes of the events as follows: You get even money for neutral currency value (i.e., you get 1X for every $1), you get 1.5X for every $1 for appreciating currency value, and you get 0.75X for every $1 for depreciating currency value.

Table 5.2 displays these outcomes as well as the probability of occurrence, the cumulative probability distribution for each event, and the interval of random numbers assigned to each event. The expected outcome (i.e., currency valuation) can be computed as follows (Note: Remember the expected value calculations from Chapter 3):

$$E(\text{currency valuation}) = (0.12)(1) + (0.45)(1.5) + (0.43)(0.75) = 1.1175$$

Therefore, in the long run, one could expect to have currency valuation of around 1.1175X/$1, or some currency appreciation.

Generating Random Numbers and Simulating Currency Values

Random numbers may be generated for simulation problems in different ways. A table of random digits could be used, or the spin of a numbered wheel. We will use the RAND function in Excel to generate the random numbers for this example and to simulate the currency values.

TABLE 5.2 *Currency Example Outcomes*

EVENT X/$	OUTCOME	PROBABILITY OF OCCURRENCE	CUMULATIVE PROBABILITY	LOWER RANGE OF RANDOM NUMBERS
Currency value neutral	1X to $1	24/200 = 0.12	0.12	0.00
Currency value appreciation	1.5X to $1	90/200 = 0.45	0.57	0.12
Currency value depreciation	0.75X to $1	86/200 = 0.43	1.00	0.57

Excel Spreadsheet Simulation of Currency Value Example

Figure 5.2 contains an Excel spreadsheet program that simulates the currency value situation for 10 trials. Once operational, numerous trials with associated results can be repeated at nearly the speed of light by *refreshing* the random numbers with the F9 key.

Refreshing means to replace each random number in the simulation with a new random number. You are urged to study the codes for this spreadsheet and modify and extend them to try other strategies. The code for this program is illustrated in Figure 5.3. To complete the same operation in Excel, click on the Microsoft icon or File menu in the upper left corner of Excel, then click on Excel Options at the bottom of the menu, within the Excel Options menu click on the Advanced option on the left side of the window, scroll down to the "Display options for this worksheet" menu, under this menu click on the "Show formulas in cells instead of showing calculated values" check box.

It should be noted that the average currency valuation of 0.95X to $1 in this 10-trial simulation differs from the *expected* currency valuation, 1.1175X to $1, which was computed earlier. If this simulation were repeated hundreds of thousands of times, it is much more likely that the *simulated* currency valuation would be very close to the *expected* currency valuation.

Figure 5.3 contains the spreadsheet formulas for the currency valuation example. Cumulative probabilities are calculated via Excel formulas in column D to avoid mathematical errors that may occur through hand calculations. The = VLOOKUP function is used in column I to "look up" the random numbers generated in column H. Cell I13 calculates the average curVLOOKUP function is used in column I to "look up" the random numbers generated in column H. Cell I13

	A	B	C	D	E	F	G	H	I
1	Currency Value Example								
2		Probability	Probability Lower Range	Cumulative Probability	Currency Value (X to 1$)		Trial	Random Number	Simulated Currency Value
3		0.12	0	0.12	1		1	0.834705	0.75
4		0.45	0.12	0.57	1.5		2	0.41846	1.5
5		0.43	0.57	1	0.75		3	0.77047	0.75
6							4	0.038588	1
7							5	0.611705	0.75
8							6	0.618397	0.75
9							7	0.911885	0.75
10							8	0.971495	0.75
11							9	0.431685	1.5
12							10	0.090158	1
13								Average	0.95

FIGURE 5.2

Excel Spreadsheet for Currency Valuation Example

	A	B	C	D	E	F	G	H	I
1	Currency Value Example								
2		Probability	Probability Lower Range	Cumulative Probability	Currency Value (X to 1$)		Trial	Random Number	Simulated Currency Value
3		0.12	0	=B3	1		1	=RAND()	=VLOOKUP(H3,$C$3:$E$5,3,TRUE)
4		0.45	=D3	=D3+B4	1.5		=G3+1	=RAND()	=VLOOKUP(H4,$C$3:$E$5,3,TRUE)
5		0.43	=D4	=D4+B5	0.75		=G4+1	=RAND()	=VLOOKUP(H5,$C$3:$E$5,3,TRUE)
6							=G5+1	=RAND()	=VLOOKUP(H6,$C$3:$E$5,3,TRUE)
7							=G6+1	=RAND()	=VLOOKUP(H7,$C$3:$E$5,3,TRUE)
8							=G7+1	=RAND()	=VLOOKUP(H8,$C$3:$E$5,3,TRUE)
9							=G8+1	=RAND()	=VLOOKUP(H9,$C$3:$E$5,3,TRUE)
10							=G9+1	=RAND()	=VLOOKUP(H10,$C$3:$E$5,3,TRUE)
11							=G10+1	=RAND()	=VLOOKUP(H11,$C$3:$E$5,3,TRUE)
12							=G11+1	=RAND()	=VLOOKUP(H12,$C$3:$E$5,3,TRUE)
13								Average	=AVERAGE(I3:I12)

FIGURE 5.3

Excel Spreadsheet Formulas for Currency Valuation Example

calculates the average currency value (X to \$1) for the 10 trials by averaging cells I3 through I12. This is the number that is compared to the expected currency valuation calculation.

Simulation of a Queuing System

Waiting in a line or a queue is one of the most common occurrences in everyday life. Not only do people spend time waiting in line or in queue but so do products in a manufacturing facility, so do planes waiting for takeoff, and so on. As students of business we know that time is a valuable resource and that the reduction of waiting time or time in the queue is a very important topic for discussion. This section will study what is called the single-server waiting line system.

Single Server Waiting Line System

The single-server waiting line system is the simplest form of queuing system. It will be used to illustrate the fundamentals of a queuing system. As a practical example of this type of queuing system, think of the line at the fast-food drive-through or the line at the cashier at a smaller convenience mart.

The most important factors to consider in analyzing a queuing system are the following:

1. Where the customers come from, or what is referred to as the *calling population.*
2. The order in which the customers are served, or the *queue discipline.*

Business Decision Modeling Behind the Scenes

The Major Players and the Story Behind the Development of Monte Carlo Simulation

A Brief History of Monte Carlo Method

The method is named after the city in the Monaco principality. The name and the systematic development of Monte Carlo methods dates from about 1944, although there were many players along the way (no pun intended).

William Sealy Gosset A.K.A. Student (1876–1937)

In 1908 Student (W. S. Gosset) used experimental sampling to help him toward his discovery of the distribution of the correlation coefficient. In the same year, Student also used sampling to bolster his faith in his so-called *t* distribution, which he had derived by a somewhat shaky and incomplete theoretical analysis. Gosset discovered the form of the *t* distribution by a combination of mathematical and empirical work with random numbers. This was an early application of the Monte Carlo method.

A. N. Kolmogorov (1903–1987)

In 1931, Kolmogorov showed the relationship between Markov stochastic processes and certain integral-differential equations. In the early part of the twentieth century, British statistical schools indulged in a fair amount of unsophisticated Monte Carlo work. Most of this seems to have been of didactic character and rarely used for research or discovery.

John Von Neumann (1903–1957)

The real use of Monte Carlo methods as a research tool stems from work on the atomic bomb during the Second World War. This work involved a direct simulation of the probabilistic problems concerned with random neutron diffusion in fissile material; but even at an early stage of these investigations, von Neumann and Ulam refined these particular "Russian roulette" and "splitting" methods. However, the systematic development of these ideas had to await the work of Harris and Herman Kahn in 1948. About 1948 Fermi, Metropolis, and Ulam obtained Monte Carlo estimates for the eigenvalues of the Schrödinger equation.

Optimal Information Area

Sabri Pllana's History of Monte Carlo Method
http://www.geocities.com/CollegePark/Quad/2435/

3. How often customers arrive, or the *arrival rate.*
4. How fast the customers are served, or the *service time.*

Each of these items will be discussed next.

Where Customers Come From— The Calling Population

The calling population is the source of the customers to the marketplace. Many queuing systems have an assumed infinite calling population. In other words, there exist such a large number of possible customers in the area where the queue is located that the number of potential customers is assumed to be infinite. However, there do exist queuing systems that have finite calling populations. An example is the repair facility for a distribution and logistics company that has 30 trucks in service at any one time. The finite calling population then is 30, the number of trucks in service at that point.

The Order in Which Customers Are Served— The Queue Discipline

The queue discipline refers to the order in which customers are served. For many waiting lines this is as simple as first-come, first-served. Think of the line at the convenience store cashier. The first person in line is the first to be served. At times the queue discipline may be random. For example, a machine operator may reach into a full box of parts and select one completely at random. There are numerous queuing disciplines that exist, but the most frequent in waiting line examples is first-come, first-served. For this reason the first-come, first-served discipline will be employed in this chapter.

How Often Customers Arrive at the Queue— The Arrival Rate

The specific rate at which the customers arrive at the service facility during a specified time period is called the arrival rate. Arrival rates can be estimated empirically by watching a queue or can be calculated as the average of data over time.

For example, if 200 customers are served in 10 hours at a fast-food drive-through window, then it could be said that the arrival rate averages 20 customers per hour. This rate is an average, and in actuality no customers could arrive the first 30 minutes and then 200 customers could arrive in the second 30 minutes. It is also assumed that these arrivals are independent of each other and vary randomly over time.

It is also commonly assumed that the arrivals at a service facility conform to some probability distribution, namely the Poisson distribution. Although the Poisson distribution has been determined as the most likely distribution for modeling arrivals, any distribution that a business decision modeler deems necessary can be used.

How Fast Customers Are Served—The Service Time

The specific rate at which customers can be served during a specified time period is referred to as the service rate. The service rate is similar to the arrival rate in that it is a random variable. For example, at a certain fast-food drive-through, 60 customers can be served in an hour. Standard nomenclature in the queuing world is to refer to arrivals in terms of a rate but to refer to service in terms of time.

It is also assumed that the service time can be defined by a probability distribution. Service times are most commonly represented by the exponential distribution. However, as before, business decision modelers can use whatever distribution they deem necessary.

Lunch Wagon Simulation Example: Arrivals and Profit Determination

For a more practically oriented problem, let's consider a simple lunch wagon where we are interested in the profit derived from customer arrival. This is not exactly a single-server queuing problem, but it sets the scene for such a problem a little later in this section.

During lunch hour potential customers arrive at a rate per minute determined by a uniform distribution, with a maximum of four customers in any given minute. (If more than four per minute show up, they go somewhere else out of frustration.) For this example, we are interested only in the profit determination from the given arrival information. It is assumed that there are no congestion problems, service deterioration, or balking as more folks wait in line.

Using the scheme we have learned, we can use random numbers to simulate arrivals any given minute by utilizing Table 5.3. Although the method presented in Table 5.3 works, for this example we will simplify the spreadsheet by using a nested

TABLE 5.3 *Lunch Wagon Arrival Distribution*

EVENT—NUMBER OF CUSTOMERS ARRIVING	PROBABILITY OF ARRIVAL	CUMULATIVE PROBABILITY	LOWER RANGE OF RANDOM NUMBERS
0	0.20	0.20	0.0
1	0.20	0.40	0.2
2	0.20	0.60	0.4
3	0.20	0.80	0.6
4	0.20	1.00	0.8

TABLE 5.4 *Excel Formulas for Lunch Wagon Simulation*

CELL	FORMULAS	ACTION
B4 (hidden cell)	=rand( )	Copy to cells B5:B13
C4	=IF(B4 < 0.2,0,IF(AND(B4 >=0.2,B4 < 0.4),1, IF(AND(B4 >=0.4,B4 < 0.6),2,IF(AND(B4 >= 0.6,B4 < 0.8),3,4))))	Copy to cells C5:C13
D4	=IF(C4 >=1,NORMINV(RAND(),6.3,1.56),0)	Copy to cells D5:D13
E4	=IF(C4 >=2,NORMINV(RAND(),6.3,1.56),0)	Copy to cells E5:E13
F4	=IF(C4 >=3,NORMINV(RAND(),6.3,1.56),0)	Copy to cells F5:F13
G4	=IF(C4 >=4,NORMINV(RAND(),6.3,1.56),0)	Copy to cells G5:G13
H4	=SUM(D4:G4)	Copy to cells H5:H13
H14	=SUM(H4:H13)	—

IF statement (see Table 5.4, cell C4). This bypasses the need to input the entire set of information from Table 5.3.

Customer Spending Habits

The amount of money spent by customers is known to be normally distributed with a mean of \$6.30 and a standard deviation of \$1.56. How could these numbers be determined from cash register records? We want to simulate the cash flow at this lunch wagon over a period of time—say 10 minutes, to keep it simple.

Origination of Probability Distributions

The probability distribution determining the amount spent on a given order is formula driven, in this case the normal probability distribution with a particular mean and standard deviation.

Actually, we will use its *inverse* to determine how much is spent by a particular customer. A spreadsheet program like Excel makes this easy to accomplish. The reason we must use the inverse normal distribution is because the usual normal distribution pairs dollars spent by the customer (x, or independent variable) with probabilities ($P(x)$, or dependent variable) in that order.

We will reverse this order and use random numbers to identify the probability of a particular expenditure associated with a given order and use the inverse function to determine, as output, the dollar amount of the order. Examine the format given in Table 5.4 for this simulation. Table 5.4 displays the Excel formulas that create the simulation numbers in Figure 5.4.

◇	A	C	D	E	F	G	H
1							
2							
3	Minute	Arrivals	First Order $	Second Order $	Third Order $	Fourth Order $	Total $
4	1	0	$0.00	$0.00	$0.00	$0.00	$0.00
5	2	4	$8.15	$6.56	$9.16	$7.23	$31.09
6	3	1	$5.58	$0.00	$0.00	$0.00	$5.58
7	4	1	$4.19	$0.00	$0.00	$0.00	$4.19
8	5	0	$0.00	$0.00	$0.00	$0.00	$0.00
9	6	2	$4.19	$6.38	$0.00	$0.00	$10.57
10	7	1	$8.62	$0.00	$0.00	$0.00	$8.62
11	8	1	$7.78	$0.00	$0.00	$0.00	$7.78
12	9	1	$5.05	$0.00	$0.00	$0.00	$5.05
13	10	2	$7.90	$5.87	$0.00	$0.00	$13.77
14							$86.65

FIGURE 5.4 Lunch Wagon Example Excel Spreadsheet

Random Number and Normal Probability Generation

You can fill in the second column by using a stream of random numbers and the table above. The dollar amount of each order can be determined by using a different random number for each appropriate cell and the inverse normal distribution with a mean of $6.30 and a standard deviation of $1.56. Of course, if the number of arrivals is less than four, some number of orders will not exist and one or more cells on the right should remain blank.

Computing Relevant Simulation Statistics and Distributions

After completing the simulation you can use the last column to find relevant statistics like the mean and standard deviation and the maximum and minimum. Your accuracy will improve if you do the simulation more than 10 times. Using an Excel spreadsheet, you can quickly do this for 10,000 or more minutes.

Lunch Wagon Waiting Line Simulation

From Figure 5.4 it appears that the lunch wagon is generating a sufficient amount of revenues. However, the lunch wagon has heard some complaints regarding waiting times. The simulation run earlier gave an idea about revenue generation given that all groups of customers could be served. This is great information for the lunch wagon staff, but it does not assist them in getting a handle on waiting times during lunchtime. In situations where customer arrivals and service times are considered events that occur at discrete points in time, the simulation model that should be employed is called a *discrete-event simulation model.* This type of problem is considered a classical single-server queuing, or waiting line, problem.

Interarrival Times

The lunch wagon knows how arrivals and service times are distributed. In a waiting line simulation model, arrival times are determined by randomly generating the time between two successive arrivals. This is referred to as the *interarrival time.* The lunch wagon knows that customer group interarrival times are uniformly distributed between 0 and 3 minutes. As was stated in the previous simulation model, the lunch wagon can service a group of customers of one to four equally well, but groups of five or more balk and go to another establishment. So, interarrival times are for groups of customers instead of just one customer.

If we allow r to denote a random number between 0 and 1, an interarrival time for two successive customer groups can be simulated by using the formula:

$$\text{Interarrival time} = a + r(b - a)$$

where a is the minimum interarrival time and b is the maximum interarrival time. For the lunch wagon, the minimum interarrival time is $a = 0$ minutes and the maximum interarrival time is $b = 3$ minutes. In turn, the formula for interarrival time is

$$\text{Interarrival time} = 0 + r(3 - 0) = 3r$$

Customer group interarrival times can be calculated as:

CUSTOMER GROUP	RANDOM NUMBER, r	INTERRARIVAL TIME, MINUTES	ARRIVAL TIME MINUTES, FROM INITIAL START TIME = 0
1	0.5364	1.6092	1.6092
2	0.3562	1.0686	2.6778
3	0.1987	0.5961	3.2739

Customer Service Times

The lunch wagon also knows what customer service times are. Customer service time is the time it takes for the lunch wagon staff to take a group's order, calculate the final bill, collect the group's payment, and send them to the pickup station (i.e., the back of the wagon). The lunch wagon estimates that service times are normally distributed with a mean of 1 minute and a standard deviation of 0.1 minute.

Overall the lunch wagon waiting line simulation proceeds as follows:

1. An interarrival time for a new customer group is created.
2. That interarrival time is then added to the arrival time of the preceding customer group to determine the new customer group's arrival time.

3. The new customer group's arrival time is compared to the completion time of the preceding customer to determine whether the lunch wagon is idle or busy.
4. If the new customer group's arrival time is greater than the completion time of the preceding customer, the lunch wagon is done taking the preceding customer group's order and is idle and the new customer group can be waited on immediately.
5. The service start time for the new customer group is then calculated as the group's arrival time.
6. If the arrival time of the new customer group is not greater than the completion time of the preceding customer group, then the new customer group must wait until the preceding customer group is finished. In this case the lunch wagon is busy.
7. The service start time for the new customer group is equal to the completion time of the preceding customer group.
8. A customer group's completion time is the service start time plus the service time itself.
9. A customer group's total time in the system is the difference between the completion time and the group's arrival time.

On an Excel spreadsheet, the lunch wagon operations are simulated for 500 customer groups. The worksheet treats the first 100 customer groups as the start-up period and the summary statistics are calculated for the 400 remaining customer groups. Figure 5.5 displays the spreadsheet for the lunch wagon waiting line simulation.

The summary statistics show that 164 out of 400 lunch wagon customers had to wait. Thus, there is a 164/400 = 41% probability that a customer will have to wait for service. This appears to be a large number of people and a high probability of waiting at the lunch wagon. However, before one concludes that the lunch wagon's process is out of control, the average wait time and maximum wait time should be examined.

The average wait time from the summary statistics area is 0.2976 minutes, or about 18 seconds. The maximum wait time is approximately 3.3 minutes. From these waiting times, it does not appear that the lunch wagon's process is drastically out of control. In fact, think to yourself how you would feel if you waited 18 seconds at a fast-food restaurant on average and the longest you ever waited was about 3.3 minutes. In addition, it appears at least 90% of customer groups are being served in 1 minute or less. So the line must move quickly even when it is full. Figure 5.6 displays the formulas for the Excel spreadsheet in Figure 5.5.

Simulation's Real Payoff—The Sensitivity/What-If Analysis

The real payoff from a simulation of this type comes when we start to ask what-if questions. For example, because of anticipated changes in the economy or the

	A	B	C	D	E	F	G	H	I	J
1	**Lunch Wagon Waiting Simulation**									
2										
3	Interarrival Times (Uniform Distribution)									
4	Lower Value	0								
5	Upper Value	3								
6										
7	Service Times (Normal Distribution)									
8	Mean	1								
9	Standard Deviation	0.1								
10										
11		Waiting Line Model								
12										
13		Customer Group	Interarrival Time	Arrival Time	Service Start Time	Wait Time	Service Time	Completion Time	Time in System	Idle Time
14		1	1.8202	1.8202	1.8202	0.0000	0.9172	2.7374	0.9172	0.0000
15		2	2.2927	4.1129	4.1129	0.0000	1.0817	5.1946	1.0817	1.3755
16		3	0.4089	4.5218	5.1946	0.6728	0.9739	6.1685	1.6467	0.0000
17		4	0.9293	5.4511	6.1685	0.7175	1.0763	7.2448	1.7937	0.0000
18		5	2.0662	7.5173	7.5173	0.0000	1.0757	8.5929	1.0757	0.2725
513		500	2.0380	766.1888	766.1888	0.0000	1.0382	767.2270	1.0382	0.3428
514										
515										
516			Summary Statistics							
517			Number that Have a Wait			164				
518			Probability of Waiting			0.4100				
519			Average Wait Time			0.2976				
520			Maximum Wait Time			3.3078				
521			% of Time Lunch Wagon Busy			0.7199				
522			Number Waiting > 1 Minute			38				
523			Probability of Waiting >1 Minute			0.0950				
524			Average # in Line			0.1936				

FIGURE 5.5

Lunch Wagon Waiting Line Spreadsheet Model

	A	B	C	D	E	F	G	H	I	J
1	Lunch Wagon Waiting Simulation									
2										
3	Interarrival Times (Uniform Distribution)									
4	Lower Value	0								
5	Upper Value	3								
6										
7	Service Times (Normal Distribution)									
8	Mean	1								
9	Standard Deviation	0.1								
10										
11		Waiting Line Model								
12										
13		Customer Group	Interarrival Time	Arrival Time	Service Start Time	Wait Time	Service Time	Completion Time	Time in System	Idle Time
14		1	=$B$4+RAND()*($B$5-$B$4)	=0+C14	=D14	=E14-D14	=ABS(NORMINV(RAND(),$B$8,$B$9)	=E14+G14	=H14-D14	=0
15		=B14+1	=$B$4+RAND()*($B$5-$B$4)	=D14+C15	=IF(D15>H14,D15,H14)	=E15-D15	=ABS(NORMINV(RAND(),$B$8,$B$9)	=E15+G15	=H15-D15	=E15-H14
16		=B15+1	=$B$4+RAND()*($B$5-$B$4)	=D15+C16	=IF(D16>H15,D16,H15)	=E16-D16	=ABS(NORMINV(RAND(),$B$8,$B$9)	=E16+G16	=H16-D16	=E16-H15
17		=B16+1	=$B$4+RAND()*($B$5-$B$4)	=D16+C17	=IF(D17>H16,D17,H16)	=E17-D17	=ABS(NORMINV(RAND(),$B$8,$B$9)	=E17+G17	=H17-D17	=E17-H16
18		=B17+1	=$B$4+RAND()*($B$5-$B$4)	=D17+C18	=IF(D18>H17,D18,H17)	=E18-D18	=ABS(NORMINV(RAND(),$B$8,$B$9)	=E18+G18	=H18-D18	=E18-H17
513		=B512+1	=$B$4+RAND()*($B$5-$B$4)	=D512+C51	=IF(D513>H512,D513,H512)	=E513-D513	=ABS(NORMINV(RAND(),$B$8,$B$9)	=E513+G513	=H513-D513	=E513-H512
514										
515										
516			Summary Statistics							
517			Number that Have a Wait			=COUNTIF(F114:F513,">0")				
518			Probability of Waiting			=F517/COUNT(F114:F513)				
519			Average Wait Time			=AVERAGE(F114:F513)				
520			Maximum Wait Time			=MAX(F114:F513)				
521			% of Time Lunch Wagon Busy			=1-(SUM(J114:J513)/H513)				
522			Number Waiting > 1 Minute			=COUNTIF(F114:F513,">1")				
523			Probability of Waiting >1 Minut			=F522/COUNT(F114:F513)				
524			Average # in Line			=SUM(F114:F513)/(H513-H113)				

FIGURE 5.6

Lunch Wagon Waiting Line Spreadsheet Model Formulas

demographics of where we have our lunch wagon parked, the uniform distribution for anticipated arrivals of customers might change.

Simulation allows managers to take a look at complex processes or events and analyze them without actually building the product or waiting for the process to complete itself.

Maybe we are considering investing in an advertising campaign. For the same or different reasons we may anticipate that the mean and standard deviation of the distribution determining the amount to be spent on each order will change also. By modifying the distributions appropriately, we can anticipate what the difference will be in our conclusions. For a lunch wagon, we might want to compare different estimates for different places we can park the wagon about the city. It is important to note that asking what-if questions often maximizes the usefulness of simulation.

@RISK Tutorial

Running @Risk in Excel

This section will detail how to get @Risk up and running in Excel after @Risk is installed on your computer.

1. Click on the Start menu in Windows.
2. Click on Program Files and find the Program Folder for Palisade Decision Tools and click on the @Risk application.

After @Risk has been loaded, Excel will automatically be loaded and the user may begin using @Risk to develop a simulation model.

What @Risk Will Do for the Modeler

@Risk is an add-in for Excel that runs simulation models. It is the responsibility of the modeler/user to construct a simulation model in Excel and to instruct @Risk what functions to perform. @Risk performs two main functions:

1. Allows users to input stochastic variables or uncertainty into their models.
2. Allows users to keep track of and analyze model that are linked to these input variables.

User Responsibilities

Once the modeler/user has built the simulation model, three main decisions areas must be made regarding:

- Inputs
- Outputs
- Settings

These areas *must* be covered and decisions made regarding their makeup in order to use @Risk and have it produce simulation data for analysis. Specifically, these main areas and decisions are:

1. Identify input variables that contain uncertainty—i.e., identify the stochastic variables in the model.
2. Identify the output variables of interest—i.e., identify what outputs from your model you wish to monitor (e.g., expected profits, average time in the queue, expected costs, NPV)
3. Inform @Risk of the following simulationsettings:
   a. The type of simulation to run—Monte Carlo
   b. How many iterations to run—e.g., 100,000.

Getting Started

@RISK is an add-in for spreadsheets such as Microsoft Excel that performs risk analysis. Risk analysis is any method, quantitative or qualitative, for assessing the impacts of risk on decision situations. @RISK uses Monte Carlo simulation to perform risk analysis.

In the following example, XYZ Corporation is faced with a critical decision on whether or not to launch a new product to the market. The initial cost of the project is calculated by the accounting department at $300,000 (Cell B3); the content of the income statement, including individual cell formulas, will be discussed in detail later in this tutorial. At the bottom of the income statement (Figure 5.7), XYZ has also calculated net present value (Cell B18) of the project, using a discount value (Cell B17).

Upon loading of @Risk, a new toolbar is created in your spreadsheet. This toolbar is visible whenever @RISK is running. The toolbar buttons run many of the

	A	B	C	D	E	F
1	XYZ Corporation Foracasted Income Statement					
2						
3	Cost of Project 1	$300,000				
4						
5		2000	2001	2002	2003	2004
6	Sales Price	$50.00	$55.00	$58.00	$61.00	$64.00
7	Sales Volume	3,500	3,800	4,100	4,400	4,700
8	Revenue	$175,000	$209,000	$237,800	$268,400	$300,800
9						
10	Unit Production Cost	$10.00	$15.00	$17.33	$15.00	$10.00
11	Cost of Goods Sold	$35,000.00	$57,000.00	$71,066.67	$66,000.00	$47,000.00
12	Operating Expenses	$1,200	$1,400	$1,600	$1,500	$1,400
13	Gross Income	$138,800.00	$150,600.00	$165,133.33	$200,900.00	$252,400.00
14	Taxes	35%	35%	35%	35%	35%
15	Net Income	$90,220.00	$97,890.00	$107,336.67	$130,585.00	$164,060.00
16						
17	Discount Value	0.11				
18	Present Value	$122,595				
19						

FIGURE 5.7
Income Statement

commands you need to perform a risk analysis. If you are unfamiliar with the @RISK toolbar button, holding the cursor over a button will allow a ToolTip to appear. Figure 5.8 contains the @Risk Toolbar for Excel 2007, whereas Figure 5.9 displays the @Risk Toolbar for Excel 2010. Other than the differences in the toolbar, @Risk for Excel 2010 and Excel 2007 are almost identical in form and substance (i.e., the screens all look the same after you get past the toolbar).

Input Cells

The spreadsheet in Figure 5.7 may look like a typical spreadsheet model, but looks can be deceiving. Let's take a look at the contents of the cells:

Cells B6 through F6 contain the formula =RiskTriang(#1,#2,#3), where #1, #2, and #3 represent the three triangular distribution values starting with #1 at the lowest value, #2 the most likely value, and #3 the highest value.

This can be interpreted as follows: XYZ has determined that for every year, sales price can range between three values. For example, in year 2000, sales price (Cell B6) ranges from 20, 50, to 80. Thus the formula for cell B6 is =RiskTriang (20,50,80). For years 2001 through 2004, the same formula is used, but with different triangular distribution values. Use the following triangular distributions for 2001 to 2004 sales price (cells C6 to F6): =RiskTriang(25,55,85), =RiskTriang (28,58,88), =RiskTriang(31,61,91), and =RiskTriang(34,64,94), respectively.

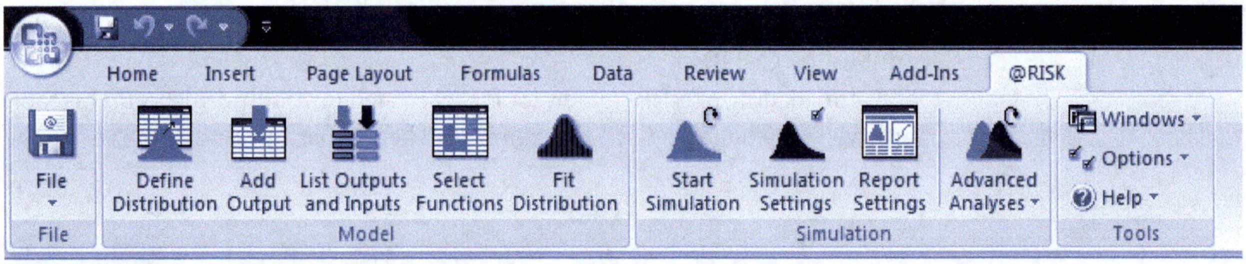

FIGURE 5.8

@Risk Toolbar for Excel 2007

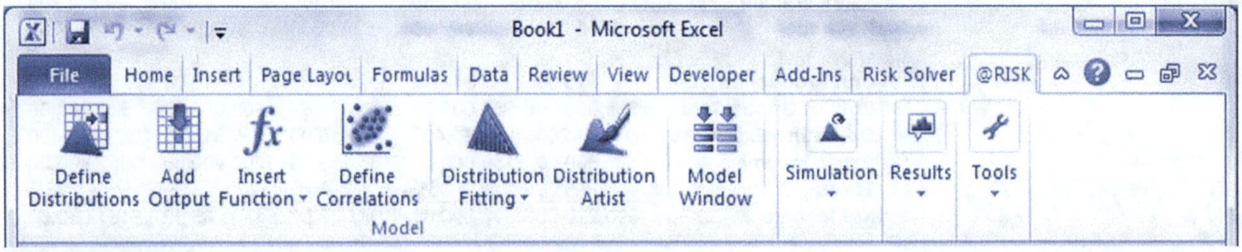

FIGURE 5.9

@Risk Toolbar for Excel 2010

The Triangular Distribution

Figure 5.10 displays the triangular distribution presented in Cell B6. Turn back to Chapter 3 for more information on distributions, especially the triangular distribution.

When a simulation is not running, @RISK will display the most likely value for the triangular distribution; thus in year 2000, 50 is displayed. During a simulation run, @RISK will sample values for cells B6 through F6 across the range of the triangular distribution. For each iteration (or recalculation of the spreadsheet) a new, randomly generated value will be placed in the worksheet cell.

Cells B10 through F10 (Unit Production Cost) and cell B17 (Discount Value) also contain the triangular distribution formula with exactly the same triangular distribution interpretation, but different high, most likely, and low parameters. For cells B10 through F10 use the following triangular distributions: =RiskTriang (7.5,10,12.5), =RiskTriang(12.5,15,17.5), =RiskTriang(14,17,21), and =RiskTriang (12.5,15,17.5), =RiskTriang(7.5,10,12.5), respectively. For cell B17 use =RiskTriang (0.10,0.11,0.12).

Cells B7 through F7 contain the formula =RiskNormal(#1,#2), where #1 represents a mean value and #2 represents the standard deviation value. The interpretation is that XYZ has determined that the volume of sales will have a normal distribution with a mean value and will fluctuate in respect to its standard deviation value.

The Normal Distribution

Figure 5.11 displays the normal distribution presented in Cell B7. Turn back to Chapter 3 for more information on distributions, especially the normal distribution.

Thus the formula in cell B7 is =RiskNormal(3500,300). This means that, in year 2000, there is a 68.26 percent chance that sales volume will fall between 3200 and 3800. For years 2001 through 2004, the same formula is used but with different normal distribution values.

When a simulation is not running, @RISK will display the mean value for the normal distribution, thus in year 2000, 3500 is displayed. During a simulation run,

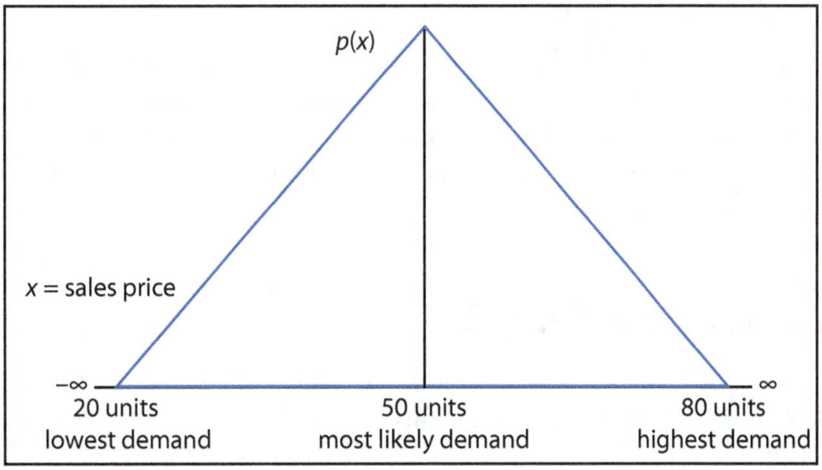

FIGURE 5.10
Triangular Distribution for Sales Price

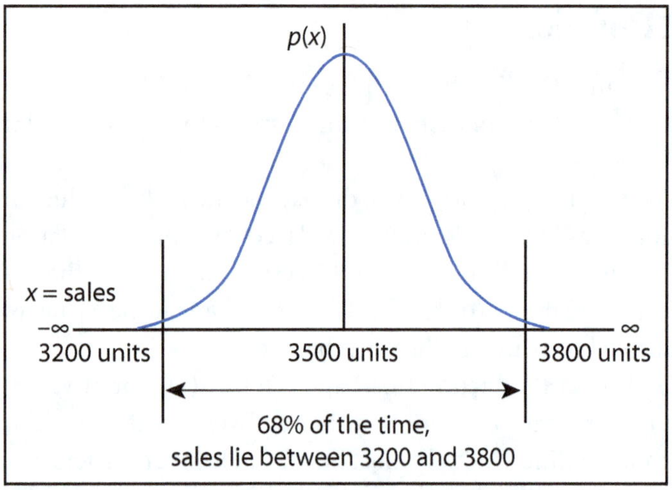

FIGURE 5.11
Normal Distribution for Sales

@RISK will sample values for those cells that fall along the normal distribution defined by their formulas.

Cells B12 through F12 (Operating Expense) also contain the normal distribution formula with exactly the same normal distribution interpretation, but different mean and standard deviation.

Note that the above-mentioned cells are called input cells, which @RISK will calculate and recalculate during a simulation run.

Output Cells

Let's take a look at the *output cells*. In @RISK, an output is a cell whose value we are interested in studying, a bottom-line value. Output cells contain formulas that reference input cells; their calculations use values from the cells containing @RISK functions you have entered. In the XYZ model, we are interested in the net Present Value, calculated in cell B18, and the Net Income value for all 5 years, calculated from cells B15 through F15.

To add cell B18 as an output, select it in the spreadsheet and click the Add Output button on the @RISK toolbar. During a simulation, each time the spreadsheet is recalculated, the value of cell B18 will be recorded. The result will be a range of possible outcome values.

XYZ is also interested in the Net Income for each year, calculated in cells B15 through F15. You can highlight the entire range from B15 through F15 and then click the Add utput" button to define these cells as outputs. By defining a group or range of cells as an output, you can study the impact of each cell individually or the impact of the whole range at once.

Summary of Inputs and Outputs

Now that we have defined uncertainty in our model and selected output cells, let's take a look at our inputs and outputs by clicking the Model Window button on the @RISK toolbar.

@Risk Window

Figure 5.12 shows that we are in the @RISK window. In addition to information on the selected inputs and outputs, simulation results and graphs are displayed here. This is discussed later in the tutorial.

The Model Window button lists three menu tabs on the upper part of the window. The tabs are Inputs, Outputs, and Correlations. The lower part of the window contains icons for graphing, sorting, and other functions regarding @Risk Inputs and Outputs.

The inputs list also shows the @RISK function contained in the cell. Now that our model is set up, we are ready to run a risk analysis.

Running a Risk Analysis

In this section, a risk analysis is run and the results studied. We will discuss the following topics associated with the risk analysis: simulation settings, running a simulation, and analyzing the results.

SIMULATION SETTINGS

Let's first discuss the settings for running a simulation, click the Simulation button at the top of the toolbar (refer to Figure 5.13a). You will see another dialog box displayed as in Figure 5.13b.

The Iteration tab defines the number of iterations to run during a simulation. At each iteration, a new set of random numbers that is generated and the worksheet is recalculated. We are currently set to run 10,000 iterations. For most simu-

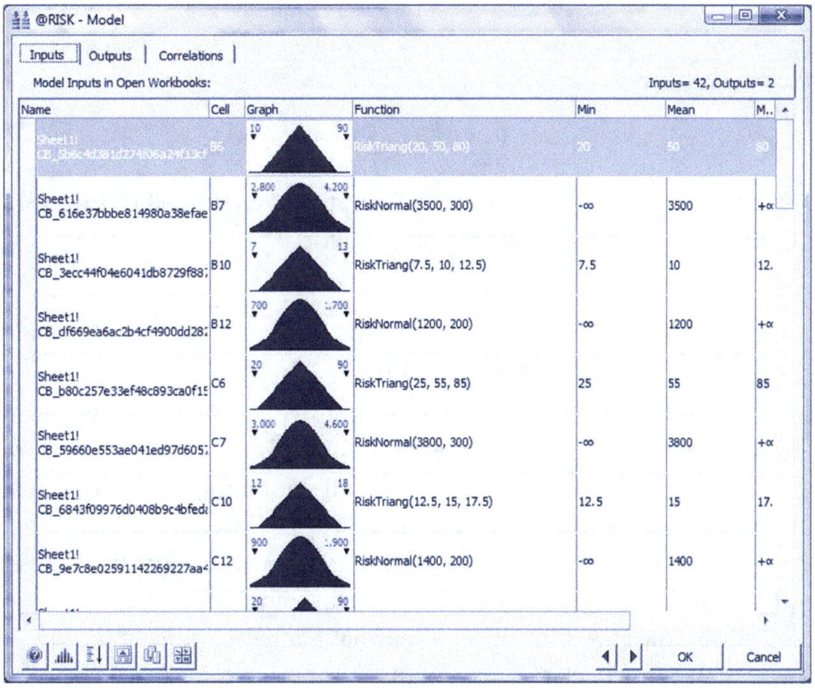

FIGURE 5.12
Inputs by Outputs List in @Risk

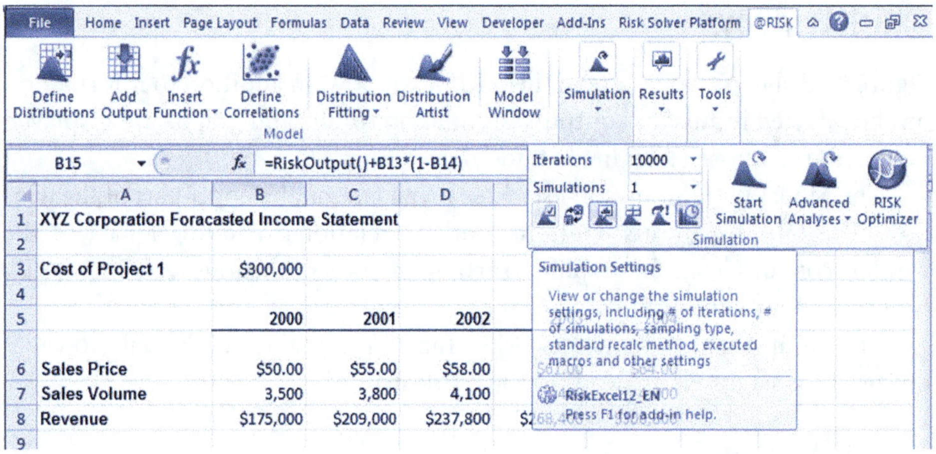

FIGURE 5.13a

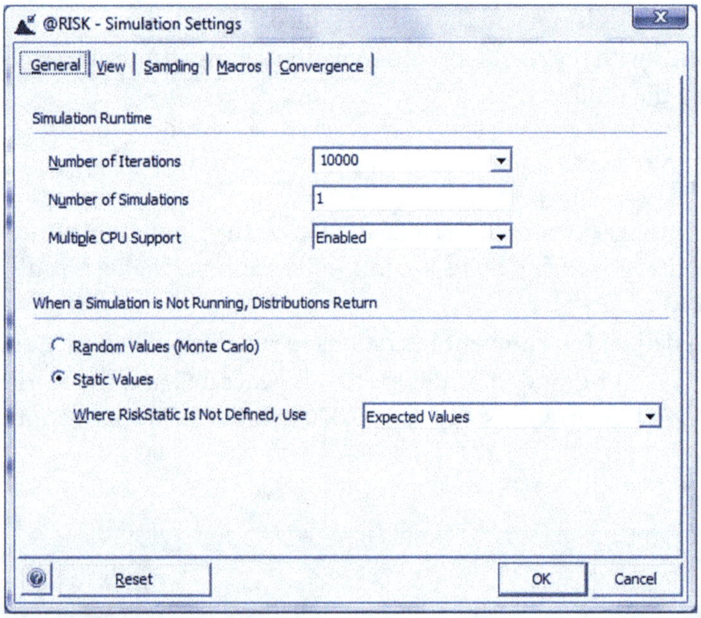

FIGURE 5.13b

Simulation Setting: General Tab

lations, you will want to run a larger number of iterations, say 100,000. However, we will use 10,000 iterations for the purpose of this tutorial.

VIEW TAB

The View tab contains two areas: the Automatic Results Display area and the Options area. The Automatic Results Display area asks what type of output from the finished simulation you want to display. Show Output Graph is the default and most chosen option. The Options area has check bodes for a number of options while the simulation runs. Any of the boxes can be checked but one that can be checked is the Update Windows During Simulation Every. This option allows you to see the random numbers in your model change as the iterations run. In the long run, this option slows down the simulation somewhat is after witnessing this once or twice you may wish to uncheck the box and turn the option off.

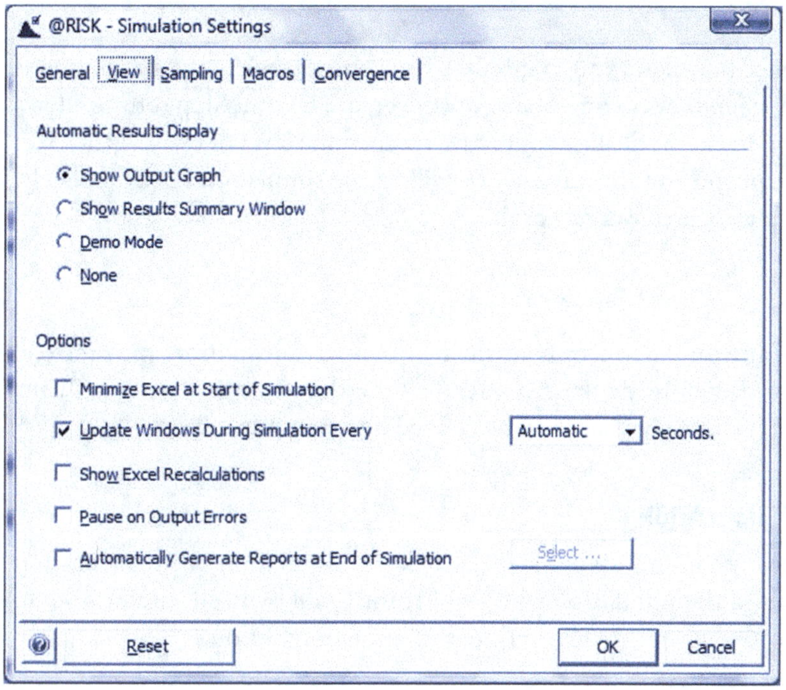

FIGURE 5.14

Simulation Settings: View Tab

SAMPLING TAB

The Sampling tab controls how each distribution in your worksheet will be sampled. We will be using the Monte Carlo sampling type, which achieves more accurate results with a larger amount of iterations. Should you be running the simulation with lesser iterations, it is recommended that you should use the default sampling type, Latin Hypercube. Figure 5.15 displays the Sampling tab.

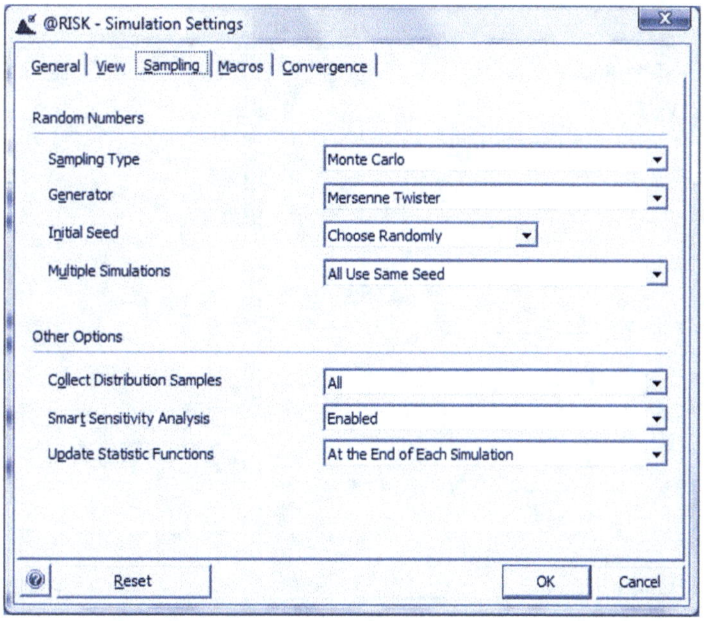

FIGURE 5.15

Simulation Setting: Sampling Tab

CONVERGENCE TAB

The Convergence tab allows you to monitor your outputs while the simulation is running to see when they become stable or converge. The AutoStop setting allows your simulation to run until all outputs have reached the level of convergence you specify. For the purpose of this tutorial, we will let the simulation run completely. Figure 5.16 displays the convergence tab.

MACRO TAB

You may continue on the Macro tab, which allows advanced users to run Excel macro commands before, during, or after a simulation. Use this feature if your model requires calculations that must be defined by macro functions.

RUNNING THE SIMULATION

You are now ready to run the simulation. Click the Simulation button at the top of the toolbar and the simulation will begin running all by itself. (Refer back to Figure 5.9 or 5.10 if you are unable to find the Simulation button.)

ANALYZE THE RESULTS

After the simulation has finished, results can be viewed by clicking the results button in the @Risk menu (see Figure 5.17a). After clicking Browse Results in the @Risk menu, a window resembling Figure 5.17b appears. Now we can take a look and interpret these results so XYZ may determine whether or not to conduct this product launch.

The Results window (top window) displays a summary of the simulation results, including minimum, mean, and maximum values calculated for each output cell and input distribution. We can see that NPV has a minimum value of

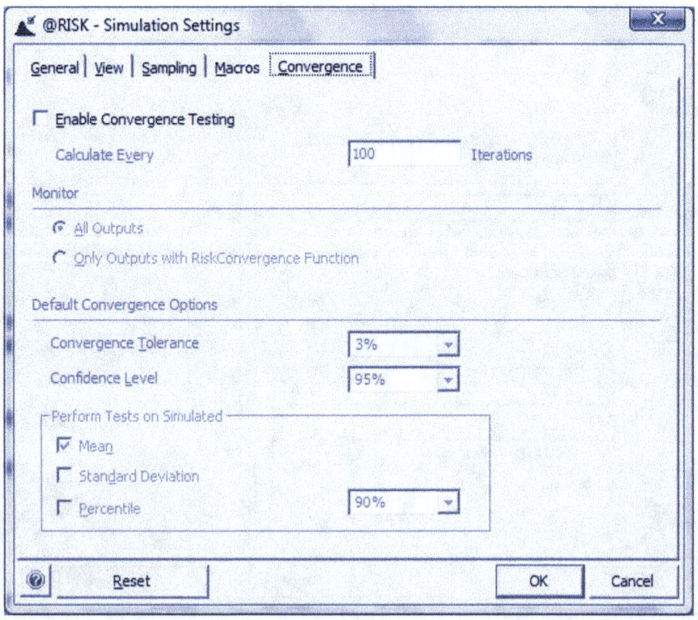

FIGURE 5.16

Simulation Setting: Convergence Tab

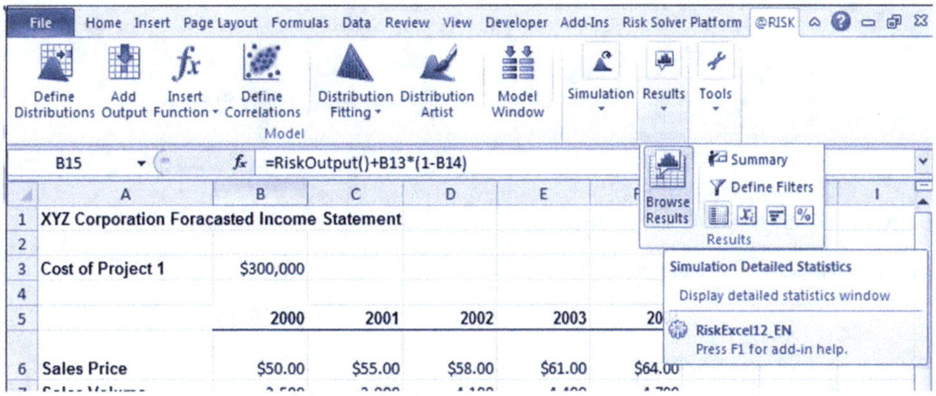

FIGURE 5.17a
Results Button in @Risk

@RISK - Detailed Statistics

Name	Net Income / 2000	Net Income / 2001	Net Income / 2002	Net Income / 2003	Net Income / 2004	Present Value Proj.
Description	Output	Output	Output	Output	Output	Output
Cell	Sheet1!B15	Sheet1!C15	Sheet1!D15	Sheet1!E15	Sheet1!F15	Sheet1!B18
Minimum	19011.29	20554.93	21707.28	41247.41	66403.98	-90286.55
Maximum	194814.3	199446.5	214192.1	244383.6	293558.5	340501.9
Mean	90287.84	97508.84	107380.4	129802.7	164692.2	122372.5
Std Deviation	29092.89	31629.11	33990.64	36247.89	38877.55	55784.15
Variance	8.463965E+08	1.000401E+09	1.155363E+09	1.31391E+09	1.511464E+09	3.111872E+09
Skewness	0.1288963	8.667336E-02	0.1163498	0.1197886	9.923776E-02	8.780136E-02
Kurtosis	2.586972	2.533338	2.539711	2.532911	2.575865	2.964252
Errors	0	0	0	0	0	0
Mode	90889.63	102552.3	103627.2	128714.7	168275.8	148562.6
5% Perc	42871.52	45105.39	51926.08	71019.1	101136.4	32344.1
10% Perc	51539.24	55055.24	62298.8	82060.04	113154.3	50767.27
15% Perc	58377.64	63041.77	70189.41	89965.31	122349.3	64354.9
20% Perc	64493.63	69424.55	76845.7	97538.02	129911.3	74916.43
25% Perc	69433.76	74797.55	82781.01	103453.2	136877.3	84546.3
30% Perc	73780.61	80037.12	88289.28	109094.3	143187.1	92506.3
35% Perc	78160.34	84528.19	93187.34	114369.6	148726.8	100195.3
40% Perc	82080.69	88509.91	97840.08	119532.7	154262.2	107556.2
45% Perc	85825.44	92938.64	102276.9	124339.1	159157.3	114337.3
50% Perc	89767.05	97191.22	106533.7	129145.8	163948.3	121201.6
55% Perc	93557.06	101419.4	110859.8	133893.7	168636.4	128274.4
60% Perc	97318.71	105461.2	115744	138767.3	174421.3	135942.3
65% Perc	101469.3	110270	120464	143873.1	179787.7	143406.6
70% Perc	106230.7	114764.6	125434	149094.6	185768.7	150904
75% Perc	110664.9	120014.7	131274.9	155012.1	191602.6	160039.9
80% Perc	115838.9	125178	137459.8	161870.7	198570.2	169667.7
85% Perc	121575.5	131489.4	144623.8	169320.5	207139.3	180587.5
90% Perc	128997	139358.3	153220.5	178601.9	216756.8	194947.8
95% Perc	139222.6	150665.5	164974.2	191154.2	230190.9	214799.1

Close

FIGURE 5.17b
Simulation Results

–90286.55, a mean value of 122372.5, and a maximum value of 340501.9. That's quite a large range of results, and depending on XYZ's tolerance for risk, it might consider this a very risky project.

Simulation Data Button

Referring back to Figure 5.17c, it is seen that there are four buttons next to the Results window, which are Simulation Statistics, Data, Sensitivities, and Scenarios.

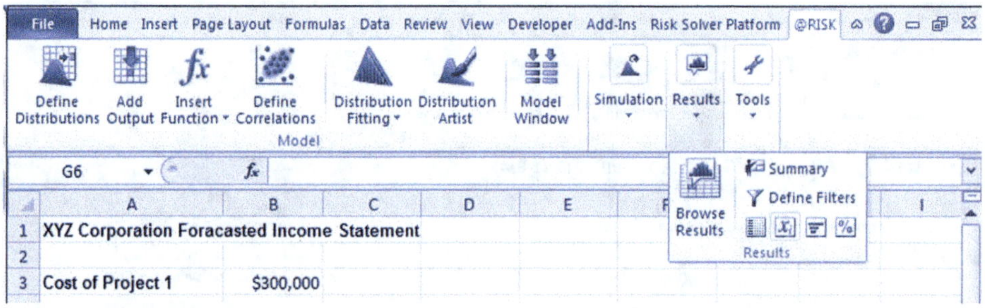

FIGURE 5.17c
Results Window Menu Buttons

Since Statistics are already displayed in the bottom window, click on the Simulation Data button. The Simulation Data button will display all the data collected and generated during each simulation for each iteration. You can transfer data and results to an Excel worksheet (Figure 5.18). Use this command to export simulation data into an Excel spreadsheet.

Simulation Sensitivities Button

Figure 5.19a displays the Simulation Sensitivities menu in the @Risk Ribbon. When the Sensitivities option is chosen, a sensitivity analysis is completed for your simulation. Figure 5.19b displays what the Sensitivity Anaylsis screen resembles.

In the "Sensitivity" window, Figure 5.19, the outputs are listed on the left. On the right, the inputs are ranked in order of their effect of the selected output. From the Rank list on the left of Figure 5.19b, we see that Sales Price is the most important input affecting the NPV.

@RISK uses two methods to measure sensitivity: multivariate stepwise regression measures the change in the selected output due to a unit change in the input variable (in units of standard deviations from the output mean), and rank-order correlation measures the rank-order correlation between the input and output data sets.

For either measurement, a value of 0 indicates that changes in the input variable have no effect on the output. The greater the magnitude of the value, the bigger the effect the input has on the output.

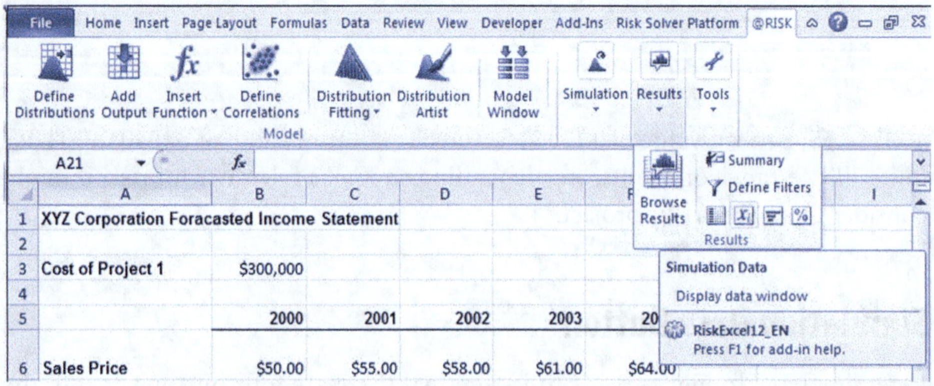

FIGURE 5.18
Simulation Data Button

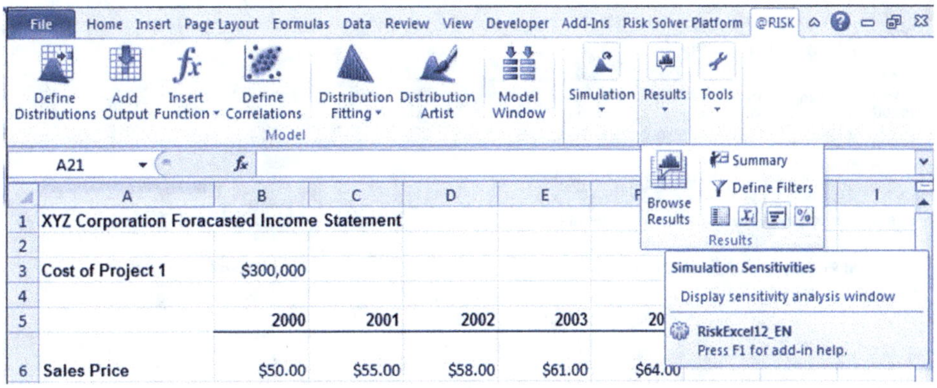

FIGURE 5.19a
Simulation Sensitivities Button

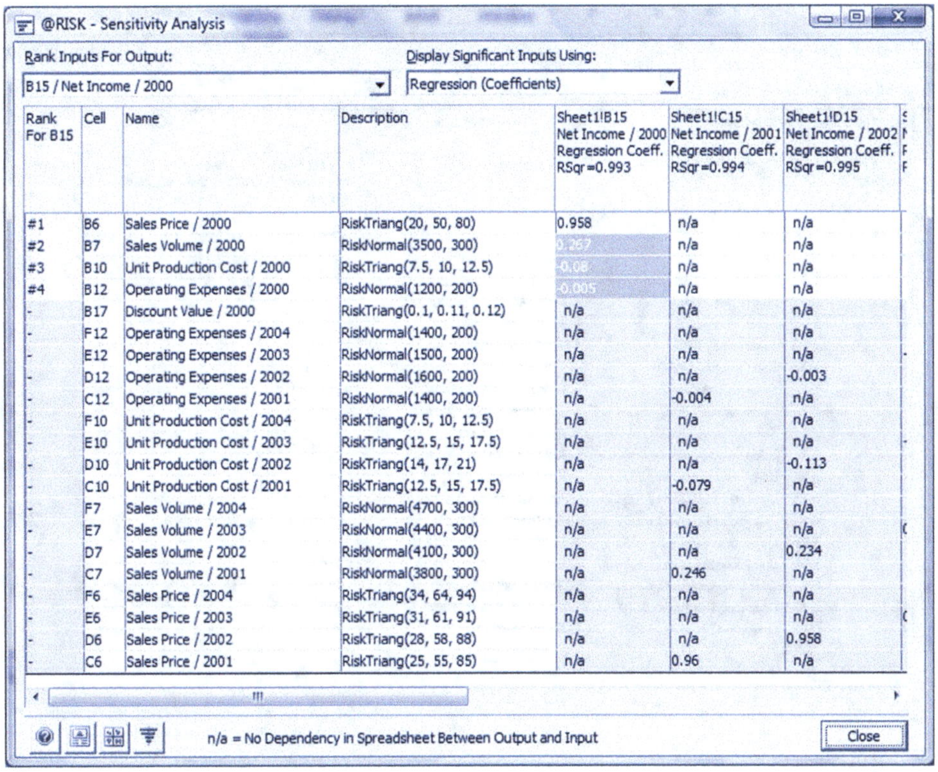

Rank For B15	Cell	Name	Description	Sheet1!B15 Net Income / 2000 Regression Coeff. RSqr=0.993	Sheet1!C15 Net Income / 2001 Regression Coeff. RSqr=0.994	Sheet1!D15 Net Income / 2002 Regression Coeff. RSqr=0.995
#1	B6	Sales Price / 2000	RiskTriang(20, 50, 80)	0.958	n/a	n/a
#2	B7	Sales Volume / 2000	RiskNormal(3500, 300)	0.267	n/a	n/a
#3	B10	Unit Production Cost / 2000	RiskTriang(7.5, 10, 12.5)	-0.08	n/a	n/a
#4	B12	Operating Expenses / 2000	RiskNormal(1200, 200)	-0.005	n/a	n/a
-	B17	Discount Value / 2000	RiskTriang(0.1, 0.11, 0.12)	n/a	n/a	n/a
-	F12	Operating Expenses / 2004	RiskNormal(1400, 200)	n/a	n/a	n/a
-	E12	Operating Expenses / 2003	RiskNormal(1500, 200)	n/a	n/a	n/a
-	D12	Operating Expenses / 2002	RiskNormal(1600, 200)	n/a	n/a	-0.003
-	C12	Operating Expenses / 2001	RiskNormal(1400, 200)	n/a	-0.004	n/a
-	F10	Unit Production Cost / 2004	RiskTriang(7.5, 10, 12.5)	n/a	n/a	n/a
-	E10	Unit Production Cost / 2003	RiskTriang(12.5, 15, 17.5)	n/a	n/a	n/a
-	D10	Unit Production Cost / 2002	RiskTriang(14, 17, 21)	n/a	n/a	-0.113
-	C10	Unit Production Cost / 2001	RiskTriang(12.5, 15, 17.5)	n/a	-0.079	n/a
-	F7	Sales Volume / 2004	RiskNormal(4700, 300)	n/a	n/a	n/a
-	E7	Sales Volume / 2003	RiskNormal(4400, 300)	n/a	n/a	n/a
-	D7	Sales Volume / 2002	RiskNormal(4100, 300)	n/a	n/a	0.234
-	C7	Sales Volume / 2001	RiskNormal(3800, 300)	n/a	0.246	n/a
-	F6	Sales Price / 2004	RiskTriang(34, 64, 94)	n/a	n/a	n/a
-	E6	Sales Price / 2003	RiskTriang(31, 61, 91)	n/a	n/a	n/a
-	D6	Sales Price / 2002	RiskTriang(28, 58, 88)	n/a	n/a	0.958
-	C6	Sales Price / 2001	RiskTriang(25, 55, 85)	n/a	0.96	n/a

FIGURE 5.19b
Sensitivity Analysis Window

Simulation Scenarios Button

Figure 5.20a displays the Simulation Sensitivities menu in the @Risk Ribbon. When the Sensitivities option is chosen, a sensitivity analysis is completed for your simulation. Figure 5.20b displays what the Sensitivity Analysis screen resembles.

Scenario analysis allows you to determine which input values contribute significantly toward reaching a goal. For example, scenario analysis can be used to determine which variable contributes to an exceptionally high or low NPV. In Figure 5.20b, we see the results of a scenario analysis when the NPV is greater than 75 percent (that is, when the NPV is at or above its 75th percentile value).

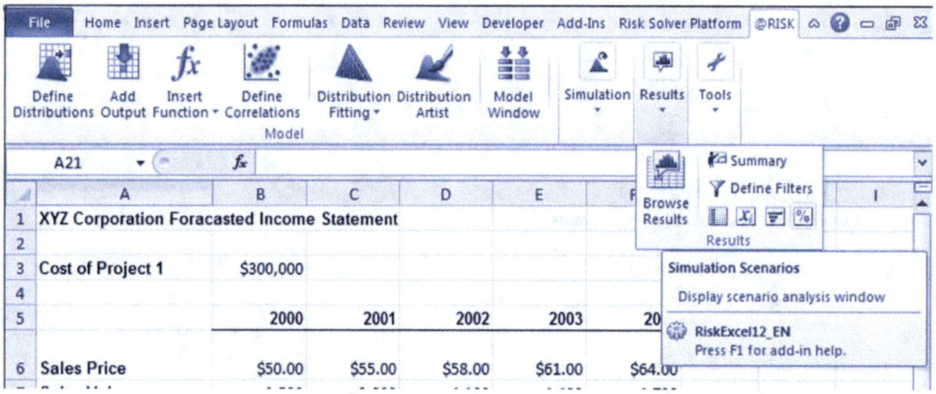

FIGURE 5.20a
Simulation Scenarios Button

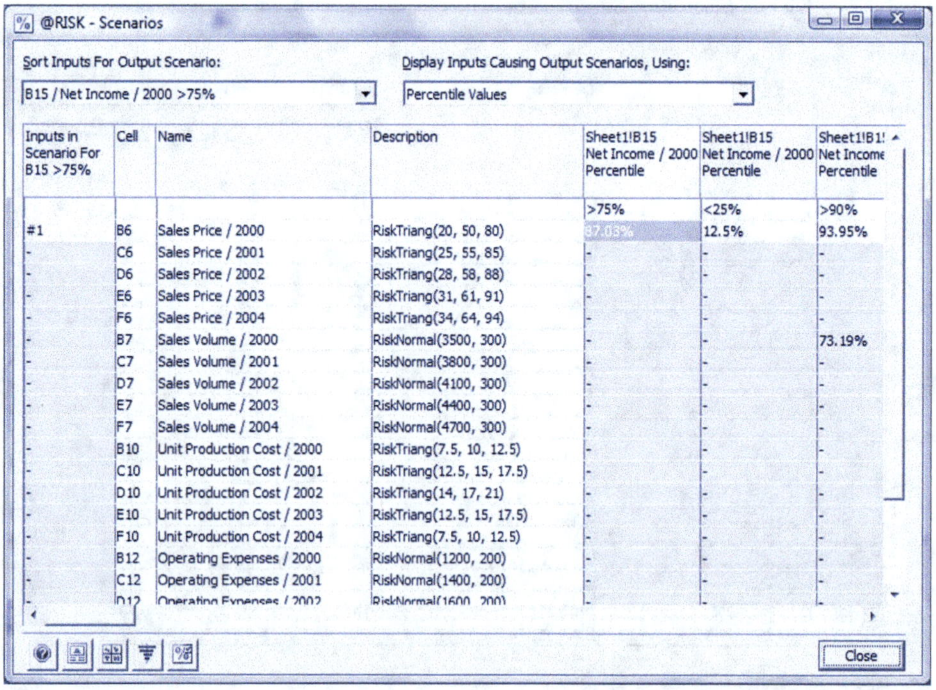

FIGURE 5.20b
Scenario Results

Scenario target values are entered in the Simulation Statistics window. According to the simulation, Sales Price is the most significant input variable when the NPV is at or above the 75th percentile value

Graphing the Results in @Risk

In this section, we will take a look at the different techniques in graphing the results from the simulation and how to interpret these graphs. We will examine the topics of histograms, graph format commands, summary graphs, tornado graphs, and graphs in the Excel spreadsheet.

Graphing: Understanding the Data More Clearly

The whole idea of graphing statistical results is to offer a method of better understanding the enormous amount of data that you have generated thus far. It is a way to put everything together and manipulate your data to make it more understandable.

Although @RISK will generate graphs for you, they may be difficult to understand; thus you can always choose to transfer your data to the Excel spreadsheet and graph it in a way both you and your audience can easily comprehend.

Using @Risk to Create a Histogram of NPV

We will first take a look at the graph for the NPV value generated from the simulation. Make the NPV cell active in the worksheet and click on the Results Menu in the @Risk Ribbon. In turn, click on Browse Results.

Figure 5.21 is called a *histogram*. It shows the distribution of possible values for cell B18 (NPV). The height of each bar represents the number of samples that fell in the range, defined by the width of the bar. In short, the histogram is a graphic representation of the uncertainty inherent in the output variable.

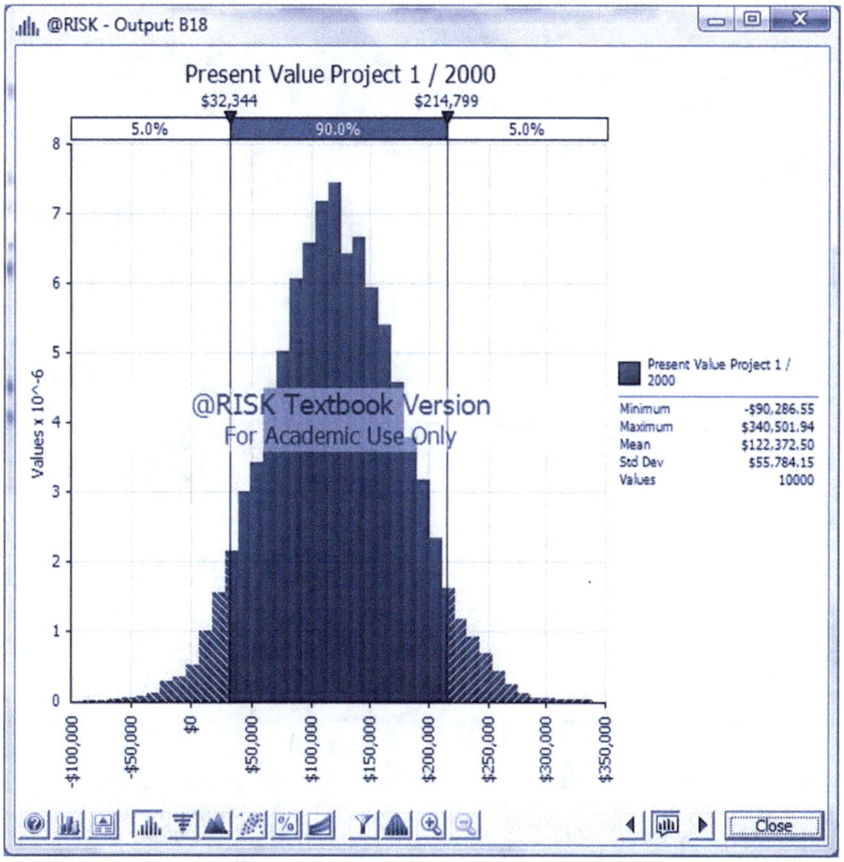

FIGURE 5.21
NPV Graph—Histogram

Using @Risk to Create a Smooth Bell-Shaped Curve of NPV

Let's view this graph in a different format. Right click on the graph, click Graph Options, click on the Curves tab, change the Style to Line, and Interpolation to Linked Midpoint.

Now we can see that the NPV statistics calculated from the simulation is very close to a simple bell curve (see Figure 5.22). This should make interpretation of the graph easier and not so esoteric.

Using @Risk to Create a Cumulative Distribution Graph of NPV

Let's view the graph in a cumulative distribution format. Right-click on the graph, click on Graph Options, Distribution and change the Distribution Format to Cumulative Ascending, then click on the Curves Tab, and change Style to Solid (see Figure 5.23).

The graph is now displayed as a cumulative probability curve (Figure 5.24). The graph shows the probability of a result less than or equal to any value in the range. For example, there is a 20 percent probability that the NPV will be less than approximately $75,000.

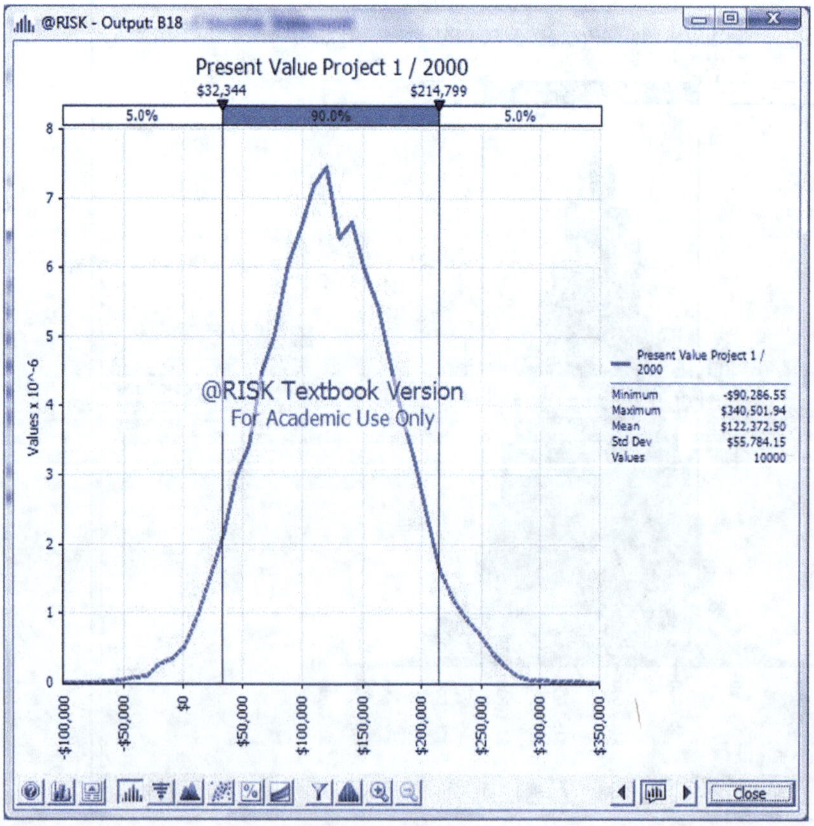

FIGURE 5.22
Smooth Bell-Shaped Curve of NPV

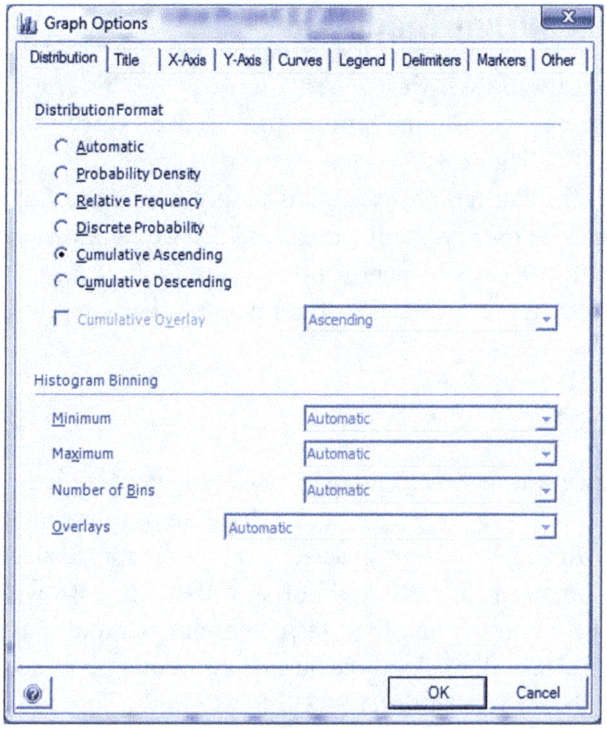

FIGURE 5.23
Cumulative Distribution Graph Options

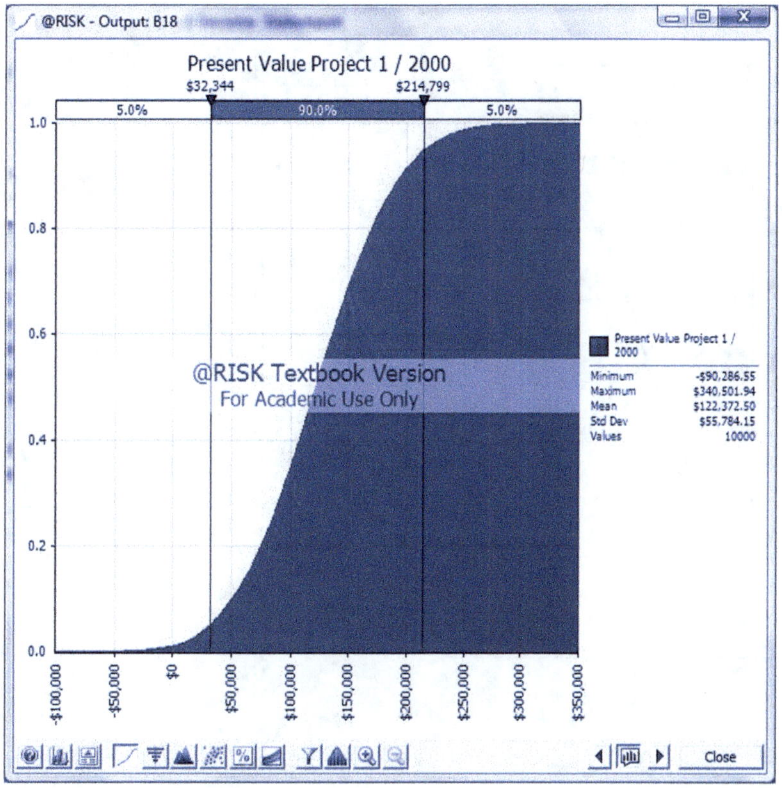

FIGURE 5.24
Cumulative Distribution Graph

Cumulative Distribution Outline Graph

Let's change the format once again to see if we can better understand this graph. Right-click on the graph again, click on Graph Options, then click on Curves tab and change Style to Line. Click OK. Figure 5.25 resembles the new graph.

You may notice that this is the same graph, except it is simply an outline of the previous graph. This graph may be more visually pleasing, since we can now see how the value of the NPV starts low, climbs steeply, and then levels off at the top. This graph presents the same idea as the normal distribution graph (bell curve).

Summary Output Graphs

What about the output range we selected in our model, the Net Income? We mentioned earlier that one advantage of selecting a range of cells as an output is that you can study changes of the whole group at once. Select a cell in the spreadsheet model and click the Results menu in the @Risk ribbon and then click Browse Results. At the bottom of the results graph find the Create Summary Graph in the New Window button (see Figure 5.26a). Click on the Summary Trend option and a menu simular to Figure 5.26b will appear. Enter $B$15:$F$15 in the Summary Graph options box and click OK.

The Summary Graph (Figure 5.27) summarizes the distributions generated for the cells in the selected output range—in this case for the five Net Income cells (B15 through F15).

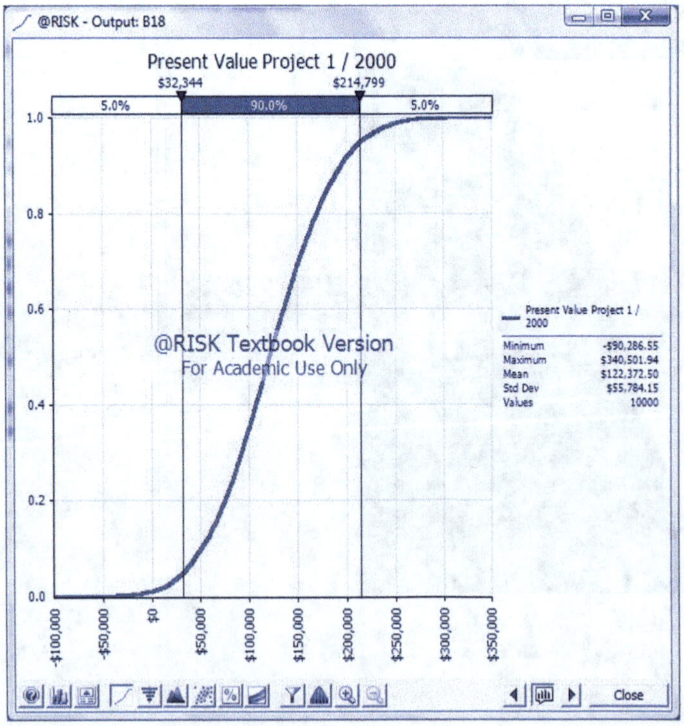

FIGURE 5.25
Cumulative Distribution Graph—Outline

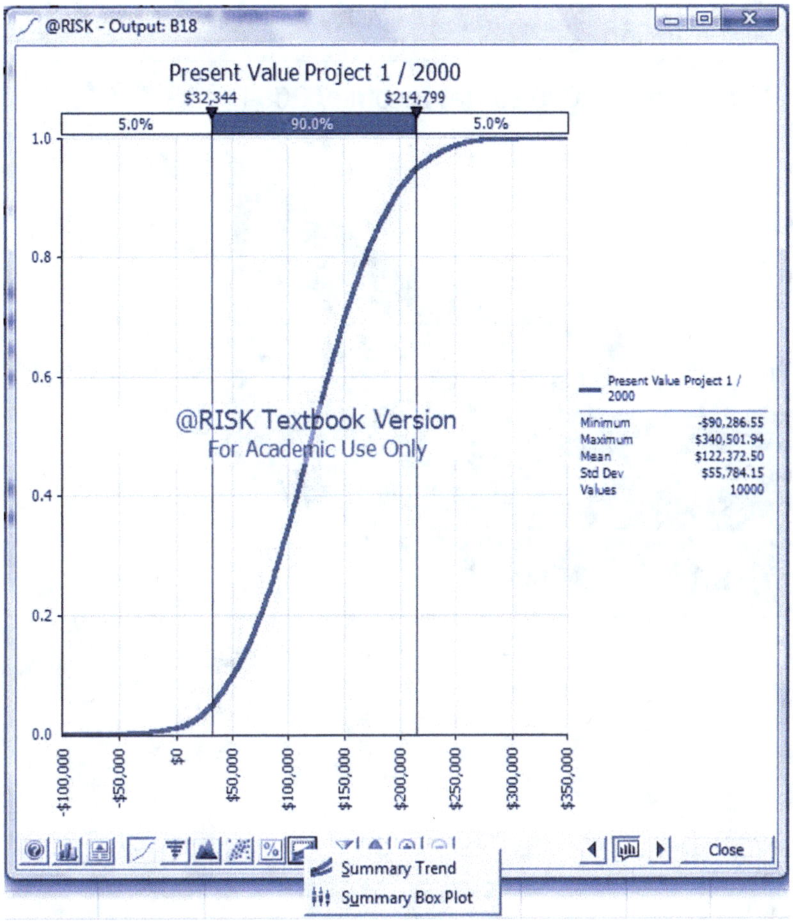

FIGURE 5.26a
Summary Trend Button

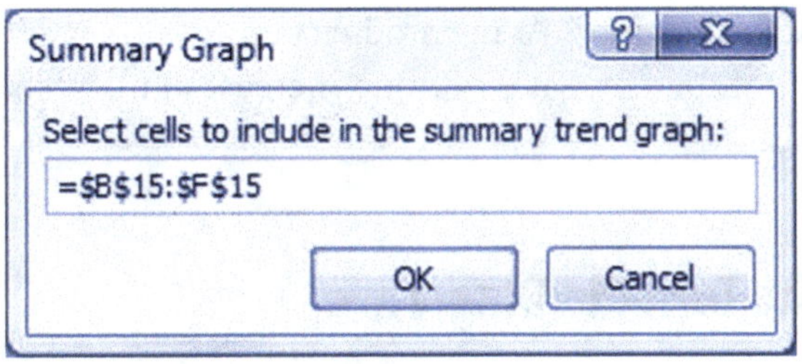

FIGURE 5.26b
Selecting Cells for Summary Graph

The lighter line in Figure 5.27 represents the trend in the mean of the distribution over 5 years, as described in the model. The darker band extends for one standard deviation about the mean. The outer medium color band extends to the 5th and 95th percentiles. The Summary Graph is useful for looking at how values change across an output range.

Interpretation of the Summary Graph

In this example, the graph demonstrates a steady upward trend for the first 2 years and then the trend picks up rapidly after the third year. This is atypical in a product life cycle, from a marketing perspective. As a product first becomes available to

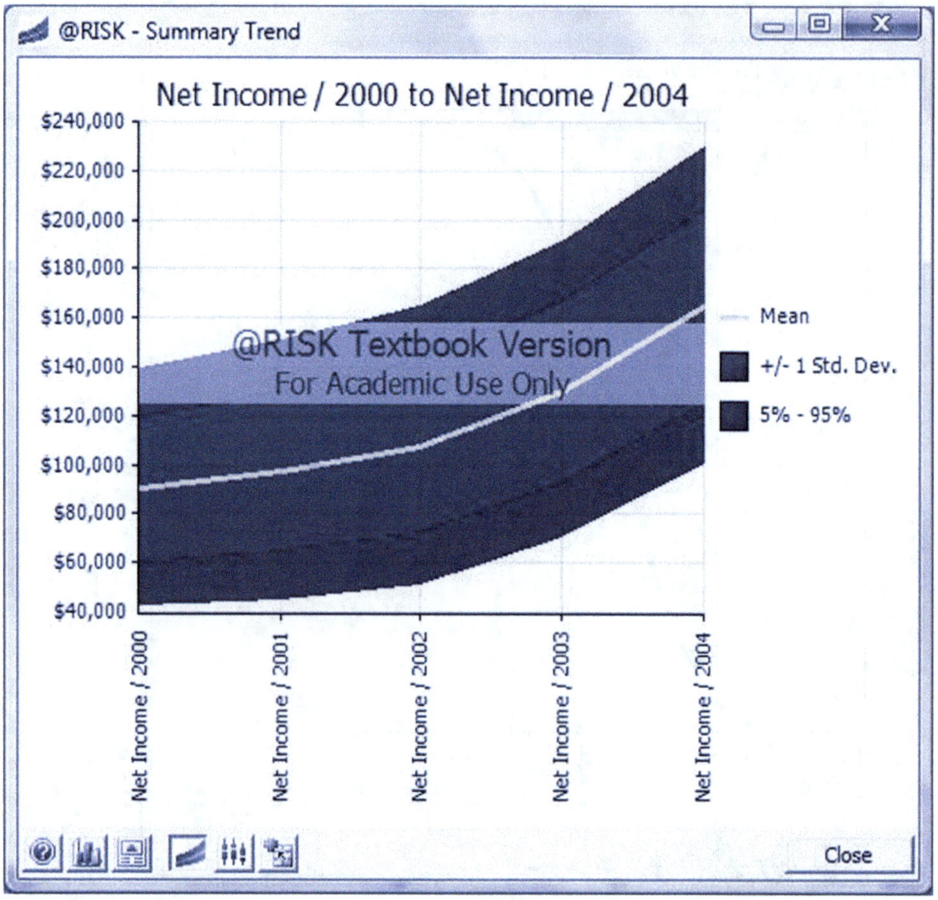

FIGURE 5.27
Summary Trend Graph

the public, it takes 1 to 2 years to gain recognition. As the product becomes accepted and management becomes more competent, sales volume increases and costs decrease, thus net income increases.

Sensitivity Analysis and the Tornado Diagram

Next, let's look at the sensitivity analysis in a graphical format called a Tornado Diagram. Click on cell B18 (the NPV cell) and then click on the Results Menu in the @Risk Ribbon. Next, click on the Simulation Sensitivities icon and the Sensitivity Analysis screen similar to Figure 5.19b will appear. From this screen click on the Tornado Graph icon on the bottom left of the screen. A figure that resembles Figure 5.28 will appear.

You can choose between Regression Coefficients or Correlation Coefficients. For the purpose of this tutorial the default is Regression Coefficients and that is what we will analyze.

As you can see from the tornado graphs in Figures 5.28, Sales Price for year 2000 is the most significant input, which is drawn at the top of the graph with the longest bar. The correlation coefficients are represented along the *x* axis, and each input variable is charted on the *y* axis.

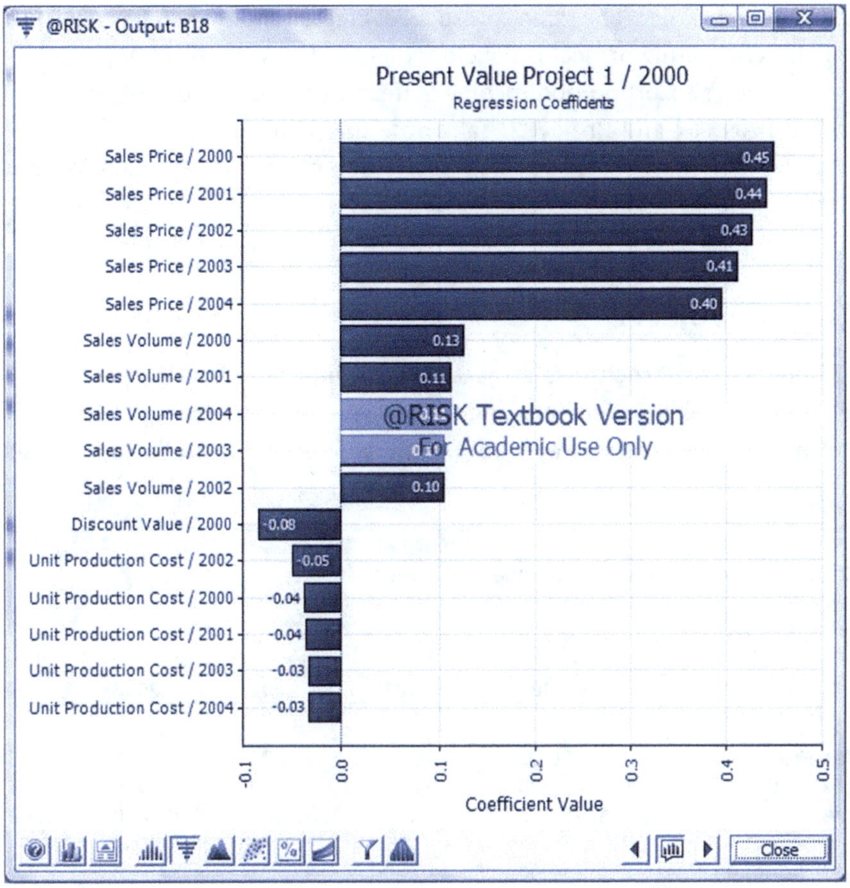

FIGURE 5.28
Tornado Graph

The tornado graph summarizes the effect of variables in a neat, simple graph. We can easily compare the magnitude of the effect of each input by the size of the bar and whether the effect is positive or negative in the direction of the bar (right or left, respectively).

Graphing in Excel

There may be times when you want to take data into an Excel spreadsheet or a different program for graphing. @RISK makes it easy to convert any graph to the native chart format of your spreadsheet via the Graph in Excel command.

Referring back to Figure 5.17, right-click on the graph, click Chart in Excel, and the graph will automatically be created in your Excel spreadsheet. Not only does @RISK create a histogram as an Excel chart, it will also copy all the data points to the same worksheet. You can use Excel's Chart features to customize the graph as you would any other chart.

@Risk Example with Multiple Decision Alternatives

Many times managers are faced with multiple projects that they must compare. The analysis completed for the XYZ Corporation can also be completed if the firm was faced with competing projects. This section adds to the XYZ Corporation example presented earlier. The same spreadsheet created in Figure 5.8 is used but now a second competing project is developed along the same lines. Figure 5.29 contains the new XYZ Corporation Income Statement for both projects, appropriately labeled Project 1 and Project 2. Take note that Project 1 is the exactly the model that was previously built. The next section describes the input and output cells for Project 2.

Structure of Project 2

Project 2 is identical in structure to Project 1 but the input distribution parameters are different. Project 2 has a different underlying structure for sales price, sales volume, unit production cost, and operation expenses. In addition, Project 2 costs

	A	B	C	D	E	F
1	**XYZ Corporation Foracasted Income Statement**					
2						
3	**Cost of Project 1**	$300,000				
4						
5		**2000**	**2001**	**2002**	**2003**	**2004**
6	**Sales Price**	$50.00	$55.00	$58.00	$61.00	$64.00
7	**Sales Volume**	3,500	3,800	4,100	4,400	4,700
8	**Revenue**	$175,000	$209,000	$237,800	$268,400	$300,800
9						
10	**Unit Production Cost**	$10.00	$15.00	$17.33	$15.00	$10.00
11	**Cost of Goods Sold**	$35,000.00	$57,000.00	$71,066.67	$66,000.00	$47,000.00
12	**Operating Expenses**	$1,200	$1,400	$1,600	$1,500	$1,400
13	**Gross Income**	$138,800.00	$150,600.00	$165,133.33	$200,900.00	$252,400.00
14	**Taxes**	35%	35%	35%	35%	35%
15	**Net Income**	$90,220.00	$97,890.00	$107,336.67	$130,585.00	$164,060.00
16						
17	**Discount Value**	0.11				
18	**Present Value**	$122,595				
19						
20						
21	**XYZ Corporation Foracasted Income Statement**					
22						
23	**Cost of Project 2**	$410,000				
24						
25		**2000**	**2001**	**2002**	**2003**	**2004**
26	**Sales Price**	$58.33	$63.33	$63.33	$68.33	$68.33
27	**Sales Volume**	3,800	4,100	4,400	4,700	4,700
28	**Revenue**	$221,667	$259,667	$278,667	$321,167	$321,167
29						
30	**Unit Production Cost**	$11.33	$11.33	$11.33	$11.33	$11.33
31	**Cost of Goods Sold**	$43,066.67	$46,466.67	$49,866.67	$53,266.67	$53,266.67
32	**Operating Expenses**	$1,500	$1,500	$1,500	$1,500	$1,500
33	**Gross Income**	$177,100.00	$211,700.00	$227,300.00	$266,400.00	$266,400.00
34	**Taxes**	35%	35%	35%	35%	35%
35	**Net Income**	$115,115.00	$137,605.00	$147,745.00	$173,160.00	$173,160.00
36						
37	**Discount Value**	0.11				
38	**Present Value**	$130,248				

FIGURE 5.29 XYZ Corporation Forecasted Income Statement

more up front than Project 1 (e.g., compare cell B23, $400,000, to cell B3, $300,000, in Figure 5.29).

In general, the extra money spent up front for Project 2 does have benefits. The extra money boosts overall sales price over all years compared to Project 1. Sales volumes are also higher across the years, eventually matching Project 1 levels in 2004. Project 2 also brings with it initial higher unit production and operating costs, but these costs are consistent over the years whereas Project 1's costs tend to rise and fall over time. From Figure 5.29 it appears that on average Project 2 has a higher NPV. However, intuitively we don't know what happens to NPV as the different input variables change within the model. This is a good indication that simulation would assist us in obtaining a better picture of what NPV will be for both projects.

Input Cells for Project 2

For Project 2, in year 2000, Sales Price (Cell B6) ranges from a low of 15 to a most likely value of 50 to a high of 80. Thus the formula for cell 26 is =RiskTriang (15,55,105). For years 2001 through 2004, the same formula is used, but with different triangular distribution values. Use the following triangular distributions for 2001 to 2004 Sales Price (cells C26 to F26): =RiskTriang(20,60,110), =RiskTriang (20,60,110), =RiskTriang(25,65,115), and =RiskTriang(25,65,115), respectively.

As with Project 1, Project 2 Sales Volumes are normally distributed. The formula in cell B27 is =RiskNormal(3800,300). This means that, in year 2000, there is a 68.26% chance that sales volume will fall between 3,500 and 4,100. For years 2001 through 2004, the same formula is used, but with different normal distribution values. The following distributions are used for 2001 to 2004 Sales Volume (cells C27 to F27): =RiskNormal(4100,300), =RiskNormal(4400,300), =RiskNormal (4700,300), and =RiskNormal(4700,300).

Unit production costs for Project 2 are based on triangular distributions. For cells B30 through F30 use the following triangular distribution: =RiskTriang (9.5,10,14.5). Note that the distribution for Unit Production Cost for Project 2 is the same for all years.

Cells B32 through F32 (Operating Expense) also contain the normal distribution formula. The distribution for operating expense for Project 2 remains the same for all years. The following distribution are used for 2000 to 2004 Sales Volume (cells B32 to F32): =RiskNormal(1500,200). Discount value for Project 2 is also variable but is identical to Project 1. Therefore, insert =RiskTriang(0.10,0.11,0.12) in cell B37.

Output Cells

As in the original XYZ model, we are interested in the net Present Value, calculated in cell B18 for Project 1 and cell B38 for Project 2. For this example only NPV will be analyzed.

To add cell B38 as an output, select it in the spreadsheet and click the Add Output button on the @RISK toolbar. During a simulation, each time the spreadsheet is recalculated, the value of cell B38 will be recorded. The result will be a range of possible outcome values.

Running the Simulation

As in the original example, we wish to run 10,000 iterations. So in the Iterations tab within the Simulation Settings menu make sure # Iterations is set to 10,000. Also, we wish to sample using Monte Carlo, so in the Sampling tab within the Simulation Settings menu, make sure the Sampling Type is Monte Carlo and the Standard Recalc is set to Monte Carlo. Click the OK button when done. Now the Start Simulation button can be clicked. A screen may appear that asks you if you wish to "Save current @Risk model and results before simulating?". If you wish to save then click Yes and save the model, otherwise click No and the simulation will begin.

Interpreting the Results

As with the original XYZ Corporation example, we wish to graph the simulation output statistics in Excel. Figure 5.30 displays the simulation output in graphical format. Now the three areas of sensitivity analysis can be discussed to shed some light on how the two projects stack up to each other.

Dominance

First, from Figure 5.30 it is apparent that neither project has strict dominance over the other. Let's assume in Figure 5.30 that the left hand side of the graph represents

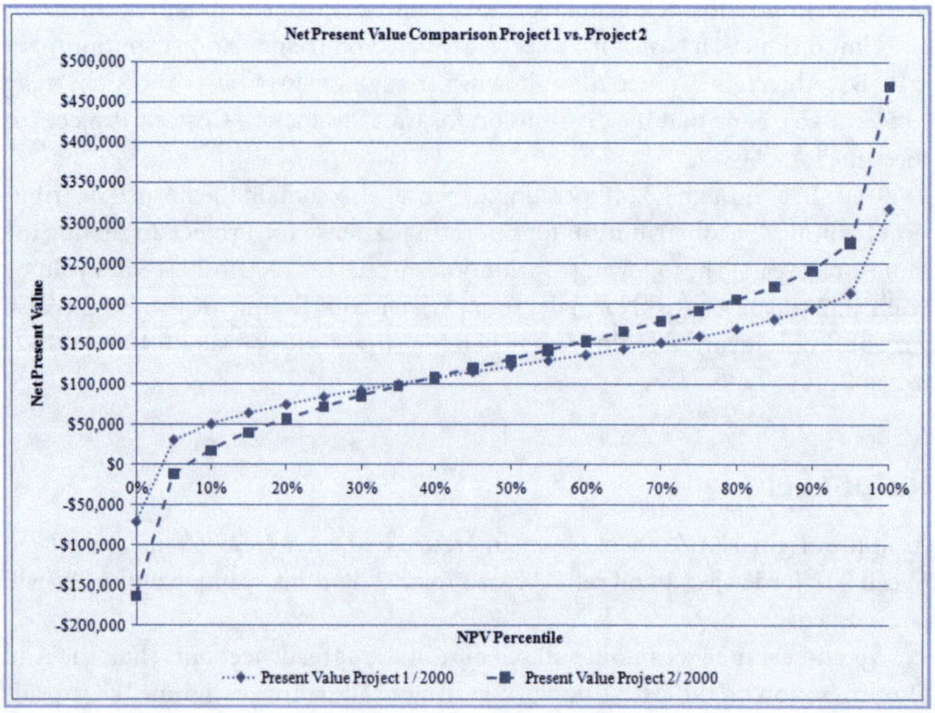

FIGURE 5.30
Simulation Output

the situation when all the "not-so-good" things happen (i.e., low sales price, low sales volume, and high costs) and that the right hand side of the graph represents when all the "good" things occur (i.e., high sales price, high sales volume, and low costs). It is clear from Figure 5.30 that at certain NPV percentiles Project 1 is the better choice and for other NPV percentiles Project 2 is the better choice. For example, although the NPV for Project 1 beings in the negative region (refer to the 0% NPV percentile in Figure 5.30), it is less negative than Project 2, making it the better choice. This better NPV position continues for Project 1 until somewhere around the 40% percentile. Around the 40% percentile Project 2 begins to overtake Project 1 in terms of NPV. Project 2 outpaces Project 1 for all percentiles up to the 100% percentile. So, it appears both projects can be considered "good" depending on what happens with the input variables.

Trade-offs

The point at which Project 1 and Project 2 trade off has been established as the principle of dominance was discussed. Somewhere around the 40% percentile Project 1 and Project 2 trade off. In other words, as the input variables change in the simulation model, Project 1 tends to be the best project around 40% of the time while Project 2 tends to be the better project around 60% of the time. One might say "Oh, 60% versus 40%, I pick Project 2 since 60 is greater than 40." However, a decision maker must be careful not to be hasty. Each project's risk must be analyzed before a decision can be made.

Risk Analysis

Although it is true that Project 2 has higher NPV more often than Project 1, it must be noted that Project 2 has more downside risk than Project 1. This is illustrated in Figure 5.30 on the left hand side of the graph. Although both projects have negative NPV values below the 5% percentile, Project 1 loses money less often and losses less money overall. In the worst case, Project 2 loses around $90,000 more than Project 1. A manager must decide whether to handle this larger downside to Project 2 versus Project 1.

With that said, Project 2 also has a larger upside gain associated with its adoption. This is illustrated in Figure 5.30 on the right hand side of the graph. Although both projects have positive NPV values above the 95% percentile, Project 2 gains more money overall. In the best case, Project 2 gains around $150,000 more than Project 1. This is a great benefit to Project 2. However, a manager must understand that in choosing Project 2 the possibility of the larger upside also comes with the possibility of the larger downside. From this analysis it could be said that Project 2 is relatively more risky than Project 1 or that Project 1 is more consistent compared to Project 2. Take note though, if a manager decides to be more conservative and take Project 1, that gives up the chance to garner superior high-end gains.

Another way to look at risk is by analyzing the project's standard deviations. Another advantage to simulation models is the ability to get a good measure of our decision alternative's standard deviations. Standard deviation can be used as a proxy for risk. Larger standard deviations can be associated with higher relative risks. The standard deviation for Project 1 is approximately 55,400 whereas the standard deviation for Project 2 is approximately 87,100. Project 2's standard deviation is higher than Project 1's and therefore could be deemed relatively more risky. This matches with the previous analysis of upside gain and downside risk.

Risk Solver Platform Tutorial

Getting Started with RSP and the XYZ Corporation Model

In the following example, XYZ Corporation is faced with a critical decision on whether or not to launch a new product to the market. The initial cost of the project is calculated by the accounting department at $300,000 (Cell B3); the content of the income statement, including individual cell formulas, will be discussed in detail later in this tutorial. At the bottom of the income statement (Figure 5.31), XYZ has also calculated net present value (Cell B18) of the project, using a discount value (Cell B17).

Input Cells

The spreadsheet in Figure 5.31 may look like a typical spreadsheet model, but looks can be deceiving. Let's take a look at the contents of the cells:

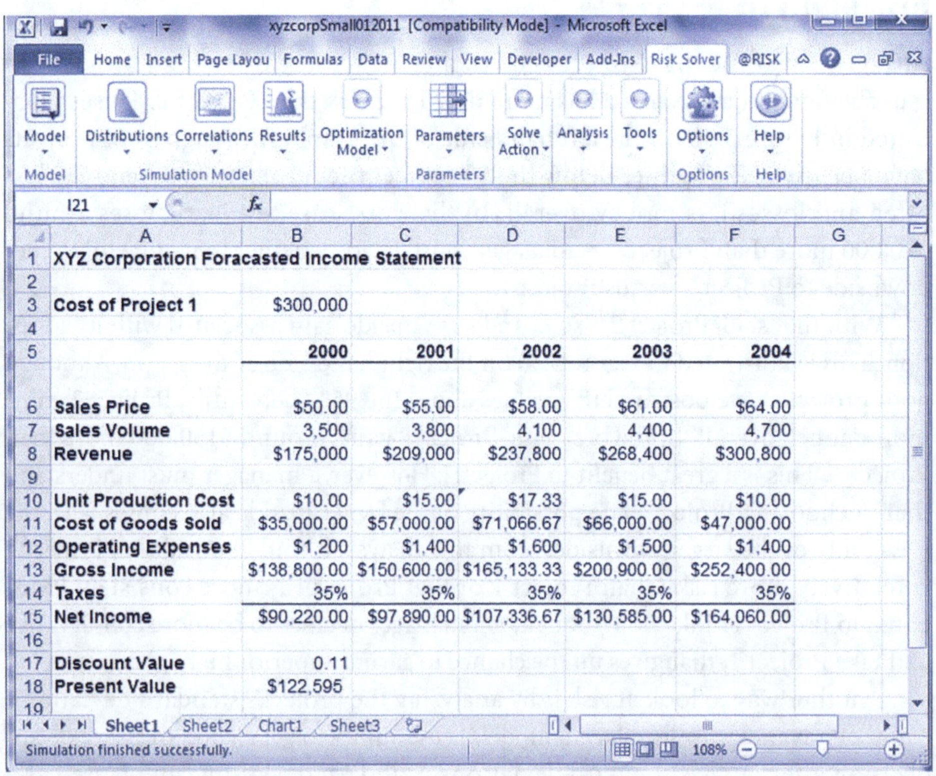

	A	B	C	D	E	F
1	XYZ Corporation Foracasted Income Statement					
2						
3	Cost of Project 1	$300,000				
4						
5		2000	2001	2002	2003	2004
6	Sales Price	$50.00	$55.00	$58.00	$61.00	$64.00
7	Sales Volume	3,500	3,800	4,100	4,400	4,700
8	Revenue	$175,000	$209,000	$237,800	$268,400	$300,800
9						
10	Unit Production Cost	$10.00	$15.00	$17.33	$15.00	$10.00
11	Cost of Goods Sold	$35,000.00	$57,000.00	$71,066.67	$66,000.00	$47,000.00
12	Operating Expenses	$1,200	$1,400	$1,600	$1,500	$1,400
13	Gross Income	$138,800.00	$150,600.00	$165,133.33	$200,900.00	$252,400.00
14	Taxes	35%	35%	35%	35%	35%
15	Net Income	$90,220.00	$97,890.00	$107,336.67	$130,585.00	$164,060.00
16						
17	Discount Value	0.11				
18	Present Value	$122,595				

FIGURE 5.31

Cells B6 through F6 contain the formula =PsiTriangular(#1,#2,#3), where #1, #2, and #3 represent the three triangular distribution values starting with #1 at the lowest value, #2 the most likely value, and #3 the highest value.

This can be interpreted as follows: XYZ has determined that for every year, sales price can range between three values. For example, in year 2000, sales price (Cell B6) ranges from 20, 50, to 80. Thus the formula for cell B6 is =PsiTriangular (20,50,80). For years 2001 through 2004, the same formula is used, but with different triangular distribution values. Use the following triangular distributions for 2001 to 2004 sales price (cells C6 to F6): =PsiTriangular (25,55,85), =PsiTriangular (28,58,88), =PsiTriangular (31,61,91), and =PsiTriangular (34,64,94), respectively.

When a simulation is not running, RSP can display the most likely value for the triangular distribution or a random number drawn from the distribution. For the XYZ spreadsheet in Figure 5.31, the most likely values for all the cells are displayed or what is called Sample Mode. During a simulation run, RSP will sample values for cells B6 through F6 across the range of the triangular distribution. For each iteration (or recalculation of the spreadsheet) a new, randomly generated value will be placed in the worksheet cell. You can use the F9 key to automatically recalculate the input cells when not in the Sample Mean mode. You can also choose which value to display within the RSP options menu. How to change the value to display option will be covered later in this section.

Cells B10 through F10 (Unit Production Cost) and cell B17 (Discount Value) also contain the triangular distribution formula with exactly the same triangular distribution interpretation, but different high, most likely, and low parameters. For cells B10 through F10 use the following triangular distributions: =PsiTriangular (7.5,10,12.5), =PsiTriangular (12.5,15,17.5), =PsiTriangular (14,17,21), and =PsiTriangular (12.5,15,17.5), =PsiTriangular (7.5,10,12.5), respectively. For cell B17 use =PsiTriangular (0.10,0.11,0.12).

Simulation Modeling

Cells B7 through F7 contain the formula =PsiNormal(#1,#2), where #1 represents a mean value and #2 represents the standard deviation value. The interpretation is that XYZ has determined that the volume of sales will have a normal distribution with a mean value and will fluctuate in respect to its standard deviation value.

The Normal Distribution

Figure 5.12 displays the normal distribution presented in Cell B7. Turn back to Chapter 3 for more information on distributions, especially the normal distribution. Thus the formula in cell B7 is =PsiNormal(3500,300). This means that, in year 2000, there is approximately a 68.26 percent chance that sales volume will fall between 3200 and 3800. For years 2001 through 2004, the same formula is used but with different normal distribution values.

In this example, when a simulation is not running, RSP displays the mean value for the normal distribution, thus in year 2000, 3500 is displayed. During a simulation run, RSP will sample values for those cells that fall along the normal distribution defined by their formulas.

Cells B12 through F12 (Operating Expense) also contain the normal distribution formula with exactly the same normal distribution interpretation, but different mean and standard deviation.

Note that the above-mentioned cells are called input cells or randomly generated cells, which RSP will calculate and recalculate during a simulation run.

Output Cells

Let's take a look at the output cells. In RSP, an output is a cell whose value we are interested in studying, in other words a bottom-line value. Output cells contain formulas that reference input cells; their calculations use values from the cells containing RSP functions you have entered. In the XYZ model, we are interested in the Net Present Value, calculated in cell B18, and the Net Income value for all 5 years, calculated from cells B15 through F15.

To add cell B18 as an output, select it in the spreadsheet and click the Results icon in the RSP ribbon, the Output option, and the In Cell option (refer to Figure 5.32). In the formula bar you should see the formula for cell B18 has changed. The cell formula should read "ì=NPV(B17,B15:F15)-B3 + PsiOutput()"î. The PsiOutput() at the end of the formula denotes that cell B18 is now an output cell in RSP. During a simulation, each time the spreadsheet is recalculated, the value of cell B18 will be recorded.

The result will be a range of possible outcome values. XYZ is also interested in the Net Income for each year, calculated in cells B15 through F15. You can highlight the entire range from B15 through F15 and then click the Result Icon, then click the Output option, and then the In Cell option to define these cells as outputs.

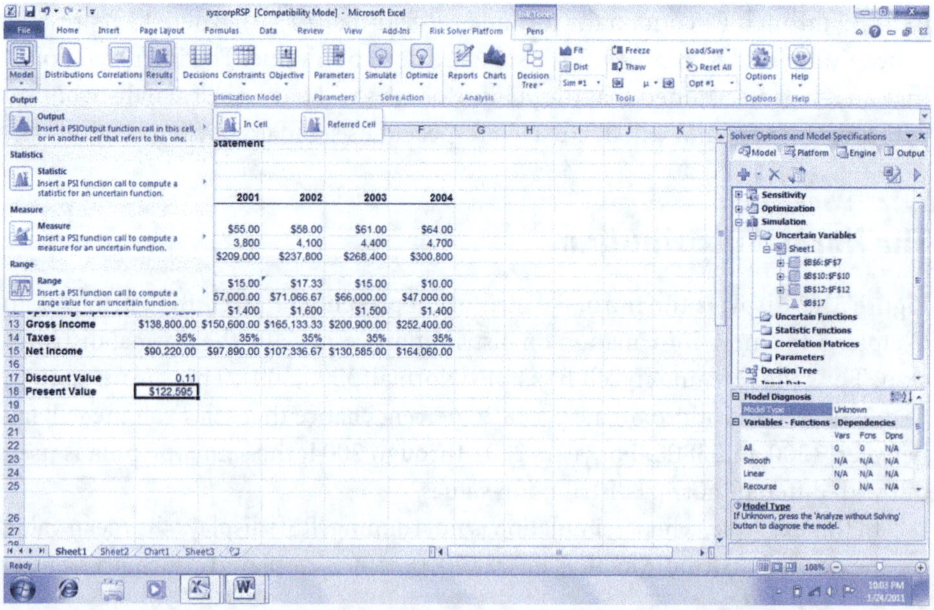

FIGURE 5.32

By defining a group or range of cells as an output, you can study the impact of each cell individually or the impact of the whole range at once.

Summary of Inputs and Outputs

Now that we have defined uncertainty in our model and selected output cells, let's take a look at our inputs and outputs by clicking the List Inputs by Outputs button on the @RISK toolbar.

Solver Options and Model Specifications Window

Figure 5.33 shows the Solver Options and Model Specifications window. This window displays the selected inputs and outputs of the simulation model. The Uncertain Variables menu lists the input variables to the model, whereas the Uncertain Functions menu lists the output variables we are interested in.

Running a Risk Analysis

In this section, a risk analysis is run and the results studied. We will discuss the following topics associated with the risk analysis: Options Menu, Simulation settings, running a simulation, and analyzing the results.

Options Menu in RSP

The Options menu in RSP contains the setting for your simulation model. Figure 5.34 displays the menu that opens when the Options icon in the RSP ribbon is clicked.

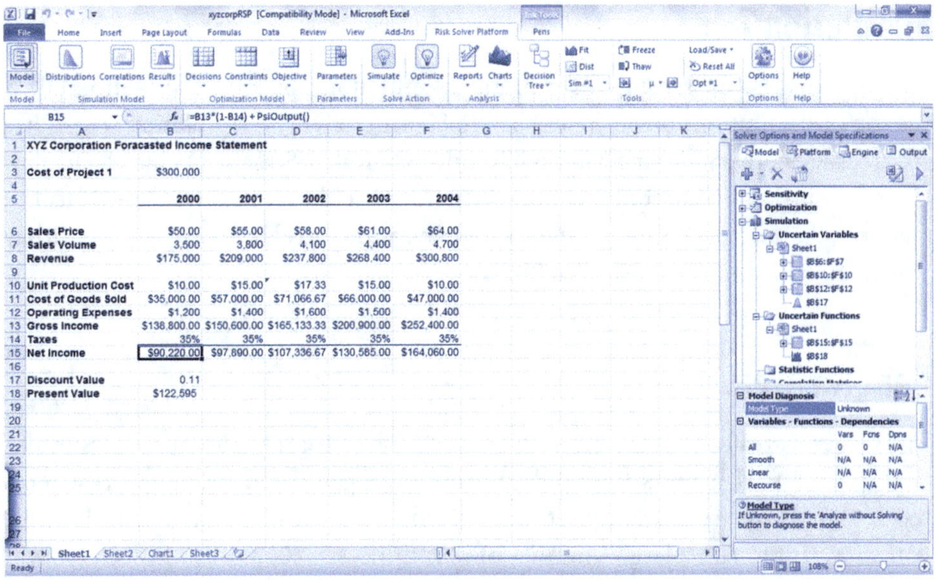

FIGURE 5.33

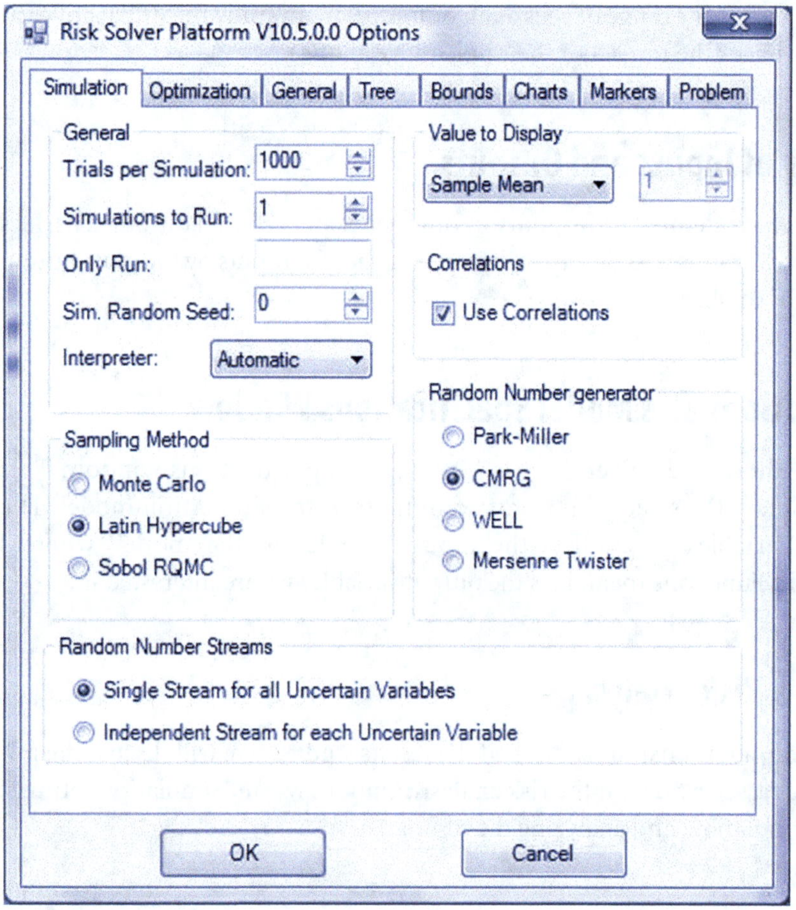

FIGURE 5.34

For our model we will concentrate on the Simulation tab. The other tabs are important for more complex models, but for our model the default settings can be used.

Simulation Tab

Let's first discuss the settings for running a simulation. Click the Simulation tab at the top of the Options menu (refer back to Figure 5.34). The Simulation screen has six areas: General, Sampling Method, Random Number Streams, Value to Display, Correlations, and Random Number Generator. This section will speak to the General, Sampling Method, Value to Display, and Correlations areas. The other two areas are left at their default settings.

General Area

The General area defines the number of iterations or trials to run during a simulation. At each trial, a new set of random numbers is generated and the worksheet is recalculated. We are currently set to run 1,000 iterations. For most simulations, you will want to run a larger number of iterations, say 100,000. However, we will use 1,000 iterations for the purpose of this tutorial. The other items in the General area can be left at their default settings.

Sampling Method Area

The Sampling area controls how each distribution in your worksheet will be sampled. We will be using the Monte Carlo sampling type, which achieves more accurate results with a larger amount of iterations. Should you be running the simulation with lesser iterations, it is recommended that you use the default sampling type, Latin Hypercube.

Value to Display Area

The Value to Display area allows the user to set what type of value is displayed in the underlying spreadsheet model. There are five options in the pull-down menu. The two options we are interested in are the All Trials and Sample Mean options. If the Value to Display pull-down menu is set to All Trials, the spreadsheet will depict a random number in each uncertain cell within the spreadsheet. If the Value to Display pull-down menu is set to Sample Mean, the spreadsheet will depict the mean of the distribution for each uncertain cell within the spreadsheet.

Correlations Area

The Correlations area is important for sensitivity analysis once the simulation has been run. The one check box is for collecting correlations between cells within the simulation model. If the correlations box is checked, correlations are collected. If the correlations box is unchecked, correlations are not collected.

Running the Simulation

You are now ready to run the simulation. Click the Simulation button at the top of the toolbar and the simulation will begin running all by itself (see Figure 5.35).

Analyze the Results in RSP

We should now take a look at how to interpret the simulation results so XYZ may determine whether or not to conduct this product launch. After the computer has completed running the simulation, the results can be displayed by double clicking on the cell that you are interested in. For our model, cell B18 is the output of interest. After double clicking on cell B18, a window resembling Figure 5.36 will appear. The default tab to be displayed is the Frequency tab and displays the simulation data for cell B18 as a frequency diagram. While this is an interesting way to view the data, we first need to take a look at the summary statistics behind the simulation for cell B18.

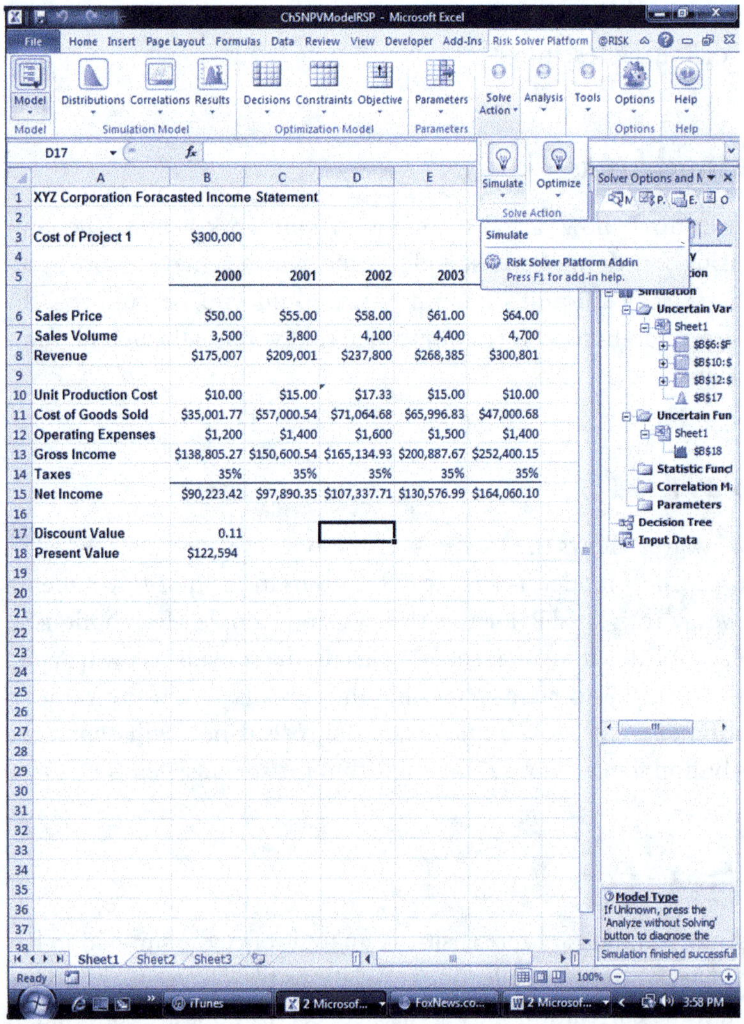

FIGURE 5.35

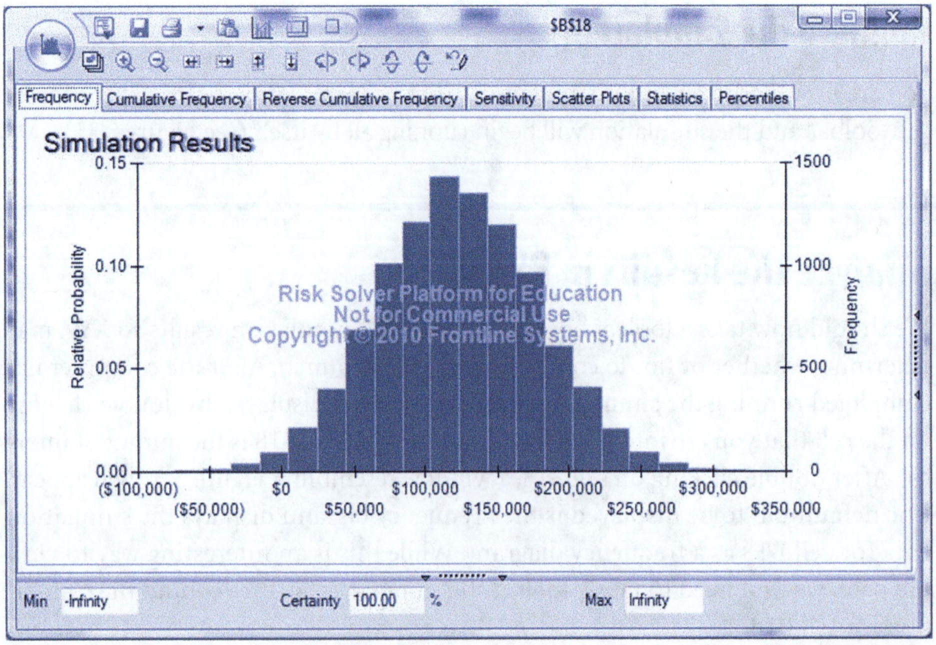

FIGURE 5.36

Click on the Statistics tab in Figure 5.36 and you can see the detailed statistics for the cell you double clicked on—in this case cell B18 (see Figure 5.37). The Statistics view displays a summary of the simulation results, including mean, median, standard deviation, minimum, and maximum values calculated for cell B18. We can see that NPV has a minimum value of (94,612), a mean value of \$122,615, and a maximum value of \$321,722. That's quite a large range of results, and depending on XYZ's tolerance for risk, it might consider this a very risky project. Look around in this window and obtain a better sense of the statistics calculated by the simulation.

Cumulative Distribution Outline Graph

The frequency diagram's format can be changed to aid in understanding the data more. Click the Cumulative Frequency tab and a graph resembling Figure 5.38 will appear. The graph displays the probability of a result less than or equal to any value in the range. For example, there is about a 20% probability that the NPV will be less than approximately \$75,000. The Cumulative Distribution graph contains the same data as the Frequency Diagram but may be visually more pleasing and gives the user a different view. It can now be seen that the value of NPV starts low, climbs steeply, and then levels off at the top of the curve/right side of the graph.

Sensitivity Analysis and Tornado Diagrams

Now let's look at the sensitivity analysis data in a graphical format. Click on the Sensitivity tab. For the purpose of this tutorial, we will take a look at the Rank Correlations within the input variables. As you can see from the tornado graphs in

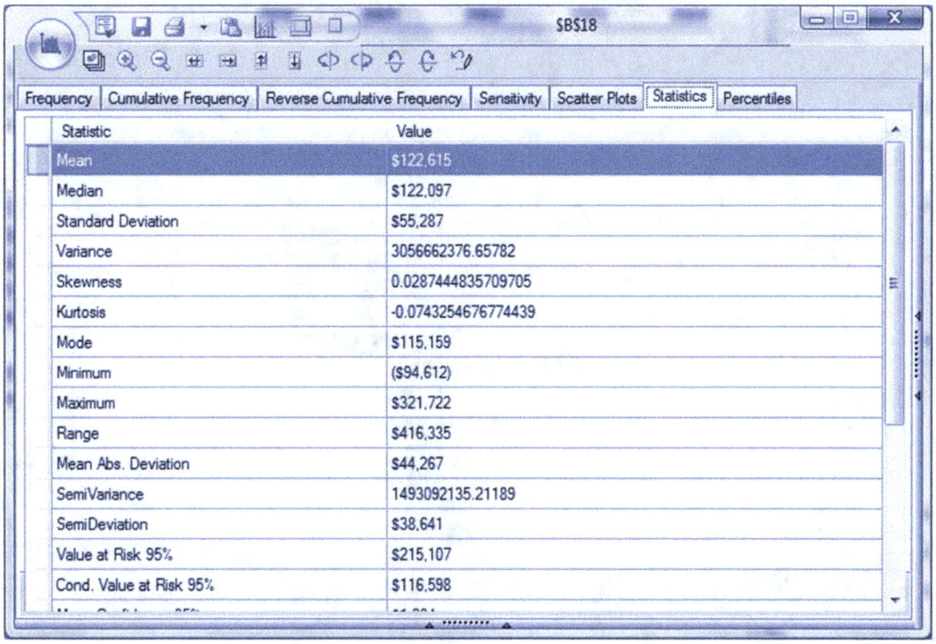

Statistic	Value
Mean	\$122,615
Median	\$122,097
Standard Deviation	\$55,287
Variance	3056662376.65782
Skewness	0.0287444835709705
Kurtosis	-0.0743254676774439
Mode	\$115,159
Minimum	(\$94,612)
Maximum	\$321,722
Range	\$416,335
Mean Abs. Deviation	\$44,267
SemiVariance	1493092135.21189
SemiDeviation	\$38,641
Value at Risk 95%	\$215,107
Cond. Value at Risk 95%	\$116,598

FIGURE 5.37

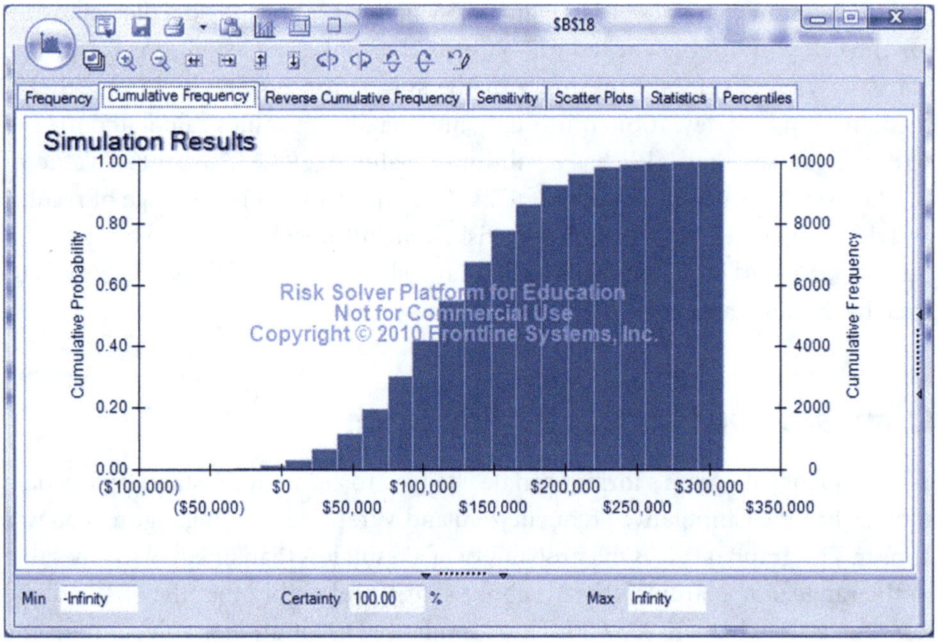

FIGURE 5.38

Figure 5.39, cell $B$6, Sales Price for year 2000, is the most significant input, which is drawn at the top of the graph with the longest bar. The correlation coefficients are represented along the *x* axis, and each input variable is charted on the *y* axis. The tornado graph summarizes the effect of variables in a neat, simple graph. We can easily compare the magnitude of the effect of each input by the size of the bar and whether the effect is positive or negative in the direction of the bar (right or left, respectively).

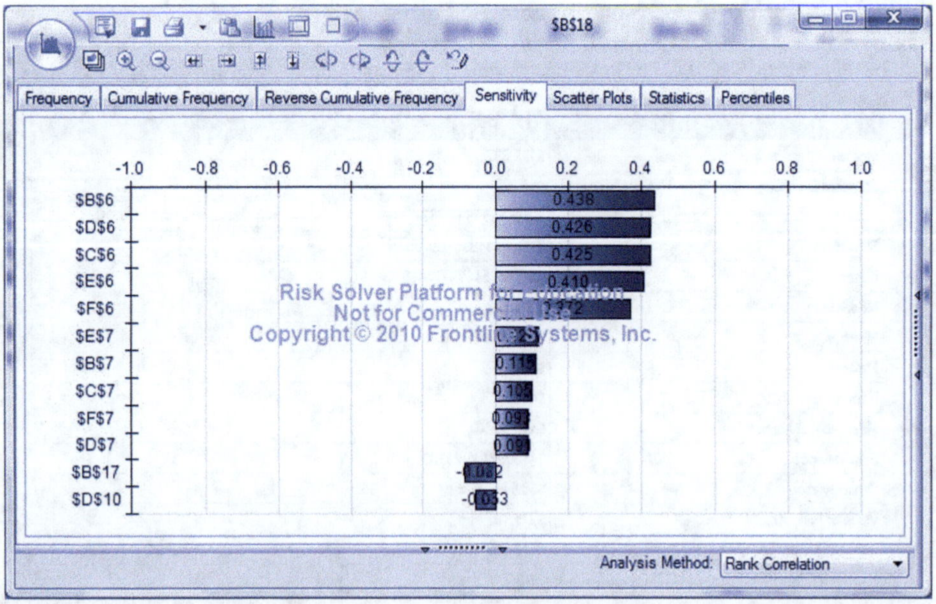

FIGURE 5.39

Summary

The results of the simulation run in RSP will not exactly match the simulation in @Risk due to the random nature of the model, but the results will be very close. For example, compare Figure 5.36 to Figure 5.21. RSP has many other options to explore regarding graphing and sensitivity analysis. This section gave an overview of the major features of creating and running a simulation in RSP.

Conclusions

Both projects have the chance to generate negative NPV. However, the chance for either project to generate negative NPV is definitely less than 5%. While Project 2 appears to generate higher NPV values more often than Project 1 (60% versus 40%) and has greater upside potential, Project 2 does have a greater downside risk (negative NPV more often and larger in magnitude). In short, if a manager believes "good" things (higher sales prices, higher sales volumes, lower costs) will be prevalent, than Project 2 is the better choice. However, if a manager believes "not-so-good" things (lower sales prices, lower sales volumes, higher costs) will be prevalent, than Project 1 is the better choice.

Now that you have just completed a basic tutorial for @RISK, it is up to you to make a decision for XYZ Corporation. It will take a few rounds of practice and some playing around to become proficient at @RISK and interpreting the results. Do you think XYZ should launch this new product? On what basis are you making your recommendation? Remember, your decision has to be based on the data and statistics you have generated, hence the name of this course, business decision modeling. Enjoy!

Summary

Overall, some very important points must be remembered when you are building, running, and interpreting simulation models. The most important points are:

- ***Randomness and random number generation.*** Simulation models must sample from distributions that exhibit random properties—i.e., correct random number generation.
- ***Run enough trials.*** Enough trials must be run when implementing simulation models—i.e., enough is usually 100,000 trials.
- ***Verify the model.*** Models must be verified with regard to inputs, outputs, and uncertainty—link uncertainty to probability distributions (Chapters 1 to 3).
- ***Validate the model.*** Models must be validated—link validation to decision structuring (Chapters 4 and 5).

- *Conduct sensitivity analysis.* Sensitivity analysis generally tends to be the most robust area for interpreting simulation results—link sensitivity analysis to Chapters 4 and 5.

The major payoffs of simulation modeling are often the result of asking what-if questions when the model is running. It is also very important to make sure your model is *valid* and that it has been *verified.* By verify, we mean to make sure the computer or spreadsheet program used in the model is not flawed. This requires checking and rechecking the work, perhaps writing it in different languages to see if similar results occur and perhaps asking independent experts to review the work.

Conducting sensitivity analysis is the real payoff in modeling and running simulations.

A simulation is valid when it models what it is supposed to model. After working long hours on a simulation and viewing results that are aesthetically pleasing, it is easy to be seduced into believing the results while losing sight of the fact that the model misses the point. To have a valid simulation model, it is important to talk to workers closest to the action, to contrast and compare other models and the experience of other experts, to utilize whatever data are available to identify trends for what-if analysis, and to keep an open mind.

The next section displays an executive summary example for the XYZ Corporation simulation modeling example detailed in the @Risk tutorial section.

EXECUTIVE SUMMARY FOR XYZ CORPORATION

TO: Delta Investing Corporation
FROM: Alan Fang, President Fang Consulting

Problem Identification

XYZ Corporation is seeking a net present value (NPV) analysis on a potential project launch. Items such as the forecasted sales price, unit production costs, and discount factor are distributed triangularly with three possible values, whereas sales volume and operating expenses are normally distributed with a mean and a standard deviation (SD). The criterion for XYZ Corporation to accept this project is positive NPV after discounting the future cash flows (Net Income) from year '00 to '04. The alternative for XYZ is not launching the project, which has a net NPV of zero.

Modeling the Problem

A spreadsheet model is constructed by utilizing basic accounting principles to calculate net income. NPV is then calculated by discounting the five forecasted net income figures, using a current discount value and subtracting the original cost of the project. To obtain a full analysis on the upside potential and the downside risk of the project, XYZ Corporation decided to employ a Monte Carlo simulation comprising 100,000 iterations. The simulation offers XYZ Corporation a detailed perspective on a range of possible NPVs for the project and the probability of the NPV to occur above $0.

Results: Sensitivity Analysis

From the simulation, the result of all possible NPVs is graphed in Figure 1.

Dominance

As we can see from the graph, the NPV has a mean value around $125,000, a low value around –$60,000, and a high value of $310,000. The project's NPV is positive approximately 95% of the time. By not launching the project, XYZ would have zero NPV and would avoid this downside loss. It appears that launching dominates not launching the project around 95% of the time.

Trade-offs

The points are read off the graph by finding the percentile of interest on the x axis (NPV percentile), let's say 50%, proceeding vertically from the 50% point until the graph is reached, and then horizontally proceeding to the y axis and reading the corresponding NPV. The trade-off point between launching or not launching the project occurs around the 5th NPV percentile (i.e., 5% on the x axis).

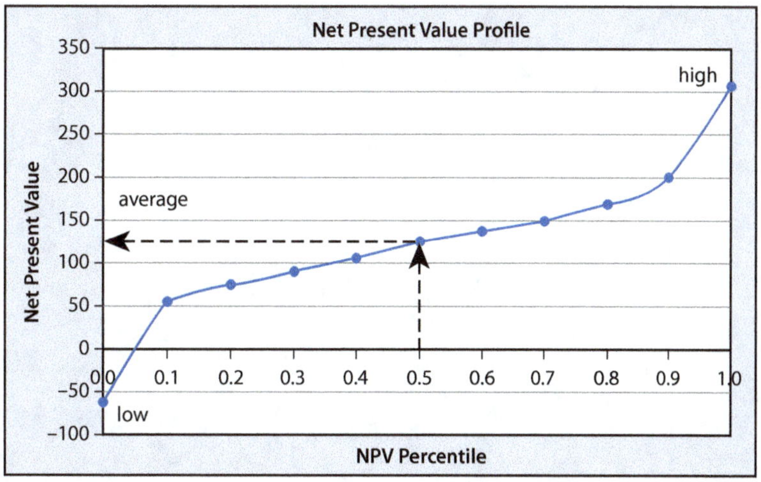

FIGURE 1

Risks

Risk for this decision can be defined and quantified in two ways, by range and by SD. The average, high, and low values are listed on the graph. Range (high–low) for launching the project is around $370,000. The range for not launching the project is $0. Although informative, range is not the best measure of risk here. SD should also be analyzed. Risk can be interpreted by declaring that out of all NPVs calculated from the simulation, few fall below $0, and overall NPV climbs steadily from around a value of $50,000 to a value of $200,000. This in essence is the SD for the NPV of launching the project. It has an actual value of $56,616.

Conclusion and Recommendations

On the basis of the criteria on whether to accept a project on NPV, XYZ Corporation has decided to accept this particular project because there is a 95% (100% to 5%) probability that NPV will be greater than $0. With mean value of around $125,000 and an SD value of around $57,000, there is a 66.68% chance that the NPV will fall between $68,000 and $182,000 and a 95% chance that the NPV will fall between $11,000 and $239,000. XYZ would be wise to accept this project.

CASE STUDY

Steve's Solar System

Background and Historical Electricity Information

Steve is considering installing a solar hot water system (SHH2OS) in his business to transfer some of his power consumption off the grid. Steve knows that the up-front costs of the SHH2OS including materials and labor are $11,600. Future operating and maintenance costs are negligible. Obviously, SHH2OSs work best and are most efficient when it is sunny outside. However, it is not always sunny outside where Steve's business currently resides. Therefore, Steve knows the SHH2OS will save him at most 80% but at least 50%, with a most likely number around 70% of the electricity he normally would use for hot water heating each month.

From past records, Steve has estimated that the business's electricity bills run about $450 a month. However, some months they could be as high as $575 or as low as $290. Steve also estimated that hot water heating in general makes up anywhere from 30% to 50% of the electricity bill with a most likely number of 40%.

Solar Incentives

Currently, there are no discounts for installing an SHH2OS. However, Steve is expecting new legislation to be passed on the federal and state levels that will allow some discounts on the cost of a system. The federal legislation would allow for a 35% discount off the total price on the SHH2OS. The state legislation would allow for a flat $1400 discount on any SHH2OS originally priced above $5000.

Payback Period Calculations and Concerns

Steve would like to know his expected payback period from the installation of the SHH2OS with and without the discounts. The payback period for an investment or project is the number of periods it takes before the investment's or project's initial investment is paid back.

Simulation Modeling and Discussion Questions

Using Excel, create a simulation model to help Steve. Given the following assumptions, run the simulation model for 100,000 trials and interpret the results. Help Steve understand:

1. What his expected monthly and annual saving could be with the new unit with and without the discounts.
2. The payback period for the SHH2OS with and without the discounts.

Distribution Assumptions

Variable	*Distribution*
Monthly electricity saving from the SHH2OS	Triangular: 50% as the low, 70% as the most likely, and 80% as the high
Monthly electricity bills	Triangular: $290 as the low, $450 as the most likely, and $575 as the high
Percent of electricity from hot water heating	Triangular: 30% as the low, 40% as the most likely, and 50% as the high

INTERACTIVE CASE

Serving the Customers at Schenck's

Background

Steve Schenck has run his family delicatessen for 10 years. The delicatessen serves food all day long from 7 A.M. until 9 P.M. and also provides customers with packaged meat and other products for take-home use. Business has always been busy, even when his father ran the business. However, two new office buildings and a new subdivision have been built nearby over the last 5 years. These additions have brought many new customers, and Steve has been hearing complaints about the wait. Specifically, the complaints have been about the wait to check out.

Current Setup

Currently Steve has one cash register to serve his customers. In general, customers place their orders at the order window and employees process the orders (e.g., make a sandwich, cut some corned beef, pack up some dill pickles). This process usually isn't the bottleneck, since the behind-the-counter employees are well seasoned, know the layout well, and manage the work easily (i.e., there are enough workers, since all can do each others' jobs).

The bottleneck comes when the customers go to check out. Steve knows that customers have complained about the wait and he has heard that some have mentioned to the cashier that they might go elsewhere in the future because of the long waits to check out. In fact, Steve stood outside the store just the other day and watched as some customers looked in the window, saw the long line at the cashier, and decided not to go into the delicatessen. Steve knows the word is getting out and wants to improve the situation before he starts losing current customers as well as future customers.

Steve is contemplating adding another cashier to the process to alleviate the long line that builds. However, his brother is telling him that it will cost too much money and overall won't solve the problem. Steve's brother believes that the cashier just needs to work faster and the problem will take care of itself.

Data Analysis and Simulation

Steve believes adding another cashier will help and he wishes to test his theory versus his brother's theory. From data that his son collected for a college business decision modeling course, Steve knows the arrival rate and service rate for his customers. The data tell Steve that his customer arrival rate is 5 customers per hour and his customer service rate is 3 customers per hour.

Steve knows that he could send his cashier to some training classes at the local business college and his service rate would improve. He estimates that after training, the cashier could process customers faster and that the service rate would go up to 4 customers per hour but no higher. However, these classes would cost Steve money, around $2000. Steve's brother speculates that training the cashier and in turn improving the service rate would cut the number of customers waiting in line by 80% and cut the time they wait by more than half. These metrics, cutting customers in line by 80% and cutting waiting time by more than half, are definitely two of Steve's goals and, if they are realized, he could justify the $2000 spent.

(continues)

INTERACTIVE CASE

Serving the Customers at Schenck's (continued)

Steve asked his son about his brother's speculation and his son didn't agree. His son does not think just by training the cashier and improving service rates that they will see these dramatic improvements. Therefore, Steve's son has suggested that they add another cashier (i.e., add another server to the queue). His son estimates that if they add another cashier in the process they will at least cut the average number of customers waiting in the line by 80% and cut the time customers wait in the line by half. However, adding another cashier will cost money too, about $400 a week in pay and benefits. Overall, Steve is willing to pay the money if his goals of cutting the number of customers in line and the waiting time could be met.

Waiting Line Simulation Settings

Three waiting line simulations (Current Setup, Training Option, Extra Cashier Option) have been suggested by Steve's son for comparison. The table below contains the parameters that should be used to test the waiting line simulation options.

PARAMETERS FOR INTERACTIVE WAITING TIME SIMULATION

Parameter	Current Setup	Training Option	Extra Cashier Option
Arrival rate	5	5	5
Service rate	3	4	3
Number of servers in phase 1	1	1	2

Run the simulation, observing the system, until 50 customers have been served. Then record, at a minimum, the performance measures of average customer waiting time and average # of customers waiting in the line for each simulation (Current Setup, Training Option, Extra Cashier Option).

Discussion Questions

1. How does the Training Option compare to the Current Setup? Are Steve's goals of cutting the number of customers waiting in line by 80% and cutting customer waiting time by more than half realized?
2. How does the Extra Cashier Option compare with both the Current Setup and Training Options? Does the Extra Cashier Option meet Steve's goals?
3. What would you advise Steve to do?

Optimal Information Area

Computational Science Education Project Introduction to Monte Carlo Methods
http://csep1.phy.ornl.gov/mc/node1.htm

History of Monte Carlo Method
http://stud2.tuwien.ac.at/~e9527412/history.html

Glossary: Monte Carlo Simulation
http://www.contingencyanalysis.com/glossarymontecarlosimulation.htm

Sabri Pllana's History of Monte Carlo Method
http://www.geocities.com/CollegePark/Quad/2435/

Palisade Incorporated simulation software
http://www.palisade.com

References

Camm, J. D., and J. R. Evans. *Management Science: Modeling, Analysis, and Interpretation.* Cincinnati, OH: South-Western Publishing Co., 1996.

Evans, J. R., and D. Olson. *Introduction to Simulation and Risk Analysis.* Upper Saddle River, NJ: Prentice-Hall, 1998.

Law, A. M., and W. D. Kelton. *Simulation Modeling and Analysis,* 2nd ed. New York: McGraw-Hill, 1991.

Leon, L., Z. Przasnyski, and K. C. Seal. "Spreadsheets and OR/MS models: An End-User Perspective." *Interfaces,* vol. 26, no. 2 (1996), pp. 92–104.

Ragsdale, C. T. *Spreadsheet Modeling and Decision Analysis, A Practical Introduction to Management Science,* 2nd ed. Cincinnati, OH: South-Western Educational Publishing.

Sheel, Atul. "Monte Carlo Simulations and Scenario Analysis: Decision-Making Tools for Hoteliers." *Cornell Hotel and Restaurant Administration Quarterly,* vol. 36, no. 5 (1995), pp. 18–26.

"'Super Flush' passes test," *USAToday,* July 16, 1998.

Uyeno, D. "Monte Carlo Simulation on Microcomputers." *Simulation,* vol. 58, vol. 6 (1992), pp. 418–423.

PROBLEMS

1. A basic skill needed to do simulation is to be able to correctly assign random numbers to a probability distribution. Do this for the circumstances described below. In each instance identify all possible outcomes and the probabilities associated with those outcomes before assigning random numbers according to the scheme described in this chapter.

   a. Rolling a die.

   b. Flipping a coin.

   c. Having a birthday in a month that begins with J. Ignore leap years and assume it is equally likely a person is born on any given day.

2. Simulate flipping two coins and rolling a die at the same time. Do 100 simulations. From your results estimate:

   a. The probability of having at least one head.

   b. The probability of the coins having the same faces and the face of the die being greater than four.

   c. The probability that the face of the die is an even number and the faces of the coins do not match.

3. Use the mathematics of probability to calculate the theoretical result for each part of Problem 2 and compare your results. Why are they different from the results of the simulation? How could you improve on the simulated results?

4. The following information was found about a credit card processing facility: a uniform maximum arrival rate of 3 units per minute and a minimum arrival rate of 0, a normally distributed average service rate of 1.2 units per minute, a standard deviation of 0.75 units per minute. Develop a simulation model in Excel to determine;

   a. What is the average number of customers in the waiting line?

   b. What is the probability of waiting?

   c. What is the average customer waiting time?

d. What is the number waiting more than 1 minute?

e. What is the percentage of time the credit card processing facility is busy?

f. What is the maximum wait time?

5. To create a probability distribution from historical data, one first needs to create a frequency distribution and then a relative frequency distribution. Suppose you track the weekly change in price for 1 year (52 weeks) of a particular stock with the results indicated in the following table. Using Excel, re-create the table and fill in the blanks.

WEEKLY CHANGE IN PRICE (NEAREST $)	NUMBER OF WEEKS	RELATIVE FREQUENCY	ASSIGNED RANDOM NUMBERS
+4	5	5/52 = 0.0962	
+3	5		
+2	6		
+1	4		
0	12		
−1	11		
−2	5		
−3	4		

6. In macho frontier times a game called Gambler's Ruin was played. In such a contest, two opponents document all their assets, obtain a supply of good whiskey and proceed to play cards, generally with a crowd watching, until one has lost all he has to the other. To simulate this as a game of pure chance is probably not accurate because in a game like poker, chance and skill combine to determine the winner. Nevertheless we can gain insights into such a set of circumstances by simulating a game of chance by flipping a coin where the assets of each player are identified by an appropriate integer. One student may start with five assets and another with two and each student is identified with either "heads" or "tails" as his or her winning circumstance. Play the game until one is ruined. Try starting with different divisions of assets and see if you can discover an underlying relationship that will predict the probability of being ruined for each player on the basis of the player's original assets. Is it to the advantage of the player with the most assets or least assets to play such a game?

7. Historical data indicate that a student's income for any month of school from work, parents, scholarships, and loans is consistent with the following probability distribution:

INCOME	PROBABILITY
$750	0.20
$950	0.36
$1150	0.30
$1350	0.14

Expenses for the same student are believed to be consistent with the following probability distribution:

EXPENSE	PROBABILITY
$900	0.40
$1000	0.25
$1100	0.20
$1200	0.15

Assuming the student begins the school year with a balance of $1200, use Excel and Crystal Ball to simulate 9 months of activity and to predict the position of the student at the end of the year.

8. Redo Problem 7 if expenses are believed to be normally distributed with a mean of $1026 and a standard deviation of $191.36. How does this change the average cash position of the student compared to what you found in Problem 7?

9. Pick a stock or commodity and establish a probability distribution like the one in Problem 7. Identify your trading strategy and, using Excel and Crystal Ball, simulate the activity of a year.

10. A particular stock has been tracked for the past year with note being made of the change in price from the beginning of the week to the end of the week. Relative frequency considerations produce the following probability distribution for the performance over the past year.

CHANGE IN PRICE, $	RELATIVE FREQUENCY
+4	0.09
+3	0.11
+2	0.11
+1	0.10
0	0.20
−1	0.20
−2	0.19

Assume you own 1000 shares of the stock, for which you paid $150 per share, and that you adopt a trading strategy of selling 100 shares each week the stock goes up and buying 100 shares each week the stock goes down. On the assumption that the probability distribution for next year will be the same as for this year, simulate your position a year hence. Set up a simulation model in Excel and use Crystal Ball to simulate the stock price and to track your trading strategy. Try asking "what if" the distribution changes in some way when you invent or try changing the trading strategy, or both, and contrast and compare your results.

11. A one-person-operated food stand finds that on a Monday morning its customers arrive at the maximum rate of 12 per hour (i.e., a lower interarrival time of 5 minutes) and a minimum rate of 2 per hour (i.e., an upper interarrival time of 30 minutes). The average time to serve a customer is normally distributed and is 7 minutes with a standard deviation of 1 minute. Develop a simulation model in Excel to determine the following:

a. What is the average number of customers in the waiting line?

b. What is the probability of waiting?

c. What is the average customer waiting time?

d. What is the number waiting more than 1 minute?

e. What is the percentage of time the food stand is busy?

f. What is the maximum wait time?

12. The daily demand for newspapers at a particular vending machine is either 20, 21, 22, or 23, with probabilities 0.4, 0.3, 0.2, or 0.1, respectively. Assume the following random numbers have been generated: 08, 54, 74, 66, 52, 58, 03, 22, 89, and 85. Using these numbers, set up an Excel spreadsheet that generates daily newspaper sales for 10 days.

13. The number of machine breakdowns per day at ASQ's factory is either 0, 1, or 2, with probabilities 0.5, 0.3, or 0.2, respectively. Using Excel and the Crystal Ball add-in simulate 100 days of business for the factory. What proportion of these days had at least 1 breakdown?

14. The number of cars arriving at Nathan Hunt's self-service gasoline station during the last 50 hours of operation is as follows:

NUMBER OF CARS ARRIVING	PROBABILITY
6	0.25
7	0.45
8	0.15
9	0.15

Using Excel and the Crystal Ball add-in, simulate 100 days of business for the station. What is the average number of arrivals during this period? What is the range of arrivals (i.e., the difference between the high and the low)?

15. The time between arrivals at the drive-through window of Hugh Leach's fast-food restaurant follows a uniform distribution with a lower bound of 0 minutes and an upper bound of 5 minutes. The service-time distribution is also uniform with a lower bound of 0.5 minutes and an upper bound of 3.0 minutes. Simulate the utilization of the drive-through over 500 minutes. Use Excel to construct the model and Crystal Ball to simulate the 500 minutes. What is the average wait at the drive-through? What is the longest someone will wait in line? On average, how many people are in line at the drive-through?

16. J. J. Stakem sells papers at a newspaper stand for $0.75. The papers cost $0.15 each, giving her a $0.60 profit on each one she sells. From past experience J. J. knows that

    20% of the time she sells 100 papers
    20% of the time she sells 150 papers
    30% of the time he sells 200 papers
    30% of the time he sells 250 papers

    Assuming that J. J. believes the cost of a lost sale to be $0.15 and any unsold papers cost her $0.35, simulate her profit outlook over 100 days if she orders 200 papers for each of the 100 days. Use Excel to construct the model and Crystal Ball to simulate the 100 days.

17. Billy O'Boyle's liquor store has noted the following figures with regard to the number of people who arrive at the store's checkout stand and the time it takes to check them out. Interarrival times tend to be uniformly distributed with a lower bound of 0 minutes and an upper bound of 4 minute, and service times tend to be uniformly distributed with a lower bound of 1 minute and an upper bound of 2 minutes.

    Simulate the utilization of the checkout stand over 500 minutes. Use Excel to construct the model and Crystal Ball to simulate the 500 minutes. What is the average wait at Billy's liquor store? What is the longest someone will wait in line? On average, how many people are in line at Billy's store?

CHAPTER

8 Introduction to Optimization Models

Using Risk Solver Platform in Excel

- Defining Optimization Model in RSP
- Defining the Objective Cell in RSP
- Defining the Variable Cells in RSP
- Defining the Constraint Cell in RSP
- Defining the Non-Negativity Conditions in RSP
- Reviewing the Models in RSP
- Solving the Model in RSP
- Summary of Optimization Using RSP

A Brief Discussion of the Simplex Method

- Simplex and Slack Variables
- How the Simplex Method Finds the Optimal Solution
- Summary

Classical Linear Optimization Problems

- Network Flow/Transportation Problems

The Transportation Problem: Pirate Logistics

- Characteristics of the Transportation LP
- The General LP Formulation for the Transportation Problem
- Setting Up the Transportation LP in a Spreadsheet
- Description of the Spreadsheet
- Decision Variables
- Supply and Demand Constraints
- The Objective Function
- Non-Negativity Assumptions

Setting Up Solver to Find Solutions to the Pirate Logistics LP Problem

- Answer Report in Excel
- Sensitivity Report in Excel
- Constraints Section
- Summary of Pirate Logistics LP Problem

Integer Linear Programming

- Stating Integer Properties and Solving ILPs
- Basics of Binary ILP Problems
- The Capital Budgeting Problem
- Summary of Integer Programming
- Summary of Linear Programming

Case Study: Chris's Capital Budgeting Ballyhoo

Optimal Information Area

Problems

Appendix 8A: Review of Graphical Solutions to Optimization Problems

Business Decision Modeling in Action

Spreadsheet Optimization Models in Use, or Why Use Spreadsheets to Optimize?

Weighing the Pros and Cons of Optimization Modeling Using Spreadsheets

It was once stated that, in spite of the drawbacks spreadsheets have, 30 million users favor using spreadsheets as the analytical vernacular of management. In a sense, can that many business folks be completely wrong?

Spreadsheets: Today's Modeling Tool of Choice

The spreadsheet has become the modeling tool of choice for today's business problems. Custom linear optimization packages did exist before the first copies of Lotus 1-2-3 or Excel had ever shipped. However, as any business decision modeling student today can testify, everyone knows how to use spreadsheets. In addition, in most cases "the computer already comes loaded with a spreadsheet program."

Around 1985, linear optimization packages were being released for Lotus 1-2-3. These early optimization packages were highly acclaimed and won numerous awards including *PC Magazine*'s prestigious Technical Excellence Award. Soon after this, mainstream business and computer publications such as the *Wall Street Journal* and the *New York Times* began to bring widespread attention to these packages and their unique abilities.

Solving Larger-Scale Optimization Problems

Many of the current spreadsheet optimization packages have their roots in tackling large-scale, real-world problems. As early as 1991, a utility company in England was using an optimization package to solve spreadsheet models in excess of 100,000 variables. By 1994, spreadsheet add-ins capable of solving large-scale nonlinear models had been developed. Today, graduate as well as undergraduate business and engineering students use spreadsheets to assist in solving constrained optimization problems in many different areas.

Optimal Information Area

@RISK, Palisade Corp., Newfield, N.Y.; http://www.palisade.com.

Crystal Ball, Decisioneering Inc., Boulder, Colo.; http://www.decisioneering.com.

Excel Solver, Frontline Systems, http://www.frontsys.com.

What'sBest!, Lindo Systems, http://www.lindo.com

Introduction to Optimization Models

This chapter investigates a powerful area of business decision modeling, spreadsheet optimization. Many situations arise in business activities that call for optimal decisions. Models called optimization models generate these optimal decisions. The definition of an optimization model is:

> A deterministic decision model consisting of a single performance measure (an objective function) to be optimized subject to satisfaction of a given set of constraints

Specific techniques are used to identify the optimal solution to this objective function. The technique, which will be described in this chapter, is known as *mathematical programming*. Hence, the author refers to models that use mathematical programming to identify the optimal solution as an optimization model.

An optimization model is a decision model that seeks to optimize a given performance measure while meeting some set of given constraints.

It is important to note the difference between a descriptive model, a model that merely describes alternatives or outcomes, and an optimization model, a model that actually finds the "optimal" alternative or outcome. In addition, this chapter will discuss using spreadsheets in a manner to develop, construct, and solve optimization models.

How Does an Optimization Model Find an Optimal Solution?

A good question for the reader to ask is "How does an optimization model find this optimal solution?" In fact, there are a number of good questions to be asked right about now, such as:

- How is an optimization model constructed?
- Can descriptive models be transformed into optimization models?
- What is an objective function?
- What are constraints?
- Do I need to understand complex mathematics to construct and solve optimization models?

Actually, let's answer the last question first. With the advent of readily available computing power and user-friendly software, it is feasible to construct and solve optimization models without an explicit understanding of higher-order mathematics. However, it is important to familiarize the reader with a basic set of core components that make up optimization models. This chapter introduces these components and uses spreadsheets to illustrate how these components fit together and result in a final optimal solution.

The chapter also defines the classic constrained resource problem and describes a specific type of mathematical programming called linear programming (LP). In addition, LP formulation, two LP solution approaches, LP sensitivity analysis, and general LP problem types, are presented. Spreadsheets are used throughout to illustrate LP concepts.

Descriptive Models: The Foundation for Optimization Models

A good descriptive model is cornerstone to the development of an optimization model.

Building the framework for an optimization model is critical to solution success. A good descriptive model is cornerstone to the development of an optimization model. The descriptive model is the foundation from where an optimization model directs its search for a solution. Therefore, a working descriptive model is a necessity for constructing, solving, and analyzing an optimization model.

Transforming a Descriptive Model into an Optimization Model

Descriptive models get their name from their function; they describe a situation or circumstance. Models that describe a situation or circumstance are very valuable but lack a basic necessity for business decision making, the ability to provide a recommendation that is "best" or "optimal." To do so, descriptive models must be transformed into what the author refers to as *optimization models*. The next section provides an example of a descriptive model and its transformation into an optimization model.

Classic Descriptive Economic Order Quantity Model

A classic example of a descriptive model is the economic order quantity model.

A classic example of a descriptive model is the economic order quantity (EOQ) model used in many economics and operations management courses. The EOQ model is derived from the total annual cost formula for a unique product. The term EOQ refers to the quantity that should be ordered, so setup costs are balanced with carrying costs, resulting in the lowest possible overall annual cost of purchasing and carrying inventory of a product.

EOQ models provide an optimal order number by balancing holding and setup costs.

The EOQ model is a classic descriptive model because it describes what the components of total annual costs are and how they are aggregated. However, the basic total annual cost and EOQ descriptive model provide a business decision maker with only the means to describe costs. They do not provide a true optimal cost or EOQ value.

By using basic algebra to construct the total annual cost equation and some elementary calculus to minimize total annual costs with regard to order quantity, an optimal answer can be found. Thereby, one transforms the descriptive model into an optimization model. This can be done with paper and pen, as has been the case for decades. However, with the advent of spreadsheets, the process of finding the optimal solution to the EOQ model has not only changed, it has also improved.

The next section details a unique example of an EOQ problem and illustrates its solution by using a spreadsheet optimization model.

EOQ EXAMPLE: KAYE'S FLORAL OPTIMAL ORDER QUANTITY PROBLEM

Kaye's design studio purchases glass vases for floral arrangements. Each vase is then hand painted and sent to the distributor for resale through a number of outlets. Each vase's purchase cost is \$15. Annual demand for the vases is 15,000 units, evenly distributed throughout the year. Kaye's holding costs or costs to carry inventory are 10% of the purchase cost per year. Each order has a fixed setup cost of \$200 per order, no matter how many units are purchased.

Kaye wishes to know the number of vases to order so as to minimize total annual costs. She thinks she can figure out how to calculate total annual costs associated with the ordering of the vases, but is having trouble finding the optimal number of vases to order so as to minimize the cost.

Kaye has listed all the variables associated with total annual costs below and set up a preliminary descriptive model. In addition, Kaye is currently ordering 1100 units per order.

Purchase cost = P = \$15
Annual demand = D = 15,000 units/year
Carrying costs = C = 10% of the purchase price/year
Setup costs = S = \$200
Order quantity = Q

$$\text{Orders per year} = \frac{D}{Q}$$

$$\text{Average annual inventory} = \frac{Q}{2}$$

Therefore,

$$\text{Annual purchase cost (APC)} = P \times D = \$15 \times 15{,}000 = \$225{,}000$$

$$\text{Annual carrying costs (ACC)} = P \times C \times \frac{Q}{2} = \$15 \times 0.10 \times \frac{1{,}100}{2} = \$825.00$$

$$\text{Annual setup costs (ASC)} = S \times \frac{D}{Q} = \$200 \times \frac{15{,}000}{1{,}100} = \$2727.27$$

and

$$\text{Total annual costs} = \text{APC} + \text{ACC} + \text{ASC}$$

or, in functional form,

$$\text{Total annual costs} = (P \times D) + \left(P \times C \times \frac{Q}{2}\right) + \left(S \times \frac{D}{Q}\right) = \$3552.27$$

The descriptive model for Kaye's EOQ provides measures for the different costs associated with purchasing vases and holding vases in inventory. It also gives Kaye a total annual cost number, in this case $3552.27. However, the descriptive model does not inform Kaye if she is ordering the optimal amount of vases so to minimize total annual costs.

In order to find the optimal number of vases to order to minimize total annual total costs, Kaye's descriptive model must be transformed into an optimization model. Specifically, a spreadsheet optimization model can assist Kaye in determining her optimal order quantity or EOQ. The next section develops a spreadsheet optimization model and describes how to use Excel's Solver tool to optimize the model, i.e., find Kaye's optimal order quantity or EOQ.

EOQ Spreadsheet Optimization Model

Figure 8.1 displays the spreadsheet optimization model for Kaye's floral EOQ problem. At an order quantity of 1100, Kaye's annual carrying cost is $825.00, while the annual setup cost is $2727.27. In an EOQ model that is optimal, the carrying cost

	A	B	C
1			
2	Purchase Price	P	$15.00
3			
4	Annual Demand	D	15,000
5			
6	Carrying Cost	C	10%
7			
8	Setup Cost	S	$200.00
9			
10	Order Quantity	Q	1,100
11			
12	Annual Purchase Cost	APC	$225,000.00
13			
14	Annual Carrying Cost	ACC	$825.00
15			
16	Annual Setup Cost	ASC	$2,727.27
17			
18	Total Annual Cost	TAC	$228,552.27

FIGURE 8.1

EOQ Spreadsheet Model for Kaye's Floral Problem

	A	B	C
1			
2	Purchase Price	P	15
3			
4	Annual Demand	D	15000
5			
6	Carrying Cost	C	0.1
7			
8	Setup Cost	S	200
9			
10	Order Quantity	Q	1100
11			
12	Annual Purchase Cost	APC	=C2*C4
13			
14	Annual Carrying Cost	ACC	=C2*C6*C10/2
15			
16	Annual Setup Cost	ASC	=C8*C4/C10
17			
18	Total Annual Cost	TAC	=C12+C14+C16

FIGURE 8.2
Spreadsheet Formulas for Kaye's Floral EOQ Problem

is equal to the setup cost. Therefore, we know Kaye's order quantity of 1100 is not the optimal order quantity because carrying cost and setup cost are not equal. Figure 8.2 displays the formulas associated with Kaye's EOQ spreadsheet.

Finding the Optimal EOQ

Using the spreadsheet model presented in Figures 8.1 and 8.2, an optimal order quantity could be found by trial and error. However, this method is very tedious and inefficient. A much better approach is to employ a built-in Excel tool, called Solver. The next section will discuss how to use Solver to find the optimal order quantity for Kaye's Floral problem.

A better method in approaching the solution to the EOQ problem is to use a tool in Excel called Solver.

Excel's Solver

Solver is an add-in to Excel that allows users to find an optimal value for a formula in one cell, called the target cell, on a worksheet. Solver works with related group of cells, either directly or indirectly, to solve the target cell formula. To produce the result you specify from the target cell formula, Solver adjusts the values in the changing cells you specify, called the adjustable cells. You can apply constraints to restrict the values Solver can use in the model, and the constraints can refer to other cells that affect the target cell formula. The next section describes how to set up Solver in Excel. The terms *target cell*, *adjustable cells*, and *constraints* will be used from this point forward.

The Solver add-in is located in the Excel Tools menu.

Solver as an Add-In to Excel

Solver is an add-in to Excel that allows users to find an optimal value for a formula in one cell, called the target cell, on a worksheet. Solver works with a related group of cells, either directly or indirectly, to solve the target cell formula. To produce the result you specify from the target cell formula, Solver adjusts the values in the changing cells you specify, called the adjustable cells. You can apply constraints to restrict the values Solver can use in the model, and the constraints can refer to other cells that affect the target cell formula. The next section describes how to set up Solver in Excel. The terms target cell, adjustable cells, and constraints will be used from this point forward.

The Solver add-in is located in the Data Tab and the Analysis Group.

SETTING UP SOLVER IN EXCEL

The following steps should be followed to set up Solver in an Excel spreadsheet.

1. On the Data Tab and the Analysis Group, click Solver. Figure 8.3 displays the Tools menu.

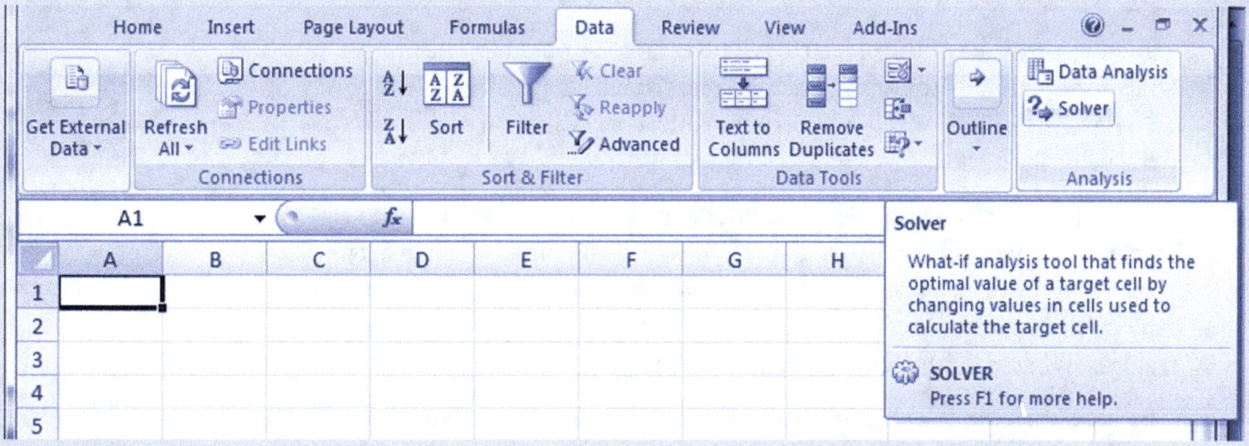

FIGURE 8.3
Solver Add-In Location in Excel

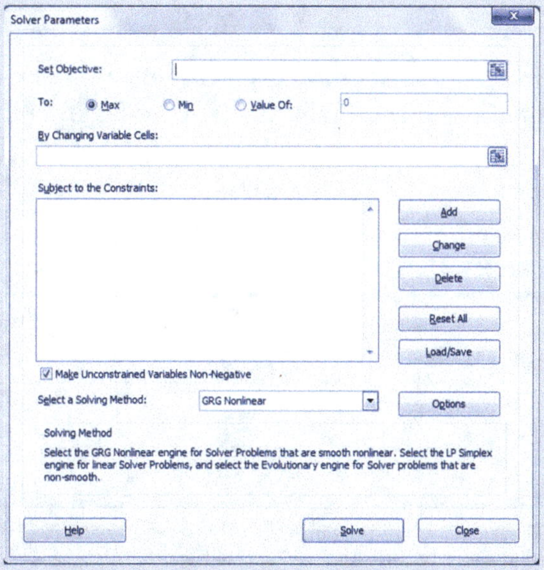

FIGURE 8.4
Excel Solver Dialogue Box for Excel 2010

2. If the Solver command is not listed in the Analysis Group, you need to install the Solver add-in. Follow the procedure to install Excel Add-Ins previewed in Chapter 2, the section entitled Using Excel's Solver in Excel.

If the Solver command is not on the Add-Ins option in the Tools menu, run the ValuePack installer from your original Microsoft Office CD and install Solver.

USING SOLVER TO FIND SOLUTIONS TO A SPREADSHEET OPTIMIZATION MODEL

This section discusses how to use Solver to optimize a spreadsheet model in Excel. It is assumed that the user has already built a spreadsheet optimization model in Excel (refer to Figures 8.1 and 8.2).

After you click on Solver in the Analysis Group, the Solver dialog box, shown in Figure 8.4, will appear. For Excel 2007, the Solver Dialogue box looks a bit different but is analogous in function to Figure 8.4. The following steps enable Solver to find solutions to optimization spreadsheets.

1. In the Set Objective Cell box, enter a cell reference or name for the objective cell. The objective cell must contain a formula.
2. To have the value of the objective cell be as large as possible, click Max. To have the value of the objective cell be as small as possible, click Min. To have the objective cell be a certain value, click Value of, and then type the value in the box.
3. In the By Changing Variable Cells, enter a name or reference for each variable cell, separating nonadjacent references with commas. The variable cells must be related directly or indirectly to the objective cell. You can specify up to 200 variable cells. To have Solver automatically propose the variable cells based on the objective cell, click Guess.
4. In the Subject to the Constraints box, enter any constraints you want to apply.
5. Click Solve.

Applying these steps to the Kaye's Floral spreadsheet problem defines a objective cell, variable cells, and constraints as shown in Table 8.1 (refer to Figures 8.1 and 8.2).

TABLE 8.1 *Solver Cell Definitions*

Set Objective Cell	$C$18
To	Min
Variable Cells	$C$10
Constraints*	$C$10>=0

*Specifying a constraint is a must, as order quantity must be a positive number. This can also be accomplished via the Options menu in Solver by clicking the Assume Non-negativity check box (refer to Figure 8.20).

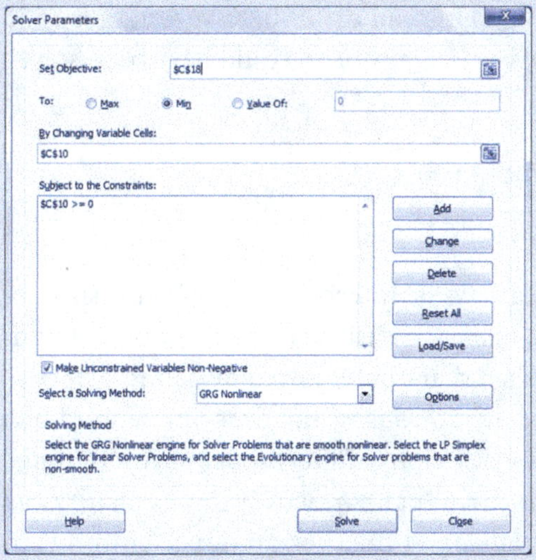

FIGURE 8.5 Final Solver Parameters for Kaye's Floral EOQ Model for Excel 2010

The Solver menu will resemble Figure 8.5 after the values from Table 8.1 have been entered into the Solver dialog boxes.

Figure 8.6 displays the final EOQ spreadsheet model for Kaye's Floral problem with the optimal order quantity, 2000 (refer to cell C10). Cell C10 is of special interest, as it contains the optimal order quantity, which minimizes Total Annual Cost (cell C18). If the value in cell C18 ($228,000) from Figure 8.6 is compared to cell C18 ($228,552.27) in Figure 8.2, Total Annual Costs for the order quantity of 2000 (cell C10, Figure 8.6) are less by approximately $553.

	A	B	C
1			
2	Purchase Price	P	$15.00
3			
4	Annual Demand	D	15,000
5			
6	Carrying Cost	C	10%
7			
8	Setup Cost	S	$200.00
9			
10	Order Quantity	Q	2,000
11			
12	Annual Purchase Cost	APC	$225,000.00
13			
14	Annual Carrying Cost	ACC	$1,500.00
15			
16	Annual Setup Cost	ASC	$1,500.00
17			
18	Total Annual Cost	TAC	$228,000.00

FIGURE 8.6 Optimized EOQ Spreadsheet Model for Kaye's Floral Problem

Thus, by ordering in quantities of 2000 instead of 1100, Kaye will save $553 annually in carrying and setup costs. Kaye's EOQ problem could have been solved via the age-old EOQ formula

$$EOQ = \sqrt{\frac{2DS}{CP}} = \sqrt{\frac{2 \times 15{,}000 \times 200}{1.50}} = 2000$$

The descriptive model for EOQ can always be solved without a spreadsheet or an optimization model. So why would a manager waste time and resources building a complicated spreadsheet for a problem that can be solved by hand?

A spreadsheet model allows a manager to perform "what if" analysis and test changes in underlying assumptions.

The answer lies in the underlying assumptions of the descriptive model. A number of assumptions are implicit to the descriptive EOQ model, such as enough capacity to hold the optimal order quantity. What happens if Kaye's facility can only hold a maximum of 1500 units at any one time (i.e., an upper bound constraint on the EOQ model)? Also, how does the model change if the supplier requires customers to purchase a minimum number of units with each order, i.e., a lower bound constraint on the EOQ model?

If these underlying assumptions change, or constraints are added, then the descriptive model is fairly impotent to adjust and find an optimal answer. However, this is exactly what a spreadsheet optimization model is used for. The next section introduces two constraints to Kaye's Floral EOQ problem and discusses the implementation in the spreadsheet optimization model and impact on the "optimal" order quantity.

EOQ EXAMPLE: KAYE'S FLORAL OPTIMAL ORDER QUANTITY PROBLEM WITH CONSTRAINTS

Kaye has just thought of two new pieces of information regarding her optimal order quantity problem. She has realized that her facility can not hold 2000 units because of space constraints. In fact, the largest amount of units she can hold at one time is 1500. This is an upper limit placed on the optimal order quantity, in other words, an upper constraint.

Kaye has also heard that the company supplying her with vases will not take orders for less than 1000 units without increasing the setup cost, in other words, a lower constraint. This seems to negate the earlier answer for the optimal order quantity of 2000, as a result of Kaye's inability to hold 2,000 units because of space constraints. What is Kaye to do?

Kaye could attempt to approximate the optimal order quantity by enumerating various order quantities, but that would be tedious and it might not deliver the true optimal answer. To assist Kaye, let's refer back to the spreadsheet optimization model constructed earlier (see Figures 8.1 and 8.2).

In order for Kaye to use the spreadsheet optimization model presented in Figures 8.1 and 8.2 in light of the two new constraints introduced, a few modifications of the original model must be made. Specifically, the upper and lower constraints on order quantity must be added into the spreadsheet and into the Solver menu. Figure 8.7 displays an example of what the new spreadsheet may look like after adding the two constraints.

	A	B	C	D	E
1					
2	Purchase Price	P	$15.00		Note: The order quantity listed here is the optimal order quantity without the upper and lower constraints. As the constraints are taken into account, this number will be adjusted.
3					
4	Annual Demand	D	15,000		
5					
6	Carrying Cost	C	10%		
7					
8	Setup Cost	S	$200.00		
9					
10	Order Quantity	Q	2,000		
11					
12	Order Quantity Upper Limit	Qu	1,500		
13	Order Quantity Lower Limit	Q_l	1,000		
14					
15	Annual Purchase Cost	APC	$225,000.00		
16					
17	Annual Carrying Cost	ACC	$1,500.00		
18					
19	Annual Setup Cost	ASC	$1,500.00		
20					
21	Total Annual Cost	TAC	$228,000.00		

FIGURE 8.7

EOQ Spreadsheet Model for Kaye's Floral Problem with Constraints

The two modifications to the original spreadsheet are rows 12 and 13 in Figure 8.7. These two rows contain the upper and lower order quantity limits for Kaye's EOQ problem. The second area that must be modified is within Solver. The following steps must be taken to inform Solver that the spreadsheet model now contains additional constraints on the variable cell C10.

The Solver add-in allows for constraints to be added to any optimization model by using the Add Constraint feature.

1. Open Solver inside the EOQ spreadsheet and click on the Add button in the Subject to the Constraints area (refer to Figure 8.5).
2. A dialog box resembling Figure 8.8 will appear. This dialog box is used to inform Solver that the variable cell order quantity has an upper limit.
3. In the Cell Reference: box, identify or type in the variable cell, cell C10.
4. In the Constraint: box identify or type in the cell reference for the upper bound, cell C12.
5. The Add Constraint dialog box should resemble Figure 8.9 after you have completed these entries.
6. Repeat steps 1 to 5 for the lower constraint, using cell C10 again as the Cell Reference and C13 as the Constraint cell. Figure 8.10 displays what the Add Constraint dialog box should resemble after these entries have been completed.

After these two constraints have been added into the model, the solver menu will resemble Figure 8.11.

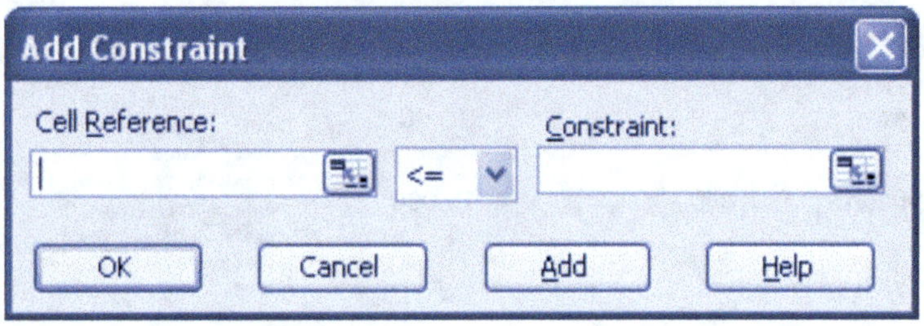

FIGURE 8.8
Solver Add Constraint Dialogue Box

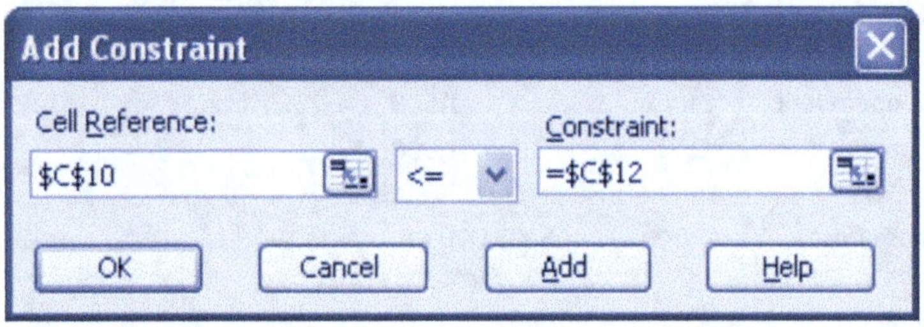

FIGURE 8.9
Solver Add Constraint Dialog Box for Upper Constraint

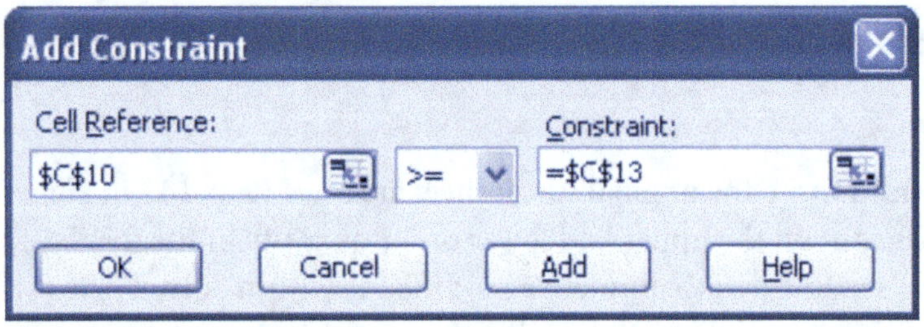

FIGURE 8.10
Solver Add Constraint Dialog Box for Lower Constraint

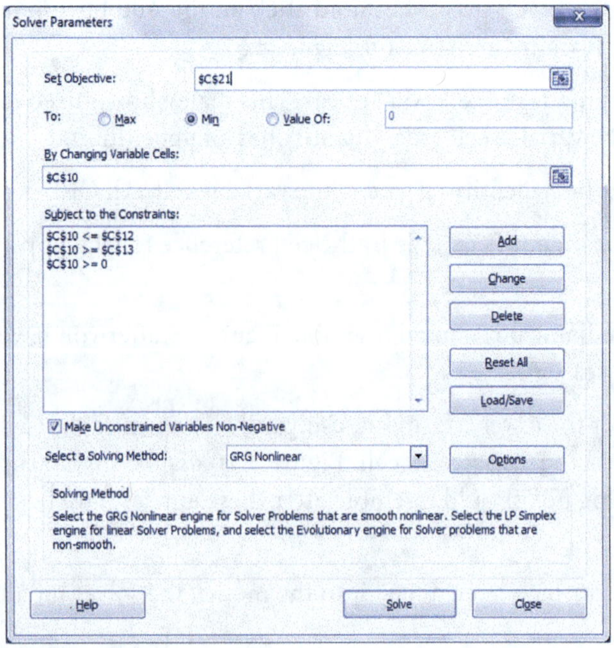

FIGURE 8.11
Final Solver Parameters for Kaye's Floral EOQ Model with Constraints for Excel 2010

	A	B	C
1			
2	Purchase Price	P	$15.00
3			
4	Annual Demand	D	15,000
5			
6	Carrying Cost	C	10%
7			
8	Setup Cost	S	$200.00
9			
10	Order Quantity	Q	1,500
11			
12	Order Quantity Upper Limit	Qu	1,500
13	Order Quantity Lower Limit	Q_l	1,000
14			
15	Annual Purchase Cost	APC	$225,000.00
16			
17	Annual Carrying Cost	ACC	$1,125.00
18			
19	Annual Setup Cost	ASC	$2,000.00
20			
21	Total Annual Cost	TAC	$228,125.00

FIGURE 8.12
Optimized EOQ Spreadsheet Model for Kaye's Floral Problem

Figure 8.12 displays the final EOQ spreadsheet model for Kaye's Floral problem including constraints. It should be noted the optimal order quantity is 1500 (refer to cell C10). Cell C10 is of special interest, as it contains the optimal order quantity, which minimizes Total Annual Cost (cell C21 in Figure 8.12). If the value in cell C21 ($228,125) from Figure 8.12 is compared to cell C18 ($228,000) in Figure 8.6, Total Annual Costs for the order quantity of 1,500 (cell C10, Figure 8.12) are more by approximately $125.

Thus, by having to order in quantities no greater than 1500 and no less than 1000 (the upper and lower order quantity limits—see cell C12 and C13 in Figure 8.12) instead of the optimal EOQ of 2000 found earlier (see Figure 8.9), Kaye incurs $125 extra in total annual cost.

It should be noted that the total annual cost given in cell C21 in Figure 8.12 is optimal with regard to the constraints imposed on Kaye's ordering amount (refer to cells C12 and C13 in Figure 8.12). The issue of constraints is very important to optimization and spreadsheet modeling. In fact, constraints are really what brings us to the concept of mathematical programming, or what many refer to as *constrained resource planning*.

Mathematical Programming

The term mathematical programming refers to a class of models in which levels of various activities are selected, subject to a set of constraints, to maximize or minimize an objective such as total profit or total cost. In Kaye's Floral example with constraints, the activity is the order quantity, and the purpose of the model is to find the order quantity that minimizes total annual cost subject to the upper and lower bounds on order quantity itself.

The term *mathematical programming* refers to a class of models that contain a general objective statement subject to a set of constraints.

The word programming used here does not mean a computer program which must be written or developed, but originates from the British term *programme*, which can be defined as a plan or a schedule of operations.

Linear Programming Models

A special subset of mathematical programming models exists called linear programming models. Linear programming models are commonly referred to as LP models. In fact, the word linear really gives away the uniqueness of LP. All objectives and constraints must be linear in order for an optimization model to be considered an LP model.

A special subset of mathematical programming problems is linear programming problems.

Properties of LP Models

More specifically, linear programming models are a unique subset of mathematical programming models because of three important properties: proportionality, additivity, and divisibility. The next sections will briefly discuss these properties.

Linear programming problems are unique in three properties: proportionality, additivity, and divisibility.

PROPORTIONALITY

Proportionality deals with the relation of the level of any activity to another activity. An assumption of proportionality is made when an LP model is used. This proportionality is said to be met when the following is true: When the level of any activity is multiplied by a constant factor, then the contribution of this activity to the objective, or to any of the constraints in which the activity is involved, is multiplied by the same factor. For example, if the optimal value of an activity is cut in half, then the amounts of resources it uses should also be cut in half.

Proportionality deals with the relation of any activity to another activity.

Proportionality deals directly with the linear concept of linear programming. If the last statement was not true, let's say if the optimal value of an activity were cut in half and the amounts of resources used decreased by an amount larger than one-half, then the proportionality assumption is violated. In fact, a relationship such as the one just described would be considered a nonlinear relationship.

ADDITIVITY

Additivity refers to the sum of contributions from the various activities to a particular constraint. The additivity assumption is said to hold when the sum of the contributions from the various activities to a particular constraint equals the total contribution to that constraint. In addition, additivity applies to the objective as well.

Additivity refers to the sum of contributions from the various activities of a particular constraint.

An example of the additivity is as follows: four separate activities each take 100, 200, 300, and 400 units of constraint 1 to complete, therefore the total units used is the sum of these amounts, 1000 units. In regard to the objective, the sum of the contributions from the various activities is the value of the objective itself. Additivity implies that the contribution of any activity to the objective or to any constraint is independent of the levels of the other activities.

DIVISIBILITY

Divisibility encompasses the concept of integer and noninteger levels of activities.

Divisibility encompasses the concept of integer and noninteger levels of activities. We assume that activities can take on all values greater than zero, integer and noninteger included. However, there are many instances in reality where noninteger activity values do not make sense. For example, if the optimal order quantity of vases for Kaye's Floral shop were 1501.98, Kaye could not order 0.98 of a vase. Kaye must order in integer quantities, as vases do not come in fractional quantities. Conversely, there are activities, such as water measured in gallons, where a noninteger value like 1501.98 gallons makes sense.

When activities need to be integer values, there are two approaches: (1) solve the linear model without an integer constraint, and if the solution turns out to contain noninteger values, an attempt to round them to integer values may be successful, or (2) the LP can be explicitly constrained so certain activities are required to be integer values. This latter approach is considered integer programming, a more difficult subset of LP problems that is studied at the end of this chapter.

Activity Scaling and LP Models

Errors that occur in Solver even when all three properties of LP problems have been met are typically attributed to round-off error.

There are times when all three properties have been met and a true linear model has been formulated, but an error still occurs in the Solver. For some reason, Solver is not convinced that the model that has been defined has met all the LP assumptions. This is typically due to round-off error within Solver.

Round-off error can occur when activities have vastly different scales. For example, if activity A is in thousands of units, whereas activity B is in hundredths of units (a factor of five difference), the model is poorly scaled. Poorly scaled models lead to increases in round-off error and may result in error messages regarding the linearity of the LP model. Employing the automatic scaling feature in Solver and/or redefining all activities units to a similar magnitude can ameliorate round-off error.

Modeling a Real Problem and the LP Assumptions

In general, whenever a manager creates a model for a real-life problem, some simplifying assumptions are made. The three properties discussed above may or may not all be satisfied for every model. In fact, models are many times simplified to meet the three properties and therefore provide solutions more quickly.

Overall, real-life problems are frequently nonlinear. However, LP models have been successfully applied in the real world, in applications such as shipping, personnel scheduling, food processing, and petroleum processing. LP models are useful even when the solutions are only approximations of reality. Much of the insight gained by managers from LP models is in the formulation and sensitivity analysis that occurs after a solution is obtained. Unless one suspects major violations of the three properties discussed earlier—proportionality, additivity, and divisibility— LP models can be used effectively to describe and solve constrained resource problems.

Three Parts of an LP Model

Every LP model has three distinctive parts:

- The objective function
- Constraints
- Non-negativity assumptions

Every LP model has three distinct parts: objective function, constraints, and non-negativity assumptions.

As a modeler, you are required to define each of these parts. A short introductory section defining some terms is next, followed by a section defining and describing the three parts of an LP model.

Definition of LP Terminology

Before the three parts of an LP are defined and described, a few terms must be defined. The following are the appropriate terms and definitions:

Decision variables. Symbols used to represent an item of interest to the user that can take on any value (e.g., x_1 = labor hours, x_2= number of workers).

Decision variables are items of interest to the user, such as how much labor to use or how much raw material A to use.

Parameters. Known constant values that are defined for each problem (e.g., price of a unit, production capacity).

Modified standard form. A standard form that LP models are converted into that allows the solution process to proceed and provides easy understanding of the overall problem formulation.

Students should take note that formal LP nomenclature makes reference to the term *standard form* instead of modified standard form. The latter terminology is due to the author's use of spreadsheet models, and its import will become apparent later in this chapter. Do not let this confuse you as you attempt to build LP models. It should also be noted that decision variables and parameters must be defined for each unique LP model, and the responsibility of defining these decision variables and parameters falls upon the modeler.

The Objective Function

The objective function of an LP model is always defined as a linear relationship of decision variables describing the problem objective. In other words, the objective function is what you are trying to accomplish, such as maximizing profit or minimizing costs.

By definition, the objective function always consists of maximizing or minimizing some value (e.g., maximize profit, minimize cost) and is customarily given the designation Z. Examples of typical objective functions are

The objective function of an LP problem always consists of a maximize or minimize statement.

$$\text{Maximize profit} = Z = 3x_1 + 5x_2$$

$$\text{Minimize cost} = Z = 6x_1 + 15x_2$$

where x_1 and x_2 would be decision variables defined for the LP model and the coefficients would be profits or costs associated with each of the decision variables.

For example, in the first objective function, Maximize profit $= Z = 3x_1 + 5x_2$, the coefficient of x_1, 3, is interpreted as follows: If x_1 increases by one unit (all things held constant) then the objective function will increase by 3 units ($3 \times 1 = 3$). This same logic holds for each decision variable and coefficient pair.

It should be noted that in this text the author works within the realm of single objective optimization and single objective spreadsheet models. Multiple objective optimization and multiple optimization models do exist in the real world but are not covered here.

The Constraints

Constraints are defined as physical limitations or restrictions on the LP problem.

Constraints are defined as physical limitations or restrictions on the LP problem. Constraints are constructed as linear relationships of decision variables representing these physical limitations or restrictions. Physical limitations or restrictions could include limited resources such as labor or capital, hours in the workday, or amount of a commodity such as corn or wheat that can be purchased or stored.

It is the responsibility of the LP modeler to construct the constraint functions. Constraints come from knowledge about an activity or a set of activities. LP modelers are confronted with phrases such as

"Total labor hours must be less than or equal to 50" or
"x_1 must use at least 20 pounds of corn."

These phrases are actually statements of restrictions of the LP model and must be defined as linear relationships of decision variables. For the aforementioned phrases, the following linear relationships can be developed, assuming two decision variables $x_1 + x_2$:

"Total labor hours must be less than or equal to 50"

is transformed into

$$x_1 + x_2 \leq 50$$

and

"x_1 must use at least 20 pounds of corn"

is transformed into

$$x_1 \geq 20$$

A fully formulated LP model may have tens, even hundreds, of constraints, involving all or any combination of decision variables. Constraints can consist of greater than or equal to (≥), less than or equal to (≤), and/or strictly equal to (=) operators. Constraints can also contain additive (+) and/or subtractive (–) operators within their construction.

A fully formulated LP model may contain tens, even hundreds, of constraints.

The Non-Negativity Assumptions

The third and final part of an LP model is one of the simplest and most logical parts of the LP formulation. Non-negativity assumptions basically define the decision variables as always being positive in quantity. This is logical because negative decision variables are inconceivable in most LP problems For example, minus 10 units of production, a negative consumption, or scheduling less than zero employees make no sense Non-negativity assumptions are written as follows, assuming two decision variables $x_1 + x_2$:

The third and final part of an LP model is the non-negativity assumptions.

$$x_1, x_2 \geq 0$$

Although non-negativity assumptions are the simplest part of the LP formulation, they are easy to forget. Solver attempts to remedy this problem by providing a menu option in Solver automatically defining all decision variables as non-negative. However, the LP modeler still needs to remember to check the menu box for this option in Solver.

Putting It All Together—Steps in Formulating an LP Model

1. **Define the decision variables**—identify the key variables whose values we wish to determine.
2. **Determine the objective function**—determine what we are trying to do (i.e., Maximize profit, Minimize total cost).
3. **Formulate the constraints**—determine the limitations of the decision variables.

LP formulation steps: (1) Define decision variable, (2) determine objective function, (3) formulate constraints.

The steps listed above must be completed for each LP model developed. In addition, it is the responsibility of the modeler to perform the steps. Many times the completion of the steps is a tedious process. The next section addresses ways to formulate LP problems.

Putting It All Together—Modified Standard Form

The preceding sections discussed definitions and nomenclature associated with LP models. As with any discipline, mastering the nomenclature or jargon for any technique is part of the learning process. LP modeling combines the aforementioned nomenclature using what is called modified standard form.

Modified standard form combines decision variables, the objective function, and non-negativity assumptions together in one place.

Modified standard form combines decision variables, the objective function, the constraints, and non-negativity assumptions. LP modelers use modified standard form to communicate the structure of the LP problem. Overall, each LP model should be transformed into modified standard form. Transforming each LP model into standard form accomplishes two main goals: (1) provides a common form to communicate the structure of LP models and (2) provides an easy form for spreadsheet entry and solution using Solver.

In general, modified standard form for an LP model is as follows where the three parts of the LP model are numbered as follows: Equation (8.1) objective function, Equation (8.2) constraints, and Equation (8.3) non-negativity assumptions:

$$\text{Maximize} \quad Z = c_1x_1 + c_2x_2 + \cdots + c_nx_n \tag{8.1}$$

$$\text{subject to} \quad a_{11}x_1 + a_{12}x_2 + \cdots + a_{1n}x_n \leq b_1 \tag{8.2}$$

$$a_{m1}x_1 + a_{m2}x_2 + \cdots + a_{mn}x_n \leq b_m$$

$$x_1, x_2, x_n \geq 0 \tag{8.3}$$

where

x_i = decision variable i

c_i = coefficient of contribution for decision variable i

a_{ni} = coefficient of contribution for constraint n, decision variable i

b_m = total amount of constraint m

The equations presented for modified general form may look somewhat daunting. However, modified standard form contains all parts of an LP model in compact form, which allows for easy spreadsheet entry and solution. To aid in the understanding of modified standard form and the process of formulating LP models, an example is given next.

Mark's Bats LP Example—The Story

Mark's firm produces two types of baseball bats, the Wooden Wonder and the Aluminum Ally. Mark's firm makes \$7 profit for each Wooden Wonder and \$10 profit for each Aluminum Ally it produces. The bats go through three processes before they are ready to be shipped: shaping, stamping, and packing.

The first process is shaping. Each type of bat is shaped on a different machine. The machine used to shape the Wooden Wonder has a finite capacity of 100 hours per week, whereas the machine used to shape the Aluminum Ally has a finite capacity of 120 hours per week. Each Wooden Wonder bat uses 1.5 hours of shaping machine capacity, while each Aluminum Ally uses 2 hours of shaping machine capacity.

The second process is stamping, and both bats can be stamped on the same machine. The stamping machine has 60 hours of capacity a week. The Wooden Wonder bats take 15 minutes to stamp whereas the Aluminum Ally takes 30 minutes to stamp because of the metal exterior.

Both styles of bats are packed on the same machine and each requires the same amount of time, 15 minutes. The packing machine has a finite capacity of 25 hours a week. Finally, Mark's firm has already agreed to produce 30 Wooden Wonders for a preferred customer.

Mark's firm needs assistance in figuring out how many Wooden Wonders and how many Aluminum Ally bats to produce to maximize total profits. Mark believes an LP model will aid in solving this problem.

LP Example—The Formulation Process

The problem that Mark is faced with is a typical problem that can be solved by using an LP model. This type of problem is referred to as a *product mix problem*. It occurs in many industries, including furniture, automobile, and electronics manufacturing.

Identifying Decision Variables

The first step in formulating Mark's bat production problem is to identify the decision variables. The best way to identify the decision variables is to ask the question "What are the activities that Mark must decide on?"

The best way to identify decision variables is to ask "What are the activities that I must decide on?"

In the bat production problem, it is clear that Mark wishes to know how many of each bat to produce. The entire problem would be moot if Mark could just produce an infinite amount of both bats and in turn make an infinite amount of profit. However, as has been stated earlier and as reality dictates, Mark's firm has constraints on its capacity and therefore cannot produce an infinite amount of bats.

The decision variables for Mark's bat production problem are then defined as:

$$\text{Decision variable 1} = x_1 = \text{number of Wooden Wonders}$$

$$\text{Decision variable 2} = x_2 = \text{number of Aluminum Allys}$$

Take note that each of the above decision variables is in number produced per week. This per week measure must be followed throughout the LP formulation for proper scaling.

Objective Function Formulation

The next step in Mark's bat production LP model is the formulation of the objective function. We know that, for each Wooden Wonder produced, \$7 of profit is realized and, for each Aluminum Ally produced, \$10 of profit is realized. It is also known that Mark's firm wishes to maximize profits. The objective function is formed from the profit gained from each style of bat being multiplied by the appropriate decision variable and added together.

An objective function always contains a maximize or minimize statement.

Therefore, the objective function takes on the form

$$\text{Maximize } Z = \$7x_1 + \$10x_2$$

Business Decision Modeling throughout the Ages

The History of Mathematical Programming

Definition and Essence of Mathematical Programming

Mathematical programming, or constrained optimization, or math programming for short, is a mathematical procedure for determining optimal allocation of scarce resources. Math programming, and its most popular special form, linear programming (LP), has found practical application in almost all facets of business, from advertising to production planning. Transportation and aggregate production planning problems are the most typical objects of LP analysis.

Limited Resources and Activities

For most optimization problems, one can think of two important classes of objects. The first of these is limited resources, such as land, plant capacity, and sales force size. Second are activities, such as "produce low carbon steel," "produce stainless steel," and "produce high carbon steel." Each activity consumes or possibly contributes additional amounts of the resources. The problem is to determine the best combination of activity levels that does not use more resources than are actually available. Many managers are faced with this task every day, and hence the birth of the field of mathematical programming.

The Diet Problem

The diet problem is one of the first optimization problems to be studied dating back to the 1930s and '40s. It was first motivated by the Army's desire to meet the nutritional requirements of the field GIs while minimizing the cost. One of the early researchers to study this problem was George Stigler. He made an educated guess of the optimal solution to linear program by using a heuristic method. His guess for the cost of an optimal diet was \$39.93 per year (1939 prices).

In the fall of 1947, Jack Laderman of the Mathematical Tables Project of the National Bureau of Standards undertook solving Stigler's model with the new simplex method. It was the first "large scale" computation in optimization. The linear program consisted of nine equations in 77 unknowns. It took nine clerks using hand-operated desk calculators 120 worker-days to solve for the optimal solution of \$39.69. Stigler's guess for the optimal solution was off by only 24 cents per year.

Goal of the Diet Problem

The goal of the diet problem is to find the cheapest combination of foods that will satisfy all the daily nutritional requirements of a person. The problem is formulated as a linear program where the objective is to minimize cost and meet constraints that satisfy nutritional needs. Constraints that regulate the number of calories and amounts of vitamins, minerals, fats, sodium and cholesterol in the diet are also included. The mathematical formulation is simple, but you will find out by running the model that people do not actually choose their menus by solving this model. Humans' nutritional requirements can be met, yet their concerns for taste and variety go unheeded. No one would never drink gallons of vinegar nor include a few bouillon cubes in our meals; however, such "optimal" menus have been created by using this model.

Practical Computing Methods and Linear Programming Models

The systematic development of practical computing methods for linear programming began in 1952 at the Rand Corporation in Santa Monica, under the direction of George B. Dantzig. After 1956, the work continued at CEIR, Inc., in Washington for some years and later in many places by many individuals and firms. By the late 1960s, elaborate systems of programs known as mathematical programming systems (MPS) had become a standard part of the available software for a number of mainframe computers. Work still continues and substantial improvements have been made in speed, reliability, supporting data management and control systems, and application techniques including the use of desktop PCs and spreadsheets to design and solve LP models.

George Dantzig's Take on the History of Linear Programming Models

"In retrospect," Dantzig wrote in the 1991 history book, "it is interesting to note that the original problem that started my research is still outstanding—namely the problem of planning or scheduling dynamically over time, particularly planning dynamically under uncertainty. If such a problem could be successfully solved it could eventually through better planning contribute to the well-being and stability of the world."

The nature of that original problem is also detailed in the book. Dantzig's contributions, he explained, grew out of his experience in the Pentagon during World War II, when he had become an expert on programming—that is, planning methods done with desk calculators. In 1946, as mathematical adviser to the U.S. Air Force Comptroller, he was challenged by his Pentagon colleagues to see what he could do to mechanize the planning process, "to more rapidly compute a time-staged deployment, training and logistical supply program.." In those pre–electronic computer days, mechanization meant using analog devices or punch-card machines. "Program" at that time was a military term that referred not to the instructions used by a computer to solve problems, which were then called "codes," but rather to plans or proposed schedules for training, logistical supply, or deployment of combat units. The somewhat confusing name "linear programming," Dantzig explained in the book, is based on this military definition of "program."

Optimal Information Area

Abstracted primarily from "A History of Mathematical Programming in the Petroleum Industry" by C. E. Bodington and T. E. Baker, *Interfaces*, vol. 20, no. 4 (1990), pp. 117–127.

Lenstra, J.K., Rinnoy, A.H.G., and Schrijver, A. (1991) *History of Mathematical Programming: A Collection of Personal Reminiscences*, Elsevier Science Publishers B.V.: Amsterdam, The Netherlands.

Constraint Formulation

Formulation of the constraints restricting the production of each style of bat is the next step in developing the LP model. From the earlier narrative about Mark's bat production process, we know that three capacity limits exist. These limits translate into three constraints: one constraint for shaping, a constraint for stamping, and a constraint for packing.

In addition, Mark's firm has promised one of its clients 30 Wooden Wonders. This means that there must be at least 30 Wooden Wonders produced. This may not seem like a constraint limiting production at the outset. However, one must keep in mind that constraints not only limit but also may define minimum levels of activity.

SHAPING CONSTRAINTS

To formulate the constraints, the words from the narrative must be transformed into linear equations. Let's first look at the shaping process. The Wooden Wonder requires 1.5 hours to shape and the machine used in shaping the Wooden Wonder has a maximum of 100 hours. Therefore, the total hours used to shape Wooden Wonders cannot exceed 100 hours per week. The constraint takes on the form

$$1.5x_1 \leq 100 \quad \text{Wooden Wonder shaping constraint}$$

Constraints can be formulated as $\geq$, $\leq$, or $=$ relationships.

The constraint is formed by taking the amount of hours required for a single Wooden Wonder multiplied by the respective decision variable, x_1, and setting the result less than or equal to the maximum amount of Wooden Wonder shaping hours available.

The same logic then applies to the Aluminum Ally constraint. Each Aluminum Ally requires 2 hours of shaping, and the machine used to shape the Aluminum Ally has a maximum of 120 hours. Therefore, the constraint takes on the form

$$2.0x_2 \leq 120 \quad \text{Aluminum Ally shaping constraint}$$

STAMPING CONSTRAINT

The constraint for the stamping process is based on similar logic but takes on a slightly different form. First, only one machine is used in the stamping process. Therefore, both the hours used to stamp the Wooden Wonder and the Aluminum Ally must be related to the total stamping hours available. According to the clues given in the narrative, the stamping constraint takes on the form

$$0.25x_1 + 0.5x_2 \leq 60 \quad \text{Stamping constraint}$$

The constraint is constructed from the two decision variables, the stamping time associated with each decision variable, and the total stamping time available.

The same logic used in the shaping constraints is employed here also. However, the coefficients for each decision variable must be discussed. It should be noted in the stamping constraint that the coefficient of x_1 is 0.25. This is because 15 minutes is a quarter of an hour and the coefficient for x_1 must be in the same units as the total number of stamping hours available. Thereby the units of the coefficients and the total constraint amount match. Overall, for any constraint, the constraint coefficients and the total constraint amount must be in the same units.

PACKING CONSTRAINT

The constraint for the packing process follows the same construction as the stamping constraint. According to the information given in Mark's bat production narrative, the packing constraint takes on the form

$$0.25x_1 + 0.25x_2 \leq 25 \quad \text{Packing constraint}$$

The issue of unit matching of the coefficients and the total packing time is also relevant here. Take note of the constraint coefficients for x_1 and x_2.

MINIMUM WOODEN WONDER PRODUCTION CONSTRAINT

Since Mark has agreed to produce 30 Wooden Wonders for a client, there must be a constraint formulated for this information. Basically, no matter how many Aluminum Ally bats Mark's firm produces, 30 Wooden Wonders must be produced to meet the preferred customer demand. Therefore, a minimum Wooden Wonder constraint must be formulated. According to the clues given in the narrative, the minimum Wooden Wonder production constraint takes on the form

$$x_1 \geq 30 \quad \text{Minimum Wooden Wonder production constraint}$$

Take note that this constraint contains a greater than or equal to operator. Relate this to the discussion regarding the preferred customer's order. This completes the formulation of the constraints associated with Mark's production problem. The next section provides the final part of the LP model to be constructed, the non-negativity assumptions.

Non-Negativity Assumptions

Since there are two decision variables, x_1 and x_2, the non-negativity assumptions are basic and take on the following form:

Non-negativity assumptions state that all decision variables must be equal to or greater than zero.

$$x_1, x_2 \geq 0$$

Remember that, even though the non-negativity assumptions are the simplest part of the LP model, they must be included. The next section combines all three parts of the LP model together into modified standard form.

Modified Standard Form—Mark's Bat Production Problem

Modified standard form for Mark's bat production LP model is as follows where the three parts of the LP model are numbered as follows: Equation (8.4) objective function, Equations (8.5a) to (8.5e) constraints, and Equation (8.6) non-negativity assumptions.

When an LP model is formulated and transformed into modified standard form, a method for solving the LP model can be employed. The next section details two methods for solving LP models and provides both solution types for Mark's Bat Production problem.

Maximize $Z = \$7x_1 + \$10x_2$ **(8.4)**

subject to $1.5x_1 \leq 100$ Wooden Wonder shaping constraint **(8.5a)**

$2.0x_2 \leq 120$ Aluminum Ally shaping constraint **(8.5b)**

$0.25x_1 + 0.5x_2 \leq 60$ Stamping constraint **(8.5c)**

$0.25x_1 + 0.25x_2 \leq 25$ Packing constraint **(8.5d)**

$x_1 \geq 30$ Minimum Wooden Wonder production constraint **(8.5e)**

$x_1, x_2 \geq 0$ **(8.6)**

Methods of Solving LP Problems

Two methods of solving LP problems exist: the graphical method and the simplex method.

Once the LP model is in modified standard form, two basic approaches to solving the LP model exist. The first method is the graphical method, and the second is called the simplex method. The next section describes the graphical method and the subsequent solution to Mark's bat production LP model. A section describing the simplex method follows the description of the graphical method and the solution generated by Solver for Mark's bat production LP model.

The Graphical Method

The graphical method is simple, but is limited to smaller LP models (i.e., two or three decision variables). The limitation on decision variables is due to the nature of the graphical method. When presented with an LP model with two decision variables, the graphical method produces a two-dimensional graph. In turn, when presented with an LP model with three decision variables, the graphical method produces a three-dimensional graph.

This logic makes it clear that when an LP model contains four or more decision variables, it is impossible to use the graphical method of solution, as no n-dimensional graph can be developed for n greater than 3. The next section provides a set of steps to follow when the graphical method is to solve LP models.

Steps to Implementing the Graphical Method

The following set of steps is used for implementing the graphical method of solving LP models. Before the steps are detailed, however, a few terms must be defined.

Feasible region. The region mapped by the constraints containing values of the decision variables that are allowed by the constraint set.

The feasible region is defined as the region mapped by the constraints containing values of decision variables that are allowed by the constraint set.

Corner point. A point where a set of constraints intersect.

Corner point feasible solution. A point where a set of constraints intersect that is on the edge of the feasible region.

The steps are presented next. Their application to Mark's bat production problem can be found in Appendix 8A.

1. Construct an *x-y* coordinate plane/graph.
2. Plot all constraints on the plane/graph.
3. Identify the feasible region dictated by the constraints.
4. Identify all corner point feasible solutions of the feasible region.
5. Identify the optimum solution by plotting a series of objective functions over the feasible region.
6. Determine the exact solution values of the decision variables and the objective function at the optimum solution.

A six-step process can be followed to solve LP problems graphically.

Using Spreadsheets to Model LP Problems

As was demonstrated earlier in this chapter, spreadsheets can be used to model optimization problems. This is also true for LP problems. The next section details how to create and solve an LP spreadsheet model for Mark's bat production LP problem.

Creating the LP Spreadsheet Model

This section describes how to create the underlying spreadsheet LP model for Mark's bat production problem. Figure 8.13 displays the basic spreadsheet model in Excel. Figure 8.14 displays the spreadsheet formulas associated with the LP model. The decision variables are defined in words in cells C3 and C4 and then defined as variables in cells D3 and D4. The objective function is defined in row 8 and specifically represented in words in cell C8 and as a mathematical function in cell D8.

The terms LHS and RHS are used in Figure 8.13 to denote left-hand side of a constraint and right-hand side of a constraint, respectively. It should be noted that, since the decision variables are currently set at zero, the objective function and all LHS constraints are zero.

	A	B	C	D	E
1	Decision Variables				
2					
3			x_1= # of Wooden Wonders to Produce	0	
4			x_2 = # of Aluminum Allys to Produce	0	
5					
6	Objective Function				
7					
8			Max Z = \$7x_1 + \$10x_2	0	
9					
10	Constraints			LHS	RHS
11			Wooden Wonder Shaping		
12			$1.5x_1 \leq 100$	0	100
13			Aluminum Ally Shaping		
14			$2.0x_2 \leq 120$	0	120
15			Stamping		
16			$0.25x_1 + 0.5x_2 \leq 60$	0	60
17			Packing		
18			$0.25x_1 + 0.25x_2 \leq 25$	0	25
19			Minimum Wooden Wonder Production		
20			$x_1 \geq 30$	0	30

FIGURE 8.13 Spreadsheet LP Model for Mark's Bat Production Problem

Figure 8.14 displays the spreadsheet formulas associated with the LP model. Specific formulas for the objective function and individual LHS constraints are found in column D.

	A	B	C	D	E
1	Decision Variables				
2					
3			x_1=# of Wooden Wonders to Produce	0	
4			x_2=# of Aluminum Allys to Produce	0	
5					
6	Objective Function				
7					
8			Max Z = \$7x_1+\$10x_2	=7*D3+10*D4	
9					
10	Constraints			LHS	RHS
11			Wooden Wonder Shaping		
12			$1.5x_1 \leq 100$	=1.5*D3	100
13			Aluminum Ally Shaping		
14			$2.0x_2 \leq 120$	=2*D4	120
15			Stamping		
16			$0.25x_1 + 0.5x_2 \leq 60$	=0.25*D3+0.5*D4	60
17			Packing		
18			$0.25x_1 + 0.25x_2 \leq 25$	=0.25*D3+0.25*D4	25
19			Minimum Wooden Wonder Production		
20			$x_1 \geq 30$	=D3	30
21					

FIGURE 8.14 Spreadsheet Formulas Associated with Mark's Bat Production Problem

Using Solver to Find Solutions to a Spreadsheet Optimization Model

This section discusses how to use Solver to optimize a spreadsheet LP model in Excel. It is assumed that the user has already built a spreadsheet optimization model in Excel (refer to Figures 8.13 and 8.14). After clicking on Solver in the Tools menu, the Solver dialog box (Figure 8.15) will appear. For Excel 2007, the Solver dialogue box is quite similar in looks. The following instructions apply to both Solver in Excel 2007 and 2010 as the menu options are analogous.

Solver allows you to input an objective function, a set of constraints, and non-negativity assumptions within a spreadsheet.

The following steps enable Solver to find solutions to optimization spreadsheets.

1. In the Set Objective box, enter a cell reference or name for the target cell. The target cell must contain a formula.
2. To have the value of the objective be as large as possible, click Max. To have the value of the objective be as small as possible, click Min. To have the objective be a certain value, click Value of and then type the value in the box.
3. In the By Changing Variable Cells, enter a name or reference for each adjustable cell, separating nonadjacent references with commas. The adjustable cells must be related directly or indirectly to the target cell. You can specify up to 200 adjustable cells.
4. In the Subject to the Constraints box, enter any constraints you want to apply. Click on the Add button and add your constraints as follows:
   a. Click in the Cell Reference box and add the cell reference for the LHS portion of the constraint in the spreadsheet.
   b. Adjust the operator menu to match the constraint's operator (e.g., ≤, =, or ≥).
   c. Click on the Constraint box and add the cell reference for the RHS portion of the constraint in the spreadsheet.

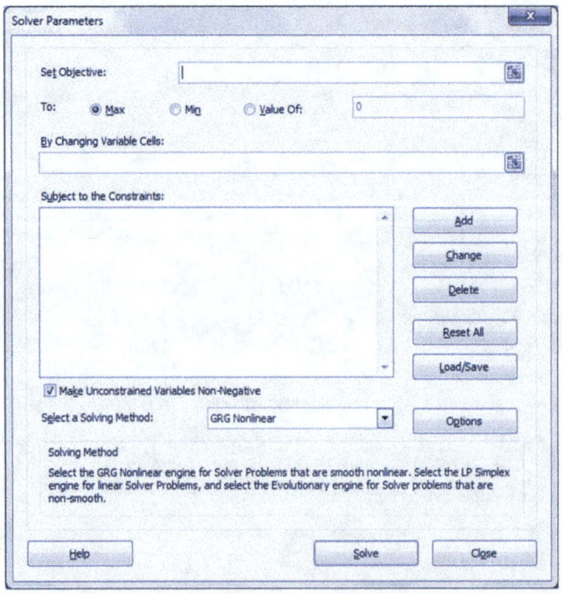

FIGURE 8.15

Excel Solver Dialog Box for Excel 2010

TABLE 8.2 *Solver Cell Definitions*

Set Objective Cell	$D$8
To:	Max
By Changing Variable Cells	$D$3:$D$4
Subject to the Constraints:	
Wooden Wonder shaping	$D$12< =$E$12
Aluminum Ally shaping	$D$14< =$E$14
Stamping	$D$16< =$E$16
Packing	$D$18< =$E$18
Minimum Wooden Wonder production	$D$20 > =$E$20

d. Click OK when finished adding the constraint. You will be taken back to a screen that resembles Figure 8.15

5. Click Solve.

Applying these steps to Mark's bat production spreadsheet LP problem, an objective cell (the objective function), variable cells (the decision variables), and constraints are defined as shown in Table 8.2 (refer to Figures 8.13 and 8.14):

In entering the solver cell definitions for the constraints, follow the same procedure as detailed in Figures 8.8, 8.9, and 8.10, using the constraints for Mark's LP model. The solver menu will resemble Figure 8.16 after you have entered the values from Table 8.2 into the Solver dialog boxes.

Since Mark's bat production problem contains only linear constraints, Solver must be notified. This is in most cases a formality, but it is good form to follow. Notifying Solver of a linear model is simple:

1. From the Select Solving Method: drop down menu, choose Simplex.
2. Check the box labeled Make Unconstrained Variables Non-Negative.

NOTE: See Figure 8.16 for both of these commands.

After the linear assumption and non-negativity assumption have been enabled, Solver is ready to be employed to solve Mark's bat production LP problem. From the Solver menu (refer to Figure 8.16), click the Solver button to commence the solution process.

Figure 8.17 displays the final spreadsheet model for Mark's bat production LP problem. The optimal production quantities of 40 Wooden Wonders and 60 Aluminum Allys and the maximum objective function value of $880 are shown (refer to cells D3, D4, and D8 respectively).

Cell D8 is of special interest as it contains the optimal value of the objective function. If Mark produces 40 Wooden Wonders and 60 Aluminum Allys, he will maximize his profit. The maximum profit generated, $880, is identical to the maximum objective function calculated by the graphical method (refer to Appendix 8A).

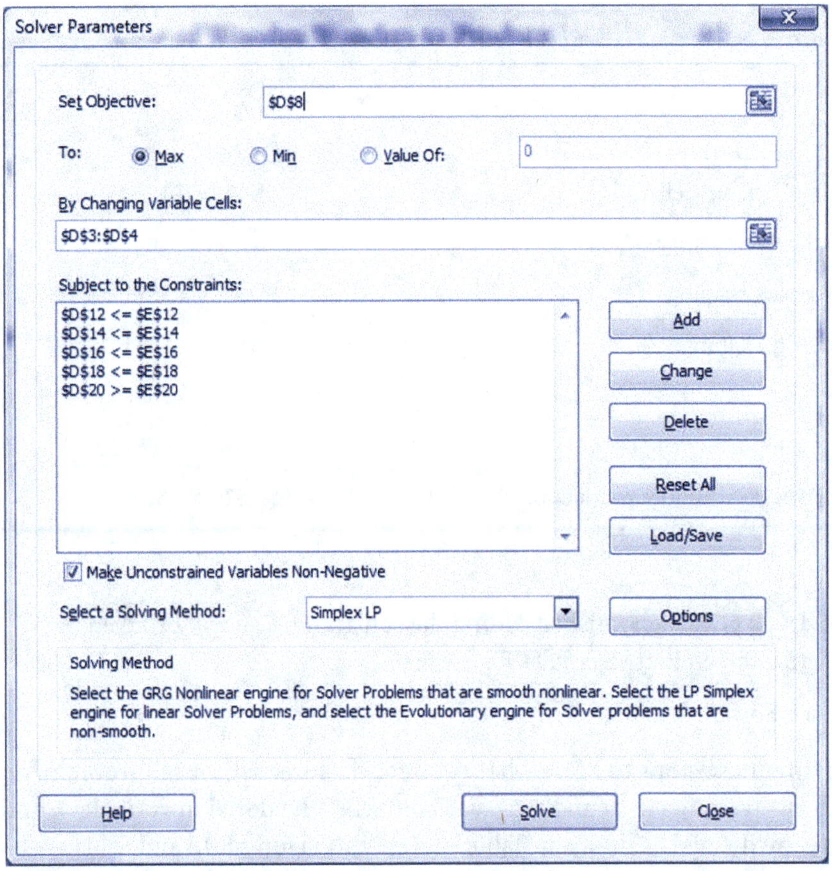

FIGURE 8.16

Final Solver Parameters for Mark's Bat Production Problem for Excel 2010

	A	B	C	D	E
1	Decision Variables				
2					
3			x_1=# of Wooden Wonders to Produce	40	
4			x_2=# of Aluminum Allys to Produce	60	
5					
6	Objective Function				
7					
8			Max Z = \$7x_1+\$10x_2	880	
9					
10	Constraints			LHS	RHS
11			Wooden Wonder Shaping		
12			$1.5x_1 \leq 100$	60	100
13			Aluminum Ally Shaping		
14			$2.0x_2 \leq 120$	120	120
15			Stamping		
16			$0.25x_1 + 0.5x_2 \leq 60$	40	60
17			Packing		
18			$0.25x_1 + 0.25x_2 \leq 25$	25	25
19			Minimum Wooden Wonder Production		
20			$x_1 \geq 30$	40	30

FIGURE 8.17

Optimized Spreadsheet Model for Mark's Bat Production LP Problem

Comparison of Constraints and Sensitivity Analysis

Another area of interest is comparison of LHS and RHS cells (refer to columns D and E). In comparing the cells, it can be seen that some cells labeled LHS are equal to the cells labeled RHS. This occurs because an LP model contains only linear relationships and the corner point feasible solutions must be found on the perimeter of the feasible region. As discussed earlier, the optimal solution will lie at the intersection of a set of constraints that make up the perimeter of the feasible region. The constraints that intersect to form the optimal solution are indicated when LHS cells equal the RHS cells. The next section will discuss the implications when the LHS and RHS are equal and when they are not equal.

The optimal solution to an LP model will generally lie at the intersection of a set of constraints.

Binding and Nonbinding Constraints

Information about the relationship between the optimal solution and the constraints is contained in the LHS and RHS cells. From the LHS and RHS cells, it can be determined which constraints are "binding" and which constraints contain "slack." A binding constraint can be defined as a constraint that is "used up"; in our example, the LHS cell would equal the RHS cell. A constraint that has slack is not used up, and, in our example, the LHS would not be equal to the RHS cell. This information is important, as it tells the user on which constraints the optimal solution lies. It must be noted that word slack is used in a different sense from what is defined as a slack variable and/or a surplus variable in the simplex method. The term slack is used in the present context to characterize constraints.

A binding constraint is considered to be used up or have no slack.

From Figure 8.17, it is seen that the LHS and RHS for the Aluminum Ally shaping constraint and for the packing constraint are equal (see cells D14, E14, D18, and E18). The intersection of the Aluminum ally shaping constraint and the packing constraint defines a feasible corner point solution and the optimal solution (40, 60). In turn, since the optimal solution lies at the intersection of these two constraints, they are completely used up. In being used up, all resources for Aluminum Ally shaping and packing are consumed. In turn, the constraints where the LHS is not equal to the RHS (Wooden Wonder shaping, stamping, and minimum Wooden Wonder production) are not used up and contain slack. In other words, there is leftover Wooden Wonder shaping time, stamping time, and more than enough Wooden Wonders produced to meet the minimum requirement.

A constraint that has slack is not fully used up.

Results and Sensitivity Analysis in Excel

Excel has the capability to produce reports containing information about LP results and constraint sensitivity analysis. To generate the answer and sensitivity reports, follow these steps:

1. After Solver has completed its solution process, a screen like that in Figure 8.18 will appear. For Excel 2007, an analogous Solver Results window will appear.
2. In the Solver Results window, select the Answer and Sensitivity options in the Reports menu.

Solver will generate answer and sensitivity reports for an LP solution.

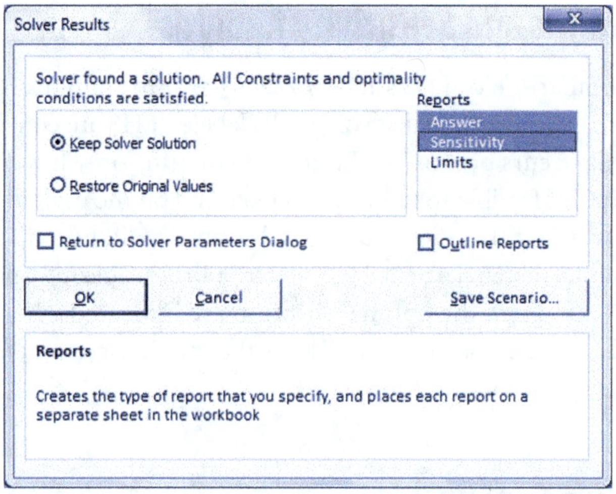

FIGURE 8.18
Excel Solver Results Window for Excel 2010

3. Two new worksheets will be generated, one for the answer report and one for the sensitivity report

The answer report is the first report discussed, followed by the sensitivity report.

Answer Report in Excel

The answer report generated within Solver details three areas: objective cell, variable cells, and constraints. Figure 8.19 displays the answer report generated for Mark's bat production LP problem.

Microsoft Excel 14.0 Answer Report
Worksheet: [MarksBarProduction.xls]Sheet1
Report Created: 2/28/2011 2:29:01 PM
Result: Solver found a solution. All Constraints and optimality conditions are satisfied.
Solver Engine
Engine: Simplex LP
Solution Time: 0.015 Seconds.
Iterations: 3 Subproblems: 0
Solver Options
Max Time 100 sec, Iterations 100, Precision 0.000001
Max Subproblems Unlimited, Max Integer Sols Unlimited,
Integer Tolerance 5%, Solve Without Integer Constraints, Assume NonNegative

Objective Cell (Max)

Cell	Name	Original Value	Final Value
$D$8	Max Z = $7x1+$10x2	0	880

Variable Cells

Cell	Name	Original Value	Final Value	Integer
$D$3	x1=# of Wooden Wonders to Produce	0	40	Contin
$D$4	x2=# of Aluminum Allys to Produce	0	60	Contin

Constraints

Cell	Name	Cell Value	Formula	Status	Slack
$D$12	1.5x1 < 100 LHS	60	$D$12<=$E$12	Not Binding	40
$D$14	2.0x2 < 120 LHS	120	$D$14<=$E$14	Binding	0
$D$16	0.25x1 + 0.5x2 < 60 LHS	40	$D$16<=$E$16	Not Binding	20
$D$18	0.25x1 + 0.25x2 < 25 LHS	25	$D$18<=$E$18	Binding	0
$D$20	x1 > 30 LHS	40	$D$20>=$E$20	Not Binding	10

FIGURE 8.19
Excel Solver Results Window

OBJECTIVE CELL SECTION

The Objective Cell section in Solver's answer report contains information about the objective function.

The first section of interest is the Objective Cell section. The Objective Cell section contains information regarding the objective function. Cell C8 contains the objective function defined in the original spreadsheet LP model, whereas cell D8 contains the original value of the objective function. The original value for Mark's bat production problem is zero, since the decision variables were set to zero (see the Adjustable Cell section).

Cell E8 contains the final value of the objective function. In this LP model the final value of the objective function is 880. This value is the same as the value calculated by the graphical method detailed in the Appendix 9A. Overall, the Objective Cell section provides information about the objective function, specifically its final and optimal value.

VARIABLE CELLS SECTION

The Variable Cells section in Solver's answer report contains information about the decision variables.

The Variable Cells section provides information about the decision variables x_1, the number of Wooden Wonders to produce, and x_2, the number of Aluminum Allys to produce. Cells D13 and D14 contain the original values of the decision variables. The values in the cells are zero, as the decision variables were set to zero originally. Cells E13 and E14 contain the final values of the decision variables, 40 Wooden Wonders and 60 Aluminum Allys. In sum, the Variable Cells section informs the decision maker of the optimal number of bats to produce.

CONSTRAINTS SECTION

The Constraints section in Solver's Answer Report contains information about the constraints or limitations on the decision variables.

The Constraints section contains information about the constraints or limitations on the decision variables. This section should be linked to the earlier discussion involving the LHS and RHS columns in Figure 8.17. The Constraints section contains the same information as the LHS and RHS columns in Figure 8.17. However, the Constraints section organizes constraint information more efficiently and provides information on slack. As defined earlier, slack is defined as an amount of a constraint that is not used up.

The Constraint section in Figure 8.19 contains the constraint formulas, cells C19 to C23; the final constraint value, labeled Cell Value and contained in cells D19 to D23; and the Excel constraint formulas labeled "Formula" in cells E19 to E23. In addition, the Constraint section contains information about whether the constraint is binding or not binding in cells F19 to F23, labeled Status.

The cells labeled Slack, cells G19 to G23, contain information about how much of a constraint is left over and are related to cells F19 to F23. If a cell in the Status section is labeled Binding, the corresponding Slack cell will be zero. Likewise, if a cell in the Status column is labeled Not Binding, the corresponding Slack cell will contain a positive value.

Slack values correspond to the amount of a constraint that is not used up.

Slack values correspond to the amount of the respective constraint that is not used up. When the slack value is zero, the Status label will always read, Binding. A connection should be made, in that when a constraint is Binding, the optimal solution lies on that constraint and that constraint is in turn used up (i.e., slack equals zero). Refer back to the discussion "Binding and Nonbinding Constraints," above, to make this connection.

Sensitivity Report in Excel

The Sensitivity report generated within Solver details two areas: variable cells and constraints. Figure 8.20 displays the sensitivity report generated for Mark's bat production LP problem.

The Sensitivity report generated within Solver details two areas: variable cells and constraints.

The report displayed in Figure 8.20 summarizes information on how sensitive the optimal solution is to changes in various coefficients in the underlying LP model. The Variable Cells section is detailed first, followed by the Constraints section.

VARIABLE CELLS SECTION

The Variable Cells section of the sensitivity report provides information about the sensitivity of changes to the decision variables. The column labeled Final Value contains the optimal values for the number of Wooden Wonders and Aluminum Allys to produce. For Mark's bat production LP, the optimal number of Wooden Wonders to produce is 40, while 60 Aluminum Allys should be produced. These are the same values presented in the answer report (see Figure 8.19). However, the sensitivity report gives additional information on changes to the variable cells in the LP. The Reduced Cost area is discussed next.

The Variable Cells section in Solver's answer report contains information about the sensitivity of changes to the decision variables.

REDUCED COST

Specifically, the Reduced Cost column indicates how much the objective coefficient of a decision variable must improve before that decision variable could assume a positive value in the optimal solution. In the case of Excel Solver, the absolute

Microsoft Excel 14.0 Sensitivity Report
Worksheet: [MarksBarProduction.xls]Sheet1
Report Created: 2/28/2011 2:29:01 PM

Variable Cells

Cell	Name	Final Value	Reduced Cost	Objective Coefficient	Allowable Increase	Allowable Decrease
$D$3	x1=# of Wooden Wonders to Produce	40	0	7	3	7
$D$4	x2=# of Aluminum Allys to Produce	60	0	10	1E+30	3

Constraints

Cell	Name	Final Value	Shadow Price	Constraint R.H. Side	Allowable Increase	Allowable Decrease
$D$12	1.5x1 < 100 LHS	60	0	100	1E+30	40
$D$14	2.0x2 < 120 LHS	120	1.5	120	20	53.3333333
$D$16	0.25x1 + 0.5x2 < 60 LHS	40	0	60	1E+30	20
$D$18	0.25x1 + 0.25x2 < 25 LHS	25	28	25	6.66666667	2.5
$D$20	x1 > 30 LHS	40	0	30	10	1E+30

FIGURE 8.20

Excel Sensitivity Report for Mark's Bat Production LP Problem

The Reduced Cost column indicates how much the objective coefficient of a decision variable must improve before that decision variable assumes a positive value in the optimal solution.

value of the Reduced Cost column is always taken and interpreted. In Mark's bat production LP problem, both values in the Reduced Cost column are zero. This occurs because each decision variable is already a positive value (40 Wooden Wonders and 60 Aluminum Allys respectively) in the objective function.

OBJECTIVE COEFFICIENT, ALLOWABLE INCREASE, AND ALLOWABLE DECREASE

The column labeled Objective Coefficient corresponds to the coefficients that accompany each decision variable in the objective function.

The Allowable Increase and Allowable Decrease columns describe the range an objective coefficient must stay within for the optimal decision variables to be valid.

The next columns in the Variable Cell section are labeled Allowable Increase and Allowable Decrease. These columns are linked to the Objective Coefficient column. For Mark's bat production LP, the Wooden Wonder objective coefficient is 7, the allowable increase value is 3, and the allowable decrease is 7. If one adds 3 to or subtracts 7 from the current Wooden Wonder objective coefficient of 7, a range of optimality for the objective coefficient is obtained. The range for the Wooden Wonder decision variable, C_{ww}, would then be

$$0 \leq C_{\text{ww}} \leq 10$$

This range informs us that, as long as the objective coefficient (profit contribution) from Wooden Wonders remains between \$0 and \$10 inclusive, the optimal production numbers, 40 Wooden Wonders and 60 Aluminum Allys, remain optimal. The same analysis can be performed for the Aluminum Ally objective coefficient.

CONSTRAINTS SECTION

The Constraints section gives the user insight into how the constrained resources are being utilized.

The information provided in the Constraints section gives the user insight into how the constrained resources are being utilized. For example, the entries in the Final Value column display the exact units of a constraint needed to produce the optimal combination of 40 Wooden Wonders and 60 Aluminum Allys. Therefore, producing 40 Wooden Wonders and 60 Aluminum Allys takes 60 hours of Wooden Wonder shaping (refer to row 15 in the Constraints section), 120 hours of Aluminum Ally shaping (refer to row 16 in the Constraints section), 40 hours of stamping (refer to row 17 in the Constraints section), 25 hours of packing (refer to row 18 in the Constraints section), and 40 units of Wooden Wonder production (refer to row 19 in the Constraints section).

THE CONSTRAINT R.H. SIDE COLUMN

The values in the R.H. Side column are the original RHS values for each constraint: 100 hours of Wooden Wonder shaping, 120 hours of Aluminum Ally shaping, 60 hours of stamping, 25 hours of packing, and 30 units minimum of Wooden Wonder production. One should notice that the slack variables discussed in the section describing the answer report are just the absolute value of the Constraint R.H. Side column less the Final Value column. Keep in mind that the Wooden

Wonder production constraint is a minimum constraint; therefore, producing more than the minimum value of 30 is logical and the slack is the extra units produced (i.e., 10 = |30 – 40|).

SHADOW PRICE COLUMN

The Shadow Price column assists the user in determining what additional amounts of constrained resources would be worth. A Shadow Price is defined as the amount by which the objective function value changes given a unit increase/decrease in the RHS value of the constraint, assuming all other coefficients remain the same.

The Shadow Price column assists in determining what additional amounts of constrained resources would be worth.

Given that a shadow price is positive, a subsequent increase in the RHS value of the associated constraint would result in an improvement in the objective function value. Likewise, given that a shadow price is negative, a subsequent increase in the RHS value of the associated constraint would result in a declination in the objective function value. For constraints that have a shadow price of zero, it can be determined that changing the RHS of the constraint would have no effect on the objective function value, and it can be inferred that the constraint is also nonbinding (i.e., has slack).

For constraints with a shadow price of zero, it can be determined that changing the RHS of a constraint would have no effect on the objective function.

However, one must keep in mind that increases or decreases in the RHS value of a constraint must be within certain limits or else the shadow price commentary is invalid. In other words, if you change the RHS value of a constraint outside of a given increase/decrease range, the entire LP problem changes and the shadow prices are not valid anymore.

ALLOWABLE INCREASE AND DECREASE COLUMNS

For Mark's Bat Production LP problem, it can be seen in Figure 8.20 that the shadow price for the first constraint (refer to row 15 in the Constraints section) is zero. Note that the allowable increase is listed as 1E+30 (scientific notation for a very, very large number) and the allowable decrease is 40. Since the constraint is nonbinding, the RHS of the constraint could be increased infinitely with no change occurring in the objective function (i.e., a shadow price of zero). In turn, the RHS of the constraint could be decreased a maximum of 40 without changing the objective function. This logic is true for each of the constraints that have shadow prices of zero (refer to rows 15, 17, and 19 in Figure 8.20).

The Allowable Increase and Allowable Decrease columns describe the range a RHS constraint must stay within for the shadow price to be valid.

However, for constraints where the shadow price is nonzero, increases or decreases in the RHS of the constraints will change the value of the objective function. For example, the shadow price for the second constraint, the Aluminum Ally shaping constraint (refer to row 16 in the Constraints section of Figure 8.20) is 1.5.

Therefore, if the number of available shaping hours increased by any amount in the range from 0 to 20 hours (this is the amount of the allowable increase), the optimal objective function would increase by \$1.50 per hour of increase in Aluminum Ally shaping time. Consequently, if the number of Aluminum Ally shaping hours decreased by any amount in the range 0 to 53.3333 (this is the amount of the allowable decrease), the optimal objective function would decrease by \$1.50 per hour of decrease in the Aluminum Ally shaping time.

COMMENT ON SHADOW PRICES

It is important to note that if the constraint's RHS values are altered (increased or decreased), then either more or less of a key resource is available. In keeping with this logic, the optimal values of the decision variables may also change. In reality, this makes perfect sense. For example, if a user can somehow acquire more hours for shaping, stamping, or packing bats in Mark's bat production LP, it should be possible to produce more bats (all other things held constant).

Shadow price is akin to marginal value and equates to the marginal value of a resource being used with the marginal benefit of the goods being produced.

This description of shadow prices is unique to Solver in Excel. Regrettably, there does not seem to be a standard method of reporting shadow prices. When compared to Solver in Excel, different LP software packages may report shadow prices with opposite signs.

In sum, shadow price information is extremely valuable to users, as it opens up the question of efficient use of resources and cost-benefit analysis. For example, in the case of Mark's bat production LP problem, what if Mark could somehow obtain an additional amount of Aluminum Ally shaping hours? From the sensitivity report we know that for each hour of Aluminum Ally shaping resource added, Mark will see his objective function (and overall profit) increase by $1.50.

Resources that have slack will have shadow prices that are zero.

However, the real question at hand is "How much would Mark be willing to pay for those additional hours of Aluminum Ally shaping?" Some would say it definitely would not be more than the gain in increased profits (the increase in the objective function) by adding the extra resource. Numerous discussion topics could be developed here regarding evaluation based on fixed cost or variable cost assumptions. These discussions are not investigated here, and students are referred to any text detailing linear program applications for further inquiry. However, significant points regarding shadow prices to remember are:

- Shadow prices are akin to marginal value.
- Shadow prices equate the marginal value of a resource being used with the marginal benefit of the goods being produced.
- Resources that have excess supply or slack (i.e., nonbinding resources or the resource has not been used up) will have shadow prices of zero.
- Resources that do not have excess supply or slack (i.e., binding resources) will have shadow prices.

Using Risk Solver Platform in Excel

Risk Solver Platform (RSP) is an enhanced version of the standard Solver that accompanies every version of Excel. Although all of the examples in the text can be created and solved using the standard Solver, RSP includes additional capabilities that are featured here using Mark's Bat Problem.

After developing Mark's Bat Problem we can use RSP to solve. However, we must indicate in RSP which cells in the model represent the objective function, the decision variables, and the constraints (just like when we used Solver). First you must install RSP (an academic version of the software is available with this text).

After installing RSP, the user needs to invoke RSP by choosing the Risk Solver Platform tab in the Excel ribbon, as shown in Figure 8.21, and clicking on the Model option.

RSP includes a number of analytical tools (for example, Decision Trees, which we studied in Chapter 4). However, we are interested in RSP's optimization tool. The optimization tool can be expanded by double clicking on the Optimization option in the RSP task pane (see Figure 8.22).

Defining the Optimization Model in RSP

We need to define three parts of the optimization model (objective function, variables, and constraints) in RSP. We will start with the Objective cell and then discuss Variables and Constraints.

Defining the Objective Cell in RSP

Figure 8.23 displays how to define the Objective cell for our model. The following is a step-by-step set of instructions:

1. Select cell D8 as it contains our objective formula.
2. Click on the Objective option from the list in the RSP task pane and then on the green plus sign. Cell D8 will then appear under the Objective option in the RSP task pane (see Figure 8.23).

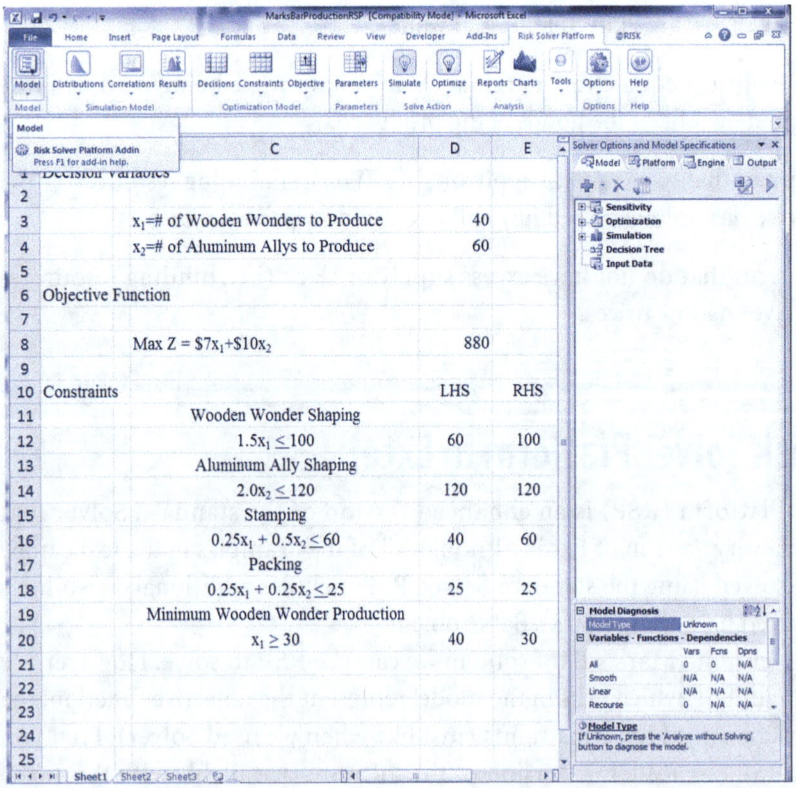

FIGURE 8.21
RSP Ribbon in Excel

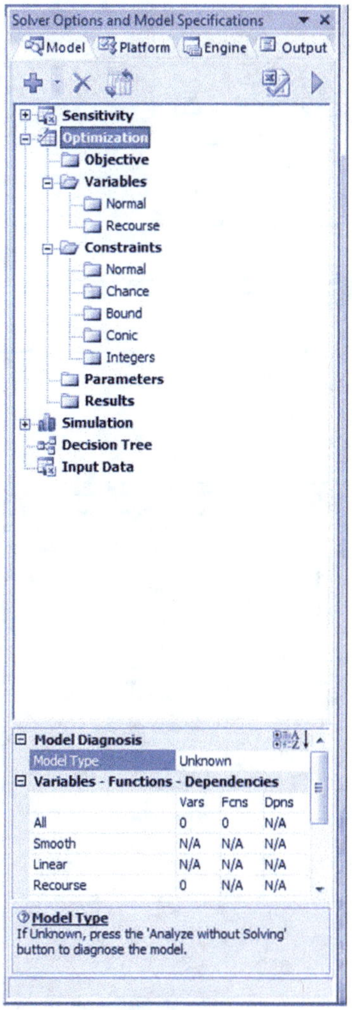

FIGURE 8.22

RSP Options and Model Specifications Window in Excel

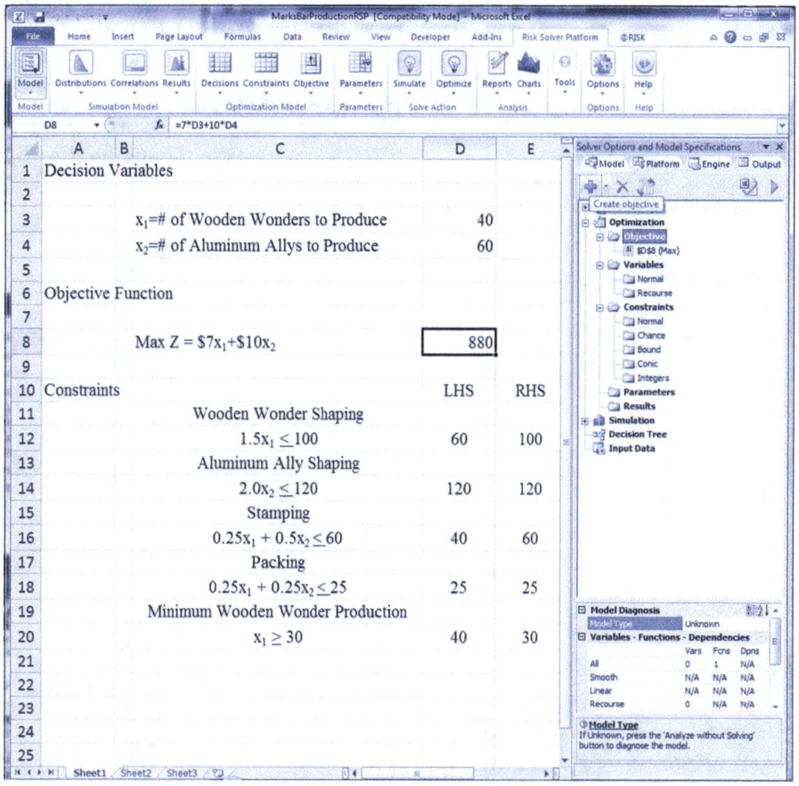

FIGURE 8.23

Mark's Bat Production LP Problem Formulation in RSP

In RSP's task pane, cell D8 is now listed as the objective for the problem. By default, RSP assumes we wish to maximize the objective's value. For Mark's Bat Problem this assumption is correct, but it may not be correct for every model created in RSP. RSP handles this with what is called the "Sense" property within the objective task pane. Refer to the bottom of Figure 8.24 and notice the "Sense" menu and the pull-down menu to its right. This pull-down menu allows the user to choose to either Maximize, Minimize, or choose a Value of for the objective. Alternately, double clicking the objective cell in the RSP task pane will launch a dialog box that can be used to change the desired optimization setting and other information regarding the objective (see Figure 8.25).

Defining the Variable Cells in RSP

To solve our optimization model, we need to identify which cells represent the decision variables. Figure 8.26 displays how to define the Variable cells for our model. The following is a step-by-step set of instructions:

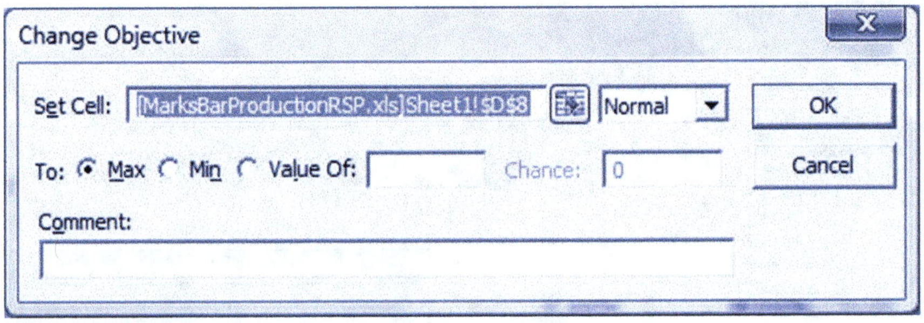

FIGURE 8.25

RSP Dialogue Box for Changing the Objective Function in Excel

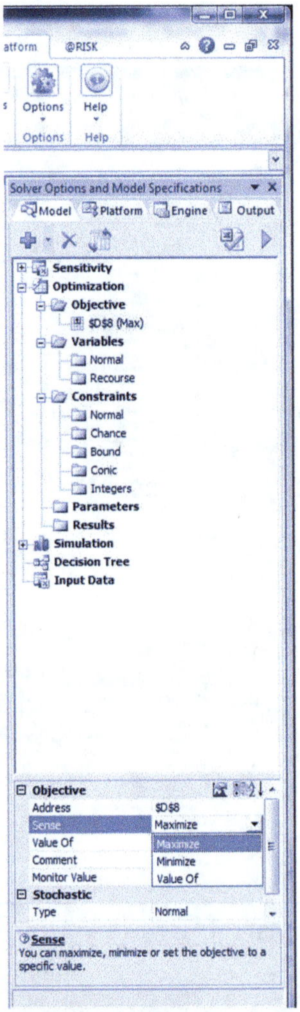

FIGURE 8.24

RSP Sense Menu in Excel

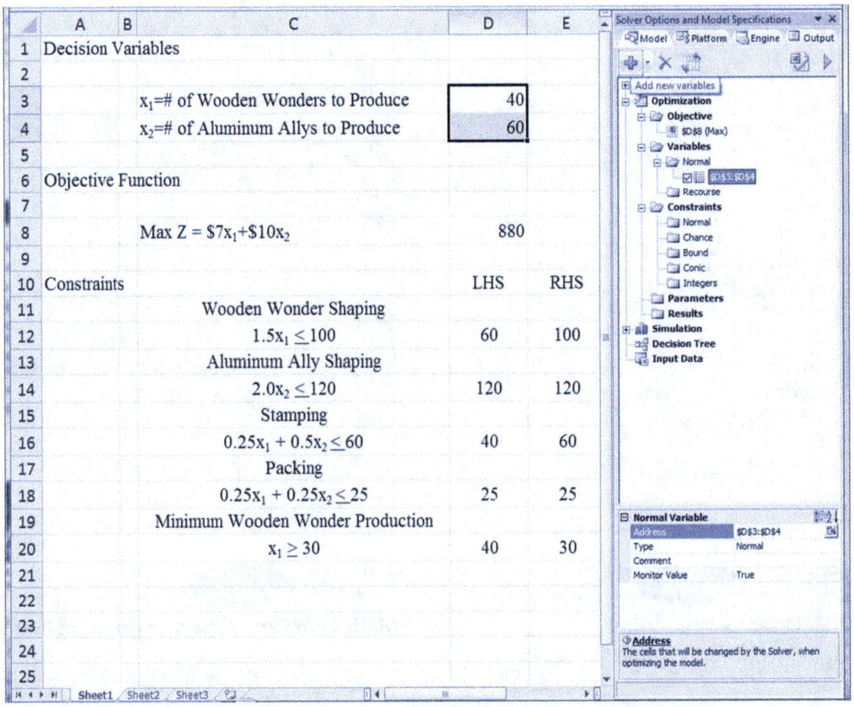

FIGURE 8.26

RSP Variables Option Menu in Excel

1. Select cells D3 and D4 as these cells contain our decision variables.
2. Click on the Variable option from the list in the RSP task pane and then on the green plus sign. Cells D3 and D4 will then appear under the Variables option in the RSP task pane (see Figure 8.26).

Cells D3 and D4 now represent the decision variables for our model. RSP will determine the optimal values of these cells when we solve the optimization model. You can select non-contiguous (not adjacent) decision variables by pressing the Crtl key while selecting the cells that contain the decision variables themselves. In general, it is good practice to juxtapose your decision variables in a contiguous range.

Defining the Constraint Cells in RSP

Finally, to complete our optimization model, we need to identify which cells represent the constraint cells or the restrictions that apply to those cells. The constraint cells are the formulae we developed as the LHS cells in our spreadsheet model. We have two different types of constraints in our model: less than or equal to and greater than or equal to. Therefore, we must input at least two constraints within RSP. However, for our specific model we will enter five separate constraints. Figure 8.27 displays how to input Constraint cells for our model. The following is a step-by-step set of instructions for the first constraint cell:

1. Select cell D12.
2. Click on the Constraints option in the RSP task pane and then click on the green plus sign. A figure resembling Figure 8.28 will appear (when the figure first appears there will be nothing listed in the "Constraint:" box).
3. Click in the "Constraints:" dialog box and then click on cell E12 in our spreadsheet model. Note that the default operator is the less than or equal to symbol. For the shaping constraint this is correct. However, for constraints that are not less than or equal to constraints, the operation must be modified using the pull-down menu associated with it. You can enter a comment if you like in the comment box or just click OK and the first constraint would be entered into RSP.

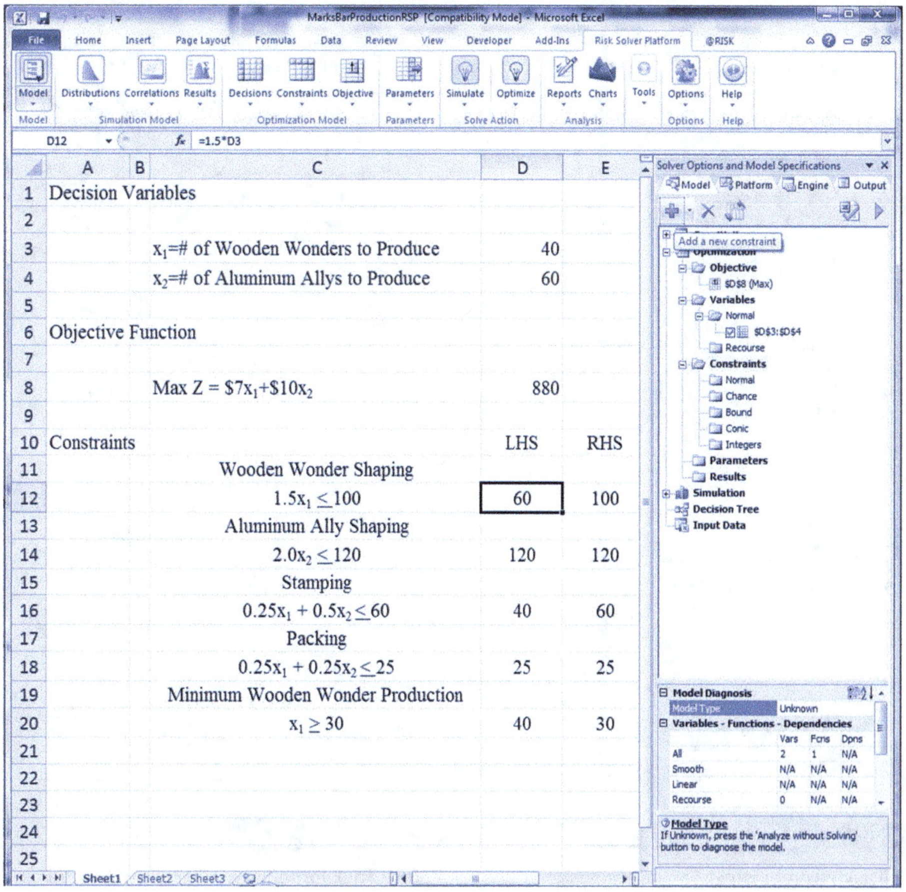

FIGURE 8.27

RSP Add a New Constraint Menu in Excel

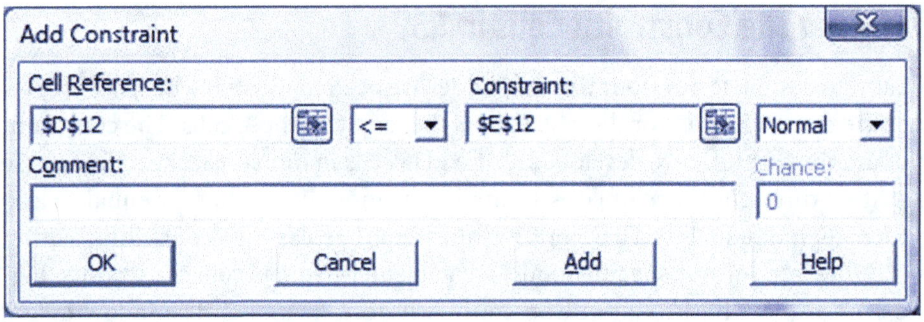

FIGURE 8.28
RSP Add a Constaint Dialogue Box in Excel

4. This same procedure would be repeated for each constraint, taking note to modify the constraint operator accordingly.

Figure 8.29 displays the RSP task pane with all the constraints for Mark's Bat Problem identified and entered.

As a note, you can also add an objective, variable, or constraint by clicking on the green plus sign in the RSP task pane and then choosing from the menu given. Figure 8.30 displays this action and associated menu.

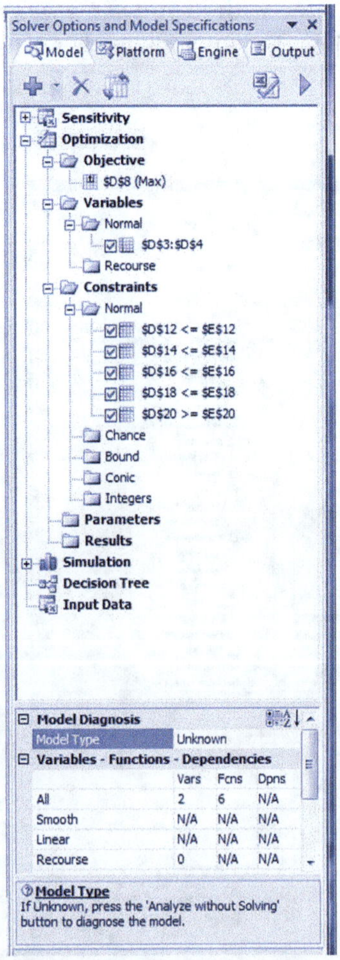

FIGURE 8.29
RSP Task Pane in Excel

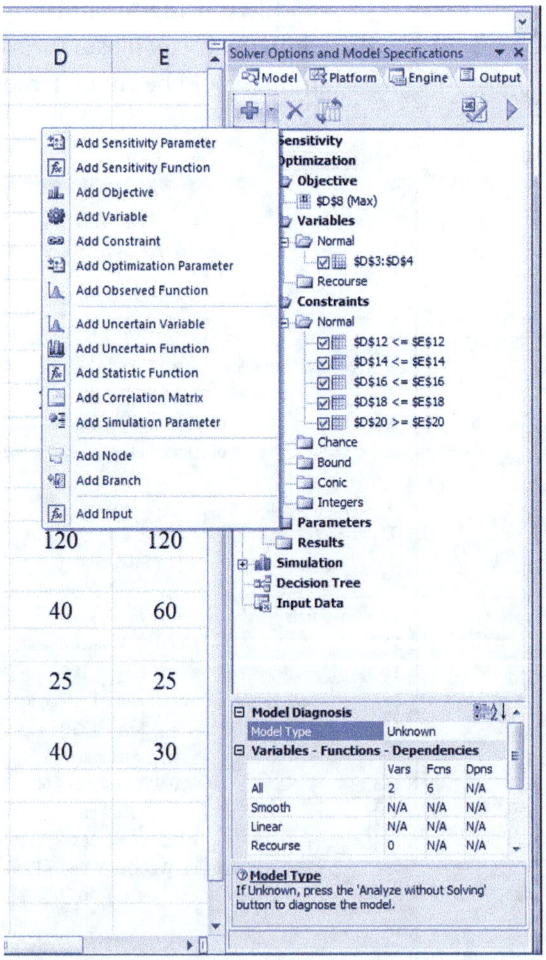

FIGURE 8.30
RSP Task Pane Menu Options in Excel

Defining the Non-Negativity Conditions in RSP

There are a number of ways to specify non-negativity conditions within RSP. One method you could use is to specify the decision variables as greater than zero constraints. This method is effective but may add more work. An easier method is to specify non-negativity properties within the RSP Engine tab. On the Engine tab in RSP's task pane, set the value to Assume Non-Negative property to True. This informs RSP to assume that all the Variables (i.e., decision variables) in our model should have lower bounds set at zero (see Figure 8.31).

Reviewing the Model in RSP

Once we have finished specifying the objective, variables, constraints, and non-negativity conditions, it is a good idea to review the model in its entirety. RSP provides a quick and easy way to do this. Before we solve the optimization model, we can click on the Analyze without Solving icon in the RSP task pane (see Figure 8.32).

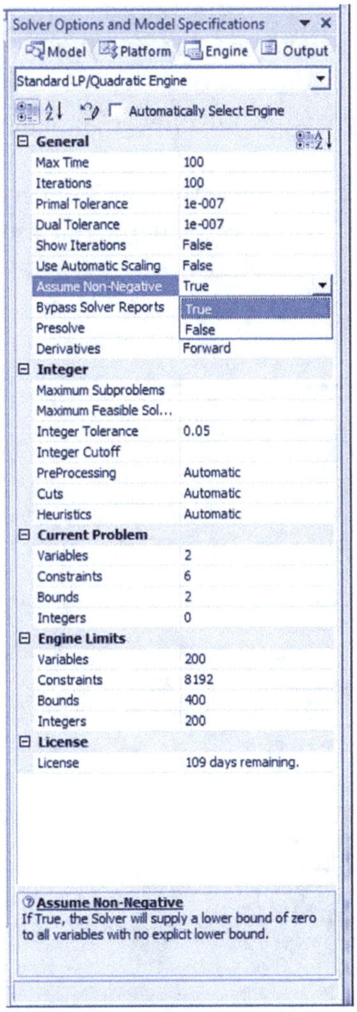

FIGURE 8.31
RSP Engine Tab in the RSP Task Pane

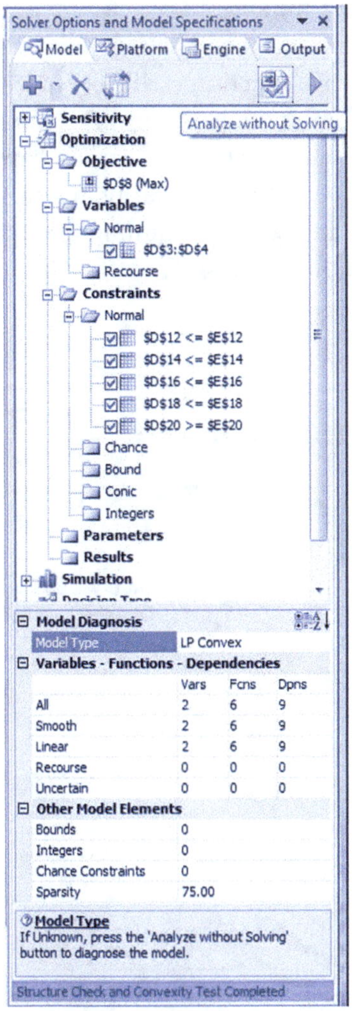

FIGURE 8.32
RSP Analyze Without Solving Option in RSP Task Pane

For our model, RSP determined that the model is a convex linear programming problem with two variables, six functions, and nine dependencies (e.g., two decision variables involved with the objective function, three constraints that contain only one decision variable, and two constraints that contain two decision variables). Note, convexity is important to optimization, and all linear programming problems are convex by definition.

Solving the Model in RSP

The next step is to solve our optimization problem in RSP. To do so, click on the Solve icon in the RSP's task pane or click on the Optimize icon on the RSP ribbon in Excel (see Figure 8.33). The Ouput tab in the RSP task pane is activated when RSP finishes solving the optimization problem (see Figure 8.34). The Output tab provides a description of the various events that occurred during the solution process. Notice the message at the bottom of Figure 8.34 indicating that RSP found a solution and that all constraints and optimality conditions were met. If RSP ever runs into a problem when solving an optimization problem, a message will appear in the area.

As shown in Figure 8.33, RSP determined that the optimal value for our objective function (cell D8) is \$880, whereas the optimal values for our decision variables (cells D3 and D4) are 40 and 60, respectively (this outcome is the same outcome from earlier in Chapter 8).

In business terms, this means Mark should produce 40 of the Wooden Wonders and 60 of the Alumimum Allys and he would garner a profit of \$880. You can also

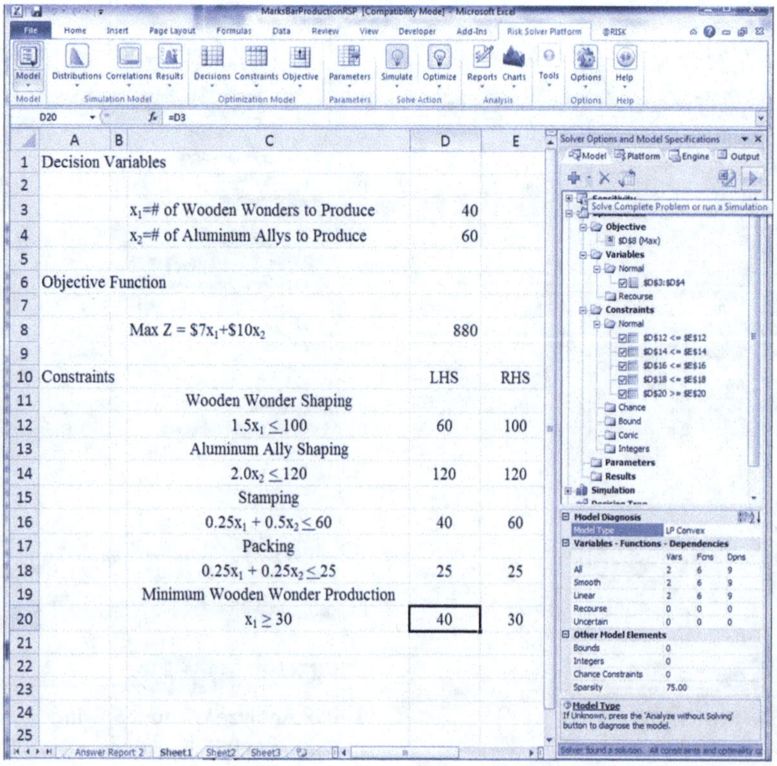

FIGURE 8.33
Mark's Bat Production LP Problem Solution in RSP

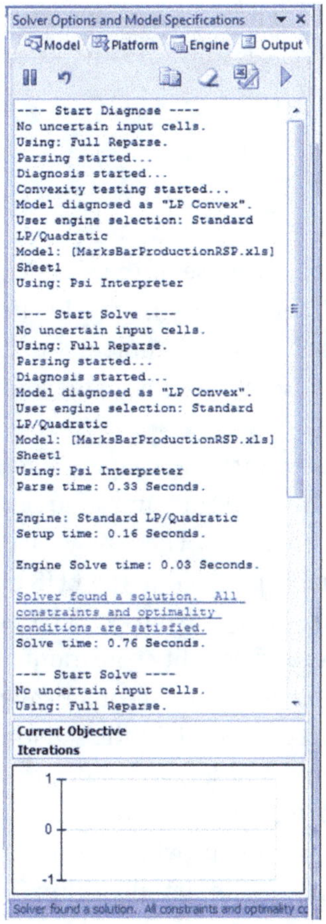

FIGURE 8.34
RSP Solver Options and Model Specifications Menu for Mark's Bat Production Solved LP Problem

see from the solution (cells D12 and E12) that only 60 of the 120 hours of shaping allocated to the Wooden Wonders is used. For the Aluminium Allys, all of the shaping time is used (cells D14 and E14). Only 40 of the 60 hours of stamping is used (cells D16 and E16), whereas all of the packing time is used (cells D18 and E18). Finally, we can see that at least 30 of the Wooden Wonders are being produced (cells D20 and E20).

Summary of Optimization Using RSP

This section illustrated the use of Risk Solver Platform to create and solve optimization problems in Excel. RSP is an enhanced version of the standard Solver that comes with every copy of Excel. Although all of the examples in this text can also be solved using Excel's standard Solver, RSP includes many added capabilities for optimization along with analytical tools for simulation and decision analysis, for example.

A Brief Discussion of the Simplex Method

The simplex method was developed by George B. Dantzig around 1952.

As was discussed earlier, the systematic development of practical computing methods for linear programming (LP) began in 1952 at the Rand Corporation in Santa Monica, under the direction of George B. Dantzig. Dantzig developed what is referred to as the *simplex method* of solving LP problems. The next section gives a brief overview of the simplex method and provides references for those interested in further study.

Simplex and Slack Variables

Slack and surplus variables are needed to turn ≤ and ≥ constraints into equality constraints when the simplex method is used.

Solver was able to solve Mark's bat production problem because of the simplex algorithm. The simplex algorithm requires that all constraints in the LP be expressed as equalities. Take a look back at step 4 under "Steps to Implementing the Graphical Method," as this step refers to corner point solutions. Relate the idea of corner point feasible solutions to equality constraints.

In turning inequality constraints into equality constraints, the simplex algorithm adds one new variable to each less-than or equal-to constraint and subtracts one new variable from each greater-than or equal-to constraint. These new variables are called slack and surplus variables. A slack variable is added to the LHS of a ≤ constraint to convert it to an equality constraint. Likewise, a surplus variable is subtracted from the LHS of a ≥ constraint to convert it to an equality constraint.

With Solver there is no need to set up slack variables, as Solver automatically completes this step. In fact, we have discussed the concept of slack in the section on Solver's answer report. It must be noted that the term *slack* used within this text is different from the term *slack variable* or *surplus variable* used in the simplex method. The values we spoke about in the answer report section provided by Solver correspond to the optimal values of the slack variables in the simplex algorithm.

How the Simplex Method Finds the Optimal Solution

Simplex identifies any corner point feasible solutions and then moves from one corner point feasible solution to an adjacent feasible corner point solution.

In adding slack or surplus variables to the LP problem, all inequalities are converted to equalities. The simplex algorithm uses this fact to its advantage. Simplex first identifies any of the corner point feasible solutions for the LP, using the relationships between equality constraints—think about how the corner point feasible solutions were found in Mark's bat problem. The algorithm then moves to an adjacent corner point feasible solution if that move improves the objective function. When no movement to an adjacent corner feasible solution improves the objective function, the current corner point feasible solution is considered optimal and the algorithm halts.

Summary

Overall, the simplex algorithm considers only the corner point feasible solutions and is a very efficient way to solve linear constrained problems. Slack variables are introduced to convert inequality constraints to equality constraints, so the simplex method can move systematically from corner point feasible solution to corner point feasible solution in the attempt to improve the objective function. When no improvement can be achieved by this systematic movement, the algorithm stops and the last identified corner point feasible solution is then the optimal solution to the LP problem.

Classic Linear Optimization Problems

Some classic LP problems are categorized as blending, assignment, transportation, and network problems.

In the area of business decision making, LP models have been one of the most successful quantitative approaches over the last few decades. Applications of LP modeling are widespread in almost every industry from production operations to financial services and planning to marketing. We have already uncovered a classic problem type where LP models prove extremely valuable: Mark's bat production problem successfully illustrated the use of an LP model to determine the mix of bats Mark should produce and sell. This type of LP model is referred to as a *product mix* or *blending* LP formulation. This is a classic linear optimization application area. The next section details another classic linear optimization application area: the network flow/transportation model.

Network Flow/Transportation Problems

Network flow problems are common in business and can be modeled by LP.

Many network flow problems are common in business. Network flow problems have similar common characteristics and in general can be described via a network flow diagram or graph. Network flow problems are also at times referred to as transportation problems, shortest path problems, or assignment problems. The next section details a common network flow or transportation problem.

The Transportation Problem: Pirate Logistics

The transportation problem appears in many places in real life. Shipping companies, freight forwarding companies, the U.S. Postal Service, and the railways all have transportation problems to solve. In general, a network of supply nodes and demand nodes characterizes the transportation problem. Figure 8.35 displays an example of a network of supplying nodes and receiving nodes for the Pirate Logistics Company. The Pirate Logistics Company example is used to illustrate the transportation problem and LP formulation. The company has three supply locations: Wilmington, New Bern, and Lynchburg. In turn, Pirate Logistics ships goods to three demand locations: Grand Island, Omaha, and Sioux Falls.

Characteristics of the Transportation LP

The one-way flow of goods makes network problems unique LP problems.

What makes the transportation problem a unique network problem is the one-way flow of goods. From the direction of the arrows in Figure 8.35, it can be seen that goods flow from the supply locations to three demand locations. Other unique characteristics of the basic transportation problem are:

- A unique shipping cost is associated with each supply locale.
- Limited supply amounts are provided at any supply locale.

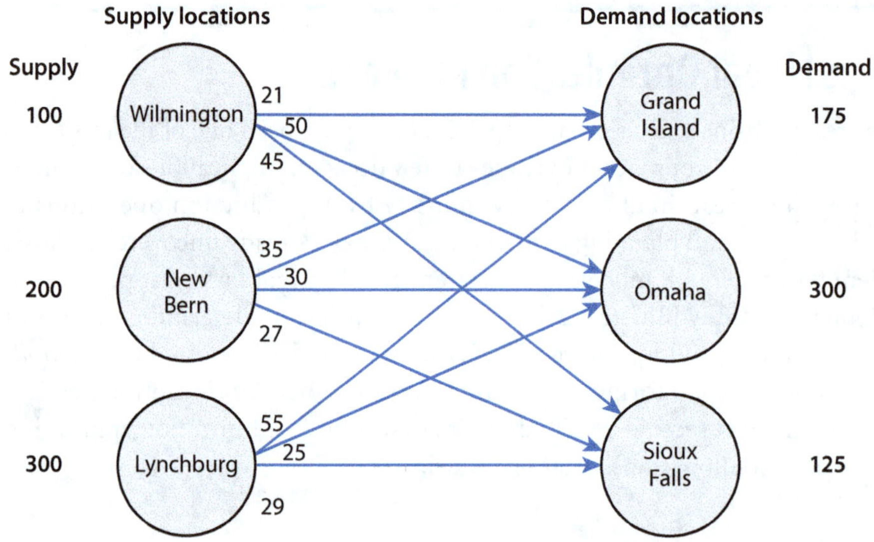

FIGURE 8.35
Network for Pirate Logistics Company

- Each demand locale must meet a required demand amount.
- Amount supplied must equal amount demanded.
- Cost minimization is the objective.

These characteristics are common in real-life transportation problems. Each locale a firm ships to has its own cost structure, depending on distance, geographic region, highway accessibility, etc. Also, a firm can ship only a limited amount of goods, usually based on what it has in stock (i.e., the limited supply caveat). In turn, when a company orders goods to be delivered, it wants delivered only what it ordered, no more or no less (i.e., the required demand amount). The idea of equating amount supplied and amount demanded links the supply amount directly to the demand amount. Finally, it is just common sense that a business would wish to ship all goods at the lowest cost possible, hence the cost minimization objective.

Transportation LP problems appear regularly in shipping companies.

The General LP Formulation for the Transportation Problem

The following notation details the general linear programming formulation for the transportation model.

i = index for supply locations, i = 1 to m

j = index for demand locations, j = 1 to n

x_{ij} = number of units shipped from supply location i to demand location j

c_{ij} = cost per unit shipped from supply location i to demand location j

s_i = supply or capacity in units at location i

d_j= demand in units at location j

The general transportation LP model for m-supply locations and n-demand destinations is

$$\text{Min} \sum_{i=1}^{m} \sum_{j=1}^{n} c_{ij} x_{ij}$$

$s.t.$

Most transportation LP models contain a minimize cost objective function.

$$\sum_{j=1}^{n} x_{ij} = s_i \quad \text{for } i = 1 \text{ to } m \quad \text{Supply constraint}$$

$$\sum_{i=1}^{m} x_{ij} = d_j \quad \text{for } j = 1 \text{ to } n \quad \text{Demand constraint}$$

$$x_{ij} \geq 0 \quad \text{for all } i \text{ and } j$$

Setting Up the Transportation LP in a Spreadsheet

The basic transportation LP can be formulated, solved, and analyzed very easily in a spreadsheet. Figure 8.36 displays the spreadsheet formulation for the Pirate Logistics transportation LP problem.

Description of the Spreadsheet

In the spreadsheet, the shipping costs per unit for each supply and demand location are summarized first (cells C5 through E7, Figure 8.36). Supply and demand requirements are summarized next in cells C16 to E16 and G12 to G16, respectively.

Decision Variables

In most transportation LP models, the decision variables are defined as the amount to ship from one locale to another.

The actual amounts to be shipped from supply locations to demand locations are defined by cells C12 to E14. These nine cells correspond to the nine decisions that must be made in the original problem "How much should be shipped from each supply locale to each demand locale?"

Supply and Demand Constraints

Three supply locales multiplied by three demand locales gives nine decision variables. To see this, take a look back at Figure 8.35 and you will notice nine lines connecting the six nodes. Figure 8.36 displays how the spreadsheet will look when you are finished. However, there are a number of formulas throughout the spreadsheet itself. Figure 8.37 displays the formulas behind the spreadsheet in Figure 8.36.

In terms of RHS and LHS variables, which were used earlier to describe LP model constraints, cells C12 to E14 would be considered LHS variables, whereas cells C16 to E16 and G12 to G14 would be considered RHS variables.

	A	B	C	D	E	F	G
1							
2			Shipping Cost per Unit				
3				Demand Location			
4		Supply Location	Grand Island	Omaha	Sioux Falls		
5		Wilmington	21	50	45		
6		New Bern	35	30	27		
7		Lynchburg	55	25	29		
8							
9			Supply and Demand Requirements				
10			Demand Location to Ship to				
11		Supply Location	Grand Island	Omaha	Sioux Falls	Total Shipped	Supply Available
12		Wilmington	0	0	0	0	100
13		New Bern	0	0	0	0	200
14		Lynchburg	0	0	0	0	300
15		Total Received	0	0	0		
16		Demand Required	175	300	125		
17							
18		Objective Function-Minimize Shipping Costs from Supply Locations to Demand Locations					
19		Cost=	0				

FIGURE 8.36

Spreadsheet Formulation for Pirate Logistics

The Objective Function

Cell C19 contains the objective function. The objective in the Pirate Logistics problem is to meet shipping requirements at the lowest cost. The formula in cell C19, Figure 8.37, is

Formula for cell C19: =SUMPRODUCT(C5:C7,C12:E14)

The SUMPRODUCT() function in Excel multiplies the elements of two ranges and sums those products. In the Pirate Logistics case, it is the range of supply and demand shipping costs (cells C5 to C7) multiplied by the actual amounts to be shipped from supply to demand locations, i.e., the decision variables (cells C12 to E14), and summed.

A transportation LP's objective function is usually a cross product of shipping costs and amounts shipped.

Non-Negativity Assumptions

Simply put, it does not make sense to have negative amounts shipped from one locale to another. Therefore, it is implicit in the model that the nine decision variables (cells C12 to E14) will always be greater than or equal to zero. However, we must inform Excel of this when Solver is set up.

	A	B	C	D	E	F	G
1							
2				Shipping Cost per Unit			
3				Demand Location			
4		Supply Location	Grand Island	Omaha	Sioux Falls		
5		Wilmington	21	50	45		
6		New Bern	35	30	27		
7		Lynchburg	55	25	29		
8							
9				Supply and Demand Requirements			
10				Demand Location to Ship to			
11		Supply Location	Grand Island	Omaha	Sioux Falls	Total Shipped	Supply Available
12		Wilmington	0	0	0	=SUM(C12:E12)	100
13		New Bern	0	0	0	=SUM(C13:E13)	200
14		Lynchburg	0	0	0	=SUM(C14:E14)	300
15		Total Received	=SUM(C12:C14)	=SUM(D12:D14)	=SUM(E12:E14)		
16		Demand Required	175	300	125		
17							
18		Objective Function-	Minimize Shipping Costs from Suppl y Locations to Demand Locations				
19		Cost=	=SUMPRODUCT(C5:E7,C12:E14)				

FIGURE 8.37

Spreadsheet Formulas Associated with Pirate Logistics' LP Problem

Setting Up Solver to Find Solutions to the Pirate Logistics LP Problem

This section discusses how to use Solver to optimize the spreadsheet LP model for Pirate Logistics. It is assumed that the user has already built a spreadsheet optimization model in Excel (refer to Figures 8.36 and 8.37). After clicking on Solver in the Tools menu, the Solver dialog box resembling (Figure 8.38) will appear. For Excel 2007, a simliar looking screen will appear. The following instructions apply to Solver in both Excel 2007 and 2010 as the menu options are analogous. The following steps enable Solver to find solutions to optimization spreadsheets.

1. In the Set Objective box, enter a cell reference or name for the objective cell. The objective cell must contain a formula.
2. To have the value of the objective cell be as large as possible, click Max. To have the value of the objective cell be as small as possible, click Min. To have the objective cell be a certain value, click Value of, and then type the value in the box.
3. In the By Changing Variable Cells box, enter a name or reference for each adjustable cell, separating nonadjacent references with commas. The changing variable cells must be related directly or indirectly to the target cell. You can specify up to 200 changing variable cells.
4. In the Subject to the Constraints box, enter any constraints you want to apply.
5. Click Solve.

In the Pirate Logistics spreadsheet LP problem, the objective cell (the objective function), changing variable cells (the decision variables), and constraints are defined as shown in Table 8.3 (refer to Figures 8.36 and 8.37).

APPENDIX

8A Review of Graphical Solutions to Optimization Problems

Modified Standard Form—Mark's Bat Production Problem

Modified standard form for Mark's bat production LP model is as follows, where the three parts of the LP model are numbered as follows: Equation (8A.1) objective function, Equations (8A.2a) to (8A.2e) constraints, and Equation (8A.3) nonnegativity assumptions.

When an LP model is formulated and transformed into modified standard form, a method for solving the LP model can be employed. The next section details two methods for solving LP models and provides both solution types for Mark's Bat Production problem.

Maximize $Z = \$7x_1 + \$10x_2$ **(8A.1)**

subject to $1.5x_1 \leq 100$ Wooden Wonder shaping constraint **(8A.2a)**

$2.0_2 \leq 120$ Aluminum Ally shaping constraint **(8A.2b)**

$0.25x_1 + 0.5x_2 \leq 60$ Stamping constraint **(8A.2c)**

$0.25x_1 + 0.25x_2 \leq 25$ Packing constraint **(8A.2d)**

$x_1 \geq 30$ Minimum Wooden Wonder production constraint **(8A.2e)**

$x_1, x_2 \geq 0$ **(8A.3)**

Methods of Solving LP Problems

Once the LP model is in modified standard form, two basic solution approaches to solving the LP model exist: the graphical method and the simplex method. This appendix describes the graphical method and the subsequent solution to Mark's

Two methods of solving LP problems exist: the graphical method and the simplex method.

bat production LP model. The main text of Chapter 8 describes the simplex method.

The Graphical Method

The graphical method is simple, but is limited to smaller LP models (i.e., two- or three-decision variables). The limitation on two to three decision variables is due to the nature of the graphical method. When presented with an LP model with two decision variables, the graphical method produces a two-dimensional graph. In turn, when presented with an LP model with three decision variables, the graphical method produces a three-dimensional graph.

This logic makes it clear that, when an LP model contains four or more decision variables, it is impossible to use the graphical method of solution, as non-dimensional graph can be developed for *n* greater than three. The next section provides a set of steps to follow when using the graphical method to solve LP models.

Steps to Implementing the Graphical Method

The feasible region is defined as the region mapped by the constraints containing values of decision variables that are allowed by the constraint set.

The following steps are used for implementing the graphical method of solving LP models. Before the steps are detailed, a few terms must be defined.

Feasible region. The region mapped by the constraints containing values of the decision variables that are allowed by the constraint set.

Corner point. A point where a set of constraints intersect.

Corner point feasible solution. A point where a set of constraints intersect that is on the edge of the feasible region.

The steps are presented next and their application to Mark's Bat Production problem follows.

A six-step process can be followed to solve LP problems graphically.

1. Construct an x-y coordinate plane/graph.
2. Plot all constraints on the plane/graph.
3. Identify the feasible region dictated by the constraints.
4. Identify all corner point feasible solutions of the feasible region.
5. Identify the optimum solution by plotting a series of objective functions over the feasible region.
6. Determine the exact solution values of the decision variables and the objective function at the optimum solution.

Application to Mark's Bat Production Problem

The following section details the application of the LP graphical solution method to Mark's Bat Production Problem.

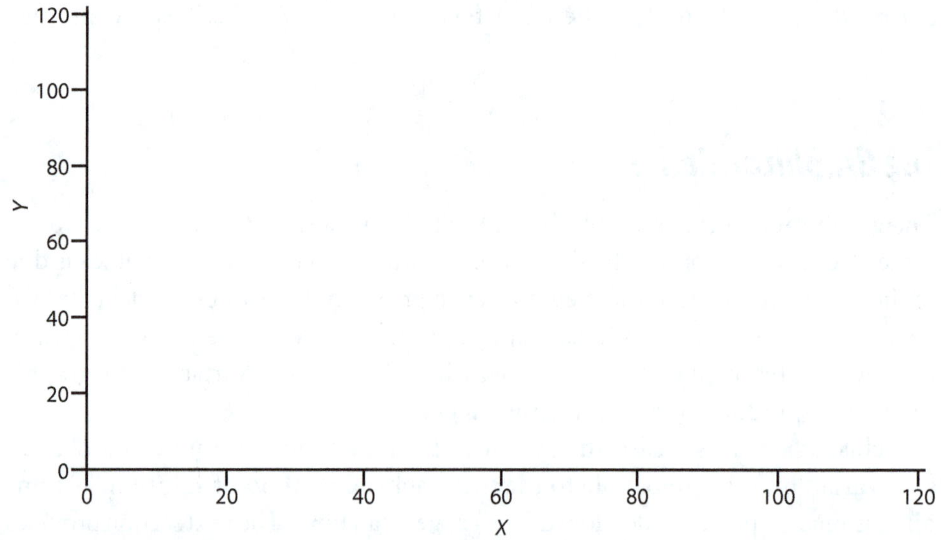

FIGURE 8A.1
x-y Coordinate Plane

STEP 1: CONSTRUCT AN *X-Y* COORDINATE PLANE/GRAPH

This step is by far the easiest. It involves constructing a simple *x-y* coordinate plane. This should be familiar from past algebra or geometry courses. Figure 8A.1 displays an example of an *x-y* coordinate plane.

Drawing an *x-y* coordinate plane is the first step in solving an LP problem graphically.

STEP 2: PLOT ALL CONSTRAINTS ON THE PLANE/GRAPH

The second step to solving an LP model graphically is to plot all constraints on the *x-y* coordinate plane. This is accomplished by calculating where each constraint crosses the coordinate axis. From this point forward the y axis is referred to and labeled x_2, whereas the x axis is referred to and labeled x_1. This is done to coincide with standard LP modeling nomenclature and the two constraints defined earlier in Mark's bat production problem.

Plotting the constraints on the *x-y* coordinate plane is the second step in solving an LP problem graphically.

Constraint 1. Let's begin with the first constraint. Constraint 1 in functional form is

$$1.5x_1 \leq 100$$

Note that constraint 1 contains only decision variable x_1. Therefore, constraint 1 never intersects the x_2 axis. In addition, the decision variable x_2 can take on any value with regard to constraint 1.

Constraint 1 actually has an upper boundary, since the constraint contains a less than or equal to sign. This upper bound is found by dividing both sides of the constraint by 1.5 (the coefficient of x_1 in the constraint). The resulting equation is $x_1 \leq 66.67$and is graphed in Figure 8A.2.

Constraint 2. Constraint 2 in functional form is

$$2.0x_2 \leq 120$$

Note that constraint 2 contains only decision variable x_2. Therefore, constraint 2 never intersects the x_1 axis. In addition, the decision variable x_1 can take on any value with regard to constraint 2.

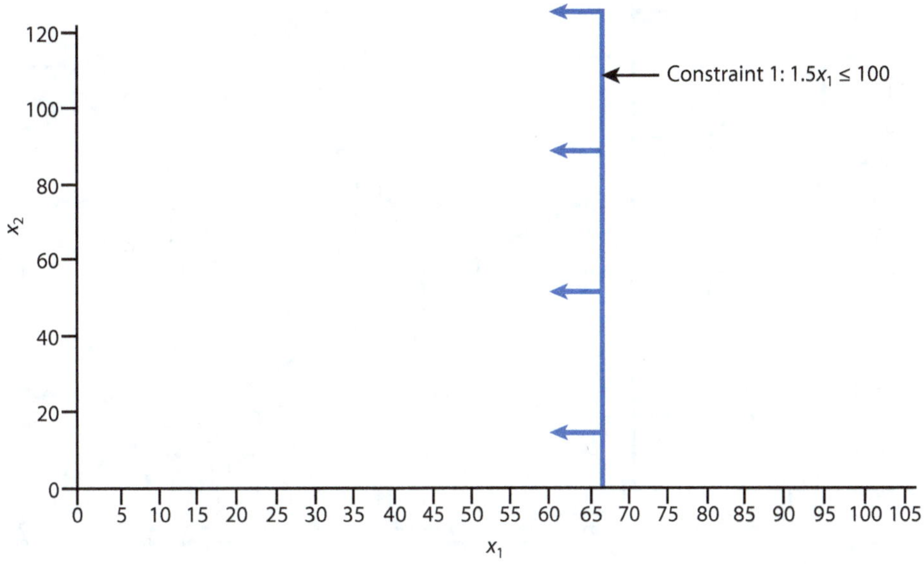

FIGURE 8A.2
Mark's Bat Production Problem with Constraint 1

Constraint 2 actually has an upper boundary, since the constraint contains a less than or equal to sign. This upper bound is found by dividing both sides of the constraint by 2.0 (the coefficient of x_2 in the constraint). The resulting equation is It is graphed, along with constraint 1, in Figure 8A3.3.

Constraint 3. Constraint 3 in functional form is

$$0.25x_1 + 0.5x_2 \leq 60$$

Constraint 3 has an upper boundary, since the constraint contains a less than or equal to sign. In addition, this upper bound is a line with a certain slope. The equation of this line is found easily by finding where the constraint crosses the x_1 and x_2 axes. These intercepts are found by setting one decision variable equal to

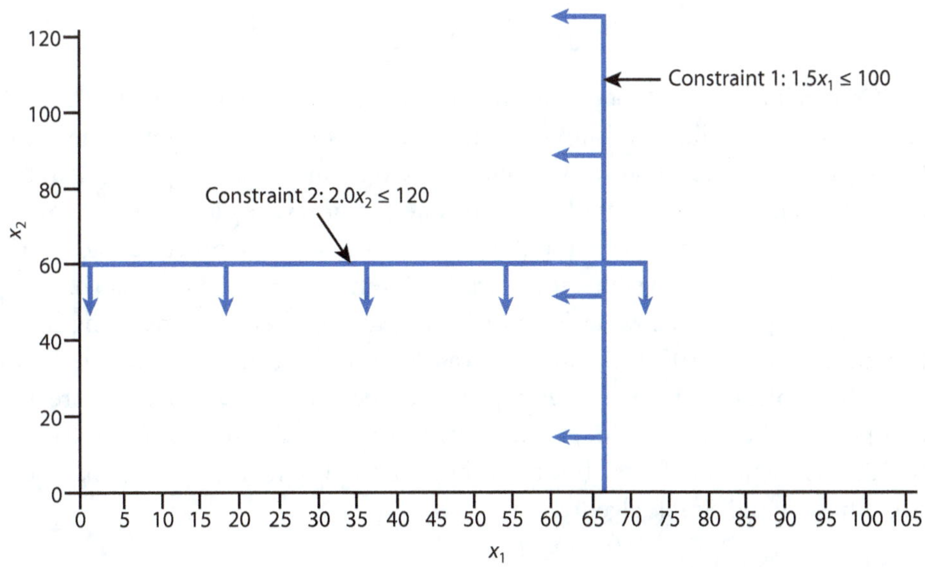

FIGURE 8A.3
Mark's Bat Production Problem with Constraints 1 and 2

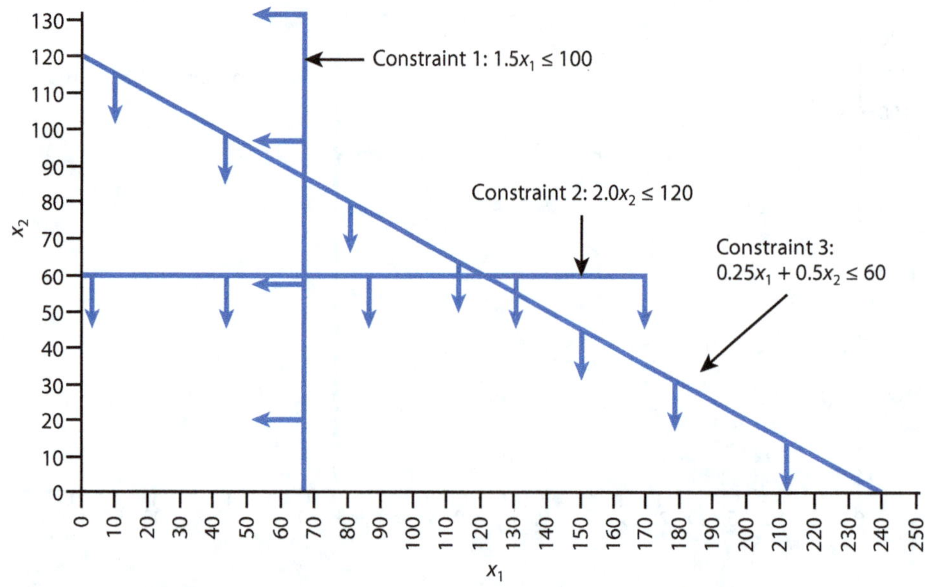

FIGURE 8A.4

Mark's Bat Production Problem with Constraints 1, 2, and 3

zero and dividing both sides of the constraint by the coefficient of the other constraint, and then performing the same operation for the other decision variable.

For example, let's allow decision variable x_1 to equal zero; the resulting equation becomes $x_2 \leq 120.00$. Continuing with the same logic and allowing decision variable x_2 to equal zero, we find the resulting equation becomes

$$x_1 \leq 240.00$$

Therefore, the two points where constraint 3 intersects the x_1 and x_2 axes are (240, 0) and (0, 120). The equation for the line of the upper bound is then found by using these two numbers and simple algebra.

$$x_2 \leq 240 - 0.5x_1$$

It is graphed, along with constraints 1 and 2, in Figure 8A.4.

Constraint 4. Constraint 4 in functional form is

$$0.25x_1 + 0.25x_2 \leq 25$$

Constraint 4 has an upper boundary, since the constraint contains a less than or equal to sign. In addition, this upper bound is a line with a certain slope. The equation of this line is found easily by finding where the constraint crosses the x_1 and x_2 axes. These intercepts are found by setting one decision variable equal to zero and dividing both sides of the constraint by the coefficient of the other decision variable, and then performing the same operation for the other decision variable.

For example, let's allow decision variable x_1 to equal zero. The resulting equation becomes $x_2 \leq 100$. Continuing with the same logic and allowing decision variable x_2 to equal zero, the resulting equation becomes $x_1 \leq 100$; therefore, the two points where constraint 3 intersects the x_1 and x_2 axes are (100, 0) and (0, 100). The equation for the line of the upper bound is then found by using these two numbers and simple algebra.

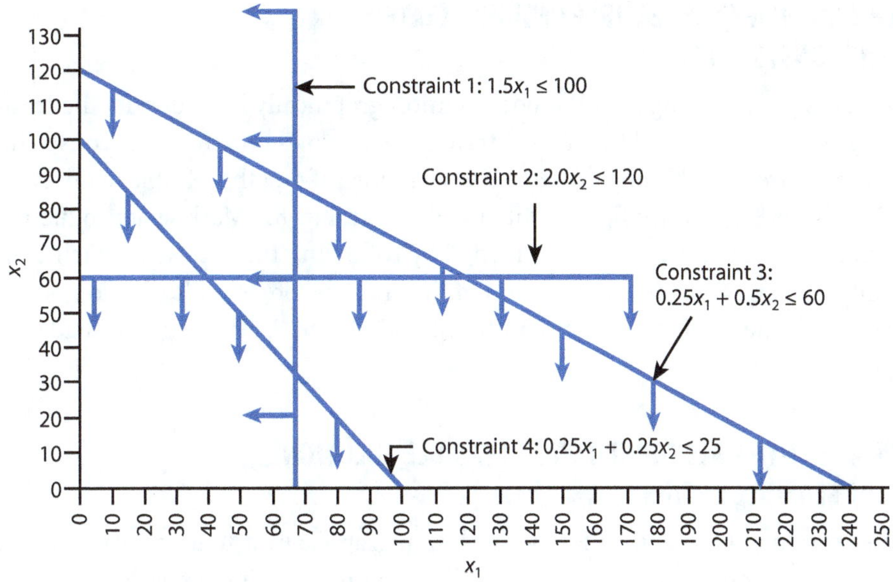

FIGURE 8A.5 Mark's Bat Production Problem with Constraints 1, 2, 3, and 4

$$x_2 \leq 100 - 1.0x_1$$

It is graphed, along with constraints 1, 2, and 3, in Figure 8A.5.

Constraint 5. Constraint 5 in functional form is

$$x_1 \geq 30$$

Note that constraint 5 contains only decision variable x_1. Therefore, constraint 5 never intersects the x_2 axis. In addition, the decision variable x_2 can take on any value with regard to constraint 5.

Constraint 5 has a lower boundary, since the constraint contains a greater than or equal to sign. Since constraint 5 is in its simplest form, the constraint is graphed as in Figure 8A.6.

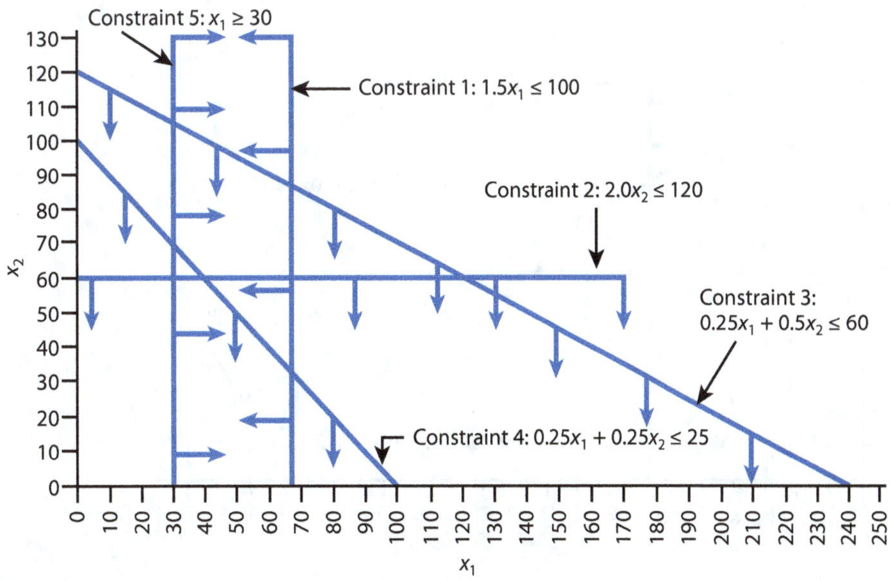

FIGURE 8A.6 Mark's Bat Production Problem with All Constraints

STEP 3: IDENTIFY THE FEASIBLE REGION DICTATED BY THE CONSTRAINTS

The next step in finding the LP model solution graphically is to identify the feasible region that is dictated by the constraints. The arrows on any of the constraint graphs (Figures 8A.2 through 8A.6) guide us in identifying the feasible region.

Identifying the feasible region dictated by the constraints is the third step in solving an LP problem graphically.

In Figure 8A.6, which figure contains all constraints for Mark's bat production problem, the feasible region is identified by following the arrows on each constraint and narrowing down the region of the graph where feasible solution points exist. This is the area bordered by constraints 1, 2, 4, and 5. This region is shaded in Figure 8A.7.

STEP 4: IDENTIFY ALL CORNER POINT FEASIBLE SOLUTIONS OF THE FEASIBLE REGION

The next step in finding the LP model solution graphically is to identify the corner point feasible solutions. Since an LP model contains only linear relationships, the corner point feasible solutions must be found on the perimeter of the feasible region. Take a look at the shaded region of Figure 8A.7. This shaded region is referred to as the *feasible region*. The points where any two constraints intersect within the feasible region reveal a corner point feasible solution.

Identifying the corner point feasible solutions of the feasible region is the fourth step in solving an LP problem graphically.

This text does not delve deeply into why only these corner points are part of the feasible solution set. However, since we are attempting to optimize by using linear relationships, the feasible region identified is considered a convex set. Therefore, mathematically speaking, the optimal solution to any convex set must lie on the solution set's boundary and most likely at a unique corner point. This text chooses to explain how each of the corner point feasible solutions is found to aid in the underlying geometric and algebraic layout of an LP problem. However, it is well known that this process is not necessary to obtain the optimum. For

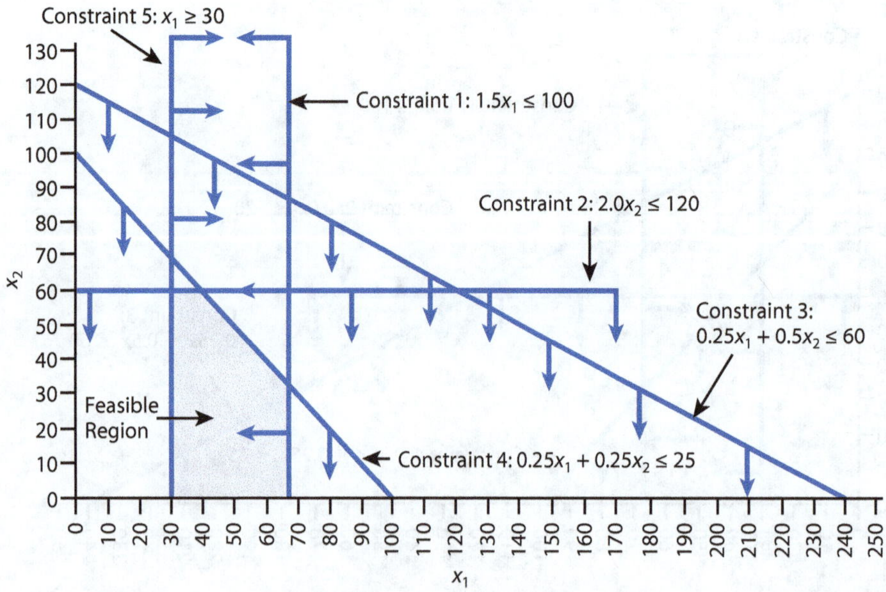

FIGURE 8A.7 Feasible Region Identification for Mark's Bat Production Problem

those wishing to omit this section, please skip to Figure 8A.9 and read the discussion on passing the objective function through the feasible region to obtain the optimum.

To find the exact corner points of the feasible region in Figure 8A.7, some basic algebra must be employed. In short, we need to find the coordinates (x_1, x_2) of where each constraint intersects another constraint over the feasible region. To accomplish this, let's first identify all corner point feasible solutions on a graph. Figure 8A.8 displays an enlarged view of the feasible region from Figure 8A.7.

The corner point feasible solutions are denoted by circles in Figure 8A.8. The coordinates of each of these corner points must be identified. The next section details how to determine the coordinates of the five corner point feasible solutions.

Determining Exact Corner Point Feasible Solutions

To find the exact corner points of the feasible region, the coordinates where each constraint intersects must be found.

To find the exact corner points of the feasible region in Figure 8A.8, some basic algebra must be employed. In short, we need to find the coordinates (x_1, x_2) of where each constraint intersects another constraint over the feasible region.

Corner Point Feasible Solutions 4 and 5

In general, exact corner point feasible solution points are where constraints intersect on the boundary of the feasible region.

Let's start with the obvious intersection points from Figure 8A.8. Corner point 5 intersects the x_1 axis at 30 and the x_2 axis at 0. Therefore, the coordinates for corner point feasible solution 5 are (30, 0). In turn, corner point 4 intersects the x_1 axis at $66.6\overline{6}$ and the x_2 axis at 0. Therefore, the coordinates for corner point feasible solution 4 are $(66.6\overline{6}, 0)$. Mathematically speaking, this corner point feasible solution is allowed. With regard to Mark's bat production problem, one-third of a wooden bat would not be a feasible production amount. However, for this example and the entirety of this problem, fractions of bat production are allowed.

Corner Point Feasible Solution 1

Finding the coordinates of corner point feasible solution 1 is also simple. The coordinates are the intersection of two constraints. From Figure 8A.8, follow the two constraints that make up corner point feasible solution 1 (constraints 2 and 5)

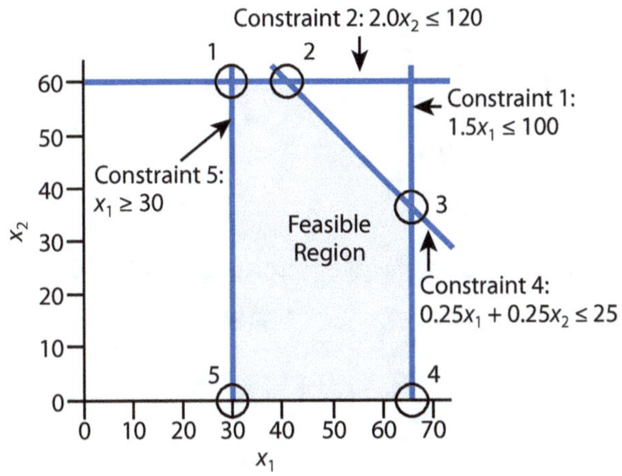

Constraint 3 is not graphed, as it is not part of the feasible region.

FIGURE 8A.8 Corner Point Feasible Solutions to Mark's Bat Production Problem

from the corner point to the respective axis. For example, follow constraint 5 down toward the x_1 axis and note the value at the intersection point of the constraint and the x_1 axis. This value is 30. Therefore, the x_1 coordinate of corner point feasible solution 1 is 30.

In turn, follow constraint 1 to the left towards the x_2 axis and note the value at the intersection point of the constraint and the x_2 axis. This value is 60. Therefore, the x_2 coordinate of corner point feasible solution 1 is 60. The coordinates for corner point feasible solution 1 are (30, 60).

Corner Point Feasible Solution 2

In order to find the coordinates for corner point feasible solution 2, the equations for the two intersecting constraints must be identified. It can be seen from Figure 8A.8 that constraint 2 and constraint 4 intersect at corner point feasible solution 2. The equations of constraints 2 and 4 are respectively as follows:

$$2.0x_2 \leq 120$$

$$0.25x_1 + 0.25x_2 \leq 25$$

To find the point at which these two equations intersect, the equations must be simultaneously solved. This can be accomplished in a number of ways. The author uses the method of substitution and solving for the intersection point. The following algebra and mathematical manipulations solve for the intersection point.

1. Replace each inequality with an equality sign:

$$2.0x_2 = 120$$

$$0.25x_1 + 0.25x_2 = 25$$

2. Solve for x_2 in constraint 2:

$$2.0x_2 = 120$$

$$x_2 = 60$$

3. Substitute the value of x_2 found in step 2 into constraint 4:

$$0.25x_1 + 0.25(60) = 25$$

and solve for x_1

$$0.25x_1 + 15 = 25$$

$$0.25x_1 = 10$$

$$x_1 = 40$$

Therefore, the coordinates for corner point feasible solution 2 are (40, 60).

Corner Point Feasible Solution 3

The process for finding the coordinates for corner point feasible solution 3 is the same as for corner point feasible solution 2. In order to find the coordinates, the equations for the two intersecting constraints must be identified. It can be seen from Figure 8A.8 that constraint 1 and constraint 4 intersect at corner point feasible solution 3. The equations of constraint 1 and 4 are respectively as follows:

$$1.5x_1 \leq 100$$

$$0.25x_1 + 0.25x_2 \leq 25$$

To find the point at which these two equations intersect, the equations must be simultaneously solved. This can be accomplished in a number of ways. The author uses the method of substitution and solving for the intersection point. The following algebra and mathematical manipulations solve for the intersection point.

1. Replace each inequality with an equality sign:

$$1.5x_1 = 100$$

$$0.25x_1 + 0.25x_2 = 25$$

2. Solve for x_2 in constraint 1.

$$1.5x_1 = 100$$

$$x_1 = 66.6\overline{6}$$

3. Substitute the value of x_1 found in step 2 into constraint 4:

$$0.25(66.6\overline{6}) + 0.25x_2 = 25$$

and solve for x_1:

$$16.6\overline{6} + 0.25x_2 = 25$$

$$0.25x_2 = 8.3\overline{3}$$

$$x_2 = 33.3\overline{3}$$

Therefore, the coordinates for corner point feasible solution 3 are ($66.6\overline{6}$, $33.3\overline{3}$). Mathematically speaking, this corner point feasible solution is allowed. With regard to Mark's bat production problem, one-third of a wooden or aluminum bat would not be a feasible production amount. However, for this example and the entirety of this problem, fractions of bat production are allowed.

Summary of Corner Point Feasible Solution Coordinates

Table 8A.1 displays the coordinates of the five corner point feasible solutions. It should be noted from Table 8A.1 that all corner point feasible solutions are listed for this example.

Now that all the corner point feasible solutions are identified, an optimum solution can be found. Step 4 identifies the optimum solution by plotting a series of objective functions over the feasible region

TABLE 8A.1 *Corner Point Feasible Solution Coordinates*

CORNER POINT FEASIBLE SOLUTION	COORDINATES (x_1, x_2)
Corner point 1	(30, 60)
Corner point 2	(40, 60)
Corner point 3	$(66.6\overline{6}, 33.3\overline{3})$
Corner point 4	$(66.6\overline{6}, 0)$

STEP 5: IDENTIFY THE OPTIMUM SOLUTION

This step calls for plotting a series of objective functions over the feasible region in order to identify the optimum solution. This means physically plotting successive objective functions starting at or near the origin and moving away from the origin on both axes until an optimum solution is identified. The optimal solution will be the last corner point feasible solution that the objective function intersects with before leaving the feasible region altogether.

It is not necessary to calculate the profit for each feasible solution. Instead we can select an arbitrary value for profit and identify all the feasible solutions (x_1, x_2) that yield the selected value. For example, what feasible solutions provide a profit of $300? The solution is given by the value of (x_1, x_2) in the feasible region that will make the objective function

$$7x_1 + 10x_2 = 300$$

This expression is simply the equation of the profit line where profit equals $300. Thus all feasible solution points (x_1, x_2) yielding a profit of $300 must be on the line. From "Determining Exact Corner Point Feasible Solutions," above, we learned how to graph a line such as the profit equation. We let $x_1 = 0$ and solve for x_2, with the resultant solution point at $(x_1 = 0, x_2 = 30)$. Similarly, by setting $x_2 = 0$ and solving for x_1, we find the resultant solution point is $(x_1 \simeq 42.86, x_2 = 0)$. The graph of this line is represented by Z_1 in Figure 8A.9.

Figure 8A.9 displays what step 4 produces. The dashed lines (labeled Z_1, Z_2, Z_3, Z_4) represent the successive objective function plots and the arrow identifies the optimum solution at different levels of profit. Z_1 represents the profit line at $300, Z_2 represents the profit line at $500, Z_3 represents the profit line at $700, and Z_4 represents the profit line at $880. The heart of this method lies in understanding the relationship between the feasible region, the corner point feasible solutions, and the objective function.

Objective Function Slope

Looking at Figure 8A.9, one notices that the profit lines are all parallel to each other and that profit increases the farther one moves away from the origin. These observations can be expressed algebraically as a line in *slope-intercept form.* If π represents profit, then the objective function is

$$\pi = 7x_1 + 10x_2$$

Solving for x_2 in terms of x_1 and π, we obtain

$$x_2 = \frac{-7}{10}x_1 + \frac{\pi}{10}$$

This equation is in *slope-intercept form* for a linear equation relating x_1 to x_2. The coefficient of x_1, $-7/10$, is the slope of the line, and the term $\pi/10$ is the intercept.

Although the objective function plotting method is effective, it is obtuse in its actual manifestation. A far easier method for solving smaller LP problems once the corner point feasible solutions have been identified is available. This method consists of calculating the objective function value by plugging in each of the corner point feasible solutions (see Step 6).

In this example, the number of feasible corner point solutions is small enough that we can enumerate the profit generated from each pair of feasible corner points. Let's begin with the maximization case and at the origin, i.e. (0, 0). In short, as the objective function passes through the feasible region, the objective function's value increases until the objective function entirely leaves the feasible region. The arrow in Figure 8A.9 demarcates this point and the solution to the LP problem.

In sum, Figure 8A.9 displays the essence of the graphical method of solving an LP model. The relationship between the objective function, the constraints, the feasible region, the corner point feasible solutions, and the optimal solution itself is manifested in Figure 8A.9.

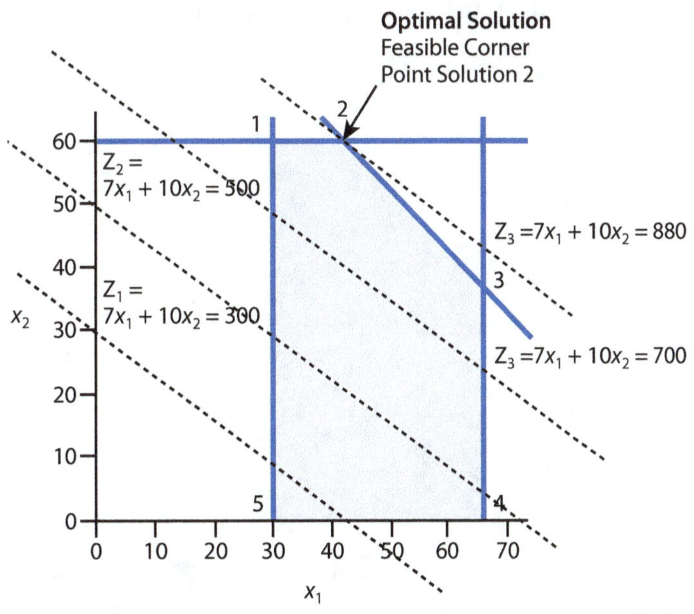

FIGURE 8A.9
Successive Objective Function Plots

TABLE 8A.2 *Objective Function Values*

CORNER POINT FEASIBLE SOLUTION	COORDINATES (x_1, x_2)	OBJECTIVE FUNCTION VALUE
Corner point 1	(30, 60)	\$810
Corner point 2	(40, 60)	\$880
Corner point 3	$(66.6\overline{6}, 33.3\overline{3})$	\$800
Corner point 4	$(66.6\overline{6}, 0)$	$\$466.6\overline{6}$
Corner point 5	(40, 0)	\$280

STEP 6. AN ALTERNATIVE TO PASSING THE OBJECTIVE FUNCTION THROUGH THE FEASIBLE REGION

Enumeration of the feasible corner point solutions to find profit works well when the LP has a small number (i.e., five to ten) of feasible corner point solutions. We will find profit for one feasible corner point solution now. Given $x_1 = 30$ and $x_2 = 60$, the objective function value is

$$Z = \$7x_1 + \$10x_2 = (\$7 \times 30) + (\$10 \times 60) = \$810$$

The same method is used to calculate the value of the objective function for each of the corner point feasible solutions. Table 8A.2 displays the objective values for each corner point feasible solution.

In the case of a maximization LP, the corner point feasible solution that produces the largest objective function value is defined as the LP optimum.

As in step 4, the largest value from the last column in Table 8.2, \$880, denotes the optimal solution to the LP problem objective function. The coordinates $x_1 = 40$ and $x_2 = 60$ produce the objective value of \$880 and are the true answers to Mark's bat production problem. In other words, based on the LP formulation given, Mark should produce 40 Wooden Wonder bats and 60 Aluminum Ally bats. Mark would garner a profit off \$880 at these production levels and is the maximum profit attainable, given the profit per bat amounts and constraints.

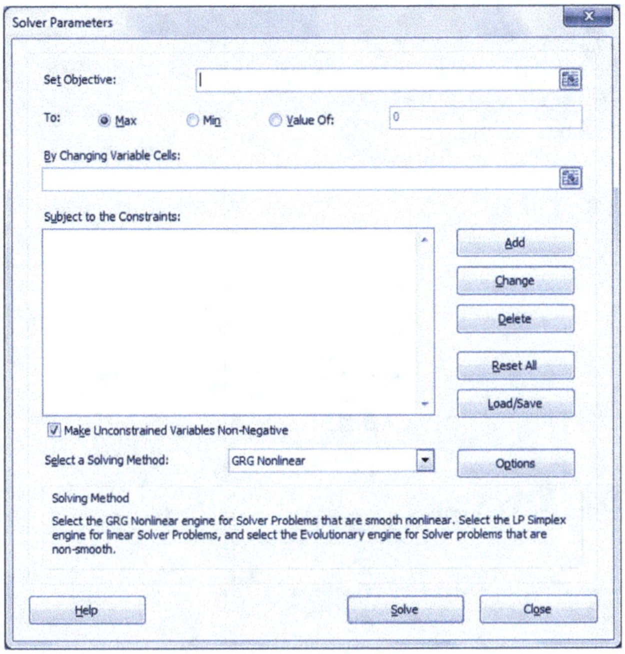

FIGURE 8.38

Excel Solver Dialog Box in Excel 2010

TABLE 8.3 *Solver Cell Definitions*

Set Objective	$C$19
To:	Min
By Changing Variable Cells:	$C$12:$E$14
Subject to the Constraints:	
Demand required	$C$15:$E$15=>$C$16:$E$16
Supply available	$F$12:$F$14<=$G$12:$G$14

In entering the Solver cell definitions for the constraints, follow the same procedure as detailed in Figures 8.8, 8.9, and 8.10 for Mark's bat production problem, using the constraints for Pirate Logistics supply and demand requirements. The Solver menu will resemble Figure 8.39 after you have entered the values from Table 8.3 into the Solver dialog boxes.

The Pirate Logistics LP model contains only linear constraints; therefore, Solver must be notified. This is in most cases a formality, but it is good form to follow. Notifying Solver of a linear model is simple:

1. From the Select Solving Method: drop down menu, choose Simplex.
2. Check the box labeled Make Unconstrained Variables Non-Negative.

NOTE: See Figure 8.39 for both of these commands.

After the non-negativity and linear assumptions have been enabled (refer to Figure 8.16), Solver is ready to be employed to solve Pirate Logistics' LP problem. From the Solver menu, refer to Figure 8.39, and click the Solver button to commence the solution process.

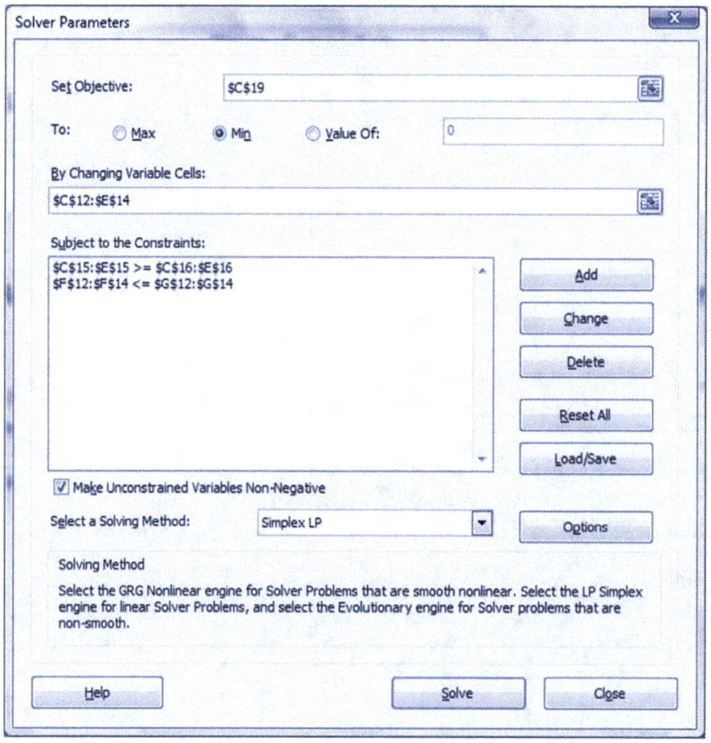

FIGURE 8.39

Final Solver Parameters for Pirate Logistics LP Problem in Excel 2010

Figure 8.40 displays the final spreadsheet model for the Pirate Logistics LP problem. The optimal shipping quantities are shown in Table 8.4, and Figure 8.40 shows the minimum objective function value of $15,600 (refer to cell C19).

Answer Report in Excel

The answer report generated in Solver details three areas: Objective Cell, Variable Cells, and Constraints.

The answer report generated within Solver details three areas: target cells, adjustable cells, and constraints. Figure 8.41 displays the answer report generated for the Pirate Logistics LP problem.

OBJECTIVE CELL SECTION

The Objective Cell section of the answer report contains information about the objective function.

The first section of interest is the Objective Cell section. The Objective Cell section contains information about the objective function. Cell D8 contains the original value of the objective function. The original value for the Pirate Logistics LP problem is zero since the decision variables were set to zero (see the Adjustable Cell section).

Cell E8 contains the final value of the objective function. In this LP model, the final value of the objective function is 15600. Overall, the Objective Cell section provides information regarding the objective function, specifically its final and optimal value.

VARIABLE CELLS SECTION

The Variable Cells section provides information about the decision variables x_1 through x_9. Cells D13 to D21 contain the original values of the decision variables. The values in the cells are zero, as the decision variables were set to zero originally.

TABLE 8.4 *Optimal Shipping Quantities*

SHIPPING LOCALE TO RECEIVING LOCALE	CELLS	OPTIMAL SHIPPING AMOUNT
Wilmington to Grand Island	C12	100
New Bern to Grand Island	C13	75
Lynchburg to Grand Island	C14	0
Wilmington to Omaha	D12	0
New Bern to Omaha	D13	0
Lynchburg to Omaha	D14	300
Wilmington to Sioux Falls	E12	0
New Bern to Sioux Falls	E13	125
Lynchburg to Sioux Falls	E14	0

Cells E13 to E21 contain the final values of the decision variables (100, 0, 0, 75, 0, 125, 0, 300, and 0 respectively). In sum, the Variable Cells section informs the decision maker on the optimal number of units to ship from a supply locale to a demand locale.

	A	B	C	D	E	F	G
1							
2			Shipping Cost per Unit				
3			Demand Location				
4		Supply Location	Grand Island	Omaha	Sioux Falls		
5		Wilmington	21	50	45		
6		New Bern	35	30	27		
7		Lynchburg	55	25	29		
8							
9			Supply and Demand Requirements				
10			Demand Location to Ship to				
11		Supply Location	Grand Island	Omaha	Sioux Falls	Total Shipped	Supply Available
12		Wilmington	100	0	0	100	100
13		New Bern	75	0	125	200	200
14		Lynchburg	0	300	0	300	300
15		Total Received	175	300	125		
16		Demand Required	175	300	125		
17							
18		Objective Function-Minimize Shipping Costs from Supply Locations to Demand Locations					
19		Cost=	15600				

FIGURE 8.40

Optimized Spreadsheet Model for the Pirate Logistics LP Problem

CONSTRAINTS SECTION

The Constraints section contains information about the constraints or limitations on the decision variables. This section should be linked to the earlier discussion involving the LHS and RHS columns. The Constraints section contains the same information as the LHS and RHS columns. However, the Constraints section organizes constraint information more efficiently and provides information about slack. As defined earlier, slack is the amount of a constraint that is not used up.

The Constraint section in Figure 8.42 contains the final constraint value, labeled Cell Value contained in cells D26 to D31, and the Excel constraint formulas labeled Formula in cells E26 to E31. In addition, the Constraint section contains information as to whether the constraint is binding or not binding. Cells F26 to F31, labeled Status, detail whether a constraint is binding or not binding.

The cells labeled Slack, cells G26 to G31, contain information about how much of a constraint is left over. They are related to cells F26 to F31. If a cell in the Status section is labeled Binding, the corresponding Slack cell will be zero. Likewise, if a cell in the "Status" column is labeled "Not Binding," the corresponding Slack cell will contain a positive value.

Slack values correspond to the amount of the respective constraint that is not used up. When the slack value is zero, the Status label will always read Binding. A connection should be made in that, when a constraint is Binding, the optimal solution lies on that constraint and that constraint is in turn used up (i.e., slack equals zero). Refer to "Binding and Nonbinding Constraints," above, to make this con-

Microsoft Excel 14.0 Answer Report
Worksheet: [Pirate Logistics - Sample.xls]Sheet1
Report Created: 3/2/2011 10:26:42 AM
Result: Solver found a solution. All Constraints and optimality conditions are satisfied.
Solver Engine
Engine: Simplex LP
Solution Time: 0.047 Seconds.
Iterations: 11 Subproblems: 0
Solver Options
Max Time 100 sec, Iterations 100, Precision 0.000001
Max Subproblems Unlimited, Max Integer Sols Unlimited, Integer Tolerance 5%,
Solve Without Integer Constraints, Assume NonNegative

Objective Cell (Min)

Cell	Name	Original Value	Final Value
$C$19	Cost = Grand Island	0	15600

Variable Cells

Cell	Name	Original Value	Final Value	Integer
$C$12	Wilmington Grand Island	0	100	Contin
$D$12	Wilmington Omaha	0	0	Contin
$E$12	Wilmington Sioux Falls	0	0	Contin
$C$13	New Bern Grand Island	0	75	Contin
$D$13	New Bern Omaha	0	0	Contin
$E$13	New Bern Sioux Falls	0	125	Contin
$C$14	Lynchburg Grand Island	0	0	Contin
$D$14	Lynchburg Omaha	0	300	Contin
$E$14	Lynchburg Sioux Falls	0	0	Contin

Constraints

Cell	Name	Cell Value	Formula	Status	Slack
$C$15	Total Received Grand Island	175	$C$15>=$C$16	Binding	0
$D$15	Total Received Omaha	300	$D$15>=$D$16	Binding	0
$E$15	Total Received Sioux Falls	125	$E$15>=$E$16	Binding	0
$F$12	Wilmington Total Shipped	100	$F$12<=$G$12	Binding	0
$F$13	New Bern Total Shipped	200	$F$13<=$G$13	Binding	0
$F$14	Lynchburg Total Shipped	300	$F$14<=$G$14	Binding	0

FIGURE 8.41
Excel Answer Report for Pirate Logistics LP Problem

nection. For the Pirate Logistics LP, we stated that supply must equal demand; therefore, all constraints are binding and there are no leftover units to be supplied or extra units to be demanded.

Sensitivity Report in Excel

The sensitivity report generated within Solver details two areas: Variable cells and constraints. Figure 8.42 displays the sensitivity report generated for the Pirate Logistics LP problem.

The report in Figure 8.42 summarizes information on how sensitive the optimal solution is to changes in various coefficients in the underlying LP model. The Variable Cells section is detailed first, followed by the Constraints section.

ADJUSTABLE CELLS SECTION

The Variable cells section of the sensitivity report provides information about the sensitivity of changes to the decision variables. The column labeled Final Value contains the optimal values for the number of units to ship from a supply locale to a demand locale. For the Pirate Logistics LP, the optimal number of units to ship from Wilmington to Grand Island is 100, from New Bern to Grand Island is 75, from New Bern to Sioux Falls is 125, and Lynchburg to Omaha is 300 (all the other supply-to-demand locales are zero). These are the same values presented in the answer report (see Figure 8.41). However, the sensitivity report gives additional

Microsoft Excel 14.0 Sensitivity Report
Worksheet: [Pirate Logistics - Sample.xls]Sheet1
Report Created: 3/2/2011 10:26:42 AM

Variable Cells

Cell	Name	Final Value	Reduced Cost	Objective Coefficient	Allowable Increase	Allowable Decrease
$C$12	Wilmington Grand Island	100	0	21	14	1E+30
$D$12	Wilmington Omaha	0	34	50	1E+30	34
$E$12	Wilmington Sioux Falls	0	32	45	1E+30	32
$C$13	New Bern Grand Island	75	0	35	25	14
$D$13	New Bern Omaha	0	0	30	34	5
$E$13	New Bern Sioux Falls	125	0	27	7	27
$C$14	Lynchburg Grand Island	0	25	55	1E+30	25
$D$14	Lynchburg Omaha	300	0	25	5	1E+30
$E$14	Lynchburg Sioux Falls	0	7	29	1E+30	7

Constraints

Cell	Name	Final Value	Shadow Price	Constraint R.H. Side	Allowable Increase	Allowable Decrease
$C$15	Total Received Grand Island	175	35	175	0	75
$D$15	Total Received Omaha	300	30	300	0	0
$E$15	Total Received Sioux Falls	125	27	125	0	125
$F$12	Wilmington Total Shipped	100	-14	100	75	0
$F$13	New Bern Total Shipped	200	0	200	1E+30	0
$F$14	Lynchburg Total Shipped	300	-5	300	0	0

FIGURE 8.42
Excel Sensitivity Report for Pirate Logistics LP Problem

information regarding changes to the adjustable cells in the LP. The Reduced Cost area is discussed next.

REDUCED COST

Specifically, the Reduced Cost column indicates how much the objective coefficient of a decision variable must improve before that decision variable could assume a positive value in the optimal solution. In the case of Excel Solver, the absolute value of the Reduced Cost column is always taken and interpreted. In the Pirate Logistics LP problem, four decision variables have nonzero numbers in the Reduced Cost column whereas the others are zero. We can interpret the Reduced Cost column as follows: To become a positive value in the optimal solution, the values following the objective coefficients must improve: Wilmington to Omaha must fall by 34, Wilmington to Sioux Falls must fall by 32, Lynchburg to Grand Island must fall by 25, and Lynchburg to Sioux Falls must fall by 7.

OBJECTIVE COEFFICIENT, ALLOWABLE INCREASE, AND ALLOWABLE DECREASE

The column labeled Objective Coefficient corresponds to the coefficients that accompany each decision variable in the objective function. The next columns in the Variable cell section are labeled Allowable Increase and Allowable Decrease. These columns are linked to the Objective Coefficient column.

For the Pirate Logistics LP, the Wilmington to Grand Island objective coefficient is 21, the allowable increase value is 14 while the allowable decrease is 1E+10 (scientific notation for a very large number). If one adds 14 to the current objective coefficient of 21, the upper range of optimality for the objective coefficient is obtained. The lower range of optimality is unbounded, meaning you can decrease the coefficient infinitely and the decision variables will still be optimal. The range for the Wilmington to Grand Island decision variable, $C_{W\text{-}GI}$, would then be

$$\infty \leq C_{W\text{-}GI} \leq \$35$$

This range informs us that as long as the objective coefficient (cost contribution) from Wilmington to Grand Island remains below \$35, the optimal shipping numbers remain optimal. The same analysis can be performed for the other objective coefficients.

Constraints Section

The information provided in the Constraints section gives the user insight into how the constrained resources are being utilized. For example, the entries in the Final Value column display the exact units of a constraint needed for shipping the optimal combination units. Since we assumed supply must equal demand in the Pirate Logistics problem, the values found in the Final Value column all match the R. H. Side column. In the prior LP problem we did not see this (i.e., there were nonbinding variables or there were constraints that had slack or units left over).

THE CONSTRAINT R.H. SIDE COLUMN

The values in the R.H. Side column are the original RHS values for each constraint. One should notice that the Slack variables discussed in "Answer Report in Excel," above, are just the absolute value of the Constraint R.H. Side column less the Final Value column (zero for the Pirate Logistics problem).

SHADOW PRICE COLUMN

The Shadow Price column assists the user in determining what additional amounts of constrained resources would be worth. A Shadow Price is defined as the amount by which the objective function value changes, given a unit increase/decrease in the RHS value of the constraint, assuming all other coefficients remain the same.

Given that a shadow price is positive, a subsequent increase in the RHS value of the associated constraint would result in an increase in the objective function. Likewise, given that a shadow price is negative, a subsequent increase in the RHS value of the associated constraint would result in a decrease in the objective function. For constraints that have a shadow price of zero, it can be determined that changing the RHS of the constraint would have no effect of the objective function value and it can be inferred that the constraint is also nonbinding (i.e., has slack).

However, one must keep in mind that increases or decreases in the RHS value of a constraint must be within certain limits or else the shadow price commentary is invalid. In other words, if you change the RHS value of a constraint outside of a given increase/decrease range, the entire LP problem changes and the shadow prices are not valid anymore.

ALLOWABLE INCREASE AND DECREASE COLUMNS

For the Pirate Logistics LP problem, it can be seen in Figure 8.42 that the shadow price for the fifth constraint (refer to row 26 in the Constraints section) is zero. Note that the allowable increase is listed as 1E+10 (scientific notation for a very, very large number) and the allowable decrease is 0. The RHS of the constraint could be increased infinitely with no change occurring in the objective function (i.e., a shadow price of zero). In turn, the RHS of the constraint could not be decreased without changing the objective function.

However, for constraints where the shadow price is nonzero, increases or decreases in the RHS of the constraints will change the value of the objective function. For example, the shadow price for the fourth constraint, the Wilmington Total Shipped (refer to row 25 in the Constraints section, Figure 8.42) is –14. Therefore, if the number of available units Wilmington can ship increases by any amount in the range from 0 to 75 units (this is the amount of the allowable increase), the optimal objective function would decrease by $14 per unit of increase in demand. Consequently, since the allowable decrease is zero, no decrease in the amount Wilmington ships can be allowed for the current shadow price to be valid.

For an additional example, let's take a look at the Total Recieved Grand Island constraint (refer to row 22 in the Constraints section, Figure 8.42). The shadow price for this constraint is 35. The allowable increase is zero, while the allowable decrease is 75. Therefore, if we were somehow able to decrease the amount demanded by Grand Island, up to 75 units, the objective function would increase by $35 for every unit increase. Keep in mind that we have stated that supply must equal demand; consequently, if we increase or decrease supply or demand in one area, a similar increase or decrease must occur elsewhere to keep the balance.

Summary of the Pirate Logistics LP Problem

In sum, Pirate Logistics should ship 100 units from Wilmington to Grand Island, 75 units from New Bern to Grand Island, 125 units from New Bern to Sioux Falls, and 300 units from Lynchburg to Omaha. The total amount shipped equals the amount received; therefore, the Supply Available and Demand Required constraints are both met. The total shipping cost Pirate Logistics incurs is $15,600.

Integer Linear Programming

Integer linear programming (ILP) is characterized by some or all of the decision variables in a linear program being restricted to only integer values. Many practical business problems are restricted to solutions that contain only integer values. Problems dealing with the scheduling of employees, allocating assets, and/or producing items that cannot be broken into fractional units are all examples. This section discusses how to construct and solve optimization problems that contain integer variables.

Stating Integer Properties and Solving ILPs

Although it is fairly simple to state variables as integers, often it makes finding solutions to the subsequent optimization problem much more difficult. In fact, Excel's Solver is at times unable to solve some ILP problems even when an optimal solution exists. A specific type of ILP, the binary ILP, will be examined in this section.

Basics of Binary ILP Problems

Some problems naturally are suited for ILP modeling (e.g., the employee scheduling problem). However, at times business managers have only two options they can choose from. This type of decision problem is at times referred to as a "go, no-go" decision problem and is characterized as a binary ILP. In a binary ILP, the decision variables can take on only two integer values: 0 or 1.

The Capital Budgeting Problem

A common binary ILP is the capital budgeting problem, where a decision maker is presented with several potential investment types of projects to choose from. The investments or projects typically require different levels of capital, labor, or other resource and produce different levels of cash flow. The objective of ensuing optimization problem is to select the investments or projects that maximize the net present value (NPV) of these cash flows.

THE BASIC INFORMATION

In general, a capital budgeting binary ILP begins as a regular capital budgeting problem. Consider the following example:

Clem Gathman is a director of research and development for iTech Consulting and is responsible for evaluating and ultimately choosing among numerous and competing R&D investments/projects. Clem has just finished looking at the seven investment/projects that made it past the engineers and accountants. Although all the investments/projects look good (positive NPV), Clem knows he cannot pick all of them, since there is not enough money (i.e., capital) to go around. Clem must determine which of the investments/projects to accept to maximize potential NPV but yet stay within company capital budgets. The expected NPV and capital requirements for each of the seven investments/projects are listed in Table 8.5.

iTech Consulting has $300,000 in capital to invest right now and has budgeted $150,000 for continued operational expenses for years 2–3 and $90,000 for years 4–5. Surplus funds in any year cannot be carried over from year to year. The next sections will define the parts of the ILP and construct the final ILP model in Excel.

IDENTIFYING AND DEFINING THE DECISION VARIABLES

There are seven investments/projects from which Clem may choose. In turn, six decision variables can be defined to represent the seven alternative investments/projects. $X_1, X_2, \ldots, X_7$ therefore represent the seven decision variables for the problem and operate as follows:

$$X_i = \begin{cases} 1, \text{if project is accepted} \\ 0, \text{otherwise} \end{cases} \qquad i = 1, 2, \ldots, 7$$

TABLE 8.5 *NPV and Capital Requirements for iTech's R&D Investments/Projects*

		CAPITAL (IN $000) REQUIRED PER YEAR				
INVESTMENT/PROJECT	EXPECTED NPV ($000)	YEAR 1	YEAR 2	YEAR 3	YEAR 4	YEAR 5
1	$74	$22	$20	$18	$16	$14
2	$233	$100	$20	$20	$20	$20
3	$177	$50	$25	$12.5	$6.25	$3.125
4	$190	$40	$30	$20	$10	$0
5	$287	$90	$90	$45	$45	$45
6	$107	$30	$15	$15	$15	$15
7	$301	$120	$120	$60	$60	$60

A binary value is assigned to each decision variable in the problem. A value of 1 is assigned if the investment/project is accepted, whereas a value of 0 is assigned if the investment/project is not accepted.

DEFINING THE OBJECTIVE FUNCTION

Clem's objective is to choose the set of investments/projects that maximize NPV. This is stated mathematically as follows:

$$\text{Maximize } Z = \$74X_1 + \$233X_2 + \$177X_3 + \$190X_4 + \$287X_5 + \$107X_6 + \$301X_7$$

Simply put, the objective function sums the NPV numbers together for the selected investments/projects.

DEFINING THE CONSTRAINTS

Since iTech Consulting has capital limitations for years 1 to 5, one capital constraint must be constructed for each year to ensure that the accepted investments/projects do not exceed the available capital. The capital constraints (cc) are as follows:

$$\$22X_1 + \$100X_2 + \$50X_3 + \$40X_4 + \$90X_5 + \$30X_6 + \$120X_7 \leq 300 \qquad \text{year 1 cc}$$

$$\$20X_1 + \$20X_2 + \$25X_3 + \$30X_4 + \$90X_5 + \$15X_6 + \$120X_7 \leq 150 \qquad \text{year 2 cc}$$

$$\$18X_1 + \$20X_2 + \$12.5X_3 + \$20X_4 + \$45X_5 + \$15X_6 + \$60X_7 \leq 150 \qquad \text{year 3 cc}$$

$$\$16X_1 + \$20X_2 + \$6.25X_3 + \$10X_4 + \$45X_5 + \$15X_6 + \$60X_7 \leq 90 \qquad \text{year 4 cc}$$

$$\$14X_1 + \$20X_2 + \$3.125X_3 + \$0X_4 + \$45X_5 + \$15X_6 + \$60X_7 \leq 90 \qquad \text{year 5 cc}$$

DEFINING THE BINARY ASSUMPTIONS

Each decision variable is assumed to be a binary variable. A formal statement of this assumption must be included in the ILP model. The binary assumption is stated as follows:

All X_i must be binary for all i

BINARY ILP IN MODIFIED STANDARD FORM

The binary ILP for Clem's problem is as follows:

$$\text{Maximize } Z = \$74X_1 + \$233X_2 + \$177X_3 + \$190X_4 + \$287X_5 + \$107X_6 + \$301X_7$$

Subject to:

$$\$22X_1 + \$100X_2 + \$50X_3 + \$40X_4 + \$90X_5 + \$30X_6 + \$120X_7 \leq 300$$

$$\$20X_1 + \$20X_2 + \$25X_3 + \$30X_4 + \$90X_5 + \$15X_6 + \$120X_7 \leq 150$$

$$\$18X_1 + \$20X_2 + \$12.5X_3 + \$20X_4 + \$45X_5 + \$15X_6 + \$60X_7 \leq 150$$

$$\$16X_1 + \$20X_2 + \$6.25X_3 + \$10X_4 + \$45X_5 + \$15X_6 + \$60X_7 \leq 90$$

$$\$14X_1 + \$20X_2 + \$3.125X_3 + \$0X_4 + \$45X_5 + \$15X_6 + \$60X_7 \leq 90$$

All X_i must be binary for all i.

DEVELOPING THE SPREADSHEET MODEL

The binary ILP for Clem's problem is shown in Figure 8.43.

Cells B6 to B12 contain a value of zero to indicate that they are decision variables from the binary ILP model we constructed. The capital constraint LHS formula is entered in cell D13 and then copied to cells E13 to H13. The RHS values for the capital constraints are listed in cells D14 to H14 as:

Formula for cell D13: =sumproduct(D6:D12,$B$6:$B$12)

The objective function is contained in cell D16 and is represented as:

Formula for cell D16: =sumproduct(C6:C12,$B$6:$B$12)

Each of the formulas for the constraints and objective function are displayed in Figure 8.44.

SOLVING THE BINARY ILP MODEL

We will employ the Solver Add-In that accompanies Excel to solve Clem's binary ILP model. In order to do this, we must tell Solver where the objective function, the decision variables, and constraints are located within the spreadsheet.

The Solver Parameters dialog box in Figure 8.45 indicates the following:

Objective function (Set Target Cell): Cell $D$16

Decision variables (By Changing Cells): Cells $B$6:$B$12

Constraints (Subject to the Constraints): $B$6:$B$12 = binary
$D$13:$H$13<=$D$14:$H$14

The objective function is located in cell D16, the decision variables in cells B6 to B12, and the constraints are located in cells B6 to B12 and D13 to H13. The first set of constraints ensures the binary condition and the second set of constraints ensures we meet the maximum capital expenditure limits.

	A	B	C	D	E	F	G	H
1	Clem Gathman's Capital Investment Problem							
2								
3								
4	Investment/	Select?			Capital per Investment/Project Required in			
5	Project	(0=No, 1=Yes)	NPV	Year 1	Year 2	Year 3	Year 4	Year 5
6	1	0	$74	$22	$20	$18	$16	$14
7	2	0	$233	$100	$20	$20	$20	$20
8	3	0	$177	$50	$25	$12.50	$6.25	$3.13
9	4	0	$190	$40	$30	$20	$10	$0
10	5	0	$287	$90	$90	$45	$45	$45
11	6	0	$107	$30	$15	$15	$15	$15
12	7	0	$301	$120	$120	$60	$60	$60
13			Capital Required	$ -	$ -	$ -	$ -	$ -
14			Capital Available	$ 300	$ 150	$ 150	$ 90	$ 90
15								
16			Total NPV	$ -				

FIGURE 8.43

Spreadsheet Model for Clem's Binary ILP Selection Problem

	A	B	C	D	E	F	G	H
1	Clem Gathman's Capital Investment Problem							
2								
3								
4	Investment/	Select?				Capital per Investment/Project Required in		
5	Project	(0=No, 1=Yes)	NPV	Year 1	Year 2	Year 3	Year 4	Year 5
6	1	0	74	22	20	18	16	14
7	2	0	233	100	20	20	20	20
8	3	0	177	50	25	12.5	6.25	3.125
9	4	0	190	40	30	20	10	0
10	5	0	287	90	90	45	45	45
11	6	0	107	30	15	15	15	15
12	7	0	301	120	120	60	60	60
13			Capital Required	=SUMPRODUCT(D6:D12,$B$6:$B$12)	=SUMPRODUCT(E6:E12,$B$6:$B$12)	=SUMPRODUCT(F6:F12,$B$6:$B$12)	=SUMPRODUCT(G6:G12,$B$6:$B$12)	=SUMPRODUCT(H6:H12,$B$6:$B$12)
14			Capital Available	300	150	150	90	90
15								
16			Total NPV	=SUMPRODUCT(C6:C12,B6:B12)				

FIGURE 8.44

Spreadsheet Formulas for Clem's Binary ILP Selection Problem

Figure 8.46 displays the optimal solution for Clem's binary ILP problem. The optimal solution indicates that if Clem selects investments/projects 1,2, 3, 4, and 6 (cells B6, B7, B8, B11), iTech Consulting can achieve a total NPV of $909 (cell D16). Take note that this solution set does not use up all the capital iTech has available (compare cells D13 through H13 to cells D14 through H14).

Summary of Integer Programming

An integer linear program is a model where the constraints and the objective function are the same as a traditional linear programming problem, but the decision variables are restricted to integer values. Overall, there are three types of integer programming models:

1. Pure integer programming problems—all decision variables are required to be integer values.
2. Mixed integer programming problems—some, but not all, decicion variables are required to be integer values.

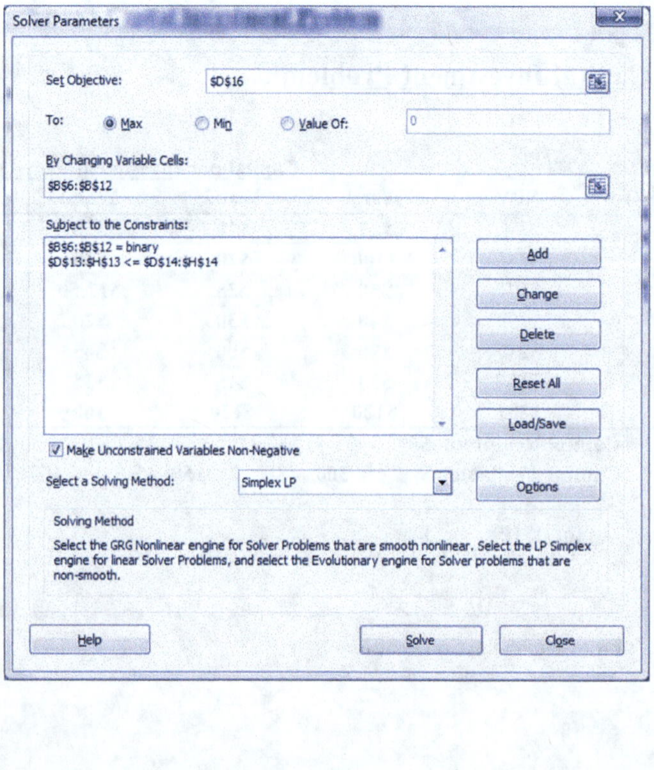

FIGURE 8.45

Solver Parameter Dialog Box for Clem's Binary ILP Model in Excel 2010

TABLE 8.6 *Solver Definitions for Clem's ILP*

Set Objective	$D$16
To:	Max
By Changing Variable Cells:	$B$6:$B$12
Subject to the Constraints:	
Project Selction (0 or 1)	$B$6:$B$12=binary
Capital Required versus Capital Available	$D$13:$H$13<=$D$14:$H$14

	A	B	C	D	E	F	G	H
1	Clem Gathman's Capital Investment Problem							
2								
3								
4	Investment/	Select?		Capital per Investment/Project Required in				
5	Project	(0=No, 1=Yes)	NPV	Year 1	Year 2	Year 3	Year 4	Year 5
6	1	1	$74	$22	$20	$18	$16	$14
7	2	1	$233	$100	$20	$20	$20	$20
8	3	1	$177	$50	$25	$12.50	$6.25	$3.125
9	4	1	$190	$40	$30	$20	$10	$0
10	5	0	$287	$90	$90	$45	$45	$45
11	6	1	$107	$30	$15	$15	$15	$15
12	7	0	$301	$120	$120	$60	$60	$60
13			Capital Required	$ 282	$ 150	$ 106	$ 87	$ 72
14			Capital Available	$ 300	$ 150	$ 150	$ 90	$ 90
15								
16			Total NPV	$ 909				
17								

FIGURE 8.46 Optimal Integer Solution to Clem's Selection Problem

3. Binary integer programming problems—special cases where all decision variables are required to have integer values of 0 or 1.

We studied the third type of model in this chapter. In general, integer programming problems are much more difficult to solve than traditional linear programming problems. The solution time required to solve integer programming problems is excessive even for very fast computers.

Summary of Linear Programming

This chapter addressed three types of linear programming problems. The first was the traditional linear programming problem for a resource allocation problem. The second was a transportation problem for a logistics applictation. The third was an integer programming problem with an application to investment opportunities. The basic steps for formulating these types of linear programs were developed within Excel using Solver and Risk Solver Platform. The development of these models included defining the problem, identifying the objective and constraints, defining the decision variables, and finally creating a spreadsheet model. Answer and sensitivity reports from Excel were also detailed and analyzed.

Business Decision Modeling Behind the Scenes

The Development of Spreadsheet Optimization Programs

Introduction

There have been many optimization packages marketed over the years. In fact, many a graduate engineering, mathematics, or computer science student has been tasked with "coding" up a simple linear optimization algorithm based on the simplex method. However, it wasn't until the early 1990s that an optimization package for spreadsheets was marketed on a large scale.

VisiCalc, VINO, and What's Best!

However, before the first copies of spreadsheet applications such as 1-2-3 or Excel had shipped, a company called LINDO Systems debuted VINO. VINO was the predecessor to their popular program called What'sBest!, and could be designated the first spreadsheet solver. The program was written for the first popular spreadsheet, VisiCalc.

In 1985, LINDO Systems and General Optimization jointly completed development on the first release of What'sBest! for Lotus 1-2-3 Release 1a. What'sBest! soon became recognized by *PC Magazine*'s prestigious Technical Excellence Award and received attention from other computer publications and such mainstream publications as the *Wall Street Journal* and the *New York Times*. What'sBest! specializes in tackling large-scale, real-world spreadsheet models with more than 100,000 variables and with nonlinear constraints.

What-If Solver

In 1990, a company called Frontline introduced What-If Solver, an add-in for Lotus 1-2-3 and Symphony. What-If Solver was the precursor of the modern spreadsheet solver add-ins. The advent of the desktop PC and the proliferation of the spreadsheet drove this new software innovation and led to what many now know as simple Solver in Microsoft Excel.

What-If Solver solved both linear and nonlinear problems, at speeds much greater than competitors. In 1991, What-If Solver won the Editor's Choice in its category in *PC Magazine*'s roundup of spreadsheet add-ins. As the popularity of the spreadsheet add-in increased, it became well known among MBA students wishing to solve complex mathematical programming problems within spreadsheets in less time.

The Excel Solver

The introduction of Lotus's spreadsheet solver in 1-2-3/G motivated other spreadsheet vendors to develop or acquire solvers of their own. In 1990—well before the launch of Windows 3.0—Frontline became the developers for creating a solver on an OEM basis for Microsoft Excel 3.0. In the next year, with the introduction of Windows 3.0 and Excel 3.0, a period of rapid adoption and growth for the Microsoft products began.

In fact, the Solver program now is the optimization program of choice by the main spreadsheet programs, Microsoft's Excel, Corel's Quattro, and Lotus's 1-2-3, as well as Mathsoft's Mathcad, which provides visual display, editing, and computational power for technical mathematics.

Evolutionary Solver

In 1997 and 1998, other vendors developed "solver" products for Microsoft Excel that were based on genetic algorithms. Although slower than the standard optimization add-in, which used classical optimization methods, they did have an advantage. These genetic algorithms could handle arbitrary Excel functions, such as IF and CHOOSE, and could obtain a more precise global optimum than classical methods.

Inclusion in Texts and Student Versions

By the early 1990s, Frontline developed the Student Edition of What-If Solver, distributed by Addison-Wesley Publishing Company for colleges and universities. The Student Edition of What-If Solver is the parent of the Excel Solver add-in used today by numerous business decision modeling students, spreadsheet users, and practitioners across the world.

Also by 1995, educational licenses for the What's Best! Solver Suite were made available at a price students could afford. As more and more students today have their own computers, the spreadsheet optimization add-in has allowed many of them to run the software on their own machine rather than having to visit the university's computer lab or "code up" up their own.

The Future

The spreadsheet has become the modeling tool of choice for today's business problems. Overall, optimization add-ins for spreadsheets have become commonplace. Almost all new textbooks being published include a version of a solver-type program or an upgraded Solver add-in program. Look for the optimization package in this text and other texts you use in your course work.

Optimal Information Area

History of Lindo page, http://www.mpassociates.gr/software/distrib/science/lindo/history.html.

http://www.solver.com/presshist.htm.

EXECUTIVE SUMMARY FOR PIRATE LOGISTICS

TO: Braxton "Pitbull" Davis
FROM: Business Decision Modeling Consulting Group

This executive summary presents the suggested distribution schedule of Pirate Logistics. A transportation network was constructed and a linear programming (LP) model developed to minimize distribution costs while maintaining required supply and demand constraints. The basic LP, a shipping schedule, and expected costs are presented next.

Basic Transportation Network and LP

Pirate Logistics wishes to minimize the costs of distribution. The Pirate Logistics Company has three supply locations: Wilmington, New Bern, and Lynchburg. In turn, Pirate Logistics ships goods to three demand locations, Grand Island, Omaha, and Sioux Falls. Specific supply and demand constraints on Pirate Logistics exist. The distribution network including the supply and demand constraint is displayed in Figure 1.1.

In Figure 1.1, the shipping costs per unit for each supply and demand location are juxtaposed on the lines connecting supply and demand locales (e.g., to ship from Wilmington to Grand Island it costs Pirate Logistics $21 per unit. Supply and demand requirements are listed on the far left and far right of Figure 1.1, respectively.

Pirate Logistics is interested in learning how much to ship from each supply locale to each demand locale. The LP model answers this question while providing the least costly solution. Table 1.1 displays the lowest cost shipping schedule for Pirate Logistics.

Shipping Schedule and LP Model Solution

Table 1.1 contains the optimal shipping amount for Pirate Logistics to ship from each supply locale to each demand locale (nonzero shipping amounts are in bold). For example, the amount to ship from Wilmington to Grand Island is 100 units. Likewise, no units are shipped from Lynchburg to Sioux Falls.

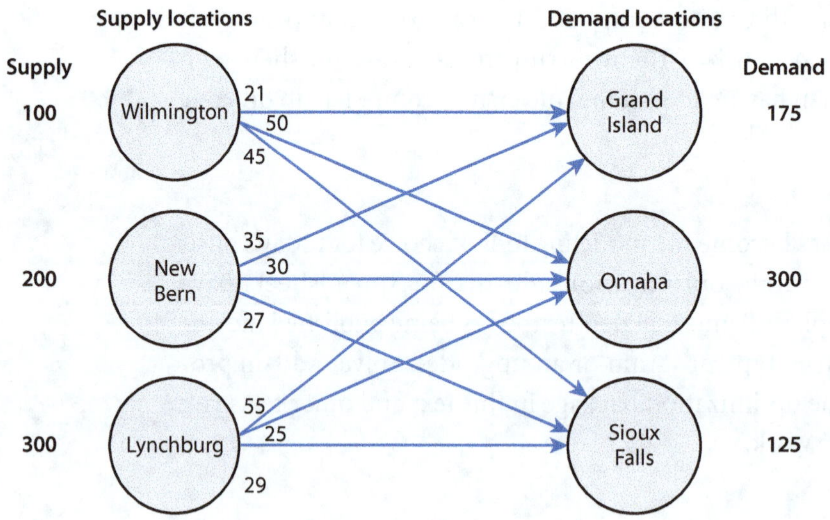

FIGURE 1.1 Distribution Network for Pirate Logistics

EXECUTIVE SUMMARY FOR PIRATE LOGISTICS (CONTINUED)

This shipping schedule results in a cost to Pirate Logistics of $15,600. Take note that total supply equals demand (i.e., total amount shipped equals 600) and that all individual supply and demand constraints are met (e.g., Wilmington has the ability to supply only 100 units and exactly 100 units are shipped, whereas Grand Island demands 175 units and exactly 175 units are shipped).

TABLE 1.1: PIRATE LOGISTICS SHIPPING SCHEDULE

Shipping locale to receiving locale	Optimal shipping amount
Wilmington to Grand Island	**100**
New Bern to Grand Island	**75**
Lynchburg to Grand Island	0
Wilmington to Omaha	0
New Bern to Omaha	0
Lynchburg to Omaha	**300**
Wilmington to Sioux Falls	0
New Bern to Sioux Falls	**125**
Lynchburg to Sioux Falls	0

Shipping Schedule Sensitivity and What-If Scenario

The shadow price assists in performing what if analysis. For the Pirate Logistics distribution problem, a shadow price is defined as the amount by which the total cost changes, given a unit increase/decrease in the supply or demand amounts. Shadow prices associated with supply are of most concern to Pirate Logistics, since amount shipped and shipping locale are more readily under its control than demand amount or location. Table 1.2 displays the shadow prices for the three shipping locales; take note that Lynchburg has the largest Shadow Price.

As Pirate Logistics' main objective is to maintain low shipping costs, it would be beneficial if units shipped could be transferred from the higher-cost Lynchburg locale to a lower-cost locale, such as Wilmington or New Bern. The logic here is as follows: As units are shifted from Lynchburg to Wilmington, overall shipping costs will decrease by $9 per unit (i.e., from $30 to $21). However, before this can occur, Pirate Logistics must verify that Wilmington can accommodate the extra units to be shipped and that overall supply equals overall demand.

TABLE 1.2: SHIPPING LOCALE SHADOW PRICES

Shipping locale	Shadow price
Wilmington	21
New Bern	31
Lynchburg	30

CASE STUDY

Chris's Capital Budgeting Ballyhoo

Background

Chris's firm, Tennessee Oil Ventures Inc. (TOVI), has $12,400,000 to invest in oil drilling exploration in the Gulf of Mexico over the next 5 years. Six investment opportunities have arisen since the latest round of hurricanes took out some production capacity in the Gulf. Table 8.7 displays the details of the six investments.

TABLE 8.7 *Investment Details*

INVESTMENT/PROJECT	EXPECTED NPV ($000)	CAPITAL (IN $000) REQUIRED PER YEAR				
		YEAR 1	YEAR 2	YEAR 3	YEAR 4	YEAR 5
1	$2700	$975	$350	$200	$100	$50
2	$3330	$1200	$200	$200	$200	$200
3	$7010	$2500	$1200	$850	$400	$400
4	$5770	$1550	$1350	$675	$337.5	$168.75
5	$2900	$1400	$350	$87.5	$21.875	$0
6	$4870	$1900	$1900	$350	$350	$350

The $14,400,000 in investment capital is spread over the 5 years as follows:

CAPITAL (IN $000) ALLOCATED PER YEAR				
YEAR 1	YEAR 2	YEAR 3	YEAR 4	YEAR 5
$5800	$3500	$1300	$900	$900

Problem at Hand

Chris had just finished looking at the six investment/projects that made it past the engineers and accountants. Although all the investments/projects look good (positive NPV), Chris knows TOVI cannot pick all of them since there is not enough money (i.e., capital) to go around. Chris and in turn TOVI must determine which of the investments/projects to accept to maximize potential NPV but yet stay within company capital budgets. However, a few caveats have cropped up regarding some federal and state laws regarding these projects.

1. Surplus capital funds in any year cannot be carried over from year to year.
2. If TOVI decides to invest in the second investment/project, it must also invest in the fourth.
3. If TOVI decides to invest in the first investment/project, it cannot invest in the fifth investment/project.

Discussion Questions

1. Help Chris and his firm, TOVI, solve this problem by defining the parts of an ILP, constructing an ILP model in Excel, and using Excel's Solver to find a solution.
2. What projects should Chris and his firm invest in? How much capital do they use? Why are certain projects being left out?

Optimal Information Area

@RISK, Palisade Corp., Newfield, N.Y.
http://www.palisade.com

Bodington, C. E., and T. E. Baker, "A History of Mathematical Programming in the Petroleum Industry,", C. E. Bodington and T. E. Baker, *Interfaces,* vol. 20, : no. 4 (1990), pp. 117–127.

Crystal Ball, Decisioneering Inc., Boulder, Colorado
http://www.decisioneering.com

Essbase, Arbor Software
http://www.arborsoft.com

Excel Solver, Frontline Systems
http://www.frontsys.com

Frontline Systems, Solver history page
http://www.solver.com/presshist.htm

History of Lindo
http://www.mpassociates.gr/software/distrib/science/lindo/history.html

Neuwirth, Erich, Web page on Spreadsheets in Education
http://sunsite.univie.ac.at/Spreadsite/

Savage, Sam L., *"Fundamental Analytic Spreadsheet Tools for Quantitative Management,"* New York: McGraw-Hill, 1993.

Savage, Sam L., Web home page with downloadable software
http://www-leland.stanford.edu/~savagehttp://www.stanford.edu/~savage/faculty/savage/

What'sBest!, Lindo Systems
http://www.lindo.com

PROBLEMS

1. The Waikiki Enterprise Corporation produces two types of computers at its manufacturing plant in Torrance, California. Profit on computer A is $900 per unit and for computer B it is $600. The manufacturing plant can produce not more than 50 of computer A and 100 of computer B a day. The following table displays the capacity for the manufacturing plant.

PLANT	CAPACITY TO PRODUCE COMPUTER A	CAPACITY TO PRODUCE COMPUTER B	MAXIMUM AVAILABLE CAPACITY
A Riverview Plant	51	101	18000
Unit profit	$900	$600	

   a. What are the decision variables?

   b. What is the objective function?

   c. What are the constraints?

   d. What are the non-negativity assumptions?

2. Firebridge's new radial tires come in two styles. The Fire Hawk uses 20 pounds of rubber and 6 pounds of steel. The Tiger Claw requires 15 pounds of rubber and 1 pound of steel. They currently have 3000 pounds of rubber and 300 pounds of steel. Firebridge is obligated to provide these tires to the government in the following minimum quantities: at least 20 Tiger Claws and at least 10 Fire Hawks. However, the government stipulates that of all the tires provided, twice as many must be Tiger Claws as Fire Hawks. In addition, Firebridge must provide at least 100 tires total. There is a cost of $10 for the Fire Hawk and $10 for a Tiger Claw.

	UNITS PER FIRE HAWK	UNITS PER TIGER CLAW	AVAILABLE PRODUCTS
Steel	6	1	300
Rubber	20	15	3000
Cost	$10	$10	

   a. What are the decision variables?

   b. What is the objective function?

   c. What are the constraints?

d. What are the non-negativity assumptions?

e. Solve the LP via Excel's Solver

3. The Backpack Corporation makes two types of backpacks for students, regular and deluxe. The company has a prior pricing agreement with the distributor, who is willing to buy as much of each kind of bag as Backpack could conceivably make. There are two steps in making a bag, first assembling it and then packaging it. Each regular bag requires 3 hours of assembling and 1 hour of packaging. On the other hand, the deluxe requires 4 hours in assembling and 2 hours in packaging. The profit obtained for each regular bag is of $15, while that for each deluxe bag is $25. In order to maximize the profit for the company, how many bags of each type should Backpack manufacture? The data are summarized in the table below.

	MAKING BAG	PACKAGING BAG	PROFIT
Regular	3 hours	1 hour	$15
Deluxe	4 hours	2 hours	$25
Total Available Hours	300	200	

a. What are the decision variables?

b. What is the objective function?

c. What are the constraints?

d. What are the non-negativity assumptions?

e. Solve the LP via Excel's Solver.

4. A senior class of 420 students will rent buses and vans for a class trip. Each bus can transport 50 students plus 3 chaperones, and costs $1200 to rent. Each van can transport 10 students and 1 chaperone, and costs $100 to rent. There are only 36 chaperones available (so they can't all go in vans). How many vehicles of each type should be rented in order to minimize the cost?

	STUDENT	CHAPERONES	COST
Bus	50	3	$1200
Van	10	1	$100
Totals	420	36	

a. What are the decision variables?

b. What is the objective function?

c. What are the constraints?

d. What are the non-negativity assumptions?

e. Solve the LP via Excel's Solver.

5. Solve the following linear programming problem via Excel's Solver

Maximize	$30X + 10Y$
Subject to	$4X + 10Y \leq 28$
	$1X + 5Y \leq 50$
	$Y \geq 1$
	$X, Y \geq 0$

6. Solve the following linear programming problem via Excel's Solver.

Maximize	$4X + 4Y$
Subject to	$3X + 3Y \leq 85$
	$X - 4Y \leq 40$
	$Y \geq 5$
	$X, Y \geq 0$

7. Tire World produces two different series, the 50 series and the 65 series, at two plants. The profit for sale of a 50 series is \$20 per tire and the profit from the sale of a 65 series is \$30 no matter what plant they are produced at. The 50 series uses 800 units of capacity per tire while the 65 series uses 1000 units of capacity per day at plant 1. At the second plant the 50 series uses 600 units of capacity while the 65 series uses 400 units of capacity per tire at plant 2. Maximum daily capacity for each plant is listed in the table below. Tire World must produce at least fifty 50 series tires overall. How many of each series should Tire World produce to at each plant to maximize profit? The following table displays the capacity of Tire World plant.

PLANT	CAPACITY PER 50 SERIES	CAPACITY PER 65 SERIES	MAXIMUM DAILY AVAILABLE CAPACITY
1	800	1000	70000
2	600	400	32000
Profit per tire	\$20	\$30	

a. What are the decision variables?

b. What is the objective function?

c. What are the constraints?

d. What are the non-negativity assumptions?

e. Solve the linear programming problem via Excel's Solver.

8. Polaski Petro Chemical Corp. produces two types of jet fuel: JP-2 and JP-3. For each gallon of JP-2 produced, a profit of $4.20 is earned; for each gallon of JP-3, a profit of $3.18 is earned. In its diffraction separator, Polaski has the capacity to produce a total of 60,000 gallons a week. A gallon of JP-2 takes 15 gallons of crude oil, and a gallon of JP-3 takes 12 gallons of crude oil. Polaski Petro Chemical receives 700,000 gallons of crude oil a week. Because of border disputes with the Hungarian Peoples Front, the Romanian Air Force has requested that JP-2 production be increased to fuel its MIG-29 fighter aircraft for the upcoming war. The government responded by limiting JP-3 production to 30,000 gallons a week. Which mix of fuels produced will maximize profits for the Polaski Petro Chemical Corporation? The table below lists the relevant data.

PLANT	CAPACITY USED PER GALLON OF JP-2	CAPACITY USED PER GALLON OF JP-3	MAXIMUM GALLON CAPACITY
1	8	6.5	62000
Unit profit	$4.20	$3.18	

a. What are the decision variables?

b. What is the objective function?

c. What are the constraints?

d. What are the non-negativity assumptions?

e. Solve the LP via Excel Solver.

9. Digitex is a small computer start-up company. At present it has an opportunity to enter the market by providing two types of server computers, one powered by Windows NT and the other backed by the up-and-coming Linux OS. The profits from these products are $1000 from a single Windows NT server and $999 from one Linux server. For cost and resource reasons, the company can produce only 88 Windows NT servers and 96 Linux servers. How much of each server should Digitex produce to maximize profit?

PLANT	CAPACITY USE PER WINDOWS NT SERVER	CAPACITY USED PER LINUX SERVER	MAXIMUM AVAILABLE CAPACITY
A	88	96	2000
Unit profit	$1000	$999	

a. What are the decision variables?

b. What is the objective function?

c. What are the constraints?

d. What are the non-negativity assumptions?

e. Solve the LP via Excel Solver.

10. The local bakery sells three different kinds of bread mixes by the sack: Whiteness, Wheatness, & Multiness. The bakery has 5000 lb of flour and 3010 lb of sugar available. The white bread needs 2 lb of flour and 1.75 lb of sugar per sack, and the profit is $2.50 per sack. The wheat bread takes 3 lbs. of flour and 0.75 lbs. of sugar and garners $7.00 in profit per sack. Finally, the Multiness bread takes 2.5 lbs. of flour and 2 lb of sugar but gets $9.00 in profit per sack. However, the marketing department has informed the operations manager that no more than 50 sacks total of Wheatness and Multiness combined will be sold and warned not to overproduce the two types. In addition, the marketing department has promised a customer 10 sacks of Wheatness mix. Partial sacks of mix can be produced. Help the bakery to find the best combination to maximize profit.

	WHITENESS	WHEATNESS	MULTINESS	AVAILABILITY
Flour	2.0	3.0	2.5	5000
Sugar	1.75	0.75	2.0	3010
Profit	$2.5	$7.0	$9.0	

a. What are the decision variables and what is the objective function?

b. What are the constraints and what are the non-negativity assumptions?

c. Solve the LP via Excel Solver.

11. A firm services different types of computerized equipment (items 1, 2, 3, 4, 5), choosing from components A, B, C, D, and E to service the equipment. The firm determines that some components in service inventory will not be used in the process during the upcoming year. However, the firm wants certain components to be used in the current year since this will increase profitability. If not, then these service components must be sent to an auxiliary production location and no profit will be gained. The level of components in the inventory is as follows;

COMPONENT ITEM	UNITS IN INVENTORY
A	20000
B	18000
C	7500
D	5000
E	22300

The level of each component that is used per each service process is as follows:

	COMPUTERIZED EQUIPMENT				
	1	2	3	4	5
COMPONENT	NUMBER USED IN SERVICE PROCESS				
A	30	40	0	30	50
B	20	30	20	20	60
C	10	10	10	10	20
D	10	10	10	0	20
E	20	30	20	40	80

The maximum service process forecasts for each service process is 2000, 1500, 500, 4000, 5000 for items 1, 2, 3, 4, 5, respectively. The profitability per unit (items 1, 2, 3, 4,) is \$20, \$40, \$80, \$60, \$20. The objective is to maximize profit. The question is how many of each of the five items should be used. Thus, the maximum possible number can be used for inventory to meet current service needs.

a. What are the decision variables and what is the objective function?

b. What are the constraints and what are the non-negativity assumptions?

c. Solve the LP via Excel Solver.

12. The following report has been generated in Excel by using Solver.

Microsoft Excel 14.0 Answer Report
Worksheet: [Ch8-Prob12.xlsx]Sheet1
Report Created: 3/2/2011 11:18:34 AM
Result: Solver found a solution. All Constraints and optimality conditions are satisfied.
Solver Engine
Engine: Simplex LP
Solution Time: 0.015 Seconds.
Iterations: 2 Subproblems: 0
Solver Options
Max Time Unlimited, Iterations Unlimited, Precision 0.000001, Use Automatic Scaling
Max Subproblems Unlimited, Max Integer Sols Unlimited, Integer Tolerance 1%, Assume NonNegative

Objective Cell (Max)

Cell	Name	Original Value	Final Value
$B$4	Objective Function	0	5816.666667

Variable Cells

Cell	Name	Original Value	Final Value	Integer
$B$1	Gallons of S1	0	3.333333333	Contin
$B$2	Gallons of S2	0	18.33333333	Contin

Constraints

Cell	Name	Cell Value	Formula	Status	Slack
$B$10	Hand Mixing Constraints LHS	35	$B$10<=$C$10	Binding	0
$B$9	Processing Constraints LHS	40	$B$9<=$C$9	Binding	0

Microsoft Excel 14.0 Sensitivity Report
Worksheet: [Ch8-Prob12.xlsx]Sheet1
Report Created: 3/2/2011 11:18:34 AM

Variable Cells

Cell	Name	Final Value	Reduced Cost	Objective Coefficient	Allowable Increase	Allowable Decrease
$B$1	Gallons of S1	3.33333333	0	150	1300	5
$B$2	Gallons of S2	18.3333333	0	290	10	260

Constraints

Cell	Name	Final Value	Shadow Price	Constraint R.H. Side	Allowable Increase	Allowable Decrease
$B$10	Hand Mixing Constraints LHS	35	1.11111111	35	165	15
$B$9	Processing Constraints LHS	40	144.444444	40	30	33

Answer the following questions from the output above:

a. What is the objective function optimal value?

b. What are the final values of the decision variables at this optimal value?

c. Explain which constraints are binding and not binding and what that means.

d. What is the maximum increase in the objective coefficient of the first variable that can occur without changing the optimal product mix?

13. The following report has been generated in Excel by using Solver.

Worksheet: [Ch8-Prob12.xlsx]Sheet2
Report Created: 3/2/2011 11:29:13 AM
Result: Solver found a solution. All Constraints and optimality conditions are satisfied.
Solver Engine
Engine: Simplex LP
Solution Time: 0.031 Seconds.
Iterations: 4 Subproblems: 0
Solver Options
Max Time Unlimited, Iterations Unlimited, Precision 0.000001, Use Automatic Scaling
Max Subproblems Unlimited, Max Integer Sols Unlimited, Integer Tolerance 1%, Assume NonNegative

Objective Cell (Max)

Cell	Name	Original Value	Final Value
$B$5	Objective Function	0	4605

Variable Cells

Cell	Name	Original Value	Final Value	Integer
$B$1	Whiteness	0	1670	Contin
$B$2	Wheatness	0	10	Contin
$B$3	Multiness	0	40	Contin

Constraints

Cell	Name	Cell Value	Formula	Status	Slack
$B$10	Sugar Constraint LHS	3010	$B$10<=$C$10	Binding	0
$B$11	Wheatness Constraint LHS	10	$B$11>=$C$11	Binding	0
$B$8	Multiness Contraint LHS	50	$B$8<=$C$8	Binding	0
$B$9	Flour Constraint LHS	3470	$B$9<=$C$9	Not Binding	1530

Microsoft Excel 14.0 Sensitivity Report
Worksheet: [Ch8-Prob12.xlsx]Sheet2
Report Created: 3/2/2011 11:29:13 AM

Variable Cells

Cell	Name	Final Value	Reduced Cost	Objective Coefficient	Allowable Increase	Allowable Decrease
$B$1	Whiteness	1670	0	2.5	0.3	2.5
$B$2	Wheatness	10	0	7	0.21428571	1E+30
$B$3	Multiness	40	0	9	1E+30	0.21428571

Constraints

Cell	Name	Final Value	Shadow Price	Constraint R.H. Side	Allowable Increase	Allowable Decrease
$B$10	Sugar Constraint LHS	3010	1.428571429	3010	1338.75	2922.5
$B$11	Wheatness Constraint LHS	10	-0.214285714	10	40	10
$B$8	Multiness Contraint LHS	50	6.142857143	50	1461.25	40
$B$9	Flour Constraint LHS	3470	0	5000	1E+30	1530

Answer the following questions from the output above:

a. What is the objective function optimal value?

b. What are the final values of the decision variables at this optimal value?

c. Explain which constraints are binding and not binding, and their meaning.

d. What is the shadow price for the flour constraint? Explain its meaning.

e. What would happen to the objective function if you could increase the flour constraint from 5000 to 5500?

APPENDIX

A Useful Information

Standard Normal Distribution Table

NOTE: Entries in the following table give the area under the curve between the mean and z standard deviations above the mean. For example, for $z = 1.25$, the area under the curve between the mean and z is 0.3944.

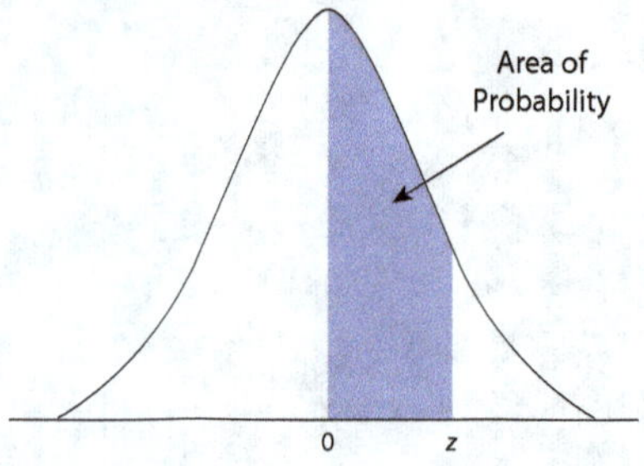

z	0.00	0.01	0.02	0.03	0.04	0.05	0.06	0.07	0.08	0.09
0.00	0.0000	0.0040	0.0080	0.0120	0.0160	0.0199	0.0239	0.0279	0.0319	0.0359
0.10	0.0398	0.0438	0.0478	0.0517	0.0557	0.0596	0.0636	0.0675	0.0714	0.0753
0.20	0.0793	0.0832	0.0871	0.0910	0.0948	0.0987	0.1026	0.1064	0.1103	0.1141
0.30	0.1179	0.1217	0.1255	0.1293	0.1331	0.1368	0.1406	0.1443	0.1480	0.1517
0.40	0.1554	0.1591	0.1628	0.1664	0.1700	0.1736	0.1772	0.1808	0.1844	0.1879
0.50	0.1915	0.1950	0.1985	0.2019	0.2054	0.2088	0.2123	0.2157	0.2190	0.2224
0.60	0.2257	0.2291	0.2324	0.2357	0.2389	0.2422	0.2454	0.2486	0.2518	0.2549
0.70	0.2580	0.2612	0.2642	0.2673	0.2704	0.2734	0.2764	0.2794	0.2823	0.2852
0.80	0.2881	0.2910	0.2939	0.2967	0.2995	0.3023	0.3051	0.3078	0.3106	0.3133
0.90	0.3159	0.3186	0.3212	0.3238	0.3264	0.3289	0.3315	0.3340	0.3365	0.3389
1.00	0.3413	0.3438	0.3461	0.3485	0.3508	0.3531	0.3554	0.3577	0.3599	0.3621
1.10	0.3643	0.3665	0.3686	0.3708	0.3729	0.3749	0.3770	0.3790	0.3810	0.3830
1.20	0.3849	0.3869	0.3888	0.3907	0.3925	0.3944	0.3962	0.3980	0.3997	0.4015
1.30	0.4032	0.4049	0.4066	0.4082	0.4099	0.4115	0.4131	0.4147	0.4162	0.4177
1.40	0.4192	0.4207	0.4222	0.4236	0.4251	0.4265	0.4279	0.4292	0.4306	0.4319
1.50	0.4332	0.4345	0.4357	0.4370	0.4382	0.4394	0.4406	0.4418	0.4429	0.4441
1.60	0.4452	0.4463	0.4474	0.4484	0.4495	0.4505	0.4515	0.4525	0.4535	0.4545
1.70	0.4554	0.4564	0.4573	0.4582	0.4591	0.4599	0.4608	0.4616	0.4625	0.4633
1.80	0.4641	0.4649	0.4656	0.4664	0.4671	0.4678	0.4686	0.4693	0.4699	0.4706
1.90	0.4713	0.4719	0.4726	0.4732	0.4738	0.4744	0.4750	0.4756	0.4761	0.4767
2.00	0.4772	0.4778	0.4783	0.4788	0.4793	0.4798	0.4803	0.4808	0.4812	0.4817
2.10	0.4821	0.4826	0.4830	0.4834	0.4838	0.4842	0.4846	0.4850	0.4854	0.4857
2.20	0.4861	0.4864	0.4868	0.4871	0.4875	0.4878	0.4881	0.4884	0.4887	0.4890
2.30	0.4893	0.4896	0.4898	0.4901	0.4904	0.4906	0.4909	0.4911	0.4913	0.4916
2.40	0.4918	0.4920	0.4922	0.4925	0.4927	0.4929	0.4931	0.4932	0.4934	0.4936
2.50	0.4938	0.4940	0.4941	0.4943	0.4945	0.4946	0.4948	0.4949	0.4951	0.4952
2.60	0.4953	0.4955	0.4956	0.4957	0.4959	0.4960	0.4961	0.4962	0.4963	0.4964
2.70	0.4965	0.4966	0.4967	0.4968	0.4969	0.4970	0.4971	0.4972	0.4973	0.4974
2.80	0.4974	0.4975	0.4976	0.4977	0.4977	0.4978	0.4979	0.4979	0.4980	0.4981
2.90	0.4981	0.4982	0.4982	0.4983	0.4984	0.4984	0.4985	0.4985	0.4986	0.4986
3.00	0.4986	0.4987	0.4987	0.4988	0.4988	0.4989	0.4989	0.4989	0.4990	0.4990

Student's *t* Table

DEGREES OF FREEDOM	CONFIDENCE LEVEL 80%	90%	95%	99%
1	3.078	6.134	12.706	63.657
2	1.886	2.920	4.303	9.925
3	1.638	2.353	3.182	5.841
4	1.533	2.132	2.776	4.604
5	1.476	2.015	2.571	4.032
6	1.440	1.943	2.447	3.707
7	1.415	1.895	2.365	3.500
8	1.397	1.860	2.306	3.355
9	1.383	1.833	2.262	3.250
10	1.372	1.812	2.228	3.169
11	1.363	1.796	2.201	3.106
12	1.356	1.782	2.179	3.055
13	1.350	1.771	2.160	3.012
14	1.345	1.761	2.145	2.977
15	1.341	1.753	2.131	2.947
16	1.337	1.746	2.120	2.921
17	1.333	1.740	2.110	2.898
18	1.330	1.734	2.101	2.878
19	1.328	1.729	2.093	2.861
20	1.325	1.725	2.086	2.845
21	1.323	1.721	2.080	2.831
22	1.321	1.717	2.074	2.819
23	1.319	1.714	2.069	2.807
24	1.318	1.711	2.064	2.797
25	1.316	1.708	2.060	2.787
26	1.315	1.706	2.056	2.779
27	1.314	1.703	2.052	2.771
28	1.313	1.701	2.048	2.763
29	1.311	1.699	2.045	2.756
30	1.310	1.697	2.042	2.750
Infinity	1.282	1.645	1.960	2.576

The F Distribution (Upper 5 Percent Points)

The numbers in the table give the critical values cutting off 5 percent in the upper tail of the F distribution. The first row gives the degrees of freedom in the numerator while the first column gives the degrees of freedom in the denominator.

	1	2	3	4	5	6	7	8	9	10	12	15	20	24	30	40	60	120	INFINITY
1	161.45	199.50	215.71	224.58	230.16	233.99	236.77	238.88	240.54	241.88	243.90	245.95	248.02	249.05	250.10	251.14	252.20	253.25	254.31
2	18.51	19.00	19.16	19.25	19.30	19.33	19.35	19.37	19.38	19.40	19.41	19.43	19.45	19.45	19.46	19.47	19.48	19.49	19.50
3	10.13	9.55	9.28	9.12	9.01	8.94	8.89	8.85	8.81	8.79	8.74	8.70	8.66	8.64	8.62	8.59	8.57	8.55	8.53
4	7.71	6.94	6.59	6.39	6.26	6.16	6.09	6.04	6.00	5.96	5.91	5.86	5.80	5.77	5.75	5.72	5.69	5.66	5.63
5	6.61	5.79	5.41	5.19	5.05	4.95	4.88	4.82	4.77	4.74	4.68	4.62	4.56	4.53	4.50	4.46	4.43	4.40	4.37
6	5.99	5.14	4.76	4.53	4.39	4.28	4.21	4.15	4.10	4.06	4.00	3.94	3.87	3.84	3.81	3.77	3.74	3.70	3.67
7	5.59	4.74	4.35	4.12	3.97	3.87	3.79	3.73	3.68	3.64	3.57	3.51	3.44	3.41	3.38	3.34	3.30	3.27	3.23
8	5.32	4.46	4.07	3.84	3.69	3.58	3.50	3.44	3.39	3.35	3.28	3.22	3.15	3.12	3.08	3.04	3.01	2.97	2.93
9	5.12	4.26	3.86	3.63	3.48	3.37	3.29	3.23	3.18	3.14	3.07	3.01	2.94	2.90	2.86	2.83	2.79	2.75	2.71
10	4.96	4.10	3.71	3.48	3.33	3.22	3.14	3.07	3.02	2.98	2.91	2.85	2.77	2.74	2.70	2.66	2.62	2.58	2.54
11	4.84	3.98	3.59	3.36	3.20	3.09	3.01	2.95	2.90	2.85	2.79	2.72	2.65	2.61	2.57	2.53	2.49	2.45	2.40
12	4.75	3.89	3.49	3.26	3.11	3.00	2.91	2.85	2.80	2.75	2.69	2.62	2.54	2.51	2.47	2.43	2.38	2.34	2.30
13	4.67	3.81	3.41	3.18	3.03	2.92	2.83	2.77	2.71	2.67	2.60	2.53	2.46	2.42	2.38	2.34	2.30	2.25	2.21
14	4.60	3.74	3.34	3.11	2.96	2.85	2.76	2.70	2.65	2.60	2.53	2.46	2.39	2.35	2.31	2.27	2.22	2.18	2.13
15	4.54	3.68	3.29	3.06	2.90	2.79	2.71	2.64	2.59	2.54	2.48	2.40	2.33	2.29	2.25	2.20	2.16	2.11	2.07
16	4.49	3.63	3.24	3.01	2.85	2.74	2.66	2.59	2.54	2.49	2.42	2.35	2.28	2.24	2.19	2.15	2.11	2.06	2.01
17	4.45	3.59	3.20	2.96	2.81	2.70	2.61	2.55	2.49	2.45	2.38	2.31	2.23	2.19	2.15	2.10	2.06	2.01	1.96
18	4.41	3.55	3.16	2.93	2.77	2.66	2.58	2.51	2.46	2.41	2.34	2.27	2.19	2.15	2.11	2.06	2.02	1.97	1.92
19	4.38	3.52	3.13	2.90	2.74	2.63	2.54	2.48	2.42	2.38	2.31	2.23	2.16	2.11	2.07	2.03	1.98	1.93	1.88
20	4.35	3.49	3.10	2.87	2.71	2.60	2.51	2.45	2.39	2.35	2.28	2.20	2.12	2.08	2.04	1.99	1.95	1.90	1.84
21	4.32	3.47	3.07	2.84	2.68	2.57	2.49	2.42	2.37	2.32	2.25	2.18	2.10	2.05	2.01	1.96	1.92	1.87	1.81
22	4.30	3.44	3.05	2.82	2.66	2.55	2.46	2.40	2.34	2.30	2.23	2.15	2.07	2.03	1.98	1.94	1.89	1.84	1.78
23	4.28	3.42	3.03	2.80	2.64	2.53	2.44	2.37	2.32	2.27	2.20	2.13	2.05	2.01	1.96	1.91	1.86	1.81	1.76
24	4.26	3.40	3.01	2.78	2.62	2.51	2.42	2.36	2.30	2.25	2.18	2.11	2.03	1.98	1.94	1.89	1.84	1.79	1.73
25	4.24	3.39	2.99	2.76	2.60	2.49	2.40	2.34	2.28	2.24	2.16	2.09	2.01	1.96	1.92	1.87	1.82	1.77	1.71
26	4.23	3.37	2.98	2.74	2.59	2.47	2.39	2.32	2.27	2.22	2.15	2.07	1.99	1.95	1.90	1.85	1.80	1.75	1.69
27	4.21	3.35	2.96	2.73	2.57	2.46	2.37	2.31	2.25	2.20	2.13	2.06	1.97	1.93	1.88	1.84	1.79	1.73	1.67
28	4.20	3.34	2.95	2.71	2.56	2.45	2.36	2.29	2.24	2.19	2.12	2.04	1.96	1.91	1.87	1.82	1.77	1.71	1.65
29	4.18	3.33	2.93	2.70	2.55	2.43	2.35	2.28	2.22	2.18	2.10	2.03	1.94	1.90	1.85	1.81	1.75	1.70	1.64
30	4.17	3.32	2.92	2.69	2.53	2.42	2.33	2.27	2.21	2.16	2.09	2.01	1.93	1.89	1.84	1.79	1.74	1.68	1.62
40	4.08	3.23	2.84	2.61	2.45	2.34	2.25	2.18	2.12	2.08	2.00	1.92	1.84	1.79	1.74	1.69	1.64	1.58	1.51
60	4.00	3.15	2.76	2.53	2.37	2.25	2.17	2.10	2.04	1.99	1.92	1.84	1.75	1.70	1.65	1.59	1.53	1.47	1.39
120	3.92	3.07	2.68	2.45	2.29	2.18	2.09	2.02	1.96	1.91	1.83	1.75	1.66	1.61	1.55	1.50	1.43	1.35	1.25
infinity	3.84	3.00	2.60	2.37	2.21	2.10	2.01	1.94	1.88	1.83	1.75	1.67	1.57	1.52	1.46	1.39	1.32	1.22	1.00

The Durbin-Watson Statistic Table

Entries in the table give the critical values for a one-tailed Durbin-Watson test for autocorrelation. For a two-tailed test, the level of significance is doubled.

	K=1		K=2		K=3		K=4		K=5	
N	D_L	D_U	D_L	D_U	D_L	D_U	D_L	D_U	D_L	D_U
15	1.08	1.36	0.95	1.54	0.82	1.75	0.69	1.97	0.56	2.21
16	1.10	1.37	0.98	1.54	0.86	1.73	0.74	1.93	0.62	2.15
17	1.13	1.38	1.02	1.54	0.9	1.71	0.78	1.90	0.67	2.10
18	1.16	1.39	1.05	1.53	0.93	1.69	0.82	1.87	0.71	2.06
19	1.18	1.40	1.08	1.53	0.97	1.68	0.86	1.85	0.75	2.02
20	1.20	1.41	1.10	1.54	1.00	1.68	0.90	1.83	0.79	1.99
21	1.22	1.42	1.13	1.54	1.03	1.67	0.93	1.81	0.83	1.96
22	1.24	1.43	1.15	1.54	1.05	1.66	0.96	1.80	0.86	1.94
23	1.26	1.44	1.17	1.54	1.08	1.66	0.99	1.79	0.90	1.92
24	1.27	1.45	1.19	1.55	1.10	1.66	1.01	1.78	0.93	1.90
25	1.29	1.45	1.21	1.55	1.12	1.66	1.04	1.77	0.95	1.89
26	1.30	1.46	1.22	1.55	1.14	1.65	1.06	1.76	0.98	1.88
27	1.32	1.47	1.24	1.56	1.16	1.65	1.08	1.76	1.01	1.86
28	1.33	1.48	1.26	1.56	1.18	1.65	1.10	1.75	1.03	1.85
29	1.34	1.48	1.27	1.56	1.20	1.65	1.12	1.74	1.05	1.84
30	1.35	1.49	1.28	1.57	1.21	1.65	1.14	1.74	1.07	1.83
31	1.36	1.50	1.30	1.57	1.23	1.65	1.16	1.74	1.09	1.83
32	1.37	1.50	1.31	1.57	1.24	1.65	1.18	1.73	1.11	1.82
33	1.38	1.51	1.32	1.58	1.26	1.65	1.19	1.73	1.13	1.81
34	1.39	1.51	1.33	1.58	1.27	1.65	1.21	1.73	1.15	1.81
35	1.40	1.52	1.34	1.58	1.28	1.65	1.22	1.73	1.16	1.80
36	1.41	1.52	1.35	1.59	1.29	1.65	1.24	1.73	1.18	1.80
37	1.42	1.53	1.36	1.59	1.31	1.66	1.25	1.72	1.19	1.80
38	1.43	1.54	1.37	1.59	1.32	1.66	1.26	1.72	1.21	1.79
39	1.43	1.54	1.38	1.60	1.33	1.66	1.27	1.72	1.22	1.79
40	1.44	1.54	1.39	1.60	1.34	1.66	1.29	1.72	1.23	1.79
45	1.48	1.57	1.43	1.62	1.38	1.67	1.34	1.72	1.29	1.78
50	1.50	1.59	1.46	1.63	1.42	1.67	1.38	1.72	1.34	1.77
55	1.53	1.60	1.49	1.64	1.45	1.68	1.41	1.72	1.38	1.77
60	1.55	1.62	1.51	1.65	1.48	1.69	1.44	1.73	1.41	1.77
65	1.57	1.63	1.54	1.66	1.50	1.70	1.47	1.73	1.44	1.77
70	1.58	1.64	1.55	1.67	1.52	1.70	1.49	1.74	1.46	1.77
75	1.60	1.65	1.57	1.68	1.54	1.71	1.51	1.74	1.49	1.77
80	1.61	1.66	1.59	1.69	1.56	1.72	1.53	1.74	1.51	1.77
85	1.62	1.67	1.60	1.70	1.57	1.72	1.55	1.75	1.52	1.77
90	1.63	1.68	1.61	1.70	1.59	1.73	1.57	1.75	1.54	1.78
95	1.64	1.69	1.62	1.71	1.60	1.73	1.58	1.75	1.56	1.78
100	1.65	1.69	1.63	1.72	1.61	1.74	1.59	1.75	1.57	1.78

Significance Points of D_L and D_U at $\alpha = 0.05$ and Number of Independent Variables

SOURCE: Durbin. J., Watson, G. S. "Testing for serial correlation in least squares regression." *Biometrika. vol. 38.* 1951. pp. 159–177.

Writing Guide for Business Decision Modeling

The numbers in the table give the critical values cutting off 5 percent in the upper tail of the F distribution. The first row gives the degrees of freedom in the numerator while the first column gives the degrees of freedom in the denominator.

Business Decision Modeling Written Analysis Guidelines

- The executive summary is the single most important part of your analysis.
- Written analysis should be concise yet informative.
- Consider the information/space tradeoff.
- View yourselves as consultants presenting to prospective clients with the end goal of obtaining a consulting contract and getting PAID!!
- View the written analysis as a sales tool that is
  a. Readable at many levels, e.g., executives, staff members, and managers.
  b. Applicable to varying degrees of technical expertise, interests, and agendas.
- Ask yourself the following questions:
  a. "What would I want to know from this Executive Summary?"
  b. "What would grab my attention and keep me reading?"
  c. "What information needs to be included for me or my group to make a decision?"
- Remember your are telling a story,
  a. Think real life.
  b. Brief the decision makers on the problem.
  c. Provide them with a quantitative analysis.
  d. State your results and sell your recommendations.

Business Decision Modeling Basic Presentation Guidelines

- Make use of the technology provided (i.e., data projector, computer, etc.) but always be prepared in case the technology doesn't work.
  a. Concentrate on giving a concise yet informative overview.
  b. Think of your group as consultants bidding for a contract.
  c. Time is limited and you may be under pressure to get your ideas across.
  d. Too much info and you risk boring the client to death, too little info and you risk being inadequate.
  e. Strive to become more effective and efficient business writers and presenters.
- Items to remember:

a. Keep your slides simple.
b. Label all graphs, axis, and spreadsheets.
c. State your assumptions and stick by them.
d. Do not overcrowd slides (e.g., complicated spreadsheets usually confuse instead of enlightening the audience).
e. Use your time wisely, cover background material, but make sure you get to the results and recommendations with sufficient time left to discuss and make your sale.
f. Practice your presentation before you give it!

Executive Summary Tutorial

The business world uses what is called an executive summary. The following are a set of guidelines for writing executive summaries.

1. The executive summary must be short (i.e., one page).
   - An executive summary that is too long defeats its purpose.
   - An executive summary that is too short omits essential content
2. The executive summary must be a self-contained unit.
   - The executive summary must stand independently.
   - Most likely the executive summary will be separated from the report and be published or circulated independently.
3. The executive summary must satisfy your clients' needs.
   - The executive summary must contain a statement of the problem, the limitations placed on it. results, conclusions, and recommendations.
4. The executive summary must be objective, precise, and easy to read.
   - State the purpose or objective (sometimes called the thesis) of the problem clearly and early in the executive summary.
   - Clearly define assumptions and terms throughout the executive summary.
   - Reference visual aids included in the executive summary.
   - Display visual aids if they are referenced in the executive summary.
5. Rewriting is far more important than writing. Points to remember:
   - Spell-check your document.
   - Define all terms, do not assume your client "knows."
   - Have a third party read your work as a reality check.
   - Tell your story, sell and educate your client about your analysis.
   - Walk your client through the executive summary.

- Link sections and ideas together.
- Restate conclusions/recommendations—in words and in numbers.
- Concise and effective executive summaries are never written they are rewritten.

6. The executive summary should contain:
   - Headings.
   - Well-developed transitions between sections.
   - Comparison and/or summary sections.
   - Visual aids if applicable.

Visual aids such as graphs, charts, decision trees, and/or spreadsheets are highly recommended and should be used to help describe and define technical sections, comparisons, results, and/or recommendations.

Executive Summary Definitions

The following is a sample of what leading business writing scholars and practitioners have stated about executive summaries. Please read the quotes and use the references to improve your executive summaries and overall writing tasks.

An Executive Summary is a fully developed "mini" version of the report itself, intended for readers who lack time or motivation to study the complete text.

—Writing Long Reports, John Thill and Courtlanci Bovee

The Executive Summary, also called the synopsis, epitome, and précis, is the report in miniature. It concisely summarizes all of the report's essential ingredient. . . . It is designed chiefly for the busy executive who may not have time to read the whole report.

—Report Writing for Business, Raymond Lesikar and John Pettit

The Executive Summary is your most effective and important selling piece and deserves all the effort and attention you can give it. Remember, the client may receive dozens of proposals and may use the Executive Summary as an initial screening process,

—Hand book for Writing Proposals, Robert Hamper and Sue Baugh

The Executive Summary . . . should state the report in a nutshell—generally, it could include the purpose or objectives of the report, background, procedures or approach to the report, findings, and summary, recommendations, and conclusions (if any).

—How to Create High Impact Business Reports. Joyce Kupsh

Always include this [executive summary], whether you are asked for it or not.... Some readers will go no further, so it is important that you get the message across to them clearly. They are likely to include the more senior people who may have to take decisions based upon you report. It is vitally important to get it right.

—*Flow to Communicate in Business: A Handbook for Engineers, David Silk*

References

Hamper, Robert J., and L. Sue Baugh. *Handbook for Writing Proposals.* Lincoinwood, IL: NTC Publishers Group, 1995.

Holtz, Herman. *The Consultant's Guide to Proposal Writing: How to Satisfy Your Clients and Double Your Income.* New York: John Wiley & Sons, 1998.

Kupsh, Joyce. *How to Create High Impact Business Reports.* Lincolnwood, IL: NTC Publishers Group, 1996.

Lesikar, Raymond V., and John D. Pettit, Jr. *Report Writing for Business.* New York: Irwin, 1997.

Sant, Tom. *Persuasive Business Proposals: Writing to Win Customers, Clients, and Contracts,* New York: American Management Association, 1992.

Silk, David. *How to Communicate in Business: A Handbook for Engineers.* IEE Management of Technology Series 17, 1995.

Smith, Charles B. *A Guide to Business Research: Developing, Conducting, and Writing Research Projects.* Chicago: Nelson-Hall Publishers, 1991.

Tebeaux, Elizabeth. *Design of Business Communications: The Process and the Product.* New York: Macmillan, 1990.

Thill, John V., and Courtland L. Bovee. *Excellence in Business Communication.* New York: Prentice-Hall, 1998.

INDEX

D

E

S

www.ingramcontent.com/pod-product-compliance
Lightning Source LLC
LaVergne TN
LVHW080017210926
848481LV00011B/3049
* 9 7 8 1 4 6 5 2 6 8 8 7 7 *